CARRIERS OF CULTURE

CARRIERS OF CULTURE

LABOR ON THE ROAD
IN NINETEENTH-CENTURY
EAST AFRICA

Stephen J. Rockel

Social History of Africa
Allen Isaacman and Jean Allman, Series Editors

HEINEMANN
Portsmouth, NH

Heinemann
A division of Reed Elsevier Inc.
361 Hanover Street
Portsmouth, NH 03801–3912
www.heinemann.com

Offices and agents throughout the world

ISBN: 0–325–07116–0 (Heinemann cloth)
ISBN: 0–325–07133–0 (Heinemann paper)
ISSN: 1099–8098

Library of Congress Cataloging-in-Publication Data

Rockel, Stephen J.
    Carriers of culture : labor on the road in nineteenth century East Africa / by Stephen J. Rockel.
        p.   cm.—(Social history of Africa, ISSN 1099–8098)
    Includes bibliographical references and index.
    ISBN 0–325–07116–0 (cloth)—ISBN 0–325–07133–0 (paper) 1. Migrant labor—Africa, East—History—19th century. 2. Porters—Africa, East—History—19th century. 3. Caravans—Africa, East—History—19th century. 4. Africa, East—Commerce—History—19th century. I. Title. II. Series.
HD5856.A354R63   2006
331.5'440967609034—dc22   2006005584

British Library Cataloguing in Publication Data

Cover photo: Professional ivory porters at the coast. Reprinted with permission.

In Memory
of Susan Ruth Rockel
1956–1988

CONTENTS

ILLUSTRATIONS

TABLES

FIGURE

ABBREVIATIONS

AA	African Affairs
AHR	American Historical Review
AHS	African Historical Studies
AIA	Association internationale africaine
ASR	African Studies Review
A-SR	Anti-Slavery Reporter
BSG	Bulletin de la société de géographie
CI	Le Congo illustré
CJAS	Canadian Journal of African Studies
CMI	Church Missionary Intelligencer
CMS	Church Missionary Society
CSSH	Comparative Studies in Society and History
DK	Deutsche Kolonialzeitung
EHA	Etudes d'histoire africaine
HA	History in Africa
HCPP	House of Commons Parliamentary Papers
IBEAC	Imperial British East Africa Company
IJAHS	International Journal of African Historical Studies
JAH	Journal of African History
JRGS	Journal of the Royal Geographical Society
JSA	Journal of the Society of Arts
JWH	Journal of World History
KHR	Kenya Historical Review
LMS	London Missionary Society
MP	Mackinnon Papers
MSOSB	Mittheilungen des Seminars für Orientalische Sprachen zu Berlin
MT$	Maria Theresa thaler

NC	The Nineteenth Century
PM	Petermanns Mittheilungen
PRGS	Proceedings of the Royal Geographical Society
RGS	Royal Geographical Society
RH	Rhodes House
ROAPE	Review of African Political Economy
SGM	Scottish Geographical Magazine
SH	Social History
SOAS	School of Oriental and African Studies
TBGS	Transactions of the Bombay Geographical Society
TNA	Tanzania National Archive
TNR	Tanganyika Notes and Records/Tanzania Notes and Records
UJ	Uganda Journal
UMCA	Universities Mission to Central Africa
VLC	Verney Lovett Cameron Collection
ZAOS	Zeitschrift für Afrikanische und Oceanische Sprachen
ZEAG	Zanzibar and East Africa Gazette
ZGEB	Zeitschrift der Gesellschaft für Erdkunde zu Berlin
ZM	Zanzibar Museum
ZNA	Zanzibar National Archive

PREFACE

Safari. What more evocative word has entered the English language? Every Western reader has an image in mind, probably via television, of a visit to an African game reserve or national park, perhaps to see the mountain gorillas of Uganda and Rwanda, or the great herds of migrating herbivores in the Maasai Mara and Serengeti Plains, or the wildlife of South Africa's Kruger Park. Here is the safari redefined and reproduced, packaged and commodified, for the late twentieth and early twenty-first centuries. *Safari* means, of course, "journey" in Kiswahili. The verb meaning "to travel," *kusafiri,* has not crossed into English. But it is this verb and all its ramifications that underlie this book.

   Carriers of Culture has been a long time coming. It began life as a PhD thesis, then slowly gestated while I lived and taught in South Africa during some of the most exciting years of the postapartheid transition. On my return to Toronto it grew to the point of becoming unwieldy and had to be split in two, with the present volume representing, as it were, an installment. It is a study of an institution—the caravans of the central trade routes in nineteenth-century East Africa—and of the way of life of its workforce, professional caravan porters, with their specialized labor process, experience, and customs. Despite the title, this book should not be thought of as merely "culturalist." The determining factors are present in my analysis, even if not always made explicit. For those readers requiring specific treatment of economic and environmental change, including the political economy of Unyamwezi agriculture, which underwrote the caravan system, this is presented in part two of the project, published separately. Here it is the social and cultural aspects of porterage that I wish to highlight.

   As the book was written and rewritten, I searched for a way to encapsulate the world of the porters. Eventually my comparative reading led me away from Africa into maritime history and the history of my native New Zealand. Under the influence of scholars such as Marcus Rediker and James Belich, I hit on the concept of crews. Although the wooden world of mercantile shipping in the age of sail is at first glance only superficially comparable to the land-based low technology of human porterage, caravan porters seem in some ways to be like ships' crews. Sailors and porters engaged in lengthy journeys or voyages in order to facilitate trade; and both were specialists—skilled workers who lived and worked in gangs or crews. Like crews elsewhere, caravan porters developed a peculiar labor culture that drew on local genius and familiar meanings, which then became transformed in the work process. By taking the concept of crews further, one can then draw comparisons between porters and other gang laborers such as whalers, sheep shearers, forestry workers, and construction crews working in late precolonial or early colonial economies. In other words, the study of porters becomes the study of labor in the context of world history.

For all that, this work is primarily a contribution to African history. It draws on other studies of African migrant workers that have become central to African labor history, including those by Frederick Cooper, Charles van Onselen, Bill Freund, Keletso Atkins, Patrick Harries, François Manchuelle, and many others. More specifically, it extends our knowledge of the history of Tanzania and East Africa. Despite the huge importance of the caravan system to the East African past, it has received no sustained study, although Abdul Sheriff's economic history of the Zanzibari commercial empire has been of great importance. Nor have the Nyamwezi—caravanners, migrant workers, and farmers par excellence—received their due. No historian has worked on the history of this large and complex people for over a generation. Nevertheless I remain indebted to the pioneers of the 1960s and 1970s, especially Alfred Unomah, Aylward Shorter, and Andrew Roberts.

In attempting to reconceptualize categories applied to precolonial East African labor, and porters in particular, I continually ran up against recurring and recycled ideas first found in nineteenth-century humanitarian and missionary propaganda. These have overshadowed, even distorted, images of the African past. I was therefore encouraged to consider aspects of orientalist and racial thought found in earlier works, as well as recent literary and postcolonial perspectives. Thus, this book contributes, if in only a small way, to the history of the production of knowledge about Africa.

Research has practical limits, however. I have read virtually all the relevant material in English, as well as a targeted selection of the German and French sources. German, French, and Belgian travelers, missionaries, and authors largely replicated the concerns of their British, Canadian, and American counterparts. African sources, often in Swahili or translated into European languages, have been particularly valuable, sometimes illuminating aspects of experience and culture that Europeans did not notice or understand. By far the most important are the oral traditions and histories collected from Nyamwezi informants. Sadly, many of them have already passed on, taking their stories to the grave. Much of the history of western Tanzania is being lost, as very few scholars work in this neglected region.

A great many people assisted me at various stages of this project. First and foremost, I must acknowledge my enormous debt to Martin Klein, my teacher, supervisor, mentor, and friend. During my PhD studies Marty allowed me with typical good humor to stray from his own specialization in West African history. Nevertheless, his immense knowledge of the African past, grounded as it is in social and economic history, thoroughly prepared me for a work of this type. Alongside Marty, Archie Thornton, Milton Israel, Laurel McDowell, and Tim Brook were wonderful graduate teachers. Although I studied outside his discipline, Richard Stren got me interested in African urbanization, a topic related to this one. Ibrahim Abdullah gave me encouragement during the early stages of my work on porters. Paul Tiyambe Zeleza provided helpful criticism. In South Africa special thanks go to Bill Freund. Bill not only offered me a great opportunity but also read my work and helped in my exploration of another African country. Thanks also to colleagues at the University of KwaZuluNatal, Durban, for offering an exciting intellectual environment, especially at the Department of History/African Studies Seminar. In Toronto, Martin Klein, Rick Halpern, and Ansuya Chetty read and critiqued drafts of various chapters. Wayne Dowler read chapter 1 and gave me a crash course in aspects of Enlightenment and post-Enlightenment thinking. From the ranks of the international collectivity of Tanzanian specialists and enthusiasts, Thaddeus Sunseri, Laird Jones, Harald Sippel, and Sheryl McCurdy offered comradeship and assistance at crucial times. Jan-Georg Deutsch and Michael Pesek provided me with two of the photographs reproduced here.

In Tanzania special thanks go to Uphoro Shayo, Tabora Divisional Secretary, who took a personal interest in the history of the region and offered great support for my fieldwork during the dry season of 2000. Theresia Michael was an admirable research assistant. My greatest thanks go to the elders of Tabora town and its surrounding villages, who, with great enthusiasm—even passion—and goodwill, told me the traditions and histories of their families and ancestors, and the people of the region. Thanks also go to the staff of COSTECH in Dar es Salaam, and to members of the Department of History at the University of Dar es Salaam, especially Fred Kaijage and the late Josiah Mlahagwa in 1992–93 and Nestor Luanda in 2000. Without the assistance of the staff at various archives and libraries, including Robarts Library at the University of Toronto; the Tanzania National Archive, Dar es Salaam; the Africana Library at the University of Dar es Salaam; the Zanzibar National Archive; the libraries of the School of Oriental and African Studies and the Royal Geographical Society, both in London; and Rhodes House, Oxford, this book would not have been possible. Thanks also to the editors of *The Journal of African History* and *The Canadian Journal of African Studies* for permission to include in Chapters 3 and 4 material from two earlier articles. I am grateful to the University of Toronto for a Connaught Fellowship, and to the Social Science and Humanities Research Council of Canada for Doctoral, New Faculty, and Standard Research grants that funded different stages of this project. Last, but in no way least, I appreciate the careful and constructive reading of the draft manuscript by the anonymous reviewer, and the patience and encouragement of the Heinemann editors, Allen Isaacman and Jean Allman.

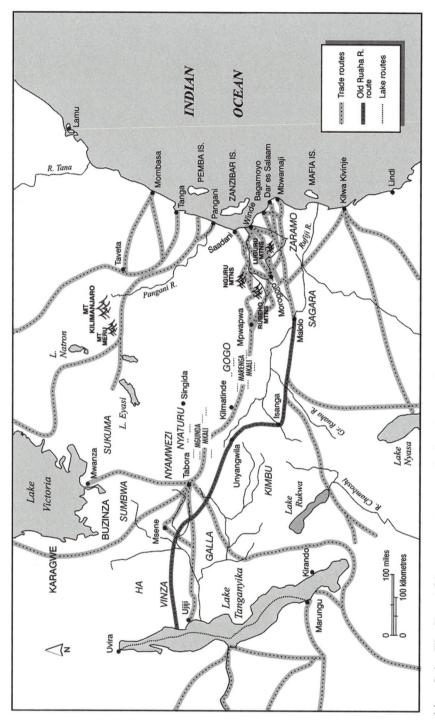

Map 0.1 The East African caravan routes in the nineteenth century.

Map 0.2   The Nyamwezi and their neighbors.

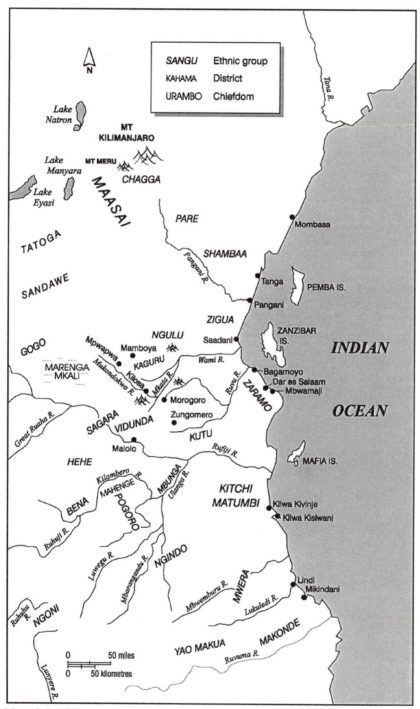

Map 0.3 The coast and eastern interior.

PART I

"SAFARI LEO!"

1

Transitional Forms of Labor

Mpagazi, n. *wa-* carrier, bearer, caravan-porter. . . . *Upagazi,* n. (1) work (profession, pay, &c.) of a caravan porter.[1]

As there are no pack animals among these people they are obliged to carry on their heads and backs the objects for the cities where they buy and sell.[2]

The success and comfort of a traveller going into the interior of Africa depended largely upon the health, strength and uprightness of the porter . . . the sole means of transport.[3]

Long-distance porters played a special role in the history of eighteenth- and nineteenth-century East Africa. Traveling on foot across vast territories, in caravans ranging in size from a dozen to three or four thousand members, they linked the large and small communities of the interior with the Muslim world of the Indian Ocean coast. The search for income and profit from the ivory trade and increasing demand for imported cloth, beads, guns, and other goods encouraged people to undertake journeys sometimes several years long, often for an agreed wage. Beginning in the mid-eighteenth century a new way of life developed, indeed a new culture, as peoples from what is now western Tanzania, especially those called by others the Nyamwezi or "people of the moon," made pioneering journeys. Their caravans at first searched out opportunities in the regional trading networks of the high plateau between Lakes Tanganyika, Victoria, and Malawi but soon reached almost every part of East and Central Africa. Many traveled east to climb the coastal ranges; cross the *nyika,* or wilderness; and reach the Indian Ocean. Others traded for ivory around the shores of the great lakes and beyond to Katanga in the south of the modern Democratic Republic of the Congo, and north to the kingdoms of Karagwe, Bunyoro, and Buganda. In the 1820s, coastal entrepreneurs—Swahili, Arab, and occasionally Indian—joined the rush for ivory, encouraged by rising international prices and stories of the interior. By the 1840s, Nyamwezi and coastal trading caravans entered the immense Congo rain forest.

This book is about the workforce of the caravans, the professional long-distance caravan porters, also known as carriers, *Träger* (in German), or *wapagazi* (in Kiswahili), upon whose heads and shoulders all trade and communications in East Africa literally rested. Travel by foot was the only possible means of transportation in nearly all of precolonial East Africa. The use of draft and pack animals was virtually precluded by the presence of the trypanosome-carrying tsetse fly in broad belts of woodland that stretched across the savanna. Donkeys, asses, horses, and oxen die within days of infection by the parasite. Water transportation was no alternative given the lack of navigable rivers in most of the region. In contrast to parts of West and Central Africa, where lakes, rivers, and lagoons made bulk transport possible, the main axis of East African commerce was along the foot tracks of the central caravan route, stretching over 950 miles through Tanzania between the entrepôts of the Mrima coast opposite Zanzibar and Ujiji on Lake Tanganyika.[4] Prior to the introduction of mechanical transport, the tens of thousands of professional wage-earning porters who worked the central and other routes played a key role in economic, social and cultural change. In the process they invented a unique working culture.

The explorer Henry Morton Stanley described the *mpagazi* as a "useful person" who was "the camel, the horse, the mule, the ass, the train, the wagon and the cart of East and Central Africa. Without him Salem would not obtain her ivory, Boston and New York their African ebony, their frankincense, myrrh and gum copal."[5] This is an understatement. Without porters, nothing would have moved. Little regional trade among African societies could have occurred (there was a great deal); the numerous small-scale societies of East Africa would have remained relatively isolated from each other, and the rest of the world, and would have found it much harder to take advantage of innovations made by their neighbors or coming from farther afield; economic development would have been impossible; no Muslims or Christians would have traveled up country, and no converts would have been made in the interior; European exploration, conquest, and colonization would have been infeasible. The historic importance of caravan porters is therefore obvious.

Caravan porters were vital to the functioning of trade, transportation, and the movement of ideas throughout sub-Saharan Africa. Beyond Africa, porterage was a fundamental institution in all parts of the world where animal power could not be utilized and waterways were inadequate. This was the case in mountainous regions such as the Himalayas,[6] in parts of the Americas, and in New Zealand until the mid-1800s. In sub-Saharan Africa, caravan porters were the first migrant laborers. They were an integral part of the spread of commerce and, indeed, modernity in many regions of the subcontinent. As Peter Linebaugh and Marcus Rediker emphasize in their work on the world of eighteenth-century sailors and slaves, who were comparable to porters in many ways, "'Principles' as well as commodities were transported on those

ships!"[7] Indeed, John Iliffe observes that in Tanzania porterage made wage
earning familiar to many Africans, particularly the Nyamwezi, the Sukuma,
and related groups. In the early colonial period these peoples dominated the
wave of labor migrations until 1908 or so, when the construction of the central railway brought other groups into wage labor.[8]

It is puzzling and somewhat ironic that we have numerous studies of
animal transportation, including horses and camel caravans; of canoes and
river transport; of railways and steamships, and even airlines;[9] but few of
porterage, the most African of transport systems. The omnipresent porter
has become almost invisible—part of the scenery. History has relegated him
or her to the background—to the "enormous condescension of posterity"—
like E.P. Thompson's English croppers, hand-loom weavers, and artisans.[10]
This is despite the fact that one can hardly find a European source from
nineteenth-century East and Central Africa that fails to mention porters. As
Cornelia Essner has noted, "the *Leitmotiv* in their [Europeans'] writings is
the long-winded discussions of complaints concerning the question of porters."[11] Indeed, carriers remained a preoccupation of many twentieth-century
travelers and ethnographers, as Mary Louise-Pratt shows for the anthropologist Evans-Pritchard in the southern Sudan.[12] For Europeans, a way of life
for hundreds of thousands, indeed millions, throughout sub-Saharan regions
became a feature denoting "backwardness,"[13] an anachronistic waste of
labor, to be made redundant by modernization and investment in railways
and then abolished as soon as possible by colonial governments.[14] Yet
long-distance caravan porters were at the center of a profound engagement
with modernity. They invented a unique but recognizably modern working
culture comparable with other labor or crew cultures of the industrializing
world found on merchant sailing ships, in the canoes of Canadian voyageurs, in whaling stations, in forest logging camps, and even military units
in their barracks or at war.

Precolonial porterage has been noticed by only a handful of scholars.[15]
Recent literature is even more unbalanced when it comes to the question of
precolonial wage labor, whether migrant, free, or otherwise. On one hand,
most accounts of migrant labor largely ignore examples from the precolonial
period, despite trade workers including porters and teamsters constituting
"the most ancient and one of the most massive forms of labor migration in
African history."[16] Indeed, porterage was the major utilizer of nonagricul-
tural labor in East Africa. On the other hand, free wage labor is generally
viewed as a creation of colonial economies, with settlers, landowners, and
the state struggling to mobilize and control labor supply, often in competition.[17] External factors are privileged, with little attention given to the precolonial dynamics of African societies.[18] This book is in part a response. The
central argument is that there was indeed a large free wage labor force in
East Africa that emerged prior to the development of the colonial capitalist

economy. The appearance of the professional or semiprofessional porter was an African response to East African conditions and environments, and not merely a belated consequence of the decline of indigenous entrepreneurship, or a process of impoverishment caused by outside forces. As Sharon Stichter has noted, the origins of the migrant labor system as the dominant form of capitalist wage labor throughout much of the twentieth century lie in conditions "specific to African pre-colonial social formations themselves," as well as in external forces.[19] In sum, we must look for the roots and preconditions of migrant labor in the late precolonial period, rather than just in the operation of colonial political economies.[20] As Frederick Cooper puts it, "power . . . was rooted in particular cultural structures."[21]

Caravan porters working the main routes in nineteenth-century Tanzania were migrants or itinerants, and most were recognizably wage workers, notwithstanding their continuing ties to the land. They were hired or mobilized through a variety of social and cultural linkages, but certainly by the middle of the nineteenth century the majority of porters worked for large merchants of Nyamwezi, coastal, or Arab origin and were paid by the month or per journey. Captive porters were rarely utilized along the central routes. Nevertheless, the emergence of Nyamwezi porterage rested partly on the employment of slaves in the domestic economy, where major contributions from women and immigrant Tutsi herders also helped release male labor power. As the caravan system became more structured and a recognized work culture emerged, custom increasingly defined working standards and regulated disputes related to working conditions, food, wages, and payment. Porters were able to force up wages at crucial junctures. Over time, Nyamwezi work norms and leisure activities created at home and on safari came to constitute the main features of a broad caravan culture. Established patterns of work survived into the early colonial period. Foreign travelers, Arab and European, had little choice but to bow to custom, with some adaptations. It was only after several years of colonial rule that new ideas about work could be successfully imposed on porters, as they were deskilled and their strategic position weakened.

How should we envisage the emergence of a labor force that seems to defy the expectations of Africanist historians? The difficulty of creating analytical categories that reflect the historically complex social relations of the large section of the African (as well as Caribbean, Latin American, and Asian) populations that is "simultaneously and ambiguously 'semiproletariat' and 'semipeasant'" is a continuing preoccupation in labor studies.[22] In nineteenth-century East Africa, wage work emerged from an indigenous labor culture with its own timetables deriving from Nyamwezi social norms and the customs of the work experience as they developed along the main routes. In this sense, East African porters developed a transitional form of wage labor shaped by indigenous precapitalist labor norms but closely linked to merchant capital and the global economy. This does not at all imply an evolution in the linear sense of a movement to full proletarianization, or that caravan porters were "partially proletarianized" and had not quite reached the level of "freedom" of wage workers in capitalist regions. Indeed, in the colonial period many of the innovative features of caravan labor were unmade as porters were deskilled and the old professionalism became rare, so that from the European perspective porterage became equated with "coolie" labor. A German observer wrote on the defeat of the Hehe of southern Tanzania in the 1890s, "The small remnant of men of pure Hehe blood who will survive will become intermingled with other tribes, and instead of remaining fearless warriors and hunters, will degenerate into *mere porters* like most of the other natives of our colony."[23] The views of the "men on the spot" thus merged with the widely held and racist assumption that Africans were good only for the manual labor of empire building: in Henry Merriman's 1894 novel, *With Edged Tools,* African porters "hired themselves out like animals, and as the beasts of the field they did their work—patiently, without intelligence. . . . Such is the African."[24]

Nevertheless, some aspects of caravan culture were necessarily accepted by new colonial employers, while others retained a life of their own in the consciousness of later migrant workers. We must therefore reject dualist theories of labor that privilege a sudden mobilization of workers directed by the colonial state and encouraged by colonial capitalism.[25] Nor does the word "transitional" imply an articulated segmentation of a worldwide labor force, as Amin and Van der Linden suggest for the term "intermediary." This formulation suggests reduced agency in non-Western societies. Rather, "transitional" suggests an indigenous form of labor organization representing a fully fledged *African* response to the world economic system. The labor culture of the caravans was transitional in that it enabled a breakthrough from a relatively isolated trading and labor system to one suited to capitalist-style accumulation. The customs, labor culture, and linkages utilized and created by long-distance caravan porters, particularly the Nyamwezi, were key to the economic, social, and cultural adaptations enabling East African societies to engage with the forces of modernity. Indeed, they were modern enough that they could be exploited in both their economic and cultural functions as they laid the basis for the migrant labor system of colonial capitalism.[26] My approach therefore differs from that of Catherine Coquery-Vidrovitch and Paul Lovejoy, who argue that African porters "shared a petty bourgeois mentality," and that their aim was to "climb the social ladder and become a merchant entirely" rather than improve "working conditions or terms of remuneration:"[27] This was true for some no doubt, and many porters did engage in small-scale trade or as partners in family concerns. But such a formulation ignores the mass of evidence from the central routes for varied types of caravan organization, professionalism, rising wages, and customary standards.

The debate about categories only goes so far, and the ideas they represent have increasingly been questioned. Given the kinds of deconstruction of imperialist categories and ideas that discourse analysis has allowed, historians can carry forward studies of work processes and labor cultures, including the development of custom. Gyan Prakash writes more generally on the possibility of a realignment of "discrepant histories and knowledges" that colonial (imperial) historiography produced. There is now a form of postcoloniality "that seizes on colonialism's contingent arrangement of values and social identification and rearranges them to reveal sources of knowledge and agency simmering beneath the calm surface of colonial history and historiography."[28] In the field of labor history, studies might now show how identifiably discreet types of recruitment and mobilization representing different relations of production nevertheless fed and were subsumed into broader labor systems with their dominant forms of organization, networks, values, and rules.[29] We might also come to a greater appreciation of the importance of mobile and often ubiquitous forms of labor that nevertheless have left scant evidence on the historical record. I am thinking of various types of crews who worked on the fringes of settled agriculture and industry, who dominated transport and communications on the oceans and rivers of the world during periods of national and colonial expansion, who did pioneering work along frontiers and linked remote districts to permanent population centers, and who staffed the extractive industries that have been so important to capitalist expansion. This type of work would add to labor histories of the colonial period and be a counterweight to the dominance of the slave paradigm, which has distorted our understanding of East African history.

LINEAGES OF SLAVERY: IMPERIALISM AND LABOR
IN EAST AFRICAN HISTORY[30]

In a revisionist interpretation of the slave trade in East Africa, Edward Alpers in 1967 drew attention to the then-unchallenged dominance of the narrative presented by the imperialist historian Sir Reginald Coupland, an influential author of scholarly books on nineteenth-century East Africa. According to Coupland, writing in the 1930s, the slave trade began with the earliest Asian contact with East Africa and from that time was a "theme which ran 'like a scarlet thread through all the subsequent history of East Africa until the present day.'"[31] This section revisits ideas about East African slavery and labor in late nineteenth- and twentieth-century Great Britain and other imperial centers, giving particular attention to an intellectual tradition that links slavery to long-distance caravan porterage. Imperial, colonial, missionary, and business documentation suggests a three-way relationship between, first, the assumptions underlying imperialist expansion in East Africa, including the requirement for a new transport infrastructure; second, the practical need to justify intervention to the European public in terms of the abolition of the slave trade; and third, the historiography of nineteenth-century East Africa.

The main assumption in question, central to post-Enlightenment (positivist) philosophy and deeply embedded in Western consciousness, was that history represents a passage from slavery to freedom. Where slavery was a natural condition there was no history. Freedom did not and could not apply where the sway of universalism seemed suspect. In the 1830s Hegel had inscribed the apparent exceptional relationship of Africa to world history in the following terms:

> The peculiarly African character is difficult to comprehend, for the very reason that in reference to it, we must quite give up the principle which naturally accompanies all *our* ideas—the category of Universality. In Negro life . . . consciousness has not yet attained to the realization of any substantial objective existence—as for example, God, or Law—in which the interest of man's volition is involved and in which he realizes his own being. This distinction between himself as an individual and the universality of his essential being, the African in the uniform, undeveloped oneness of his existence has not yet attained; so that the Knowledge of an absolute Being, an Other and a Higher than his individual self, is entirely wanting. The Negro . . . exhibits the natural man in his completely wild and untamed state. We must lay aside all thought of reverence and morality—all that we call feeling—if we would rightly comprehend him; there is nothing harmonious with humanity to be found in this type of character.

And later:

> Another characteristic fact in reference to the Negroes is Slavery. Negroes are enslaved by Europeans and sold to America. Bad as this may be, their lot in their own land is even worse, since there a slavery quite as absolute exists; for it is the essential principle of slavery, that man has not yet attained a consciousness of his freedom, and consequently sinks down to a mere Thing.[32]

With such views as part of the intellectual baggage of the nineteenth century, the continuing expansion of Europe, and ultimately the partition of Africa, was then to be a progressive campaign in which labor would be set free and bondage ended in the name of liberty.

In a stimulating discussion of the bonded labor of *kamia* agricultural workers in Bihar, in colonial India, Prakash shows how such assumptions deriving from the Enlightenment and the growth of industrial capitalism entered imperialist thought, and recast, indeed invented, the category of debt bondage where no such system of labor relations had previously existed. In the process, the reality of social relations preexisting and coexisting with colonialism was made invisible.[33] More generally, and under colonial conditions, various types of social relationships unfamiliar to Westerners in African and Asian societies, such as *kamia* servitude, were reduced and universalized by colonial writers to a form of what Marx referred to as "commodity fetishism," in which the free exchange of labor as a commodity was seen as a natural right. If the newly reified debt bondage in the Bihar case "implied that social relations were based on money" (as opposed to status and patron-client obligations), it also stood as opposed to free labor and hence had to be reformed. The social basis of debt bondage was therefore obliterated, its kinship to patron-client relations and hierarchy made invisible.[34]

None of this implies the abandonment of Enlightenment or post-Enlightenment categories in relationship to stories of engagements with modernity, imperialism, and capitalism in late precolonial East Africa. Indeed, one such category, class, is a central concept in this book. One labor historian who has grappled with questions of class in colonial contexts is Dipesh Chakrabarty, who argues that "historical debates about transition to capitalism must . . . if they are not to replicate structures of historicist logic, think of such transition as 'translational' processes."[35] Translation occurs when the narrative of the history of capital, a history in which "free labor is both a precondition of capitalist production and 'its invariable result,'" encounters narratives of the antecedents of capital that take forms not established by capital itself, but derived from their own histories. In other words, the history of the universalizing tendency of (post) Enlightenment categories, including capital, is interrupted by other histories that, although not necessarily precapitalist or incompatible with capitalism, allow "the politics of human belonging and diversity."[36] In this light, the history of the infancy of capitalism in East Africa, represented here by the mature caravan system, is modified by its noncapitalist antecedents. The resulting transition (interrupted in East Africa) is "also a process of translation of diverse life-worlds and conceptual horizons . . . into the categories of Enlightenment thought that inhere in the logic of capital."[37] The universalizing (Enlightenment) categories of the social sciences must be modified in order that the histories of noncapital and capital can both be told. The kind of free wage labor that caravan porters represented can therefore in one sense be considered part of an alternative modernity counterposed and integral to European capitalist modernity, a translated wage-labor system representing a translated modernity.[38]

As in colonial Bihar, where the contrast between "freedom" and the "bondage" of *kamias* seemed extreme in the broader Indian context, so East Africa represented to Victorians a surviving redoubt of the slave trade, an open sore on the Victorian conscience, and an anomaly in the age of progress and enlarging freedom. In the East African case, the alternative forms of labor organization that porterage took; its unique labor culture, which grew out of indigenous norms; and its engagements with the market and modernity were also not discernible to imperial eyes. This was partly the result of an outpouring of antislavery literature. Imperialist and humanitarian writers grasped the opportunity to strengthen their case for British occupation of East Africa with the rhetoric of intervention to suppress the slave trade. A large part of the antislavery campaign involved lobbying government, which was often sympathetic. Indeed, "the Foreign Office habitually explained its African moves to the ordinary voter as measures against the slave trade, for this was all he knew or cared about tropical Africa."[39] Intervention was encouraged and at the same time camouflaged by propaganda campaigns in Britain and other Western countries aimed at demonizing Arab ivory and slave traders.[40] For Britain, the mythic representation and immortalization of David Livingstone and his work is a well-documented example.[41] In Belgium, commercial interests and the megalomania of King Leopold were clearly uppermost, but those proposing intervention in East and Central Africa carefully buttressed their arguments with antislavery perspectives.[42] Germany is a separate case—Bismarck's disinterest in the arguments of the humanitarian lobby is well known, and the German antislavery society was formed only in 1888, after colonial occupation and expansion in Africa had already begun.[43] Nevertheless, German imperialists were quite happy to raise the Arab bogey after the fact, as in Frieda von Bülow's popular novel, *Im Lande der Verheißung: Ein Kolonialroman um Carl Peters*,[44] in which the conquest of German East Africa is justified by the presentation of the Arabs as the "'real' aggressors who attack unarmed German settlers and subject Africans to inhuman slavery."[45]

European conquest became in this guise an enlightened campaign for civilization on behalf of an Africa subjugated by a rapacious Orient in competition with Europe. As Adam Hochschild puts it, "righteous denunciations poured down on a distant, weak, and safely nonwhite target" rather than on the slaving powers Spain, Portugal, or Brazil.[46] The dominant systems of labor therefore had to be presented to the credulous European public as a massive mobilization of slaves by brutal Arab slavers. The Scottish missionary A. M. Mackay wrote, "The Arab with our arms and his porterage by slaves, will ever cast into the shade the freshman from Europe with his hired porters."[47] Long-distance caravans, the most obvious and largest consumers of labor, came to be seen in this light, especially as many Arab traders operated on a large scale.[48] In short, if it were admitted that free wage labor existed on a large scale in East Africa, then the whole publicly argued basis for intervention and conquest would be undermined. If slavery did not exist on a large scale—which, of course, it did—then it would have been necessary to invent it. Abolitionist rhetoric, which contributed to the "climate of imperialism," has continued even into the twenty-first century to influence academic and popular histories of the region[49] and can thus be described as a lineage of slavery and, in some respects, a language of domination. It is fascinating to consider the way that this has occurred, given that nineteenth-century writings on East Africa are far more diverse in tone and content than any single antislavery message suggests.[50] The documentation on porterage and related topics is very varied, as we shall see, and evidence often contradicts views found within the same source.

At this point it is useful to outline the commentary that connects slavery and porterage in East Africa before briefly discussing the minority of porters who were domestic slaves. In 1844, decades before annexation of East African territories, the American Michael W. Shephard wrote of trade in the East African interior, "It is the custom to buy a tooth of ivory and a slave with it to carry it to the sea shore. Then the ivory and slaves are carried to Zanzibar and sold." Shephard had never set foot on the mainland. His reportage was an early example of the belief that porterage equaled slave labor. A similar account, from the context referring to the Kilwa route, states that

> the people from the interior of Africa use Slaves to bring Ivory to the coast, and will not sell one without the other. And as soon as they hear that Slaves cannot be sold it is the custom of the first comers to return and report to other caravans on the road and they generally bury the Ivory in the ground, and return to their own country, though eventually the ivory comes to the coast.[51]

Both reports were clearly referring to a trade dominated by Africans from the interior, not coastal people. Arabs were not yet recognized as major actors in the East African slave trade, and the vilification of Muslims was to come later. In the late 1850s, the image of eastern Africa set before the British and European public was essentially that provided by Livingstone, given his heroic aura and the relatively large sales of his first book, *Missionary Travels and Researches in South Africa.*[52] Yet Livingstone barely mentioned the Arab slave trade at this point. He commented much more on the involvement of Portuguese and mulatto slave traders and only developed a greater awareness of Arab (and Yao) participation during his ill-fated Zambezi expedition from 1858 to 1864. It was then that he made the linkage, which was later accepted unquestioningly by the imperialist humanitarian lobby, that the slave trade could be defeated and the humanitarian project completed only through indirect, then direct, British intervention.[53] During these years, Livingstone's experience and the raw material for his writings concerned the heavily slaved Zambezi and Shire rivers and Lake Malawi (Lake Nyassa) regions, and despite the detailed evidence of the Nyamwezi-dominated caravan system along the central routes farther north found in Richard Burton's writings,[54] it was Livingstone's work that set the tone for a reading public not able or willing to distinguish between conditions in different parts of Africa. His leading biographer summarizes what he believed to be Livingstone's developing views in these years on the interrelationship between the ivory and slave trades:

> The slave and ivory trades were closely related. Since the Arabs used slaves captured in the interior to carry their ivory, and since both tusks and porters were sold at the coast, an increase in the demand for ivory meant that more slaves were needed as porters, and thus more slaves were sold for export at the coast.[55]

This is not actually what Livingstone wrote. The passage referred to probably comes from the *Narrative of an Expedition to the Zambesi,* in which he does discuss the use of slave porters to carry ivory, but with a qualification: he points to the trade to Portuguese controlled ports (not in the hands of Arabs) and to Kilwa, but not the main central routes.

> The trade of Cazembe and Katanga's country, and of other parts of the interior, crosses Nyassa and the Shire, on its way to the Arab port, Kilwa, and the Portuguese ports of Iboe and Mosambique. At present, slaves, ivory, malachite, and copper ornaments, are the only articles of commerce. According to information collected by Colonel Rigby at Zanzibar, and from other sources, nearly all the slaves shipped from the above-mentioned ports come from the Nyassa district. By means of a small steamer, purchasing the ivory of the Lake and the River above the cataracts . . . the Slave Trade in this quarter would be rendered unprofitable,—for it is only by the ivory being carried by the slaves, that the latter do not eat up all the profits of a trip.[56]

This is the only section in his writings where Livingstone draws a direct connection between slavery and the porterage of ivory. Given that the context is an appeal for British intervention into Central Africa, Livingstone, and his brother, Charles, probably chose their words for maximum effect. Indeed, a careful reading of David Livingstone's later work shows that he was well acquainted with the free labor system of the central routes. For example, in a section of his *Last Journals* headed "Advice to Missionaries," he writes, "It might be good policy to hire a respectable Arab to engage *free porters.*"[57] Yet the horrors he saw and attributed to Muslim slave traders in the Shire River and Lake Malawi region as well as south of Lake Tanganyika, and particularly the infamous massacre of market women in Nyangwe, in Manyema, created an impression not easily put aside by his readers.

From the 1870s, the expression of misinformed or misleading opinions on the East African slave trade became commonplace in influential imperialist circles. The contemporary literature tended to portray caravan porters as slaves, particularly in writings aimed at the general public but also in high level government pronouncements.[58] In 1877 the famous explorer Sir Samuel

Baker introduced a London presentation on East African transport routes with comments linking porterage and slave raiding.[59] Baker generalized based on his experiences in the southern Sudan and northern Uganda, where he utilized captive labor for his own caravans.[60] In the same year, Joseph Mullins, foreign secretary of the London Missionary Society (LMS), whose mainland experience was of the central route, wrote that "gangs of slaves were made almost the only means of carriage."[61] Clearly this was incorrect. Even the British consul in Zanzibar, F. Holmwood, believed that the ivory trade could be profitable only if the traders utilized slave porterage, although he was probably referring to the domestic slaves of coast-based traders as well as captives.[62] Horace Waller, one of the most forceful British antislavery activists, who was equally vigorous in his advocacy of imperialist intervention in East Africa, linked slavery and porterage directly, although he was careful to distinguish the slave supplying Lake Malawi region from others. In a propaganda piece, he used the device of the "'poor devil,' who has been marched down to market, with a tusk of ivory on his shoulder, from Nyassa" to gain the support of "John Bull" for aggressive British intervention.[63]

By the early 1890s a measure of certainty crept into some observations. One imperial servant (of the Belgians) wrote of the ivory trade that "not a tusk is brought to the coast on a free head," while with poor hindsight another, Frederick Moir, wrote "Ivory was almost the only product that would bear the cost of transport from the interior, and the only known economical means of transporting it was the slave-gang."[64] According to Moir, the rationale behind the advance into the interior of the African Lakes Company was to launch steamers on the rivers and Lake Malawi and block the routes used by the ivory caravans with their purported slave porters in order to prevent the slave trade. The company offered "fair prices" for ivory, and its steamers transported it to the coast "to obviate the necessity for raiding and slave-carrying."[65] In this fashion the aims of Christianity, commerce, and civilization could be realized. A later British consul in Zanzibar, Sir A. Hardinge (1895–1901), made the following connection between the slave trade and porterage in British East African territory:

> In the old days when the Slave Trade flourished, an Arab or Swahili trader, going up-country to get ivory, knew that even if he did not himself shoot many elephants or purchase many tusks he could always pay the cost of his journey by buying slaves of the inland tribes for retail at the ports, and that this "black ivory," quite apart from its value at the coast, would carry down for him gratis, and without him having to employ porters, any "white ivory" which he might shoot or buy.[66]

George Curzon, (later Lord Curzon, viceroy of India) brought to the question the comparison with free wage labor, returning us to the assumption with which we started this discussion. Referring to Zanzibar, the fulcrum of the caravan system, he stated in parliament in 1896 that "free labor, paid labor, is not indigenous to the place—it is an exotic, it would have to be imported, it would have to be carefully tended and watered to enable it to grow."[67]

The connection between porterage and slavery thus assumed, elaborate schemes were devised to strike a blow at the slave trade and at the same time facilitate European access to African resources and markets. Livingstone suggested that one of the consequences of an expansion of legitimate trade in cotton in the Lake Nyassa region would be the substitution of transportation by steamboat for porterage. And because slaves carried ivory to the coast, this would reduce the ravages of the slave trade.[68] Some influential writers, including a few who knew better, argued that because the system of porterage rested on slave labor, it was only right that modern forms of transportation, particularly railways, should replace it. These lines would be built by colonial governments with the purpose of developing the country.[69] In the 1870s and 1880s British and Belgian writing on East Africa became obsessed with the necessity of replacing the expensive and slow caravan system with alternative transport arrangements, including prepared roadways and ox-wagons.[70] In the Belgian case, the president of the Société de géographie d'Anvers in an overview of commercial prospects in Africa as a whole linked profits, transport problems, and slavery: "Merchandise is transported the same way; by foot like livestock, there is no freightage . . . Once produced it will be conveyed like the transport of ivory which, in caravans of black slaves, would be impracticable. In order to destroy a traffic established on such a basis, most energetic efforts are obviously necessary." European commercial penetration would encourage chiefs to keep their subjects at home to work instead of selling them as slave porters.[71] The Belgian branch of the Association internationale africaine (AIA), faced as it was with extremely long caravan journeys across East Africa to reach the Congo, in 1879–80 sponsored an experiment in the use of Indian elephants with the aim of reducing reliance on porters.[72] Many of these discussions were couched in terms of abolitionist rhetoric. In more sophisticated versions, which often came from the perspectives of commercial or evangelical mission interests, porterage was not directly equated with slavery but nevertheless was seen as a stimulus to it. According to one Manchester cotton industry spokesman, a railway would

> strike through the very heart of the slave traffic,whose hoary iniquity would hide away in shame and fly far from the track of the civilising locomotive engine; every yard of rail as laid down would increase the traffic, and extinguish the hitherto barbarous system of doing all the carrying on men's heads in loads of sixty to seventy pounds, the result of which has been that if the price of a Manchester cloth be 8s. at Zanzibar, its price at Lakes Tanganyika or Victoria Nyanza is 38s., or four times the cost.

A railway would have the happy effects, therefore, of killing the slave trade, abolishing inefficient porterage, and giving "an immediate trade with some forty or fifty millions of people occupying a country of fabulous natural resources."[73] More realistically, some businessmen and imperial and mission representatives pointed out that reliance on porterage meant dependence on "unruly" and assertive African laborers, and their customary ideas concerning wages and conditions of work. Here was the unacknowledged subtext of the imperialist and humanitarian argument, and the subject of this book.

To provide ammunition for the antislavery/anti-Arab campaign, Europeans in Africa made much of incidents connected with the slave trade, impressing their readers with the cruelty of both the trade and ivory porterage.[74] A favorite was accounts of how pitiless slavers in coast-bound caravans forced female slaves carrying their babies to bear ivory or other loads as well. If they could not, the infants were killed, so that the profits from ivory would not be lost. Perhaps the first such reportage comes from Livingstone, to be endlessly repeated, elaborated on, and "polished into myth" in antislavery propaganda. His own account is typically matter of fact. On July 16, 1861, when Livingstone and three other Europeans were at Mbame's on the Shire River, a slave caravan entered the village. Among other brutalities experienced by the slaves, "one woman had her infant's brains knocked out, because she could not carry her load and it."[75] Again, Livingstone, writing of female slaves in the eastern Congo, recollected, "Women, having in addition to the yoke and load a child on the back, have said to me in passing, 'They are killing me; if they would take off the yoke I could manage the load and child, but I shall die with three loads.'"[76] A later description by a European traveler is of the slave caravan of the Beloch trader Kabunda, which traveled from Liendwe at the south end of Lake Tanganyika toward Zanzibar in 1883:

> And the women! I can hardly trust myself to think or speak of them—they were fastened to chains or thick bark ropes, and very many, in addition to their heavy weight of grain or ivory, carried little brown babies . . . The double burden was almost too much, and still they struggled wearily on, knowing too well that when they showed signs of fatigue, not the slaver's ivory but the living child would be torn from them and thrown aside to die.[77]

Such accounts were in addition rendered in pictorial form. An excellent example comes from the *Anti-Slavery Reporter*. A sketch of "A Slave Caravan" shows a struggling line of chained slaves: women and children, backs bowed under heavy loads including infants, boxes, and bales. One of the women has fallen and pitched her load on the ground, while a threatening Muslim guard watches from the margins.[78] Dorothy Helly shows the process by which such illustrations were produced. A preliminary sketch by Horace Waller of a slave gang depicts chained women and children, slaves in slave sticks, and, in the foreground, a Muslim trader about to kill a yoked slave with an ax. One woman carries a load, probably grain. An artist then worked up this sketch for publication in Livingstone's *Last Journals,* where it appears in volume one with the caption "Slave Traders Revenging their Losses." In published form the sketch is altered for dramatic effect, so that the caravan descends a slope, and additional figures of Muslim slave traders are added.[79] The combined effect of words and pictures created an image among European readers of incessant slave raiding and violence directly connected to porterage, in which captives including women were forced to carry ivory to the coast from the far interior. These images helped prepare the way for conquest or, if described in later years, aimed to justify it. More relevant to this book, they obscured and hid the reality of free waged porterage along the central routes.

Slavery was indeed a factor in East Africa. Many coast-based porters were domestic slaves or freed slaves of various origins, islamicized and accultur-ated into coastal society, who called themselves Waungwana, "gentlemen," after the patricians of the Swahili towns.[80] They were relative latecomers to the central routes and were a minority of the caravan workforce, which con-tinued to be dominated by the Nyamwezi and related peoples, including the Sukuma, Sumbwa, and Kimbu. Coastal slave porters worked for wages, had considerable autonomy from their owners, and adopted most aspects of the

Photo 1.1 "A Slave Caravan": Porterage as depicted by the British Anti-Slavery Movement. From *Anti-Slavery Reporter,* Series 4, 1, 7 (18 July 1881), 99.

caravan culture of the interior peoples. In comparison, there is little evidence that trade slaves or captives were used for porterage, except sometimes in the south, despite the assertions of many contemporary European observers. Inexperienced, demoralized, sick, and feeble captives were hopelessly inefficient and could not be used by traders for a round-trip. In addition, slaves had a greater tendency to abscond than did free or professional porters. Even at Tabora, where Arabs and Nyamwezi alike owned many slaves, there were few slave porters around 1890.[81]

Even though observers often failed to distinguish between conditions in different regions, numerous travelers wrote accurately of captive porterage in other parts of East Africa connected to the central routes, such as the eastern Congo, where conditions were entirely different from the developing labor market on the other side of Lake Tanganyika. We have noted some examples already. Edward Hore of the LMS wrote, after discussing the use of captive porters by Kabunda, "The *buying* instead of the hiring of labour in inner Africa certainly is an Arab custom, but it is still more essentially an *African* custom."[82] Hore well knew from his own extensive experience traveling the central routes that in contrast to "inner Africa" porters were hired, not enslaved. In another part of "inner Africa"—Bemba country, in what is now northern Zambia—the demand from coastal traders for slave porters by about 1880 contributed to a burgeoning slave trade. In this case slave porters were only used because there was no free labor available.[83] It was the same in Manyema, where captive porters were commonly used to carry ivory to the shores of Lake Tanganyika, despite the preference of the coastal traders for free labor. One traveler reported that Tippu Tip and other important traders "asserted that they would be glad to find other means of transport for their goods instead of trusting it to slaves; but . . . they availed themselves of the means at their disposal." By the mid-1880s it seems that domestic slaves had replaced captives as porters between Kisangani and Nyangwe.[84] East of the lake, Manyema slaves also were used at times to carry ivory from Ujiji to Unyanyembe chiefdom, although free labor (some of it Manyema) dominated this section of the route. Some of those who reached Unyanyembe were sold along with their loads to fulfill the labor requirements of the Tabora Arabs and the Nyamwezi, and for resale to the Gogo in exchange for ivory.[85] In the south, captives were sometimes used as porters on the routes to Kilwa Kivinje and other coastal towns. In 1850 observers saw chained slave gangs carrying loads in the town, and over 30 years later the missionary W. P. Johnson traveled in a caravan in which part of the labor force consisted of yoked slaves, who carried trusses of cloth or tusks.[86] In the catchment area west of Lake Malawi, a missionary reported seeing in 1893 "a great slave caravan . . . the men carrying tusks of ivory down to the coast." He believed that young men were captured by the Arab traders specifically to carry the ivory, although they were sold along with the other slaves who were not forced to work as porters.[87] What separates all these regions from the central caravan routes was the absence of a labor market and therefore a free labor force.

The stereotype of East African slave porterage is partly dispelled by negative evidence, both qualitative and quantitative. The first category includes descriptions of slave gangs not carrying loads, sometimes in the company of apparently free porters who were. For instance, in June 1893, while marching a couple of days out of Ujiji on the central route to Tabora, a British traveler's caravan was joined by another of about 50 slaves, a similar number of Nyamwezi porters carrying ivory, and a few coastmen.[88] Professional porters were clearly preferred over slaves for the carrying of ivory.[89] Important quantitative evidence indicating that very few of the tens of thousands of porters working the central routes were captives comes from Abdul Sheriff's analysis of a list of 1,620 slaves owned by Indians in East Africa in 1860. Given that we know the ethnic origins of these slaves, it is clear that up until 1860 relatively few came from the lands through which the central caravan route passed. Unyamwezi contributed somewhere between 1 and 4 percent, Ugogo less than 1 percent, as did Unguru and Uluguru. Only the Sagara and Mrima each contributed between 5 and 9 percent of the total. By far the greatest sources of slaves were the southern peoples: the Yao (28%), the Nyasa (15%), and to a lesser extent the Ngindo.[90] These figures certainly do not suggest that a large number of slaves, whether porters or otherwise, were descending the central routes prior to 1860.[91] Nevertheless, the most powerful evidence showing that porterage by captives along the central routes was uncommon is a sustained analysis of the emergence of migrant wage labor.

Only in the late 1960s did a revised history of the East African ivory and slave trades emerge. The long hiatus in which old ideas about slavery, the ivory trade, and porterage had remained uncontested left historians a considerable amount of work to do to clear away the rubble of imperialist history.[92] In the meantime, the few historians to write in depth about East Africa, especially the huge regions under the influence of the Zanzibari "commercial empire,"[93] continued to see porterage in the same vein as had Moir, Hardinge, and the rest.[94] Coupland wrote of Arab trading caravans in the time of Burton and Speke as "a long straggling line of slaves, some of them old and tried, others newly bought or kidnapped, all carrying on their heads the bundles of all shapes and sizes that made up the baggage-bales."[95] According to Cyrus Townsend Brady, Jr., "slavery and the ivory trade were one and inseparable. The same traders handled both sorts of merchandise in the interior and at the ports, and the new-made slaves in the caravans marching to the coast each carried a load of ivory."[96] An important historian of East Africa, Kenneth Ingham, writes:

> Ivory was the main attraction which drew the Arab traders ever farther into the interior. Slaves were important, however, more particularly in view of the shortage of porters due to the increasing number of large caravans.

Slaves served a dual purpose, since they transported the ivory to the coast
and could then be sold themselves. Nevertheless, along the route to Tabora
if not in the region Lake Nyasa [Malawi], slaves appear to have been a secondary consideration, since the harsh treatment they received on their way
to the coast frequently resulted in their death, and it seems as if the Arabs
cared little so long as the ivory reached its destination safely.[97]

Generalizing about a vast territory including Uganda to the Lake Malawi
region, the otherwise admirable H.A.C. Cairns reached the same conclusion. In 1972, J.S. Galbraith reiterated what was by then almost a mantra,
stating that "goods from the interior were transported principally on the
backs of African slaves."[98] Among conservative imperialist historians, only
R.W. Beachey goes back to the sources and concludes that the notion of
"black and white ivory," meaning ivory porterage by captives, is "erroneous in its implication." Women and children made poor carriers, and adult
male slaves were burdened by their chains or slave sticks.[99] Even in Edward
Alpers's early revisionist work there are hints of the old view. Alpers points
to the revival of the internal slave trade in the 1870s as a result of the
suppression of the export trade and correctly notes the increased number
of slave caravans reported marching to the coast. He then states that "the
resulting cheapness of slave labor led caravan leaders to use slaves rather
than costlier free porters for carrying their ivory."[100] Missionaries, newly
established in 1876 at Mpwapwa on the central routes, certainly wrote of
slave caravans passing through the district and also occasionally mentioned
slaves carrying loads,[101] but these would have been a minuscule proportion
of the porters on the road.

More important, perhaps, for continued dissemination of the slave myth,
is the text written by Z.A. Marsh and G.W. Kingsnorth, designed for use
in East African schools. On "The Zanzibar Slave Trade" they write, "For
centuries slaves had been captured in the land behind the east coast of Africa
and used to transport the valuable ivory down to the coast."[102] Given the hard
death of the lineage of slavery, it is hardly surprising, then, that a minority
of my elderly informants interviewed around Tabora in 2000 told me that
Nyamwezi *wapagazi* were "caught" by the Arabs and used as slaves to carry
their ivory.[103] This is a clear case of feedback from colonial sources into the
oral record.

In sum, the legacy of an obsession with slavery has worked to the detriment
of any serious analysis of internal market conditions in late precolonial times.
Many scholars assume a lack of flexibility in African societies that prevented
the development of market relations.[104] Good evidence for the contrary view
is that a labor market for caravan porters did emerge, as many East Africans
adapted to the forces of international capitalism in a period of violence and
political upheaval. Some historians have noted increasing although uneven

commercialization of agriculture and commoditization of goods and food-stuffs in parts of nineteenth-century Tanzania.[105] Clearly this has implications for how scholars should view broader processes of economic transformation prior to the imposition of colonial rule, which cut short a series of significant indigenous innovations.[106]

In contrast to the rare use of captives or trade slaves for porterage, there is ample evidence that caravans bound for the interior often included coast-based domestic slaves or freed slaves, the Waungwana.[107] Here East Africa fits into the broader African pattern noted by Coquery-Vidrovitch and Lovejoy. Along with other subordinate groups such as poor but able members of society who wished to advance themselves, and young men frustrated by restrictive lineage ties, domestic slaves used the income-earning and trading opportunities of porterage to buy their freedom or accumulate a little capital. In this sense they were similar to free porters. As Coquery-Vidrovitch and Lovejoy note, "The difference between free and slave was defined by their social status more than by the nature of their work or even the means of payment."[108]

Whether Waungwana or free, it usually made little difference to caravan operators looking to hire porters. Most European caravans leaving Bagamoyo, Saadani, or Dar es Salaam employed a number of slave porters. They were hired on exactly the same basis as other carriers.[109] The first Royal Geographical Society expedition recruited slaves just as if they were free men. No attempt was made to ascertain or to interfere with the arrangements made between them and their owners, and according to the wage list in only two cases was half the advance wage—the usual proportion—paid directly to the master. In only "one or two cases" did the owners prohibit their slaves from departing with the caravan.[110] Another example shows how slave porters frequently evaded their owners, who in such cases had not given permission for a long absence upcountry. In June 1880, representatives of Boustead, Ridley and Company, recruiting agents for the LMS, assembled a caravan of 320 porters for the missionaries and sent the men in dhows from Zanzibar to the mainland. One Karihadyi (Karihaji) had already successfully removed three slave porters from among those already signed up, and their advance wages were returned to the company. But just as the dhows set sail, Karihadyi attempted to take two more porters from the last dhow. Muxworthy of Boustead, Ridley takes up the story:

> We could not get him to come here and examine them, but after they were all shipped he went on board and claimed two men as slaves. I told the Captain to weigh anchor but Kari dragged the men into my boat. However, as soon as the dhow was under weigh I ordered the men to jump on board which they did, and I shoved the boat off before Kari could stop them amid the cheers of the men. Karihadji [*sic*] complained to the Sultan but both Dr. Kirk and Captain Mathews said I was quite justified.[111]

At Saadani domestic slave porters were just as independent. A missionary wrote after recruiting porters that "two slave owners came up to claim their slaves—we had had three previous cases similar—but as the men preferred to go with us and held us to our agreement with them we could not move in the matter. So the owners had to carry their disappointment home."[112]

During the early 1880s the LMS developed a more conciliatory approach to slave owners who suspected their slaves had joined a mission caravan without permission. Porters were hired in the presence of an agent appointed by the sultan, and any Arab looking for runaways could attend as well. If a slave porter failed to obtain his owner's permission to join a caravan, and this was discovered by the caravan leader, the porter in question could choose release from his contract or stay with the caravan. In the latter case, a disgruntled slave owner had to produce an order from the British consul for the slave's return.[113] In the 1890s the English antislavery lobby fastened onto the use of paid slave porters by Europeans, arguing that this stimulated the slave trade.[114] The intervention had a short-lived impact on recruitment in Zanzibar. In June 1891, C. S. Smith, the British consul, restricted a large Belgian caravan departing Zanzibar to hiring only free men.[115] Yet former Consul Holmwood defended the earlier practice, observing that the technical status of domestic slaves in no way affected their work as professional caravan porters. Once a caravan was beyond the reach of coastal authorities, Waungwana porters were not compelled to return to their master.[116] The reality is that Zanzibari slave porters were quite independent, often joined caravans without their owners' permission, and did not pass on the usual half of their wages. Such behavior was symptomatic of the general expansion of opportunities for domestic slaves during this period.[117]

As Cairns noted 40 years ago, the "propagandistic context" in which nineteenth-century contact between Europeans, East Africans, and Arabs occurred and was justified looms extremely large. The standard technique was straightforward. In the case of the missionary and humanitarian lobby, "the more degraded, backward, and immoral the non-Christian world could be painted, the greater would be the difficulty of refuting the arguments for missionary expansion."[118] An exaggerated comparison in which the seemingly harsh realities of East African life could be contrasted with Christian beneficence and European progress found wide scope in the issues surrounding labor and slavery. Imperialists found ammunition for interventionist arguments in much the same way. If slavery and the slave trade underlay African economic and social life, most obviously in the triple affront of inefficient porterage by slaves, including women and children, carrying both themselves and ivory for the profit of Muslim traders, wasn't it the duty of enlightened Europe to impose modernization—Christianity, commerce, civilization—through direct occupation? The irony, and tragedy, is that the increasing European stranglehold over East Africa cut short a promising

African response to the impact of the modern world economy. Waged long-distance porterage was, of course, no answer to the problems of difficult transportation, inefficient labor utilization, and limited trading opportunities. Yet it did create the conditions for the emergence of an African modernity, admittedly one with its own contradictions and severe limitations, in which market forces, entrepreneurship, and creative cultural adaptations—including the emergence of a unique labor culture—were free for a period to find their own way.

CULTURES OF LABOR: SHIPS, CREWS, AND CARAVANS

Most East African caravan porters were wage laborers, usually migrants or itinerants, and they developed a unique African working culture. The characteristics of caravan culture—its origins in the institutions and norms of Nyamwezi society; its timetables and recruitment mechanisms; the evolution of custom regarding the organization and management of caravans, wages, rations, and disputes through experience of the labor process; its forms of resistance and control over the pace of the laboring day; its survival mechanisms and leisure pursuits; and its networks of linkages expressed in bonds of comradeship, joking relationships, and other features—are explored throughout this book. But we need to frame this culture. What kind of labor culture was it? What do we mean by "custom?" If the culture of the caravans along the central routes was an *African* culture, can it usefully be compared with the way of life of porters or perhaps different types of workers elsewhere in the world? Where else can comparable work cultures be identified?

This section, therefore, involves a necessary diversion in order to locate what I call crew culture. The workforce of a caravan can be envisaged as a crew something like, but not quite the same as, the crew of a merchant ship in the days of sail, when Jack Tar was the first proletarian during the early stages of capitalist accumulation and then industrialization. Rediker notes that merchant seamen (like caravan porters)

> were among the most footloose of workers, and they helped to link the various social and geographical particles of plebeian culture. They transcended plebeian localism; they were bearers of culture and information among far-flung groups and places. They contributed to processes of cultural standardization and communication among working people. Since service in maritime employments, whether merchant shipping, the Royal Navy, privateering, or piracy, was relatively common among workingmen, even if only for a year or two at a time, commonalities of cultural experience, and hence bases for shared consciousness, were established among the broader population of working people.[119]

But in the same way that the culture of the sailing ships diverged from the traditions of farm, workshop, and household, professional porters were different from the rest of the East African population with whom they rubbed shoulders in market towns and at caravan stops. Certain elements of caravan culture had origins in widespread institutions and customs such as hierarchies in western Tanzania, or in joking relationships grounded in kinship. But only some customs and traditions familiar to wider society were part of caravan culture, and they were modified in the process. Both localism, which was very pronounced when caravans moved into remote areas away from the main routes, and cultural standardization worked through myriad complex linkages. Further, unlike seamen, caravan porters were rarely isolated for long periods from the larger populations along the caravan routes. The very nature of porterage limited what could be carried, hence porters remained reliant on foodstuffs supplied by peasant communities, and the slowness of their journeys meant that they had plenty of opportunities for social discourse with old friends and strangers en route, or for entering into disputes and sometimes conflicts.

Before continuing with comparison, one further concept needs to be discussed. This is "custom." Here we cannot do better than start with the definition offered by E. P. Thompson, who refers to "custom in the singular (although with many forms of expression), custom not as post-anything but as sui-generis—as ambience, mentalité, and as a whole vocabulary of discourse, of legitimation and of expectation."[120] Thompson, of course, writes about eighteenth-century England and its particular class structure. English plebeian culture was handed down and reproduced through the generations and perpetuated mostly through oral transmission. Here we have a very different environment, despite the common orality of custom, and a more stable social context than the worlds of crews, which were usually more self-contained, and perhaps more innovative, due to their mobility and relative distance from the rest of the population. In eighteenth-century England,

> custom was the rhetoric of legitimation for almost any usage, practice, or demanded right. Hence uncodified custom—and even codified—was in continual flux. So far from having the steady permanence suggested by the word "tradition," custom was a field of change and of contest, an arena in which opposing interests made conflicting claims.

The plebeian culture described by Thompson, "which clothed itself in the rhetoric of 'custom' . . . had taken form defensively, in opposition to the constraints and controls of the patrician rulers." It was "located within a particular equilibrium of social relations, a working environment of exploitation and resistance to exploitation, of relations of power."[121] Custom in relation to crew culture was produced and reproduced in harsh working environments, where death was common, and retribution brutal and swift. But in such contexts men and women were often relatively free from social constraints and conventions and by controlling the workplace could often force their employers to bow to "customary" rights. So far custom might be compared with culture, but Thompson points to a second interpretation. Custom in England contributed to the development of common law as "habitual usages of the country" that might eventually become rules and precedents.[122] We shall see that this was the case in East Africa as well. Indeed, there was a brief moment when customary standards on caravans concerning rations, wages, working conditions, and punishments became embedded in the first labor legislation of at least two East African colonies.

The concept of crew culture is useful not only when thinking about eighteenth-century merchant sailors and nineteenth-century porters but also for a range of other working contexts. Let us turn to colonial New Zealand, where crews of various types were essential to what historian James Belich calls the "progress industry and its allies." The mythical New Zealand pioneers and settlers are the farmer and his family, who broke in the land and established an export-oriented pastoral economy, and the new townspeople of the burgeoning port cities. But in addition to the rural and urban legs of the colonial economy, progress industries acted as a third prop, consisting of a series of public and private works, particularly in transport and communications such as railway construction and road making, port development, and coastal steamship enterprises as well as the transplanting and settling of new white immigrants in instant townships, the military campaigns against Maori "obstacles to progress," gold rushes, and bush clearing and tree felling, as New Zealand's great native forests were stripped and the timber cut up for the construction of houses, shops, fences, and furniture.[123] Belich discusses crews in the context of a debate in New Zealand history started by the notion that mass emigration to New Zealand combined with transience within the new country, and isolation and extreme individualism resulted in bondlessness and the atomization of society. The symptoms, particularly during the decades between 1840 and 1880, were high rates of assault and arrests for drunkenness and a predilection for civil litigation compared with both contemporary Britain and post-1930 New Zealand.

The details of this debate need not detain us, but if people "hit, binged, and sued" then there had to be a reason or reasons. The debate's initiator, Miles Fairburn, blamed high crime on "bondless atoms," individuals without communities and close associates to mediate behavior. Bondlessness had damaged men's ability to interrelate cooperatively.[124] Yet Belich notes that other symptoms of an atomized society, such as suicide, mental breakdown, and imprisonment for debt, were not nearly so visible. Moreover, colonial New Zealand was an armed society; most householders owned a hunting rifle or shotgun, and revolvers were commonly carried. Yet "violent atoms," apparently unrestrained by community and convention, did not use their

guns, preferring fisticuffs to settle disputes. The evidence regarding female
crime follows the same pattern, although at one quarter of male levels,
declining as for men after 1880.[125] Belich concludes that bouts of fisticuffs,
bingeing, and whoring were central to the colonial experience because this
was the period of the "progress industries" that were staffed by crews, and
crews followed their own mores in which fighting, drinking, and casual sex
were tolerated. "Wandering crews, not drifting atoms or a highly atomised
mainstream population, were responsible for the high rate of colonial hitting
and bingeing."[126]

The subcultures and customs of crews were a substitute for community
and wider social bonds. In the age of capitalism the archetypal crews were
sailors, and this was the case in New Zealand. In the varieties of ships that
visited New Zealand (over 8,000 in the 1860s and again in the 1870s), including whalers and merchant marine vessels, sailors and crewmen served for
a season or a voyage and then were paid off and moved on. "Crews were
constantly reshuffled, a floating pool of floating labor." Each seaman could
fit easily into his new workplace due to the standardization of marine culture.
New recruits were quickly taught the ropes, and at the same time indoctri-
nated into crew culture. Even if an individual sailor boarded ship amongst
strangers, "in a sense, he ... 'knew' his new workmates." Sailors shared
similar experiences and had "the same manners, customs, slang, prejudices,
dress, leisure habits, virtues and vices—the same subculture."[127] Many sailors
abandoned ship in New Zealand and entered into other occupations, bringing
sea lore to timber mills and bush gangs, to road construction and gold mining
camps. On shore leave or when paid up, they engaged in the bingeing, fighting, and whoring reflected in the court records. Soldiers and their hangers-
on also lived and worked in crews, and like sailors, thousands settled in the
country they helped pacify.

One group with a special identity were the kauri bushmen, who worked
remote forest regions to bring down the giants of New Zealand's north island
forests.[128] They worked in stable gangs, were both Maori and Pakeha (white);
many of them were formerly sailors or soldiers, and most never married. Tree
felling, cross or pit sawing, and the construction of tramways and railways
as well as dams to float the huge logs down river was tough and dangerous
work that had to be done in teams. Bushmen were often known by nicknames,
and their former lives were their own business. They conformed to a powerful code of honor concerning police investigations. They imposed their own
camp regimens, including lights out at nine and Sunday laundry days, and
took pride in a tough masculine lifestyle, part of which was the consumption
of 15 pounds of meat a week and sleeping without bedsheets. Their historian,
Duncan Mackay, notes that "kauri bush work fostered skill specialization,
and homogeneity and interdependence amongst the men." Bushmen looked
out for each other both on the job and in town and took collections for injured

men and widows in the case of fatal accidents. "They were very orderly on the job and very disorderly off it" when periodically they descended on central Auckland for a binge of drinking and gambling. Like crews in other occupations including, as we shall see, caravan porters, they were profligate with their hard-earned wages, sometimes spending a whole paycheck in one weekend before returning to the bush to start again.[129]

Crews were not only essential to the progress industries but also to farming. Sheep shearers were organized in gangs from an early date, and their subculture has an important place in rural New Zealand life. Harvesters of grain crops and contract ploughmen made the rounds of large farms, and such mobile crews formed a counterpoint to labor on the smaller family-operated farms. All gang or crew work tended to be dangerous, and the workers lived as transients, in camps, ships, or barracks. Few women were present, and if married, men were separated from their families for long periods. Crew culture in colonial New Zealand honored strength, resilience, and mastery of a great variety of manual skills. It was transmitted orally and had its own songs, jokes, and tales. Much of this oral lore drew on the wider world of British, North American, and colonial maritime and military culture. As Belich notes, it was old, and descriptions of English sailors visiting New Zealand in 1773, sealers in the 1820s, and sheep shearers in the 1880s illustrate remarkable similarities.[130] Such cultures are clearly able to transmit themselves successfully, but they rose and fell according to economic trends.

In New Zealand, once the progress industries of colonial development had opened up the country to more sustained agricultural, pastoral, and industrial production, crew culture gave way to the labor culture of the mainstream working class. In a similar way in Tanzania, caravan culture lost its raison d'être as porters were deskilled; railway lines were built; and plantation, railway, and port work absorbed most free wage labor including many porters. Nevertheless, in both contexts, crew culture was part of the uneven and contradictory process of class formation, even as its unique characteristics dissolved under the pressures of colonial capitalism. A further comparison returns us to the idea with which this book started: that porters were engaged in a complex dialectical relationship with the forces and representatives of modernity, and that they themselves represented an African cultural adaptation to the market and international capital. Porters embodied some of the attributes of freedom in the sense discussed above. The comparison with the crews of the progress industries of colonial New Zealand highlights an obvious irony. In the New Zealand context, or in the other workplaces of burgeoning capitalism that crews dominated, such as the world of maritime labor, crews were recognized as integral to "progress" despite the ambiguity of their status in "respectable" society. In contrast, in East Africa, free wage labor in an extractive industry—ivory, like kauri trees, was a wasting resource—was subsumed into the broad category of slavery due to racist assumptions and imperialist designs.[131]

FURTHER QUESTIONS OF VOICE

Research for this book has had to cut through multiple layers of silence. As we have seen, a crippling consequence of Victorian antislavery propaganda and colonial conquest has been the effacement for nearly 100 years of stories of Africans who failed to follow the developmental trajectory expected of them by the universalizing history of "progress," and its passage from "slavery" to "freedom." Another kind of silence in the historical record is a poverty of knowledge about itinerant labor and crews of various kinds.[132] Some of the problems of representation and interpretation of the cultures of colonized and marginalized peoples have been noted above and can be followed elsewhere.[133] Nevertheless, a few comments on questions of voice and historical evidence are in order.

Because this is a study of mobile labor, it makes sense to consider both ends of the migrant labor system—the workplace and home communities. Following Cooper, we must consider what porters brought to the workplace, and what they created there, just as much as what the workplace brought to them.[134] In part, therefore, the larger project of which this book is a part is a history of rural and urban East Africa. It is an argument in favor of the assertion that precolonial societies were capable of initiative and innovation.[135] There are several advantages to such an approach. First, the totality of the labor system, including its relationship with the economy, the social relations of production, and the division of labor in the supplying areas, is more readily understood. Second, the cultural innovations of the caravan system can be fully appreciated only in the light of awareness of the political structure of Nyamwezi chiefdoms, the knowledge base of Nyamwezi society, and its institutions. Thus I take into account a reconstruction of Nyamwezi agricultural practices and the participation of women in political, economic, and social life.[136] Migrant labor rested on the work of rural women,[137] and women themselves were integral to the successful operation of caravans. Thousands of Nyamwezi women walked to the coast and back and undertook other arduous journeys as members of trading caravans, although this level of female mobility, either as individuals or with their menfolk and families, is invisible in previous histories.

"Can the subaltern speak?" Gayatri Spivak believes not, at least in the case of subordinate women in colonial India. Her intervention into the debate kick-started by the subaltern studies group is not as radical as it might seem.[138] Although postcolonial theories have been applied less to African than to South Asian history, Africanists have long championed the "African voice" and various types of neo-Marxist inspired social history "from below."[139]

The methodologies of the study of oral traditions and histories (as well as historical linguistics) have given voice to groups and individuals hidden from history.[140] In addition, feminist scholarship has a stronger voice in African than in South Asian history. Although the presence of women in caravans was noted by a number of nineteenth-century European travelers, it was only when I interviewed female elders in Tabora that I realized the degree of the sometimes stark dichotomy between male and female perceptions of history. Women told me stories of their grandmothers' journeys with their menfolk. In contrast, Nyamwezi men, when asked about female participation, denied that women had the strength or stamina to walk the 1,300-mile round-trip to the coast and back! It is a tragedy of African history that the keepers of oral texts relevant to the late nineteenth and early twentieth centuries, elderly men and women usually living in poverty, are dying before their stories are told. In the same way, the memory of porters' songs, another potentially rich resource, is fading.

Even when authoritative local voices are silenced or forgotten, there are other approaches that, combined with the use of oral and other materials, suggest that a realistic portrayal of caravan workers is possible. Megan Vaughan and Henrietta Moore show in their study of colonial northern Zambia that the construction of representations in nonverbal, nonlinguistic forms, as practices rather than discourses, permeates mission, colonial, and other records. Descriptions of practices and behaviors are not merely a record of colonial assumptions but include local knowledge that explains and represents various activities. In the case of Bemba agricultural practices,

> development documents and agricultural research papers often contain not only descriptions of the strategies people employ . . . but recognizable traces of locally constructed representations of those activities, representations that were often intended as interventions, and which would later be magically re-presented as the conclusions of the researchers and thus incorporated into the solutions posed to particular problems.[141]

In the same way in this study considerable attention will be given, for example, to the practice of desertion, endlessly reported by foreign travelers, by which porters bargained over conditions and maintained control over custom.

Given that Europeans always traveled with African caravans, sometimes for years at a time, the oppositions and objections of porters and related matters occupy a central place in their accounts. It is ironic that the less experienced European travelers often had a great deal to say on such matters, although they were usually ignorant about Africans in general. Novice travelers were surprised by the organized way in which their *pagazi* expressed demands and by the leverage that they could exert. Foreigners' writings therefore highlight much useful material, which can be deconstructed and analyzed not only for its textual content but also for what it reveals about the practices of African caravan personnel. Even in such sources the positivist categories of post-Enlightenment thinking that have dominated imperialist discourse on Africa are often subverted by what anthropologist Johannes Fabian calls "ectstasis," the intrusion of the experience of the senses and the emotions of direct relationships with Africans into the mindset of European travelers. The result is frequent contradiction between the "rational" nineteenth-century construct of Africa and revealing passages in which explorers and missionaries step outside the normative frame of their worldview.[142] Written sources on East African porterage during the period of European exploration and early missionary endeavor, that is from about 1857 onwards, and particularly after 1871, are far commoner than might be realized. I have relied particularly on the archives of the London Missionary Society and the Church Missionary Society (CMS).[143] In addition, it should not be forgotten that a great deal of what European observers learnt and recorded came from discussions with Nyamwezi, Swahili, Arab, and other traders and their caravan headmen, although no doubt translation (in the double sense) altered meanings.[144] Moore and Vaughan stress "the importance of the mutual interpenetration of coexistent practices and representations," noting that "if we do not do this we are in danger of denying local people a significant domain of action, as well as consistently excluding them from the texts produced by scholars, officials and experts on the grounds that they did not write them themselves."[145] To recognize this linkage is to give voice to the "active construction of history and agency" in which practices, evidence for custom, give clues to mentalities.

Custom is visible not only in descriptions of porters' behavior but also in other types of documents not often utilized by Africanist labor historians. European travelers recorded valuable information about their caravans in porter muster roles, wage books, and contracts according to their ideas of proper record keeping and the management of labor. What we see in these documents is less the transferal of European ideology and practices than the encoding of aspects of the customary norms of caravan culture, valid in African and European caravans. They are vital for an understanding of the contestation between custom and contract, and the background to early colonial labor legislation.[146] But the evolution of custom represented the historic agency of caravan porters, whereas codification was part of the process of creating the body of knowledge that facilitated colonial rule.[147]

The African voice is more directly heard in the dozen or so published autobiographies and travelogues by traders, porters, and Christian converts, although in a form mediated by European editorial decisions. Such works include the famous autobiography of Tippu Tip, the biography of Rashid bin Hassani, and other less-known works, such as the diary of Jacob Wainwright and the early travelogues of Lief bin Said and Said bin Habib.[148] There is also the work of the Swahili scholar Mtoro bin Mwinyi Bakari and the collection of Swahili porter and trader travelogues compiled by Carl Velten.[149] Narratives of enslavement and the freeing of individual Africans collected and edited by missionaries for home consumption also contain important details, although their primary purpose as propaganda pieces for fundraising must not be forgotten.[150]

Like earlier works, this book can be read on several levels with different layers of meaning. One level is the concept of a journey. All caravan journeys had a beginning, a middle, and an end. Thus the book is divided into three sections representing departure, the journey, and arrival. At another level the book is a conventional labor history: a history of work and workers, of the customs of the workplace, of wages and conditions, of workers' control of production, and of the culture of work and the defenses against erosion of custom. At a third level this is a history of an African cultural response to modernity represented by the international capitalist system as it encroached into the domains of preexisting histories of interior regions. At a fourth level, this book is the first stage of a history of integration, as new knowledges, networks, linkages, and customs were spread in a relatively dense form along the central routes and its branches, in remote villages, and the new urban centers of the coast and the interior. This is the beginnings of the history of twentieth-century Tanzania. The use of some poststructuralist techniques in the introduction in no way suggests that precolonial Nyamwezi society lacked coherence, or that the caravan system itself was not highly organized. Africans made a world of labor, not as subalterns, but as powerful historical actors.

In chapters 2 and 3 I discuss the pioneering stage of long-distance caravanning, the origins of porterage, and personal motivations. The emergence of professional porters and the development of the labor market are considered, as is the production of ivory, which underlay the caravan system, by specialist elephant hunters. I show how forms of caravan organization and work invented by the Nyamwezi and influenced by others became dominant along the central routes. The rising demand for porters could be met only if caravan operators offered adequate wages and observed the customs of the established work culture. Thus, market conditions contributed to the emergence of free wage labor.

Chapters 4 and 5 present aspects of the work process and caravan life. Nyamwezi work norms and leisure activities formed at home and on safari built the foundations of a common and integrating way of life along the central routes and their branches. Customary patterns of work and leisure including standard loads, the organization of the daily routine, and camp and social life survived into the early colonial period. Moreover, the safari life was always perilous, and caravan personnel faced hardships of an extreme kind. Many of the pressures of caravan life, as well as opportunities for transactions, network building, and recreation, were concentrated in market and junction towns such as Mpwapwa. The ability to transcend difficulties was central to the masculine self-identity of professional porters who, like workers in other dangerous occupations, expressed their sorrows and triumphs in lore and song. Foreign travelers, Arab and European, had little choice but to accept the custom of the caravans. It was only after several years of colonial rule that new ideas about work could be successfully imposed on porters, as their strategic position gradually weakened in a context of structural change.

Both porters and their employers developed strategies to intervene in and manage market forces. But attempts to impose on porters definitions, expectations, and patterns of work derived from European conditions were contested. Professional or semiprofessional porters acted in defense of themselves, their fellows, and their profession. They did so according to their own "work ethic," to use Keletso Atkins's words. As we see in chapter 6, authority in European caravans was expressed in different "languages": paternalistic or authoritarian. Discipline was frequently harsh and arbitrary. Whatever the management style, porters readily exploited the increasing demand for their labor. Bargaining was often collective in nature, and in order to maintain pressure on employers, porters engaged in the typical stratagems and tactics of wage workers wherever merchant capital was an increasingly powerful presence, including desertions, strikes, and slowdowns. Nevertheless, harsh reality on the mainland often diverged from customary norms, and there were constant attempts by European caravan operators to take control over the pace and length of the daily march. The violence associated with increasing imperialist intervention through the 1880s and 1890s meant that discipline in European caravans frequently assumed the brutal military style favored by travelers such as Stanley.

Caravan culture included networking systems, notably joking relationships (*utani*), a conceptual tool derived from ritual joking within kin and familial relationships in many East African societies. Nineteenth-century East Africans took *utani* and adapted it as a conscious model for use as an institution of consociation across and between wider sociocultural groups, thus serving to facilitate caravan travel across time and space. *Utani* as a premodern concept was reinvented and applied to the increasingly modern nineteenth-century caravan system. Although caravans were a special kind of community with their own customs and rules, *utani* helped solidify comradeship amongst porters of varying origins. Beyond the caravan, porters had a somewhat liminal status. They were constantly moving and usually strangers to the societies through which they passed. Ritualized *utani* joking called into being and cemented relationships between caravan porters and their temporary hosts that offered mutual aid and assistance and, at the same time, created linkages and networks that served to neutralize potential conflicts. *Utani* was not the only ritual of the road, however. Chapter 7 also considers rituals of passage associated with the crossing of marginal spaces, empty wilderness country, and the wild no-man's-land between centers of civilized life. Inventors of culture—caravan porters were men and women of the road and carried their world with them.

The book ends with a discussion of collective bargaining, contracts, and wages. Porters were paid either for the anticipated journey or by the month. Nyamwezi porters were well placed within the labor market because of their high reputation and the structural advantages of their position within the caravan system. Custom protected minimum standards and was also utilized as a bargaining tool, especially in larger caravans. Porters used their real power in order to ensure their mobility, maintain their traditional rights, and, where possible, increase their wages. At crucial junctures, when shifts in the labor market occurred and porters pressed their temporary advantage, such as when new well-funded employers hired large quantities of labor, porters seized the opportunity to push up wages. Very quickly the higher rates became customary and set a new standard. The fact that porters were usually paid in standardized lengths of cloth rather than cash made no difference. Cloth in much of East Africa was a form of money, just as cowry shells or copper bars in other regions of Africa served as currencies. Marion Johnson, Jan Hogendorn, and others have shown this for West Africa.[151] Porters bargained just as seriously over their cloth wages as workers elsewhere did over cash. Several years of German imperial government ended the period of favorable market conditions, and wages rates stagnated or even fell. Downward pressures were exerted by economic changes, colonial regulation of African caravans, and the use by the colonizers of state power.

A NOTE ON NUMBERS

During the 1950s about half the able-bodied men of many rural societies in East and Central Africa participating in migrant labor were absent at any one time. Most of the rest had migrated for work at periods in the past.[152] A similarly large percentage of Nyamwezi adult males may have participated in porterage during the second half of the nineteenth century. White Fathers missionary François Coulbois described an annual migration to the coast after harvest time of about 15,000 to 20,000. Franz Stuhlmann estimated in 1890 that about one-third of the Nyamwezi male population traveled each year to the coast.[153] Carol Sissons, historian of Ugogo, estimates that up to 90,000 Nyamwezi males could have worked as porters and traveled to the coast at any time during the second half of the nineteenth century, and perhaps 30,000 actually did so.[154] Most of these estimates do not take into account the large numbers of Nyamwezi porters who worked in eastern parts of the Democratic Congo Republic, Zambia, Uganda, and other regions. Nor do they take into account the many thousands of coastal, Manyema, Sukuma, and other porters who labored along the central route or the porters of the Pangani and Kilwa routes to the north and south.

2

PIONEERS: THE BIRTH OF A LABOR CULTURE

Caravan culture developed out of early patterns of work in the ivory trade. Little is known about the history of the first generations of caravan porters who worked the long-distance trade routes. It is unlikely that we will be able to recover the details of life and work on the caravans during the early pioneering phase of the eighteenth century. Our sources are not much better for the subsequent half century when the long-distance trading system reached maturity. In contrast to the dearth of material on caravans and porterage, we know rather more about local and regional trade, which provided the economic stimulus for the development of the caravan system. In western Tanzania, for example, people were traveling great distances to meet their own needs for basic products such as salt and iron well before the advent of the long-distance trade in ivory and slaves. The integration of such separate networks in western and eastern Tanzania to create long-distance trading systems linking the coast with the far interior is well documented thanks to the pioneering work of Andrew Roberts, Edward Alpers, Abdul Sheriff, and others.[1] Not only was the linkage a spatial one, but the two types of trading networks also interacted with each other, with "regional trade providing the capital, as it were, for long-distance enterprise, while long-distance trade provided new incentives for more-intensive regional production and exchange."[2]

Nevertheless, here and there we are given glimpses of the organization of the caravans, the origins of the porters who worked on them, and the routes they took. It is only with the publication of detailed accounts of caravan life in the works of Burton, Speke, and Grant, beginning in 1859, that a clearer picture became available. But by this time porterage on the central routes was already undergoing change, giving rise to trends toward specialization, professionalization, and the regularization of patterns of migrant labor. The unique labor culture forged by caravan porters had reached maturity, bringing its defining characteristics into sharper focus. Experience over the years and the routine expectation of certain norms and conditions solidified into custom.

The pioneering period was over by about 1850. There are three reasons for this. First, the complex and changing network of routes, market towns, and caravan stops had reached some kind of stability around this time. Second, the mid-1850s mark the beginning of a surge in ivory exports from East Africa to Great Britain, at first via India, and then directly from Zanzibar.[3] The long boom of the 1850s and 1860s contributed to an expansion of the elephant hunting frontier, a greater demand for caravan labor, and changes in the caravan system. The consequences, including the emergence of professional porters, are explored in chapter 3. Third, the 1850s saw the commencement of imperialist interest in the interior of East Africa, and the beginning of direct European participation in the caravan system. As a consequence, toward the end of the century, caravans became the site of struggles over concepts of work and control over the labor process.

Only certain peoples, usually from the interior, took to the work of porterage. They entered into labor migration due to dynamically related characteristics of their social systems, including the domestic economy, external trading relations, geographical location, political and historical experience, and culture.[4] J. Clyde Mitchell in his classic article on the causes of labor migration similarly identifies a "nexus of centrifugal tendencies" (combined with a nexus of centripetal tendencies) in which underlying economic and other forces are expressed in personal motivations.[5] The Yaos of the southeast Lake Malawi region; the Nyamwezi, Kimbu, and Sumbwa of the western plateau of Tanganyika; and the Swahili of Zanzibar and the coast all operated caravans and worked as porters. I include among the Swahili the Waungwana, the slave and freed slave porters of the coast. Their origins were varied, but most came from the heavily slaved Lake Malawi region and southern Tanzania. In this chapter these groups are treated separately. Although they all carried for the ivory trade, the origins of long-distance porterage in each case are local and regional. The second reason is that it was only during the second half of the nineteenth century that an ethnically or culturally mixed caravan workforce became the norm on the central routes, hence affecting the character of caravan labor. Prior to the 1850s the most important of these groups were those from the interior. The true pioneers were not from the coast; Muslim caravan leaders and their followers took routes well trodden by Yao, Nyamwezi, Kimbu, and Sumbwa traders and porters.

How do we explain the early dominance of peoples of the interior, whose homelands lay far from the centers of mercantile commerce? Some comparisons may be useful. In the western Sudan, the Soninke were located between the Sahara desert and the sahel and thus strategically situated for regional and long-distance trade. They also had access to centers of population in the middle Niger River valley and the Gambia River valley. In addition, the Soninke homeland was in the middle of the livestock-raising zone, south of the true desert, and north of the tsetse fly belt.[6] François Manchuelle suggests that in addition to a favorable environment and commercial opportunity, an important factor explaining trade migrations was the presence of decentralized political structures. In such societies there were few restrictions on population movements, and power lay in the ability to accumulate clients through the concentration of wealth. Conversely, if one failed to accumulate wealth, this meant dependence and thus loss of honor. Manchuelle observes: "Thus if one looks for a common denominator for peoples involved in premodern trade migrations, one such denominator may be statelessness or the weakness of the state."[7] Manchuelle also points to the reverse situation—strong state societies where mainstream populations were tied to the land, as in China, and where migrant peoples tended to come from mountainous or peripheral regions. In the case of Asante, long-distance traders were licensed to take part in officially recognized caravans.[8] A similar example is Buganda, where long-distance caravans were also officially controlled and, indeed, do not seem to have been very active. One must be cautious in making such arguments, however, as some strong state societies, for instance the Hausa, were famous for their trade migrations.[9]

Another potentially useful framework for the study of porters and pre-colonial labor history is offered by Peter Gutkind in his study of Ghanaian boatmen.[10] Gutkind's model helps explain the emergence of caravan wage labor, particularly amongst the Nyamwezi. The model rests on twin foundations: first, prior to contact with Europeans, the emergence of hierarchies and labor specialization in some African societies arising from unequal distribution of goods exchanged and accumulated through the workings of long-distance trading networks;[11] second, the entrenchment of the division of labor or the creation of a more-complex division, generated by contact with Europeans and the development of merchant capitalism on the periphery. The two interacting processes worked together to create a hierarchical social structure that over time solidified into classes or protoclasses. Sometimes new specialist occupations were created due to demands for increased production or services. With labor becoming a crucial issue at this stage, it then becomes relevant to look into its recruitment, discipline, and remuneration. Gutkind argues that in some cases wage labor was used.[12] Such cases must be regarded as exceptions to the general rule of an increase in the use of slave labor in late precolonial century Africa. Gutkind's boatmen were one such exception; caravan porters on the central routes were another.

A comparable situation to that on the Ghana coast existed on the East African coast and in Unyamwezi in the early decades of the nineteenth century. Foreign merchants arrived on the coast to find an already well-established trading system, but one with an increasing demand for slaves, gum copal, spices, and particularly ivory on the international market, and African demand for foreign imports, especially cotton textiles and guns. Arab, Indian, and European participation stimulated increased production beyond subsistence needs as well as occupational specialization. The "bug" of money making or accumulation affected some African societies, whose people expanded their trading activities or entered wage work, particularly as porters. New settlements and urban centers grew out of the expansion of long-distance trade, the life of these towns directed toward servicing those employed in trade or engaging directly in the trading economy. Such places included busy entrepôts such as Kilwa Kivinje, Tabora and Bagamoyo, and the many overnight camp stops frequented by the trading caravans. As on the coast of Ghana, it seems that an increasing specialization of labor and commoditization was engendered.[13]

The perspectives of Manchuelle and Gutkind on the emergence of wage labor are at one level reconcilable, although Manchuelle deals specifically with migrant labor. Both point to the opportunities created by mercantile capitalism, especially the expansion of the export trade, and the importance of an earlier strategic role in regional trade.[14] Manchuelle highlights the compatibility of commercial agriculture and labor migration, while Gutkind (quoting Kwame Arhin) points to increasing agricultural production on the Gold Coast beginning in the sixteenth century, as local people took advantage of the commercial opportunities presented by the new European castles, forts, and slave ships.[15] The differences between the two approaches lie at the political level. Manchuelle emphasizes the relevance of decentralized political structures for labor migration, while Gutkind argues that an increasingly hierarchical social structure contributed to a more-complex division of labor, including wage labor. Nyamwezi political structure, as we shall see, lay somewhere in between, although the largest, most centralized chiefdoms also tended to be the most commercialized.

The first sections of this chapter consist of brief accounts of the early history of Yao, Nyamwezi, Kimbu, Sumbwa, and Swahili travelers and caravanners. Following these is a discussion of the characteristics of trade migration and porterage gleaned from the extremely limited data surviving from before the 1850s, which provides a benchmark for the more-detailed analysis in subsequent chapters. The long-distance caravan system would hardly have existed without the expanding trades in imported cloth, amongst other goods, and exported ivory. Too often historians have ignored the production and procurement of ivory in the context of a moving elephant frontier.[16] Thus the chapter ends with a short account of Nyamwezi elephant hunting, which will hopefully stimulate further work on this neglected topic.

UPCOUNTRY PIONEERS: THE YAO

The first professional porters of the mainland of Tanzania were the Yao. Thanks to the research of Edward Alpers, we know that the Yao of northern Mozambique were the major players on the long-distance routes to Kilwa perhaps as early as the first quarter of the seventeenth century. It was only during the mid-nineteenth century that many Yao migrated north and established their homes in Tunduru district in southern Tanzania,[17] although smaller groups of Yao settlers had established themselves in other parts of southern Tanzania in earlier times. As in the cases of other long-distance traders and porters from the interior, the Yao began as local and regional traders: it was local trade in iron and related goods that led them to travel farther afield.[18] Eventually they made contact with another localized trading system centered on the immediate hinterland of Kilwa. Alpers believes that this connection had already occurred by the time of Gaspar Bocarro's journey in 1616. The evidence bears him out. Cloth from "the coast of Melinde," specifically Kilwa, was reaching Chief Muzura's territory north of the Zambezi via Bocarro's route.[19] A demand for imported products such as salt, cloth, beads, and other goods then developed in the Yao homeland and led to the integration of the two systems as the Yao began regular travel to the coast.[20] During the second half of the eighteenth century the Yao, and other peoples from the interior such as the Makua and Ngindo, controlled an interconnected series of regional trading systems that delivered slaves and ivory to the coast. Sometime in the late eighteenth century a colony of "Nyasa"—Masaninga Yaos—had established themselves at Kilwa Kivinje,[21] no doubt contributing to the rise of the town by attracting Yao caravans there in preference to Kilwa Kisiwani (Kilwa Island). By the 1840s, if not earlier, about 40 "large" caravans carrying ivory, rhino horns, tobacco, Maravi iron ware, and other goods arrived at Kilwa Kivinje each year from the Yao, Maravi, Nyasa, and Nyamwezi counties.[22] Around this time the Yao carrying trade to Kilwa increasingly fell into the hands of the Bisa of northern Zambia, who carried their goods the entire distance to the coast and undercut their competitors.[23] In 1849 an American merchant in Zanzibar noted reports of a "Beshu" (Bisa) caravan at Kilwa with 3,000 *frasilas*[24] of ivory, representing a huge caravan. But by the 1860s the Bisa lost their advantage due to greater competition from coastal traders and pressure on their homeland from the Bemba and Ngoni, while Yao fortunes also improved during the last decades of the century. Large Yao caravans of up to 1,000 members were reported to arrive annually at the coast near Quelimane in Mozambique during the 1890s.[25]

Experienced Yao traders and travelers were held in high esteem by their compatriots, while the "pounders of beans"[26] received scant praise. Several Yao songs celebrated the roving life of the trader and porter:

> See the traveller returning!
> "No more short rations," thinks he;
> But loaded plate, and tasty bit,
> And others at beck and call.

And:

> A-travelling I would go,
> If it were not for this grain!
> If I stay winnowing semsem here
> How can I fortune gain?[27]

Yao traders and porters traveled far for economic advantage but reveled in the status of men of the world.

WHY THE NYAMWEZI?

The context of the rise of the Nyamwezi to dominance along the central routes, as well as their importance in surrounding countries such as Buganda, Usukuma, Manyema, the Luangwa River valley, Katanga, and Urungu, is better known. First it is necessary to deal briefly with the complex question of Nyamwezi identity. Unyamwezi occupies a vast expanse of western Tanzania, beginning in the east at Tura, the first chiefdom caravans entered after crossing the Mgunda Mkali wilderness (now the Itigi Thicket), which lies between Ugogo and Unyamwezi.[28] To the west the Nyamwezi homeland extends to Usaguzi, abutting the Malagarasi River; to the north Unyamwezi includes Kahama and Bukune, and to the south, Ugunda and Ugalla. The Nyamwezi, or "people of the moon," meaning the people from the west, are of differing origins and speak variants of Kinyamwezi. The main divisions are between the Galaganza of the Ugalla River basin in the southwest, the Sagali of the territory along the Gombe River in the northwest and center of Unyamwezi, the Kahama of the north, and the Igulwibi of the south. These subsections of the Nyamwezi were never united into one political unit before the time of Mirambo, the famous Nyamwezi empire builder, but rather formed a series of chiefdoms.[29] Closely related peoples including the Sumbwa in the northwest and the Konongo in the south-southwest are sometimes included among the Nyamwezi. The name *Nyamwezi* is of foreign origin and was not used by the people themselves. The Gogo, their neighbors to the east, disparagingly called the Nyamwezi and all travelers passing through their country *Wakonongo*, "the uncircumcized."[30]

The Nyamwezi and related groups—the Sumbwa to the north and the Kimbu to the south—were alone among the peoples of the interior to take advantage of the opportunities presented by the settlement of Sagara migrants, wanderers from their mountain homeland in eastern Tanzania.[31] The arrival of the Sagara in western Tanzania during the eighteenth century, with their knowledge of the coast region, stimulated Nyamwezi traders to carry down their ivory and other goods. As Shorter puts it, "the coming of the Nyitumba from Usagara was an event of the first importance, for they opened up a route linking the interior to the hinterland of the coast, and ultimately drew the peoples of the interior to the coast in search of the new objects of value they had brought."[32] Equally, the Nyamwezi had long been operating caravans over shorter distances as part of regional trade in items such as salt and iron.[33] Significantly, it was this experience that enabled them, and not other groups, to take advantage of new opportunities.

The impact of the Sagara migrations, the distribution of natural resources in western Tanzania, and the central position of the Nyamwezi in the regional trading system all became key factors leading to the rise of the caravan system.[34] The Nyamwezi were essentially cultivators, producing, among other crops, various grains, pulses, potatoes, pumpkins, and tobacco. But because Unyamwezi is somewhat more forested than neighboring territories, inhabitants were able to hunt wildlife and harvest forest products such as honey to make baskets, wooden utensils, and bark cloth.[35] Lacking iron ore and good-quality salt, the Nyamwezi exchanged their products for Sumbwa and Konongo iron, and salt from the Uvinza pans. Other neighbors, especially the Gogo, Sukama, and Ha, kept large cattle herds. The Nyamwezi exchanged their grain, bark cloth, honey, and other products for the cattle and hides of the herders. The fortuitous position of the Nyamwezi in the center of the regional trading system of western Tanzania, between the producers of salt and iron in the west and the consumers of iron to the east and south, made them ideal intermediaries. Moreover, the organization of the gender division of labor, the absence at first of large herds of cattle, and the utilization of immigrant Tutsi and slave labor[36] left them free to travel during the dry season, when there was little work in the fields. In contrast, the nature of the local economies of other peoples in central and western Tanzania made it impossible for large numbers of people to be absent at any one time.

The geographical location of Unyamwezi became even more important when the main routes to and from the coast shifted during the 1840s from the Ruaha river line to the central route network through Ugogo and Unyanyembe chiefdom, a consequence of famine and the inability of the thinly scattered populations of Ukimbu and the Ruaha region to supply large caravans with adequate provisions.[37] As I have argued above, location is inadequate in itself to explain the central role of the Nyamwezi, but other trading peoples, including the Yao, Swahili, and the Kamba to the north, were all based in strategic positions for the caravan trade.

A secondary factor that may have encouraged long-distance migration and caravan porterage was the prevailing condition of lengthy peace and stability.[38] There is no evidence for attacks by outsiders until the mid-nineteenth century, when migrating Ngoni invaded parts of Ukimbu, Unyamwezi, and Usumbwa.[39] Prior to this, conflict was limited to occasional small-scale raiding of one Nyamwezi chiefdom by another. In contrast, peoples to the east, such as the Gogo and Sagara, were subject to raiding by the Nyaturu and Maasai, and in the case of the Sagara, the Swahili. The Nyamwezi were relatively immune because of their smaller cattle herds. To the west, the Ha accepted Tutsi over-lordship, but the Nyamwezi were left alone. By the time of the Unyanyembe civil war in the 1860s and the conflict between Unyanyembe and Mirambo in the 1870s and 1880s, the caravan system was long established.

Two other explanations for the emergence of travel and porterage as major features of Nyamwezi economy and society must be rejected. Some scholars refer to "recurrent severe famines in Unyamwezi" that made it necessary for the Nyamwezi to find additional means of support beyond agriculture and pastoralism.[40] On the surface this is a reasonable argument. There is circumstantial evidence that famine in the homeland of the Kamba of Kenya encouraged them to work as long-distance traders and porters from the late eighteenth century.[41] In contrast, Unyamwezi is less prone to drought and famine than many other parts of Tanzania, including Uzaramo, Usagara, and Ugogo along the central routes.[42] If famine did occur on a local scale, people traveled to less-affected neighborhoods to buy food. When the party bear-ing Livingstone's body to Bagamoyo passed through famine-afflicted Nguru (southeast Unyamwezi), Jacob Wainwright recorded that "many travel to [neighboring] Ugunda to buy seed corn for domestic use."[43] The numerous swamps in Unyamwezi provide reservoirs of water not present to the same degree in Uzaramo, Usagara, or Ugogo. If famine was the main reason the Nyamwezi turned to long-distance trade and porterage in such numbers, then one must wonder why other groups did not do so. In the case of the Gogo it was the nature of their economy, with its heavy emphasis on both livestock rearing and the cultivation of millet, sorghum, maize, watermelons, pump-kins, and other crops, that made porterage unattractive.[44]

The second inadequate explanation relates to culture. The success of Nyamwezi trading initiatives, which brought wealth and the taste for adventure, ensured that trekking and porterage eventually became embed-ded in Nyamwezi culture. Society's values encouraged the young to travel. Numerous nineteenth-century writers thus proposed a cultural explanation for the Nyamwezi predilection for porterage. One described the Nyamwezi as "the professional transport-agents of the East Coast," observing that "not one of them was allowed to marry before he had carried a load of ivory to the coast, and brought back one of calico or brass-wire. It was the tribal stamp of true manhood, at once making him a citizen and warrior."[45] To reflect their heightened status, Nyamwezi men who had reached the coast would often change their names to mark the significance of their visit.[46] Other Europeans who visited Unyamwezi noted that youths would copy the experienced men by walking around with mock loads.[47] Sherry Ortner has noted how in the early twentieth century, European mountaineers in the Himalayas held similar ideas about the innocence and "unmodernity" of their Sherpas, who "did not climb for money, and certainly not solely for money."[48] Such explanations concentrating on culture sometimes fail to distinguish between outward rationalizations of the tendency toward migrant labor, such as the personal search for status or gain, and the underlying socioeconomic causes.[49] This important distinction was made long ago by Mitchell, and restated by Sharon Stichter in terms similar to those used in this book, which emphasize the totality of complex factors in which the social relations of production and ideology are intertwined.[50] The origins of Nyamwezi long-distance trading activities, porterage, and attraction to migrant labor have more to do with local economic and social dynamics than culture, political history, or geography. The Nyamwezi were only able to utilize the advantages they possessed, described above, because of certain characteristics in the social and economic structure of their homeland.[51]

NYAMWEZI MIGRATIONS

The first great journeys of the Nyamwezi and Sumbwa to the coast are usually dated to about 1800, but recent research suggests that this is much too late. Owen Kalinga has shown that underlying the founding from the 1720s of the Balowoka states west of Lake Malawi was a migration of Nyamwezi ivory traders and elephant hunters. They brought with them a knowledge of the demand for ivory at the coast, dyed cotton cloth, and, seemingly, coastal styles of dress.

The Balowoka were immigrant families of differing origins, the common thread being that they all crossed Lake Malawi from what is now southwestern Tanzania over a period of about eight decades and established a number of small states in what is now the mainly Tumbuka-speaking part of Malawi. The Balowoka represented for this region a dynamic new trading interest and, according to Kalinga, asserted power over the preexisting small-scale societies through the manipulation of "a judicious mixture of social factors, religious institutions and economic monopoly." The distribution of blue-black cloth for turbans to clan heads and other people of importance cemented the cooperation of the local clans.[52]

Despite the differing origins of the Balowoka, most came from southern Unyamwezi. The first was Kakalala Musaiwila, apparently, as the name suggests, from Usaiwira, a chiefdom familiar to the earliest travelers from the coast. The traditions state that Kakalala and his followers moved toward the eastern shores of Lake Malawi, at first settling in Songea. They were perhaps drawn west from Songea by commercial opportunities deriving from the ready availability of ivory, rhinoceros horn, and valuable animal skins. It is logical to suggest, as Leroy Vail has, that Kakalala was drawn into this type of commerce through entry into the older Yao trading network to Kilwa and Mozambique Island, active since the seventeenth century.[53] Kakalala Musaiwila crossed Lake Malawi at Manda, moved up the South Rukuru Valley, and eventually established himself on the Nkhamanga Plains, near the

Luangwa River valley. In the eighteenth century, both regions teemed with game and were home to large herds of elephants.

Kakalala was followed by other Nyamwezi adventurers equally interested in the ivory trade and attracted by the rich sources west of Lake Malawi. These included Katumbi and his followers, who arrived sometime in the middle of the eighteenth century and established themselves as rivals to Kakalala. The possibility of conflict was resolved by a "merger" of the two groups' trading interests, although politically, they retained their separate identities. A third important Lowoka settler was the elephant hunter Vinkhakanima Mughogho, apparently from the emerging—and soon to be important—chiefdom of Unyanyembe, in central Unyamwezi. Arriving sometime around 1790, Mughogho settled, as his predecessors did, in the vicinity of the Luangwa River and founded the Uyombe chiefdom, in the process displacing a group of Bisa who had probably been linked to the ivory trade to the coast.[54]

Kalinga argues that the Nyamwezi Balowoka utilized the commercial knowledge of earlier groups of traders, including the Yao and the Bisa, but were able to offer more-attractive goods in exchange for ivory, thus stimulating a rush for ivory in the Luangwa Valley and surrounding regions. Once collected, ivory was sent to the eastern shores of Lake Malawi and from there carried to the Indian Ocean ports. The settlers were careful to satisfy local authorities and sent presents to the Kyungu, king of the Ngonde state, the only substantial polity in the region. Thus the typical friendly and mutually supportive relations between immigrant ivory traders and local rulers were maintained in much the same way that they were between coastal traders and African authorities in the nineteenth century.[55] With these migrations, and those to follow, it is clear that we must think in terms of a Nyamwezi diaspora that long predated the much better-known Swahili diaspora. In addition, the long-standing assumption that the far interior remained isolated during the eighteenth century is called into question.

In the middle of the eighteenth century, the Nyamwezi and Sumbwa already were experienced long-distance traders probably also working routes from their own countries to Buganda and Lake Tanganyika. According to Ganda traditions, the powerful state of Buganda was indirectly receiving goods from the east coast as early as the 1780s. Several historians have suggested that the Nyamwezi may have been involved in the transportation of these goods at least part of the distance to the lacustrine kingdom.[56] Between 1806 and 1810, Galaganza caravans had reached Kazembe's kingdom, according to reports from two Angolan *pombeiros*.[57] In 1809, while at Mesuril in Portuguese territory, Henry Salt met some "Monjou" (Yao?) traders from the interior. He writes: "They told me themselves that they were acquainted with other traders called Eveezi and Maravi, who had travelled far enough inland to see large waters, white people . . . and horses." Alpers identifies these "Eveezi" with the Nyamwezi. This must not be accepted conclusively, because as stated above, the Nyamwezi did not refer to themselves as such. But as Alpers notes, given the central location of Kazembe's kingdom in the subcontinent, and its links between the trading networks of the east and west coasts, it is quite possible that some East Africans had crossed the continent.[58] Four decades later, missionary and explorer J. L. Krapf encountered a Kimbu caravan, which had arrived at the village of Mtotana on the coast south of the Pangani River. "One of them said that he had been in Sofala, and brought copper thence," he wrote. "They seem also to be acquainted with the west coast of Africa."[59]

Certainly Nyamwezi travelers had reached Katanga, the source of copper, not long after 1820. In April 1872, Livingstone wrote while at Kwihara, Unyanyembe, in central Unyamwezi, that he "saw the chief of all the Banyamwezi (around whose *boma* it is), about sixty years old, and partially paralytic. He told me that he had gone as far as Katanga by the same Fipa route I now propose to take, when a little boy following his father, who was a great trader."[60] If the "little boy" was ten years old then, the journey would have been made about 1822. Nyamwezi and Kimbu caravans were certainly trading in Urungu, at the south end of Lake Tanganyika, during the early 1840s. It is interesting that the sources of this statement gave their home district as "Tengasha," the "king" of which was Kiswagara. They also said that "Wutumbara, a large town, and the principal one of the Monomoisy [Nyamwezi] nation, is five days' journey from them."[61] "Wutumbara" probably refers to Itumba, while the meaning of "Kiswagara" has perhaps been misinterpreted and refers instead to the district of Iswangala in central Ukimbu. Both of these districts were on the Ruaha-Isanga-Unyamwezi route.

The first certain mention of Nyamwezi people reaching the coast dates from 1811, when a British naval officer reported that Nyamwezi slaves were the most numerous of the peoples of various "tribes" sold in the Zanzibar market.[62] It is not clear whether they were brought down by Nyamwezi caravans or perhaps through a series of intermediaries. But the same source tells us that Nyamweziland, "at three months' distance, abounds in elephants' teeth," indicating that there was already a considerable trade to the coast in ivory.

By this time the Nyamwezi trading diaspora was in formation. However, the identity of the pioneers is shrouded in mystery, with the notable exception of the Balowoka. It is only the more famous of their second-, third-, and fourth-generation successors of the 1820s and 1830s who have been remembered in Nyamwezi and Sumbwa oral traditions and in a handful of written sources.[63] A clear case is that of Lief bin Said, whose itinerary from his second journey into the interior survives. He was "born in Zanzibar, of the Manmoise [Nyamwezi] tribe," yet we know nothing of his parents, except that his father was also a Muslim.[64] Among the Sumbwa, the caravan leaders Kafuku and Kasanga, both from chiefly families, have been remembered. The story of the death of Kafuku in Ugogo was told to Burton in 1857 or 1858:

> Within the memory of man one Kafuko, of Unyamwezi, a great merchant, and a Mtongi or caravan leader, when traversing Ugogo with some thousands of followers, became involved in a quarrel about paying for water. After fifteen days of skirmishing the leader was slain and the party was dispersed. The effect on both tribes has lasted to the present day. After the death of Kafuko no rain fell for some years—a phenomenon attributed by the Wagogo to his powers of magic;—and the land was almost depopulated. The Wanyamwezi, on the other hand, have never from that time crossed the country without fear and trembling.[65]

The great drought referred to led to the *Mpingama* famine.[66] We can approximately date both the famine and the death of Kafuku to sometime between 1830 and 1840, tying in with Burton's statement that the events described occurred a generation before his own arrival in Ugogo.[67] According to the traditions of the Sumbwa of Ushirombo, Kafuku was the first of their people to reach the coast,[68] so he had made at least one earlier journey. Nevertheless, it is difficult to say how accurate the tradition is when it describes him as the trailblazer. Even earlier, unnamed Sumbwa traders founded the Songo chiefdoms of northern Unyamwezi while en route to the coast. Songo traditional history tells us that the Sumbwa caravan leaders established camps, which, by about 1830, had become permanently settled villages with their own chiefs. The routes followed by the Sumbwa traders to the Mrima coast would have passed through Iramba and Ugogo.[69]

The Galaganza branch of the Nyamwezi have also kept alive traditions of caravan leaders such as Mpalangombe and Ngogomi, who, failing to secure the chiefship of Usaguzi, set off for the coast.[70] Roberts dates these journeys to sometime before 1830. The journeys of another trader from Usaguzi, Kiringawana, or Kilingabana, whose name was given to one of the routes through Usagara,[71] can be dated to the same period. In 1858 Burton and Speke met Kiringawana, chief of Kisanga, a district in Usagara on the road to the Great Ruaha River and the trading center of Isanga. Kiringawana was the son or grandson of the original Galaganza elephant hunter and trader of the same name who had established his rule over the local Sagara.[72] The first Kiringawana (Keringawarha) is mentioned in Lief bin Said's itinerary as "an usurper" at "Kesunga."[73] As MacQueen dates Lief bin Said's journey to 1831, the obvious conclusion is that Kiringawana was well established as a powerful man before that and had probably led caravans to the coast. Another example from the 1820s or 1830s comes from Kimbu traditions, which tell the story of how the Galla trader Kuti founded the Nyipito chiefdoms of Ipito and Nkololo in southern Ukimbu while attempting a journey to the Mwera (southern Tanzanian) coast.

Photo 2.1 Nyamwezi porters at the coast. Note the load of hoes carried by the porter at center-right. From Paul Reichard, *Deutsch-Ostafrika:Das Land und seine Bewohner, seine Politische und Wirtschaftliche Entwicklung* (Leipzig, 1892), opposite 424.

Nyipito literally means "traveler." At least one later chief of Ipito continued to send caravans to the coast on a regular basis.[74]

From the late 1830s into the early 1850s, one catches occasional glimpses of Nyamwezi activity along the central routes. Large caravans regularly arrived at the coast, as Nyamwezi traders took full advantage of the then-friendly relations between their home countries and the sultanate of Zanzibar. For instance, in 1839 a young Englishman in Zanzibar noted that the "Monomwezi have come down to the coast in numbers and with much ivory. They arrived about 20 days since and remain about two months."[75] In October 1842, Jairram bin Sewji, the Indian customs master at Zanzibar, told Richard P. Waters, an American merchant, that "all my Brass wire would go soon . . . as they had received news that three thousand frasillas of Ivory was on its way down to the coast." The caravans almost certainly were using the central routes rather than the southern, because Jairram also indicated that little ivory—but many slaves—was available at Kilwa. One month later, the news was received that three dhows had arrived at Zanzibar "with large lots of ivory," about 1,000 *frasilas,* belonging mostly to Arab traders who had "sent their people into the interior eighteen months since." The entry concludes, "The great Manamoise [Nyamwezi] caravan will be down in two or three months' time with much ivory," presumably the remaining 2,000 *frasilas.*[76] A few years later the arrival at the important coastal village of Mbwamaji of a

great caravan, 2,000 strong, was recorded.[77] Such caravans probably represented
the combined numbers of many smaller enterprises.

From an early date, Nyamwezi caravans traveled according to a fairly
regular timetable based on the seasonal cycle. In 1845 the geographer W. D.
Cooley wrote that

> the . . . Monomoezi . . . descend annually in large numbers to Zanzibar. The
> journey to the coast and back again takes 9 or 10 months, including the delay
> of awaiting the proper season for returning. It would appear that they start on
> the journey down in March or April, probably at the end of the heavy rains,
> and return in September.

Guillain made an almost identical observation. According to Burton
"a crowd" of Nyamwezi descended upon the coast and Zanzibar twice a
year, in the months of January through February and July through August,
to hire themselves out to "native traders" as *pagazi*.[78] Arrival at the coast in
July or August would roughly correspond with Cooley's estimate of departure from Unyamwezi in March or April, given that the journey took about
three months. The months of January and February correspond to a break
in the rainy season in the coastal regions, while July and August are in the
middle of the long dry season. Grant provides a slightly different pattern of
caravan travel:

> Natives are often obliged to travel at all seasons, but will not readily do so
> at the desire of a master; they prefer to travel during certain months, such
> as March and April, when the crops and wild fruits are about to ripen, and
> when they can help themselves as they pass the fields or go through the
> forest; or they prefer to start in August, after their crops have been gathered
> and they have had a feast on the new grain. At this time of the year they
> begin to burn down the tall grass, which might conceal wild animals. The
> seasons they naturally object to travel in are when the country is parched
> by heat in June and July, or flooded by water in December and January: in
> these times food has to be purchased, as the harvests have been gathered,
> and travellers suffer in health from hunger, heat, cold and rain.[79]

Caravans starting from the coast followed a similar pattern, departing either
before or after the rainy seasons. During the rains, the Ruvu (Kingani) River
near Bagamoyo, the main coastal entrepôt from midcentury, often flooded the
surrounding countryside and became impassable.[80]

In Unyamwezi, the rainy season, or *masika*, begins in late October or
early November and lasts until May, after which there is almost no rain
until the following October. Thus there are six months of dry weather and
six months with fairly regular—although not constant—rain. Precipitation
during the rainy season is usually so abundant that low-lying areas are

extensively flooded. During the dry season the flood waters lying on the lowlands evaporate, with regional and local variations.[81] Clearly, travel was much easier during the first dry months. In addition, most Nyamwezi porters were still attached to the land and were busy with their families in the fields during the early *masika,* which is planting time, and were not prepared for long absences when their labor was needed at home. As Burton said of his Nyamwezi *pagazi:* "Porters during the dry, these men become peasants in the wet weather."[82] Finally, seasonal variations governed the availability of provisions en route. Nyamwezi travelers (and no doubt all caravan person-nel) preferred to go on safari when the ensuing harvest guaranteed adequate food supplies. There were always exceptions to this general pattern, how-ever. Occasionally, unusually heavy rain and extensive flooding, which made travel all but impossible, interrupted the regular arrival of caravans at the coast, and hence the supply of ivory to the Zanzibar market. This was the case in the early trading season of 1849, when the Nyamwezi had been "kept back," according to Ward, because "Africa a little ways inland has been completely inundated. There has been more rain than before for 10 years."[83] Furthermore, Nyamwezi porters often went on long journeys that kept them away from home for most of the year, or even several years. The tendency toward professionalism during the second half of the century, employment on Arab and Swahili caravans, and the expansion of the elephant hunting and ivory trading frontier made caravan journeys longer.

COASTAL CARAVANNERS

Although the Bisa and the Yao, the Sumbwa, Kimbu, and Nyamwezi were the true pioneers of long-distance trade and porterage, by the late eighteenth century the Swahili and Arabs of the coast were venturing into the Kilwa hinterland. Further north, on the Mrima, the Swahili were reinforced by Omani Arabs from Zanzibar, as well as a few Indian entrepreneurs, and by about 1820, some had penetrated to the far western interior of Tanzania and had even crossed Lake Tanganyika. The Indian Khoja, Musa Mzuri (the Handsome), played a significant role. He utilized the Ruaha-Isanga route during the early 1820s, played a prominent role along the route to Karagwe and Buganda during the 1840s and 1850s, and was a founder of the trading station of Kazeh (later Tabora) in Unyanyembe in about 1852. The Arab Saif bin Said al-Muamari led the way through Ugogo, which was increasingly becoming the favored option.[84] In 1828 an American visitor to Zanzibar wrote that he had "frequently seen the elephant hunters return from thirty days' jour-ney into the interior and the governor of Zanzibar occasionally sends presents to negro kings a long distance inland."[85] By 1831 caravans from the coast regularly traveled to Ujiji or places nearby. Lief bin Said was familiar with the goods traded in the countries to the west of Lake Tanganyika.[86] Sometime during the 1830s Tippu Tip's paternal grandfather visited Uyowa in western Unyamwezi, and in the 1840s, his father married into the ruling family of Unyanyembe.[87]

The sultan of Zanzibar, Seyyid bin Said, continued to take a close interest in the caravan trade. In June 1839, a caravan of 200 of the sultan's men had left for the interior to trade on his behalf and were expected to be gone about one year. Guillain wrote of the 1840s that "the Swahili and the Arabs of Zanzibar often join these [Nyamwezi] expeditions to negotiate in the countries that they cross; and I am assured that several of them have remained two and three years in the home of the Wanyamwezi."[88] In 1844, an American visitor reported that "His Highness every year sends 100 men into the interior to explore and obtain what ivory and produce of the country . . . they can." The survivors told of having seen "a race of whites similar to the Europeans, and having vessels which are represented as being very fine and sailing on . . . large and very beautiful lakes."[89]

Such stories were not uncommon and, in fact, were heard on the coast much earlier, as we have seen with reference to the Nyamwezi. Hardy heard similar vague assertions while in Zanzibar in 1811 and reported that "Everybody I have conversed with in Zanzibar on this subject agree in their assertions of its [Zanzibar's trade] going to the other side of Africa, where they say Slaves are bought and sold the same as on this side."[90] Although it

Photo 2.2   The Livingstone Tembe at Kwihara, near Tabora, Unyanyembe chiefdom. This reconstruction, currently a museum, is typical of the fortified tembes built by Arab traders at Tabora. These structures were based on an indigenous design. (Stephen J. Rockel, 2000).

is quite possible that Swahili traders had indeed crossed the continent, the "other side" referred to may well have been the shores of either Lake Malawi or Lake Tanganyika. When in Kilwa Kivinje in March 1850, Krapf was told by the governor of the city "of a Suahili, who had journeyed from Kiloa to the lake Niassa, and thence to Loango on the western coast of Africa."[91] There is at least one case in which there is clear proof that coast-based caravan leaders crossed the continent and returned to tell their story. In early 1845 a large "Arab" caravan "under the protection of a great force" left Bagamoyo for the far interior. By the time it crossed Lake Tanganyika it consisted of several Arabs and Swahilis and "two hundred armed slaves," no doubt Waungwana. One of these Arabs was Said bin Habib of Zanzibar. Seven years later a section of this great expedition under the leadership of Said bin Habib arrived at Benguela on the west coast of the continent. François Bontinck, the historian of this epic story, writes of the climax: "The arrival at Benguela, on April 3 1852, of three 'Moors' of Zanzibar, leading a caravan of forty porters, was without doubt a sensational event for the inhabitants of that important port."[92] Said bin Habib continued his slave and ivory trading business in the interior for several more years at Kazembe's, Katanga, and the Zambezi Valley, among other places, visiting Luanda three times in the process. In 1860 he

Photo 2.3 Canoe with dhow rigging and crew, Lake Tanganyika. From Lionel Decle, *Three Years in Savage Africa* (London, 1898), 301.

arrived back in Zanzibar, completing a double crossing of the continent that had taken sixteen years.[93]

In contrast to the exploits of Said bin Habib and his followers, it was much more common for the Swahili and Waungwana of the coastal towns to combine trade and porterage over shorter distances with more-prosaic activities such as farming. A good example comes from the traditional history of Sudi, a small town near the Ruvuma River. The people of Sudi operated plantations that were worked, at least in part, by slave labor. They sold some of the surplus food to buy more slaves. They also hunted elephants for ivory. The townspeople, says "The History of Sudi," also used to borrow trade goods from merchants and travel *"to their former homes,"* where they traded for ivory and slaves.[94] Their "former homes" were probably in the Lake Malawi region, which was a major source of slaves, or perhaps nearer to Sudi in Makonde or Makua country.

From about the fourth decade of the nineteenth century, coastal traders were competing successfully on the central routes with upcountry caravan operators. Nevertheless, in the late 1850s caravans originating in the interior far outnumbered those setting out from the coast. Long-distance trade was still very much in the hands of the Nyamwezi and other upcountry peoples, who used products from their own countries or elsewhere to buy the sought-after ivory.[95] But caravans from the coast were entering new countries and expanding the elephant hunting and ivory trading frontier through Karagwe into regions north and west of Lake Victoria, and across Lake Tanganyika into the eastern Congo.[96]

EARLY PATTERNS OF PORTERAGE

By the 1850s many of the basic characteristics of caravan organization and long-distance porterage were well established. Yet around the time that Burton and Speke began their journey to the central African lakes, important structural changes were taking place, including the emergence of big Nyamwezi traders and a large corps of professional porters. This section presents the organization and work of the porters as gleaned from the earliest sources. Virtually no evidence from the northern Mrima has survived from this period,[97] therefore I will concentrate on the central and southern routes.

We know very little about the organization of Yao caravans on the Kilwa routes before the second half of the nineteenth century, despite the ancient history of Yao long-distance trade. One of the few documentary sources is from the French slaver Morice, who visited Kilwa Kisiwani several times during the mid-1770s. His description of a caravan from the interior is vague, however, and we cannot be sure to whom he is referring, although there are clues provided by the hairstyles.

> The Africans come to the coast of the mainland from the interior with their slaves carrying ivory for sale. They are naked, with only their genitals and rump covered with a skin or a piece of goat-skin dried without being tanned. Their hair is three or four inches long, and is waxed into two or three little clusters as large as pipe-stems. They are armed with knives, or with poor iron spears. By chance I fell in with a band of eighty to a hundred who had come with their slaves.[98]

For comparison, there is some evidence concerning Yao caravans further south in Mozambique. The dispatching of caravans was subject to the authority of the chiefs and headmen of villages. Considerable attention was paid to the preservation of society while the traders and porters were absent. To this end, wives of the travelers were not to engage in adulterous behavior: the belief that unfaithfulness would imperil the lives of the travelers helped ensure stability at home and peace of mind. In addition, prophylactic medicines were used and ritual bathing practiced to ensure a safe journey.[99] We will see further details of such rituals in later chapters. In the 1840s Yao slave caravans were described as "usually composed of twenty or thirty persons, without counting the captives who are often as numerous as their masters, but who rarely seek to regain their liberty by force." But because of the risk of caravan members being kidnapped while on the road, most traders joined with others and thus traveled in formidable force.[100]

We know from the earliest sources that Nyamwezi caravans made similar arrangements. For instance, Kafuku's "thousands of followers" probably represented numerous smaller ventures that, when passing through Ugogo, combined for security reasons and to save on *hongo* payments, the taxes or fees paid to chiefs for safe transit and access to local resources. Krapf provides a better example. In February 1850, while on a voyage down the coast, his dhow stopped at the Sinda Islands off Mbwamaji. There, he recorded in his journal, "we met . . . with many trading people from Uniamesi [Unyamwezi] who build little huts on the strand, and stay in them until they return homeward." Of their caravans, he wrote, they

> consist generally of from three to four thousand men, that they may be strong enough to defend themselves on the way from the attacks of hostile tribes. These people had been here for several months; for they leave Uniamesi in September, and arrive in December at the coast; and return home again in March and April.[101]

Krapf wrote of the Kimbu caravan that he encountered in 1850 at Mtotani that "These people who came with their wives and children from the interior and lived in small huts by the seashore, told me that they spent three months on the journey; and had brought slaves and ivory."[102] When we combine this information about the Kimbu with that above, it is clear that they were active caravan operators and porters during the early decades of the nineteenth century. From midcentury the Kimbu fade from the scene as the main routes shifted north of their territory.

Krapf points to an additional factor. Nyamwezi and Kimbu caravans included women and children among their numbers. A later chapter will show in detail that in many caravans the work of porterage was shared between the sexes and among different age groups. This leads us to the observation made by several contemporary travelers and modern historians that Nyamwezi caravans were relatively egalitarian in terms of relations between caravan personnel and their leaders or employers. This is sometimes compared with labor relations in the caravans of coastal and Zanzibari traders, particularly Arabs, and those led by Europeans, where there was a more-obvious hierarchy.[103] The image of a rough egalitarianism is probably more true for the first few decades of long-distance trade. We hear, for instance, that the sons of Nyamwezi chiefs sometimes worked as ivory carriers, although there is evidence of tension in the stories. Burton was told the story of how Fundikira, son of Swetu of Unyanyembe, learned of his accession to the chiefship in the early 1840s. He

> was travelling towards the coast as a porter in a caravan, when he heard of his father's death: he at once stacked his load and prepared to return home and rule. The rest of the gang, before allowing him to depart, taunted him severely, exclaiming, partly in jest, partly in earnest, "Ah! now thou art still our comrade, but presently thou wilt torture and slay, fine and flog us."[104]

Another example is Mirambo, who worked as a porter in his youth.[105] But there is no evidence from later periods that members of the aristocracy personally carried loads. A more-usual role among the Nyamwezi was for the sons of chiefs to lead caravans and act as commercial agents for their fathers, members of the indigenous merchant elite.[106] From about the middle of the century there is plenty of evidence for the rise of a Nyamwezi merchant class, the *vbandevba*, who were of mixed aristocratic and commoner origin, and who took accumulation and profit making seriously. The process is described in detail by Alfred Unomah, historian of Unyanyembe.[107] The result was the emergence of greater class divisions within Nyamwezi society, which were represented in the caravans.

A few sources tell us that the Nyamwezi sometimes used donkeys as beasts of burden, although never in sufficient numbers to replace human carriers. For one thing they were not suited to carrying ivory but were instead used to carry other trade goods and probably provisions. In 1831 Lief bin Said mentioned the numerous asses in Unyamwezi, and in 1845 Cooley noted the Nyamwezi use of donkeys.[108] Toward the end of the century, however, as ivory exports increased, their importance diminished. These animals were quite small compared with the prized white Muscat donkeys ridden by some Arab traders and were hard to manage, but they had acquired a degree of immunity to trypanosomiasis.

At the coast, as in the interior, the demand for porters by midcentury was rising. The Swahili "History of Former Times in Bagamoyo" points to the recognized value of going on safari, as opposed to staying at home. The period referred to, sometime during the reign of Sultan Majid (1856–70), is after the abolition, of the tax known as the *kanda la Pazi,* or *hongo la Pazi,* paid by the *madiwan* (headmen) of Bagamoyo and Dar es Salaam to the Zaramo.[109] The text reads, "The strongest men went on safaris up-country, while the fools occupied themselves washing their clothes and swaggering about the town—with no food in their homes."[110] The good economic sense of going on safari is emphasized, although whether this be through trade or wage earning is unclear. Profiteering from the caravan business, trade, and porterage was of interest to all levels of society, as Burton tells us:

> The coast Arabs and the Wámrímá have, besides deceiving caravans [i.e. Nyamwezi caravans], another . . . escape from poverty. The lower classes hire themselves to merchants as porters into the interior; they receive daily rations of grain, and a total hire of 10 dols., half of which is paid in advance . . . Respectable men, by promising usurious interest to the Banyans, can always borrow capital enough to muster a few loads, and then they combine to form one large caravan. The wealthier have houses, wives, and families in Unyamwezi as well as upon the coast.[111]

Clearly economic incentives were important.

But were porters themselves primarily traders, or laborers employed by others, or domestic slaves, or some combination of the three? Burton makes clear that class differences in coastal society to a large extent defined opportunity and influenced the division of labor. The key point is that the organization of caravan labor was closely connected to the relations of production in the porters' home societies and differed on each of the main route clusters. Glassman describes the contrast in terms of struggles over culture and identity politics in the coastal termini of the main routes.[112] I contend that as economic, social, and political change occurred in the interior and on the coast, the terms of caravan labor also changed, but within a cultural framework that was already well established by the middle of the century. Glassman argues that in the second half of the century the Swahili culture of the northern Mrima dominated upcountry porters at the coast, who were either passive receptors or frustrated repudiators of it. In contrast, along the central routes the universalizing culture of the caravans dominated both the interior and the coastal trading towns at all levels of society. In other words, the spread of cultural influences was multidirectional, not an essentially unidirectional diffusion of a supposedly higher coastal culture to the *washenzi* (barbarians) of the interior. Caravan culture, which was basically Nyamwezi in origin, influenced people from the coast, just as much as upcountry porters were exposed to the values of *ustaarabu* or *uungwana* (coastal civilization).

Several writers have argued, nevertheless, that among the Nyamwezi, one individual would often act as both trader and porter. Roberts writes that "a young man often used the wages earned on safari (which were usually paid in cloth) to begin trading on his own account. On his second or third expedition he might carry two small tusks of his own; with experience, he might become a caravan guide (*kiongozi*) and thus earn much more cloth for investment, and eventually he might become rich enough to fit out a caravan of his own."[113] This view is true to a point. However, for several reasons the porter described by Roberts may not be at all typical. First, the example does not take into account the relations of production in Unyamwezi, and the emergence of the entrepreneurial *vbandevba*. Second, we need to consider changes in the status of caravan porters over the nineteenth century. Third, the quote suggests that it might be normal for a Nyamwezi porter to trade "on his own account" instead of, as I suggest, as part of a "firm." Although the individual trader surely was common, and there is plenty of evidence suggesting this, there is also material showing that the smaller Nyamwezi traders-cum-porters often worked on behalf of a corporate group whose members were the household or lineage.[114] What might have appeared to casual observers as "individual" trading activities may or may not have been so. Fourth, the image portrayed does not account for increasing proletarianization of porters on the central routes, despite continuing attachment to the land.[115] Finally, the question of slavery is not addressed. Thus, the image portrayed by Roberts may well be at least partially true for the early and middle decades of the century but is rather less likely to be accurate for the last four or five decades. The transition of the caravan porter to the status of specialist and professional is the subject of the next chapter.

NYAMWEZI ELEPHANT HUNTERS

The emergence of specialist traders and porters—an aspect of the elaboration of the division of labor in Nyamwezi society—went hand in hand with increasing professionalism in the production of ivory. Elephant hunting underwent three major transformations over the course of the period covered in this book. First, it became differentiated from its earlier phase as subsistence hunting for meat utilizing preindustrial technologies and became a profession in its own right.[116] Second, it became infused with market principles as the escalating international demand for ivory spread like a wave in the East African interior. Third, Nyamwezi elephant hunters became more efficient as they gained access to firearms during the second half of the nineteenth century and, as nearer supplies of ivory were shot out, the elephant frontier expanded far beyond the *miombo* (brachystegia) woodland complex of western Tanzania and its neighboring regions. This expansion of the exploitable hinterland in itself contributed to further occupational specialization and institutional development. Indeed, some of the parallel innovations in the caravan system informed professional elephant hunting.[117] Elephant hunting and ivory trading "firms" emerged. Senior hunters frequently entered into partnerships with relatives or other members of the *vbandevba,* one specializing in the hunt while another organized the collection of ivory from sources far and wide, while perhaps a third partner recruited porters and operated caravans to the coast.

Ecological conditions and the very landscape in Unyamwezi encouraged elephant hunting. Unyamwezi is part of the central plateau of Tanzania, and most land lies at an altitude of a little above or below 4,000 feet The rolling country is in places broken by high granite outcrops but more usually consists of a succession of low ranges, shallow valleys, and broad plains. Beyond densely populated central Unyamwezi, settled areas alternate with strips of *miombo* woodland or forest from 3 to 15 miles or more wide. Here, until they were hunted out, elephants roamed. During the rainy season the valleys are flooded for months at a time, creating extensive marshlands. These marshlands, or *mbuga,* have been a mixed blessing for the Nyamwezi, hindering movement in the wet season and providing suitable breeding grounds for mosquitoes. But settlements were sited near *mbuga* because of their usefulness as water supplies during the long dry season, and the *mbuga* were also sources of small numbers of fish, poor-quality salt, and clay for pottery.[118] With the introduction of Asian rice in the middle of the nineteenth century, access to *mbuga* flood waters became much more important for Nyamwezi cultivators.[119] Large expanses of swampland, particularly in the northwest and southwest of Unyamwezi and surrounding countries, also provided ideal habitats for elephants, as did neighboring tracts of woodland. Burton wrote in 1859 that "the elephant roams in herds throughout the country, affecting the low grounds where stagnating water produces plentiful vegetation."[120]

In midcentury, despite exploitation, elephants survived near populated areas in considerable numbers, even near the coast in places, as well as in numerous regions within reach of the central caravan routes.[121] In 1859 Speke reported meeting a party of *Makua* (the generic name for elephant hunters) in western Ugogo. They had spend a year and a half there and had killed 17 elephants in that time, giving the local chief one tusk from each elephant as well as some of the meat in exchange for permission to hunt.[122] But just over 30 years later in German East Africa, informed observers believed that elephant populations were in serious decline. According to Paul Reichard, "The elephant, unfortunately, is in most regions more or less wiped out. They are found only in Kilimanjaro, in northern Massailand, a few to the north and north-east of Nyasa, and most of all in the countries to the west of Lake Victoria. Otherwise, nowhere does it pervade the wilderness except for individuals or small herds passing through."[123] Such was the impact of the demand for ivory and the consequent transformation of elephant hunting in East Africa.

Nevertheless, not all ivory entering the market was the consequence of elephant hunting. A significant proportion was so-called found ivory. Indeed, many nineteenth-century ivory traders concentrated more on looting or buying stored ivory than on hunting or employing elephant hunters. Ivory hoards could have derived from the hunt but could also have been taken from dead animals.[124] A source from the mid-nineteenth century notes of the Nyamwezi:

> The traders say they collect much of the ivory in the large swamps of their district, into which elephants have entered during the dry season in search of food, and there being overtaken by the heavy rains of the ensuing wet season have perished by drowning.[125]

No doubt many of the "drowned" elephants were those who had died of natural causes. Burton noted that the people of western Usagara, "being rarely professional hunters, content themselves with keeping a lookout for the bodies of animals that have died of thirst or of wounds received elsewhere."[126] Bridges argues from circumstantial evidence that the massive boom in East African ivory exports from the mid-nineteenth century was likely sustained only through ruthless exploitation of all sources, including significant existing stores held by chiefs and hunters more interested in meat than ivory.[127] The flaw in his argument is a tendency to underestimate the efficiency of African elephant hunters.

Before the large-scale introduction of firearms into the interior Nyamwezi hunters joined together and hunted elephants for ivory, but also for meat and because they sometimes destroyed crops.[128] The hunt was usually organized on a community basis; private expeditions were not yet common. Its preparations were of a strongly gendered character requiring considerable investment in ritual and medicine. The hunting rituals that Burton observed in Unyanyembe probably contain references to an earlier period, although many elements survived into later times. As usual the sardonic wit detracts from his keen eye:

> The hunting-party, consisting of fifteen to twenty individuals, proceeds before departure to sing and dance, to drink and drum for a consecutive week. The women form line and perambulate the village, each striking an iron jembe or hoe with a large stone, which forms and appropriate accompaniment to the howl and the vigelegele, "lullilooing," or trills of joy. At each

step the dancer sways herself elephant-like from side to side . . . The line, led by a fugle-woman . . . who holds two jembe in one hand, but does not drum, stops facing every Arab house where beads may be expected, and performs the most hideous contortions . . . imitating the actions of various animals. The labor done, the ladies apply to their pombe, and reappear after four or five hours with a tell-tale stagger and a looseness of limb . . . The day concludes with a "fackeltanz" of remarkable grotesqueness. This merrymaking is probably intended as a consolation for the penance which the elephant-hunter's wife performs during the absence of her mate; she is expected to abstain from good food, handsome cloth, and fumigation: she must not leave the house, and for an act of infidelity the blame of failure in the hunt will fall heavily upon her.[129]

Not only a failed hunting expedition but also death or severe injury to a hunter were believed to be the result of his wife's unfaithfulness.[130] Although this public ritual was similar to those practiced by the Chikunda and the Ndamba, some aspects seem particular to Unyanyembe, for example, the ritual usage of the *jembe,* the chiefdom's emblem, and the no doubt opportunistic attention given by the dancers to the Arab residents.

At the same time the hunters, themselves well under the influence of *pombe,* engaged in a dance of their own with accompanying music, circling a drum or a bark box that was beaten with sticks and fists and rubbed with stones. The box also served as a sound box for a "bow-guitar" while a fife or goat's horn added to the instrumentation. Several elephant's tails were placed around the drum.[131]

Early the next morning the men would set out, taking rations, firebrands, and their weapons with them. Before guns were common in the far interior, Nyamwezi elephant hunters used heavy spears about six and a half feet long, with a broad head and iron neck embedded in a strong wooden shaft. Attached to the spear was an *mpigi,* or charm, consisting of two pieces of wood bound together with string or animal skin.[132] In the forest the hunters might set up a base camp of hunting huts, but these were frequently abandoned or not utilized due to the great distances covered by startled elephants. Once a herd was located, the aim of the hunters was to separate a tusker and surround it. Then the *mganga*[133] would launch the first spear, with a barrage from the other hunters quickly following:

The baited beast rarely breaks, as might be expected, through the frail circle of assailants: its proverbial obstinacy is excited; it charges one man, who slips away, when another, with a scream, thrusts the long stiff spear into its hind quarters, which makes it change intention and turn fiercely from the fugitive to the fresh assailant. This continues till the elephant, losing breath and heart, attempts to escape; its enemies then redouble their efforts, and at

length the huge prey, overpowered by pain and loss of blood trickling from
a hundred gashes, bites the dust. The victors, after certain preliminaries of
singing and dancing, carefully cut out the tusks with small, sharp axes . . .
The hunt concludes with a grand feast of fat and garbage, and the hunters
return home in triumph, laden with ivory, with ovals of hide for shields, and
with festoons of raw and odorous meat spitted upon long poles.[134]

With its increasing commercialization, the developing professionalism
of Nyamwezi elephant hunters resembled in certain respects the pattern
reported in some other parts of East Africa.[135] From the 1860s onward, the
large-scale importation of firearms and gunpowder enabled big and small
chiefs, other *vbandevba,* and ambitious hunters to rearm themselves and their
followers and recruit more labor. In the process, the power and status of those
batemi (chiefs) who relied merely on their ritual powers were in comparison
reduced.[136] Many of the rising *vbandevba* organized their own hunting expeditions, no longer sharing the revenue from ivory with their community. At
the same time powerful hunters could afford to flout the claims of the local
mtemi to the ground tusk of a dead elephant, as private property rights superseded customary tribute payments. Instead, hunters presented chiefs with
a small part of their profits.[137] One informant, Shabani Kapiga, referred to
elephant hunters as "rich men"—not everyone had the resources to undertake
such work.[138] A hierarchy of hunters emerged, the most experienced and successful, known as *mafundi,* leading expeditions. The *fundi* was a master of
the hunting medicine and all the rituals followed by his party, including the
charms and songs for luring elephants.[139] In order to bring good luck on the
hunt, he wore an amulet to which two lion or leopard claws wrapped in a
piece of fleece or cotton were fixed.[140]

Mafundi and other professional elephant hunters were members of a society known as the *Vbayege,* as distinct from an older society of hunters who
used spears, the *Vbayaga.*[141] The *Uyege* title was awarded for achievement
rather than through rank or birth. A hunter became a member when he killed
his first elephant with a gun, and others more experienced recognized him.
First, they joined him in celebrating the kill by placing him on the carcass.
Then a series of rituals aimed at protecting the young hunter from misfor-
tune confirmed his status as a *Myege.*[142] In Unyanyembe, Unomah writes, the
society did not hold meetings or assemble as did the societies of porcupine
hunters (*Vbanunguli*) or snake charmers (*Vbayeye*). Thus they did not assume
a collective force. Rather, their social influence came through their achievements and evident prosperity.[143]

Unomah provides a brief biography of one of Unyanyembe's famous
elephant hunters, Kapigamiti. His life story illustrates the new professionalism of the occupation.[144] After initial success as a hunter, Kapigamiti acquired
guns and more followers and, moving from his original base in eastern

Unyanyembe, founded his own village of Igoo in Ikengo, near the site of Tabora airport. In a short time he and his slaves destroyed the local elephant population. A spatial expansion of his business followed, necessitated by the movement of the elephant frontier. His hunting expeditions to the north into Usukuma brought him fame, as a great elephant hunter, and Kapigamiti was given his nickname, "He hunted even trees," by the Nyanyembe people. His followers praised him in a song, "Mtalavbanda" (Wooden Sandal), remembered as late as 1971 by his descendents:

> The tramping of the Mtalavbanda of great hunters
> Has completely cleared the forest.
> Brother (Kapigamiti) has come.
> He has ravaged the east with his fire.
> He has gone to Mambolozi, the land of kings and princes, to hunt,
> He has gone to Milumalo, the land of kings and princes, to hunt.
> Ye young men, when you see elephants disappear in the swamps,
> It is the bullets that perform the job
> The smoke of kings and princes.[145]

Kapigamiti had a partner, his brother Mtavbo. Their partnership highlights a further development of elephant hunting and the ivory trade in Unyamwezi. While Kapigamiti remained a specialist hunter, Mtavbo sold the tusks taken from the elephants and, at the same time, traveled across the region, buying ivory to augment the brothers' stocks which were then sold to ivory traders.[146] With this arrangement, a partnership between a *fundi* and a kind of business manager, supported by their servants, employees, and slaves, we can envisage the emergence of a "firm" specializing in the production and sale of ivory.[147]

PART II

THE JOURNEY

3

THE RISE OF THE PROFESSIONALS

Driven out by poverty one man goes to hoe,
The other is like dust blown away to the coast
As porter.
For me my medicines are the coast.
I sitting at home am myself the whirlwind.
You the medicines may make foolish, but not me.[1]

Old Nyamwezi song

By the second half of the nineteenth century, long-distance caravan porters exhibited all the characteristics typical of wage laborers in areas penetrated by merchant capital. Many porters made a long-term commitment and worked on a professional or semiprofessional basis, developing specialized skills and a pride in their work. Caravan work was dominated by the Nyamwezi both numerically and in organizational terms. A mature caravan labor culture had evolved, highly influenced by Nyamwezi cultural norms, that regulated working hours and routines, conditions, and, to some degree, discipline. The models, customs, and working norms of caravan culture became the standards that were accepted by newcomers until the disruption of colonial conquest. Yet experience on the road and structural change in the emerging labor market shaped caravan culture as well. Porters bargained for their wages and rations (*posho*), developed their own techniques of persuasion, and resisted vigorously when custom was violated. A high degree of consciousness is at times indicated by collective action including slowdowns, mass desertions, and strikes. This shared way of life extended all along the central routes between the coast and Ujiji and was the main stimulus for the formation of wider intersocietal networks and linkages across Tanzania. The way porters arranged their working and domestic lives suggests that they can be compared with crews and migrant workers in other places and times. But a comparison should not ignore the high degree of control long-distance caravan porters had over the work process, and the unique East African flavor of a labor culture that emerged without substantial European input. Nyamwezi influence diminished only at the end of the nineteenth century as the power of foreign employers backed by the embryonic colonial state increased, and as structural and political change associated with early colonial rule undermined the independence and economic vitality of the peoples of the western interior.

This chapter considers aspects of specialization and increasing professionalism in the caravan system. In the first section I outline personal motivations for labor and trade migration. This should be seen as the second in a pair of related discussions, the first being "Why the Nyamwezi," in chapter 2. The second section discusses the organization of Nyamwezi caravans, including the classic model that was later taken up and copied by coastal caravan operators and Europeans. Certain skills, great stamina, and devotion to the safari were marks of a professional *pagazi* or *msafari*. The self-perception of Nyamwezi porters included conceptions of pride in their work and honor in face-to-face relations. These characteristics are considered in the third section. The fourth section is a brief overview of the wage labor market and recruitment in the second half of the nineteenth century. The increase in the numbers of wage-earning professional porters from the 1860s was due less to the pauperization of formerly independent Nyamwezi caravan operators, as has been argued by Abdul Sheriff, than to the expansion of the ivory trade and European activities in East Africa, which in turn led to an increased demand for labor. At the same time, small groups of traders carrying their own goods continued to operate caravans, as they had from the beginning of the century. The "pull" factor influencing the labor market—increasing demand for porters—worked in combination with "push" factors including the desire to ensure economic security and the satisfaction of demand in Unyamwezi for imported commodities. Recruitment, or the entry of porters into the labor market, itself became increasingly specialized.

THE WHIRLWIND: PERSONAL MOTIVES

At its most basic level, the individual struggle against the immobilizing despair of poverty—the "whirlwind"—motivated many porters. A journey to the coast was the medicine, and perhaps a cure: "You the medicines may make foolish, but not me." The profound insights of the song the chapter opens with point to personal decision making, but also to a perhaps inevitable response to opportunity opened up by deeper forces: market penetration, competition, poverty. "One man goes to hoe, the other is like dust blown away to the coast, as porter." This underlying reality should not be forgotten. But many saw beyond basic needs to personal and household enrichment, the accumulation of trade goods, and rising social status. Given the relative prosperity in nineteenth-century Unyamwezi, opportunity rather than poverty should be emphasized.

Cloth was the main commodity sought by Nyamwezi porters, although cotton and bark cloth were manufactured in Unyamwezi.[2] By the late nineteenth century local craft production had given way to the consumption of machine-made imports. Francis Nolan sees the high demand for cloth as the leading motivation for long-distance trade to the coast:

> It represented a universally acceptable form of currency and was a convenient form of storable wealth. It was a means of paying wages and gave social recognition to work values. It bestowed elegance, modesty and prestige on the wearer. A store of cotton cloth was an invaluable political asset to a chief.[3]

In 1860 mass-produced cloth was worn more by women than men. Speke describes as "their national costume" the cloth wound under the arms and over the breast. According to Grant the women of central and northern Unyamwezi were better dressed than the men: "all of them wear a cotton cloth from the waist to above the ankles." Female dress was augmented by bead necklaces, brass and copper wire armlets, the raw materials for which were imported or, in the case of copper, traded from Katanga, and thin bands made of the tail hairs of giraffes and bound with fine iron or copper wire. Men usually wore loin cloths while at home but while traveling often wore just a goat skin hanging from their shoulders "in a rather indecorous manner." Their ornaments were similar to those of the women, except that the long wire coils on the arm were replaced by thick copper or brass bracelets and might be augmented by heavy ivory bracelets. For special occasions some wore ornamental monkey or ocelot skins and a zebra mane or oxtail headdress, or a plume of ostrich, crane, or jay feathers.[4] Two decades later many Nyamwezi men were wearing "fine clothes, the produce of India, as under-garments, with long Kanzus . . . over all." By this time virtually all the men wore some kind of cloth, while the women wore "fine coloured handkerchiefs, prints, blue or white calico." Only in remote villages did anyone still wear skins.[5]

A similar transition to the consumption of imported commodities took place in neighboring Ukimbu. In 1857 the Kimbu mostly wore skins. By the 1870s imported cloth had largely replaced skins and bark cloth, and even slaves had access. Cloth came from trading expeditions to the coast, from local trade with passing caravans, or through *hongo* collected by chiefs from passing caravans, who in return were given access to the forest commons. Chiefs and clan members wore colored cloths, and commoners, bonded or free, wore plain calico. Free women also wore beads distributed by chiefs.[6]

For many porters the desire to obtain a gun was the most important motive impelling them to seek work. This was particularly the case during periods of political upheaval such as the Nyanyembe civil war (1861–64), the numerous wars instigated by Mirambo's conquests (late 1860s–84), and those in northwest Unyamwezi (1870s–early 1880s).[7] Referring to this area, Stigger writes, "The priority . . . was firstly a musket and secondly cloth, which only became the objective of a visit to the coast once the gun had been obtained and probably involved an additional journey."[8] From the 1870s porters were sometimes paid part of their wages with a musket, which might be traded for ivory, as firearms poured into the interior.[9]

The acquisition of guns, cloth, and other foreign goods was a means to very varied ends, the details of which are beyond the scope of this study.[10] But it is clear that domestic consumption was important. For a poor man, a trip to the coast might have the aim of merely acquiring sufficient cloth to wear, "because if someone does not have cloth he was regarded as a struggling man." This was the case for Mathias Ntabo's father, who, during the German period, joined a small party for the journey.[11] For many young men a prime aim was to earn sufficient wages to pay bride price. One missionary reported that the young men of his caravan worked to obtain enough cloth "to buy a wife."[12] Porters from northern Unyamwezi and Usukuma used cloth from the coast to generate wealth in cattle and perhaps enter the stock trade. Omari Musa Kagoda's grandfather invested wages from his work as a professional ivory porter in cattle, exchanging *merikani* and *kaniki* cloth as well as beads for the livestock, which, when they reproduced, added to his wealth. When he died, he reputedly had 600 cattle.[13] Some ambitious men aimed at establishing themselves as independent ivory traders or in other ventures and used their wages to buy trade goods.[14] Others of smaller means invested part of their wages in a small quantity of goods to trade on the side, which they carried over and above their employer's cloth or ivory. One such individual worked in the caravan of a European traveler in 1886, who wrote:

> Rumoago, one of my carriers, who had asked me to reduce his load, was found to have tied this to one end of a bamboo stick, with another private load of salt tied to the other. It was not because of the weight he had asked to have a smaller load, but because he wanted to speculate in salt.[15]

Some porters bought slaves with their wages, either to sell elsewhere or to work their *mashamba*.[16] Coastal slave porters could use their wages to buy their freedom. The best-known case is that of Rashid bin Hassani.[17] For specialist porters it was the wages and adventure that attracted them to the occupation, as they made the safari a way of life.

NYAMWEZI CARAVANS: A WORKING MODEL

There was no single pattern of Nyamwezi caravan organization. For porters, a range of options existed between occasional journeys and full-time specialization. Nyamwezi caravans could be small-scale ventures of a dozen or so traders and porters, or massive undertakings of 1,000 or more people. Many Nyamwezi entrepreneurs were members of the ruling class, but lesser citizens, such as subordinate chiefs, hunters, medicine men, and ordinary people, also operated trading caravans. Often the caravans were formed by individuals carrying their own trade goods, and small employers who hired just a few porters each. These numerous petty traders banded together for protection and selected from among themselves a caravan leader.[18]

Nevertheless, some common characteristics of caravan organization and the division of labor among caravan workers can be identified. The pattern for many porters of dry-season travel and priority given to agriculture during the wet season survived throughout the century. The reluctance of most Nyamwezi porters hired at the coast to travel beyond their home countries on the return journey remained typical. These points were much commented upon by European travelers. Cameron, when in Ugunda in November 1873, found it "impossible to obtain any pagazi . . . as they would not leave home during the sowing season." In 1876 a mission caravan was on its way to Lake Victoria. In December, near Nguru, the Nyamwezi porters having met the terms of their contract, left the missionaries. It was impossible to engage new porters as, "the first rains having fallen, the whole population was employed in preparing the ground for sowing, and until all the seed was sown no men would engage as porters." After the task was finished a few weeks later, "several gangs" of men signed up.[19]

The pattern of small-scale enterprise remained common throughout the century. In small chiefdoms such as Ndala, where there were no indigenous traders as rich as those in Usumbwa, Unyanyembe, or Urambo, caravans remained cooperative affairs of several small traders. A few weeks before harvest, in April, a drummer would tour the villages, broadcasting the news that a caravan would soon depart. Porters would then gather at the appointed place. Some would have their own goods to trade at the coast or elsewhere.[20] Sheriff suggests it was probably such small bands that used the northern or Pangani Valley route during the 1840s and perhaps earlier. The northern Nyamwezi and Sukuma made similar journeys to Pangani in the 1850s. During the 1870s and 1880s, they took their ivory instead to Saadani and Winde.[21] A missionary's record of an encounter in the Marenga Mkali, a desolate tract west of Mpwapwa, in August 1891, suggests the security problems that small groups of travelers faced:

> About midday a number of Wanyamwezi travellers came into our camp looking extremely excited, and told us a sad tale of murder and robbery. They said that shortly before . . . they had been attacked by a number of

predatory Wahehe . . . who had killed their leader, and carried off two tusks
of ivory and between thirty and forty goats which they had been taking to
the coast.[22]

This caravan, given the circumstances and the small quantity of stolen goods,
probably consisted of a dozen or so individuals. German records make it possible to estimate the average size of such enterprises. Over four days in May
1893, 15 African caravans passed through Mpwapwa on their way to the
coast. Fourteen began the journey in Tabora, and the other originated from
Kilimatinde, the new German post in Ugogo. All of the 14 numbered fewer
than 60 people, while the fifteenth had 256 members, for a total of 547. The
average size of the 14 smaller caravans was 21 people.[23]

A second option for porters was employment for wages by some of the
bigger Nyamwezi traders, or as a personal service. A third was exercised by
those intrepid individuals who took nothing except perhaps a few hoes on
the downward journey, joining a party hoping to find paid work in a returning caravan.[24] An account from Usambiro in northern Unyamwezi in 1891
highlights the attraction for upcountry porters of wage earning in caravans
leaving the coast:

> A drum was sent out into all the villages round about. . . . The drummer,
> on such occasions, would usually return with a crowd of followers—some
> anxious to carry loads to the coast—others wishful simply to follow in
> the . . . train, as a protection. . . . The men who did no work paid their own
> way down-country by selling tobacco or spades [hoes] of their own manu-
> facture. . . . The main object of porters and followers alike was to get to the
> coast and to carry back a load for which usually good wages were paid.[25]

During the period from about 1840 to the early 1890s, the Nyamwezi also
operated much larger caravans, representing the commercial status of the
trading elite of Unyanyembe and other large chiefdoms. Burton describes the
formation of such a caravan:

> In collecting a caravan the first step is to "make," as the people say, a
> "khambi," or kraal. The mtongi, or proprietor of the goods, announces, by
> pitching his tent in the open, and by planting his flag, that he is ready to
> travel; this is done because among the Wanyamwezi a porter who persuades
> others to enlist does it under pain of prosecution and fine-paying if a death
> or an accident ensue. Petty chiefs, however, and their kinsmen, will bring
> with them in hope of promotion a number of recruits, sometimes all the
> male adults of a village, who then recognize them as headmen.

Once the porters were assembled and all was ready, the *mtongi* oversaw the
allocation of loads.[26] The more-powerful chiefs, as members of the *vbandevba*,

could mobilize a huge workforce, drawing on their status as chief, rich trader, and warlord. As Chief Abdallah Fundikira put it:

> They [the chiefs] too went to the labor market, where people would go to ask for a job to go on a caravan as a porter. But in times of shortage, then the chief would use his influence and get the laborers induced to come, not necessarily by threats or beatings or what[ever], but they would be encouraged: "Come here, you go on the Chief's caravan . . . and you will be well rewarded for your labors."[27]

In 1882, Mirambo sent a caravan that numbered some 1,300 porters to the coast in the charge of his uncle and chief commercial agent, Mwana Seria. They carried 314 large tusks to buy cloth, guns and powder, and another 20 "fine" tusks as a present for Sultan Barghash. Soon after the return of this caravan, Mirambo dispatched several ivory-trading caravans to Buganda, Karagwe, Usukuma, Katanga, Manyema, and other places, indicating his large resources of trade goods and manpower. In September he still had sufficient porters available to send a large ivory caravan under Mwana Kapisi to Unyanyembe and the coast.[28]

Such large caravans of Nyamwezi porters were almost certainly organized according to the model adopted by the Irish caravan leader and trader Charles Stokes, who successfully managed columns of 2,500 to 3,000 porters during the 1880s and early 1890s. Stokes was unique among Europeans in East Africa in the ease with which he could attract porters, largely because he learned and applied the methods of the Nyamwezi and Sukuma. He gained a good reputation among the northern Nyamwezi and Sukuma, partly through his marriage to Limi, cousin of Chief Mtinginyi of Usongo, and partly because of his demonstrated belief in nonviolent caravan management, care for sick porters, and racial equality. Thus he was able to gain access to the labor resources of Usongo, "a land of porters," and other parts of northern Unyamwezi.[29] The future Bishop of Uganda encountered Stokes's caravan at Saadani in July 1890:

> Away from the sea . . . some 2,500 Wanyamwezi porters were encamped. These men had come down to the coast, under the leadership of Stokes, and would each carry back a load weighing some seventy pounds. They were mostly fine, stalwart-looking men. Some had brought their wives, who cooked and carried the cooking utensils and food—often no light burden. . . . Many [of the porters] were swaggering about in . . . a few yards of white calico. . . . Others had cloth . . . wrapped about their heads as a turban or folded round their waists as a loin-cloth. Others, again, were simply clad in skins. All apparently were armed with spears, bows and arrows, or antiquated muzzle loaders . . .

These 2,500 porters . . . were divided into fifteen camps and companies. For instance, there had been assigned to us for the porterage of our loads some 300 Wasukuma. These men were in [the] charge of a "nyampara," or head-man, named Simba . . . Under him were five or six subordinates who had charge of companies. Four or five, or a larger number . . . messed together. These smaller companies also had each its head. It was each man's duty in turn to cook for his fellows, draw water, and fetch firewood.

Thus the whole caravan was organized.[30]

As Tucker noted, after the merchants the most important caravan officers were the *wanyampara*,[31] literally "grandfathers." The origins of the name and function clearly lie in the political structure of Nyamwezi, Kimbu, and Sukuma chiefdoms. Northern Unyamwezi and Usukuma, according to the missionary C. T. Wilson, were divided into numerous districts, each ruled by a chief, or *monungwa*. Under the *mwanangwa* were several "lesser chiefs," or *banyampara*. "It is under these niamparas," he wrote, "that the porters or pagazi go down to the coast to engage in caravans going up into the interior."[32] Wilson was actually describing subdistricts of chiefdoms governed by *batemi*. *Nyampara* is most correctly described as "elder."[33] We have accounts from central Unyamwezi and Ukimbu of the role of *wanyampara* as members of

Photo 3.1 Irish trader Charles Stokes in Zanzibar, 1892. In the foreground are Stokes' Nyamwezi and Sukuma headmen. Standing at the rear are Zanzibari *askari*. To the left of Stokes is Indian merchant Alidina Visram. From Nicholas Harman, *Bwana Stokesi and his African Conquests* (London, 1986), 192. Reprinted with permission.

chiefs' councils.[34] It is unlikely, however, that it was the same individuals sitting on chiefs' councils who regularly went on safari, as they are described as "elders" or "elderly." Rather it seems that the title and authority were transferred to influential caravan headmen, who may later have become council members. Indeed, an elderly informant specifically distinguished between chiefs and *wanyampara,* who, he stated, were "the clever ones" taken from the ranks of the ordinary porters. Successful *wanyampara* were able to establish themselves as patrons and accumulate followers, or perhaps slaves, who would provide a source of farm labor.[35] The title was also used in caravans of coast-based porters and was therefore accepted in a multiethnic environment, where its original meaning was lost. This is the implication of O.F. Raum's statement that "the leaders of the porters, the *wanyampara,* were self-made men of great physical strength endowed with moral stamina and a sense of justice. Famous leaders spent their best years on the caravan paths, passing from one expedition to another."[36] Here, then, we have a clear example of how the caravan culture of the Nyamwezi and related peoples penetrated to the coast and dominated other caravans, albeit in modified form.

The *mganga,* or traditional doctor and diviner, another important caravan official, acted as advisor and provided ritual protection against the dangers of the road. Important diviners were sometimes also ivory merchants and organized their own caravans.[37] *Waganga* advised unsuccessful itinerant traders to carry out the "gourd of travel" ritual to improve their fortune.[38] Apart from protecting caravan personnel, the *mganga* also ritually cared for the ivory. Ivory tusks were ensured safe arrival at the coast after they had been ritually marked with spots, lines, and figures. The *mganga* carried only a light load "in view of his calling."[39]

The fourth important caravan functionary was the *kirangozi,*[40] the guide or leader on the march. The *kirangozi* was usually elected by the porters. He was not necessarily from a special rank or section of society. Any individual with experience and some standing among the porters, and with good knowledge of the road, could be chosen.[41] The *kirangozi* had no substantial power, although he had a few more opportunities for personal gain than were available to regular porters. Famous *virangozi* accumulated honor and status, sometimes recognized in naming practices. One informant's grandfather was a well-known safari leader, and his son continued to be known into his old age as Samweli Kiongozi.[42] According to Burton, a *kirangozi* had to "pay his followers to acknowledge his supremacy," and purchase "charms and prophylactics" from his *mganga.* While on the march the *kirangozi* preceded the porters, who would be fined if they stepped ahead of him. His work was to lead the caravan along the correct route, and mark off with a branch or a handful of grass, or a line drawn with the foot or spear, the paths that stragglers were not to take. Failure to mark the route for porters in the rear could lead to much wasted time and the dangerous dispersal of the caravan.[43] Despite his responsibilities, the *kirangozi* was the butt of abuse "for losing the way, for marching too far or not far enough, for not halting at the proper place, and for not setting out at the right time." He might also negotiate *hongo* with chiefs along the route. His perquisites included better rations, a lighter load, and sometimes the attendance of a slave.[44] At the beginning of a journey he was entitled to a goat "to make the journey prosperous," and perhaps other presents.[45] According to Unomah, the office was similar to that of the flag bearer of the Nyanyembe army, especially in the use of ritual implements, including a small drum.[46] A *kirangozi* at the head of a caravan made a powerful statement:

> The dignitary is robed in the splendor of scarlet broadcloth . . . with some streamers dangling before and behind: he also wears some wonderful head-dress, the spoils of a white and black "tippet-monkey" [colobus monkey?], or the barred skin of a wildcat . . . or the gorgeous plumes of the crested crane. His insignia of office are the kipungo or fly-flapper, the tail of some beast, which he affixes to his person as if it were a natural growth, the kome, or hooked iron spit, decorated with a central sausage of parti-colored beads, and a variety of oily little gourds containing snuff, simples, and 'medicine' for the road, strapped around his waist.[47]

Men such as these were professional porters, familiar with caravan life and possessing a deep knowledge of the roads.

THE PROFESSIONALS: PRIDE AND HONOR

The earliest European travelers into the far interior found that porters could readily be hired at the coast for an agreed wage, although there were variations in supply according to the extent of demand, the season, the political situation in the interior, epidemics, and other factors. This was the case not only at entrepôts such as Bagamoyo, Pangani, and Saadani, where caravans initiated and terminated their journeys, but at many of the more-important market centers and caravan stops along the central routes as well. Time and time again, they also used the term "professional" in their references to caravan porters. The use of such terminology does not contradict the ample evidence of the continuation of the older tradition of dry-season travel practiced by small upcountry traders and porters, a distinction first noted among modern historians by Robert Cummings.[48]

Many scholars have noted the earlier pattern of porterage but neglect or discount the appearance of a large corps of professional wage-earning caravan leaders, headmen, and porters. Roberts writes, "The carriage of ivory to the coast became a most important feature of Nyamwezi life, but it was not essentially a specialist activity." A more-extreme position is taken by Nolan, who argues that Nyamwezi porters cannot be considered to be specialists or wage workers before the colonial period.[49] Juhani Koponen provides in many respects the most balanced account of economic and social organization in nineteenth-century Tanganyika but writes:

> The impression created by some later historians that porterage was wage labour comparable to colonial migrant labour does not seem particularly well-founded. Rather, I should like to argue that among porters more important distinctions than those between slaves and free labourers were, first, between what might be called 'trader-porters' and 'worker-porters' and, second, between those who worked on their own and those who acted as commercial agents for their political leaders.[50]

Differing with Koponen, I argue that "worker-porters" did share many characteristics with colonial migrant laborers. From the point of labor history, it is the frequency or rate of migration or level of specialization that is important, as well as the experience of the labor process. In addition, Koponen's reformulation of categories does not clarify matters. There were, in fact, no hard and fast divisions, but considerable overlap, as we have seen. Other historians have recognized that the role of specialists was an innovation with important ramifications, including the beginnings of regular migrant labor and the transfer of capitalist ideas, as well as other cultural consequences.[51] Long-distance caravan porterage was marked by a distinct way of life and the development of professional status and pride. Specialist porters showed a long-term commitment to porterage, learned the skills necessary for success and survival, and proved their endurance and strength. A code of honor regulated customary practices. Together, custom and honor provided the "grammar" for the labor culture of the caravans, which over time, and drawing on other resources, shaped communal interactions across Tanzania. None of these characteristics were greatly affected by the continuing partial attachment of most porters to the land.

The earliest mention in the contemporary literature of professional carriers dates from 1860, when Burton, writing of his experience in 1857–59, described the Nyamwezi as "the only professional porters of East Africa."[52] Decades later, a missionary noted that the Nyamwezi were "the professional transport-agents of the East Coast." In 1879 another wrote: "Wanyamwezi take more care of their loads than Zanzibar men. The former are *professional* pagazi, the latter seldom."[53] But in time, coastal porters were also designated professionals. The former British consul at Zanzibar, F. Holmwood, had this to say concerning Zanzibari porters in 1893:

> It is true that a large proportion of the porters, guides and guards of all expeditions from Zanzibar to the interior is composed of slaves, in a technical sense. Whilst representing England at Zanzibar, I engaged, both for the

company, for Mr. Stanley, and for other travellers, more than a thousand of such porters.

These men are *professional travellers* whose livelihood is gained by such work, and the fact of their being slaves or otherwise has no bearing on their engagement, for no master can compel a slave to travel, and, practically, the moment he is outside the coast region he can desert and settle as a free man in the interior.[54]

There were more-obvious signs than status of a lifetime of physical labor. Like eighteenth-century merchant seamen, porter's bodies gave evidence of the "massive confrontation" with their physically demanding and dangerous work.[55] The traveler May French-Sheldon noted "the muscular development" of Nyamwezi porters' shoulders through their long experience carrying loads. In 1905 the German anthropologist Karl Weule described almost all his Nyamwezi men as "professional carriers, sturdy fellows with tremendous chest-measurement, broad shoulders and splendidly developed upper-arm muscles."[56] Nevertheless, by Weule's time the day of the "trained professional porter" was almost over. In later years, according to one experienced traveler, those who intermittently worked as porters rarely had the physical attributes "of the old type who made it their life's work."[57]

Photo 3.2 Professional ivory porters at the coast. Bildarchiv Preussischer Kulturbesitz, Berlin. Reprinted with permission.

The long-term commitment of specialized porters is readily evident. Many worked the caravan routes for a number of years before returning home. In 1861, Speke succeeded in acquiring the services of a specialist *kirangozi,* named Ungurue: "He had several times taken caravans to Karague, and knew all the languages well."[58] At Lumeresi's in Buzinza, south of Lake Victoria, Speke met an old acquaintance called Saim, a porter in a caravan arriving from Karagwe. "Saim told me he had lived ten years in Uganda, had crossed the Nile, and had traded eastward as far as the Masai country. . . . Kiganda, he also said, he knew as well as his own tongue; and as I wanted an interpreter, he would gladly take service with me."[59] Saim was a trader, but also a professional porter, perhaps carrying his own goods at times, but otherwise prepared to hire himself out to others. Many porters made several long safaris with the aim of accumulating enough wealth to invest in their farms or slaves or buy ivory to sell at the coast. In 1876, Mackay of the CMS noted that one of his men had traveled five times to Ukerewe island in Lake Victoria from the coast town of Wanga.[60] Even now, elderly informants remember professional caravanners such as Hamis Mbuya, a Nyamwezi Muslim who in pre-German times traveled to the coast seven times and to the Congo five.[61] In his history of Unyanyembe, Alfred Unomah interviewed several old men who had made numerous journeys to the coast during the late nineteenth or early twentieth century. One, Mwana Kakulukulu of Kazima in Unyanyembe, was over 100 years old at the time of the interview in 1968. He had traveled to the coast seven times; after the fourth safari he had enough capital to establish his cattle business.[62] Others made porterage a lifetime's work. One German writer met some elderly Nyamwezi who had walked to the coast more than 20 times.[63]

Specialist caravan leaders and porters also worked the northern and Kenyan routes. A leader of the 1,000-strong caravan from Pangani to Laikipia in 1868 had traveled to Maasailand 15 times. French-Sheldon found that many of her men had previously worked for European travelers and big game hunters. The *kirangozi* in Oscar Baumann's expedition of 1891–92 was Mkamba, a slave who "roamed uninhibited through Massailand year in year out." Baumann recognized in him "the typical 'msafari' (caravan man) of Pangani. He returns from Lake Rudolph only a few days later to set out again for Kavirondo; in one caravan his poor wages are counted out to him and in the other he names his advance for the next journey."[64] Like other experienced European travelers, Baumann admired the competence of such experts as Mkamba; his headman, Mzimba bin Omari; and other specialist caravan operators and porters. In 1892, a few days after the return to Zanzibar of W.G. Stairs's Katanga expedition, numerous headmen and porters, "unwarned by experience," signed on to a Uganda-bound caravan.[65] Many of their friends had starved to death in the famine associated with the collapse of Msiri's empire in Katanga, partly a consequence of the aggression of their employers. Another veteran was missionary A.B. Lloyd's cook, who had traveled "several times" to Uganda prior to the disastrous journey through German East Africa of the CMS caravan of 1894–95.[66]

Marcus Rediker has written at length on the similar wanderlust of eighteenth-century merchant seamen, whose rambling from port to port, ship to ship, was often seen by their superiors as symptomatic of social breakdown.[67] During early colonial times in Tanzania, German settlers and colonial officials resented the same freedom of caravan porters to "roam uninhibited," to avoid controls and evade labor ordinances, characterizing them as "drifters" who lacked stability and discipline.[68] Indeed, porterage involved social change, but the mobility of caravan porters gave them opportunities for socially constructive activities. New linkages and networks were created with far-flung communities across vast territories, and new ideas and practices introduced to remote regions. Freedom of movement enabled porters to negotiate with their feet better terms and conditions, as we shall see. Jack Tar would certainly have found in the professional *pagazi* a brother in arms.

The expansion of demand for experienced caravan personnel caused by European activities meant that many porters could move from one European caravan to another, as they were required.[69] After 1876, when Protestant and Catholic mission societies established stations upcountry, many porters found regular work on supply caravans and caravans taking up missionary reinforcements, as well as on mail services. In 1880 one LMS missionary traveling to Ujiji noted that the caravan had "a very good chief, Ulia [Ulaya]," who had worked some years before for another LMS man.[70] In the meantime, Ulaya had been employed by the French traveler, the Abbé Debaize. Other porters in the caravan had been with earlier LMS expeditions.[71] Mandara, a porter with Stairs's Katanga expedition in 1891, had previously worked for Joseph Thomson, Frederick Jackson, and Bishop Hannington. Bega and Mirabo Ngumba had survived Stanley's Emin Pasha Relief Expedition.[72] Mission societies and imperialist expeditions thus represented part of the expansion of opportunity for specialist caravan porters. Many must have worked for Arab, Swahili, and Nyamwezi caravans in addition.

Experience along with age were respected virtues among porters. Youths looked up to "gray-beards," Burton observed. "The older men, who have learned to husband their strength, fare better than their juniors, and the Africans, like the Arabs, object to a party which does not contain veterans in beard, age, and experience."[73] Such depth of experience was a resource that could be drawn on in difficult times. During the long months at Fort Bodo in the eastern Congo rainforest, the porters of the Emin Pasha Relief Expedition vented their frustrations in comparisons between their current predicament and the *saffari ya zamani*, former caravan journeys, during which there was "more food and fiercer natives, more cattle, longer marches, and bigger men."[74] Experience often showed that conditions did not live up to those on previous safaris. The result, as we will see below, was individual or collective resistance.

The work of professional caravan porters required considerable expertise and endurance, most basically for survival, but also for completion of long journeys, trade, and to deal with emergencies. One experienced European traveler wrote in praise of Nyamwezi professionals: "These Wanyamwezi are really marvellous people. . . . It is hard to imagine anything more admirable than the skill with which they manage to meet all difficulties."[75] Ivory porterage in particular was "a skilled and arduous task best performed by fit and experienced young men; undisciplined and demoralized captives would have been of very little use."[76] Certainly, familiarity with the caravan routes must have been essential for the professional porter.[77] Weule found that some of his carriers were so knowledgeable of the routes that they were able to reproduce them in rough but accurate maps covering the central route to Tabora and beyond, and branches to the north and south.[78] Expertise in the various languages of the road and knowledge of the peoples whose countries were traversed were essential. This meant some ability with Kiswahili and Kinyamwezi, as well as, for example, Kikuguru, and Kigogo. Porters on the northern routes found Kizigula, Maa, and other languages spoken in northern Tanzania and Kenya valuable.[79] A further set of skills involved the acquisition of a fund of knowledge for survival on the road and in far-off countries. Such knowledge included familiarity with practical survival techniques for coping with provisioning problems and food shortages, bad weather, and other hardships. Porters often needed hunting skills and a knowledge of edible plants and insects. Other useful practical skills included facility with food processing and knowledge of traditional medicine. Some porters specialized in hunting to provide meat at camping stops.[80] Porters also had to understand intergroup cultural support networks, including *utani,* through which aid could be provided in times of need.[81] Commercial knowledge of the long-distance trading systems would have been essential.

Remarkable stamina was another characteristic of specialist porters. Stanley believed the Nyamwezi to be superior to the Waungwana on account of their greater ability to resist disease, their enormous strength and endurance, and "the pride they take in their profession." By the early 1900s, Nyamwezi porters were "famous for their almost incredible powers of endurance."[82] But professionals from the coast were tough as well. J.A. Moloney wrote of the Mwungwana, or Zanzibari, "His powers of endurance are marvellous; they defy alike hunger, cold, rain, swamps, and malaria." Moloney put this down to "the easy fatalism" of the "patient and cheerful" coast porter.[83] Thomson wrote of his 150 "Zanzibari" porters' resilience when climbing the Uchungwe mountains west of Mahenge in 1879:

The power of lung and muscle displayed by the Zanzibari porter is certainly remarkable. With a load of from sixty to seventy pounds on the

head or shoulder, and a gun in the one hand,—the other being occupied
steadying the bale,—he will patiently toil up a precipitous mountain by the
hour together without stopping to rest, and probably shouting or singing
all the time.[84]

Thomson's Zanzibaris were in fact mostly Yao in origin, a consequence
of the vagaries of the slave trade: "The Wahyao are perhaps . . . the most
industrious and energetic people to be found in East Africa," he wrote.
"The best coast porters have been originally brought as slaves from the
Yao country. Nearly all my best men . . . are Wahyao, and the experience of
many other travelers has been the same." W. P. Johnson of the Universities
Mission to Central Africa endorsed these views: "A trained Yao will carry
a load, keep up with any European [who of course did not carry a load],
and when he has built the latter his booth to rest in, will go off to look for
honey, or if the halt be in a village, will dance all night, and come up smil-
ing next morning."[85]

Such comments carry hints of the racial and ethnic classification so typical
of the era, with tinges of an antimodern and romantic ethos finding satisfaction in descriptions of a "natural physicality" combined with the "easy fatalism" that apparently separated East Africans from Europeans. Sheryl Ortner
in her work on Nepalese Sherpas notes such a discourse in the writings of
twentieth-century European mountaineers, in which ideas of "children of
nature" loom large.[86] Consider first the following sympathetic account of the
tribulations of Zanzibari porters in Katanga written by an Irish member of an
expedition notable for its high death rate:

> There were periods when meat was not forthcoming, and then the caravan
> had to put up with very short commons indeed. For forty-eight hours they
> [the porters] did not touch a bit of food; and yet on the afternoon of the
> second day the long line of patient wayfarers toiled into camp, and every
> man began, without a murmur, to build his little grass hut, cut wood, and
> fetch water. There was something heroic about this mute resignation to
> circumstances, and I fear Tommy Atkins, under similar conditions, would
> hardly have displayed equal restraint. Indeed, Captain Stairs remarked one
> evening, that, had we been dealing with British soldiers, our work would
> have been cut out to keep them from mutiny.[87]

In 1924, Sherpa porters were cast in a similar although not so saintly mold by
a member of the British Everest expedition:

> They have the same high spirit for a tough or dangerous job; the same ready
> response to quip and jest. As with the British soldier, the rough character,
> who is perpetually a nuisance when drink and the attractions of civilization

tempt him astray, often comes out strongest when 'up against it' in circumstances where the milder man fails.[88]

In these quotations, not only was a common discourse at work, in which class, race, and an antimodern romanticism were all present, but also a snapshot across the centuries of a common process of historical categorization brought about by global capitalism. British soldiers (a quarter of whom were Irish), Zanzibari porters, and Sherpas (and may we add merchant seamen?) were subject to similar historical processes in that they had become workers of a particular type: they were all crews working at the margins of empire, with their own crew culture, customs, and ideas of honor and pride. Despite the limited nature of the discourse in most of the sources, the physical, moral, and cultural resources required for the very tough work of professional porters are revealed through careful comparison. The "children of nature"—as late as 1978, one European mountaineer described Sherpa porters as "bare-footed angels"[89]—were indeed heroic, although certainly not saintly!

Beyond mere description, burdened as it often was with orientalist assumptions, perhaps the best measure of endurance is the time taken to walk (or jog) routes commonly traversed. LMS mailmen are a case in point. Although not caravan porters in the usual sense because of their light loads and relative freedom to set their own pace, they sometimes made long journeys along the central caravan route in remarkable time. Ebenezer Southon of the LMS Urambo station, about 750 miles' march from the coast, reported that he had received letters from Zanzibar in just 33 days, an average march of almost 22 miles a day.[90] A trading company at Zanzibar reported that a letter from Ujiji, over 930 miles by foot, arrived in 45 days (an average of about 20.5 miles per day). Another from Unyanyembe took 39 days for a journey of perhaps 680 miles (over 17 miles per day). Such times were quite normal, and numerous other examples could be cited.[91] The LMS mailmen were mostly Waungwana. But the Nyamwezi were generally considered to be the strongest and most robust messengers and porters. According to Southon,

> Twenty five to thirty miles a day for ten consecutive days would be considered good walking for the average Mnyamwezi. Their pace is generally about four miles an hour.
>
> Men who are practised runners & habitually employed in carrying messages, are capable of trotting long distances, and often make short journeys in an incredibly short space of time. Forty to fifty miles are often made in one day by such men. Mirambo once told me that some of his men had made the journey from Urambo to Ujiji in six days. To do this they must have averaged about 40 miles a day. 'Runners' are almost always shod with hide sandals and are seldom loaded with a gun or other heavy weapon.

A spear or bow & arrows, are generally carried, & as the runner is not troubled with much clothing, he jogs along during the greater part of the day, and seems alike insensible to heat, hunger or fatigue.[92]

Large caravans with heavily laden porters were much slower. The LMS caravan of 1879 from Saadani to Ujiji took 100 days, including rest days, about 9 miles per day. This good time was facilitated by the few desertions and little property loss. Even better time was made by the experienced porters of the LMS caravan managed by Juma, which reached Urambo from the coast in 72 days (over 10 miles per day, including rest days).[93] One of the quickest journeys on record must be that of Bishop Tucker and his caravan, who marched from Nasa, Usukuma, to Zanzibar during the dry season of 1893. The journey took just 44 days including the passage to Zanzibar, but this was only possible because there were at least two porters for each load.[94] When an LMS caravan arrived at Saadani from Ujiji with 70 half-loaded porters, the journey had been completed in 62 days, making an average day's march of almost 15 miles. But when the 12 rest days are excluded the average daily march was slightly over 18 miles.[95] Clearly such arduous journeys could not be undertaken successfully by amateurs.

Nyamwezi, Swahili, and Arab caravans, however, usually traveled at a more leisurely pace. First, their purpose was trade, not just conveyance of the stores of explorers or missionaries. Second, Nyamwezi caravans to the coast often included herds of goats and cattle, the latter sometimes acquired from the Gogo, which necessarily slowed the march.[96] Third, upcountry porters often had to spend more time finding provisions on the march, given the more-limited quantities of barter goods available to them compared with porters working for coastal traders and Europeans.

On a more-personal level, many porters celebrated their strength and endurance. When Southon discussed the weight of some large tusks with Chief Mirambo, he casually asked, "I suppose these large tusks will be carried by two men?" Mirambo laughed and said, "No, we have plenty of men who can carry much larger ivories than these, and one man to each is plenty, in fact, some men would carry two of the small ones." "But," said Southon, "no ordinary pagazi could carry so heavy a load for any distance." "That is true", the chief replied, "but many *Wanyamwezi* men take a pride in carrying heavy weights, but then they cannot make a very long journey. Some men will carry a heavy bale but cannot carry a tusk, whilst others can carry a large tusk but are unable [to] carry a bale. It all depends upon what a man has been used to.'"[97] Livingstone saw one such Herculean porter, who carried six *frasilas*, or 210 pounds, of ivory from Unyanyembe to the coast.[98] Sometimes when loads were apportioned, especially the heaviest and most awkward, the strongest of the experienced porters were reminded of their previous deeds and were urged by their headmen to set a good example. These veteran carriers had considerable pride, which would not allow them to take the lightest burden. This was the case with Songoro, one of the porters who worked for the French explorer Giraud. Songoro told Giraud that he had gone with Stanley "from Zanzibar to the second sea [the Atlantic Ocean]" carrying a section of his boat. Working for Stanley in the Congo, he claimed to have carried no fewer than 25 boat sections from the Atlantic coast to Stanley Pool.[99] Another remarkable porter was Mnyamwezi Bundula, who habitually marched near the head of missionary S. T. Pruen's caravan. He had lost his right hand years earlier in a gun accident and "yet managed to carry his madala load (two loads tied to opposite ends of a pole), and to tie it up most skilfully [*sic*] every morning, not withstanding this defect."[100]

Specialist caravan porters were proud of their occupation and their skills and endurance. Like Rediker's merchant sailors, they were men of the world who had traveled far and experienced life to the fullest.[101] They recognized a code of honor that had developed at least as early as midcentury, particularly among Nyamwezi porters. Its most obvious expression was the custom of porters when deserting to leave their loads and sometimes their advance pay behind rather than damage their collective reputation. Burton wrote of his Nyamwezi porters that they "hold it a point of honor not to steal their packs; but if allowed to straggle forward, or to loiter behind, they will readily attempt the recovery of their goods by opening their burdens, which they afterward abandon upon the road."[102] A decade later, a French observer echoed Burton. Nyamwezi porters, he wrote, were "of a proverbial honesty and exemplary docility. However there would be danger in treating them harshly," he warned, "not because they revolt against bad treatment, but because they save themselves by abandoning their loads intact."[103]

There are many examples. On the very first day of Speke and Grant's journey to Unyanyembe in September 1860, 11 of the porters disappeared, including 10 of the freed slaves provided by Sultan Majid of Zanzibar, and one Nyamwezi *pagazi*. Only the Mnyamwezi "deposited his pay upon the ground." Later, near Zungomero, three more Nyamwezi porters deserted, leaving their loads on the path. At Kanyenye in Ugogo eight of the Nyamwezi absconded. Although they took a part of their burdens with them, this probably represented what they considered to be wages owed to that point.[104] At Bagamoyo in 1873, a number of recently hired Nyamwezi porters disappeared but "were honest enough to leave their pay behind them." In 1893 the tradition was still alive. A Nyamwezi porter deserted the caravan of Lionel Decle on the Unyanyembe border, leaving his gun, ammunition, and the 49 rupees that were owed him in wages.[105]

Whether they deserted or not, the Nyamwezi had a good reputation for honesty. Livingstone spoke highly of "Banyamwezi" porters who "as usual" carried goods "honestly to Unyanyembe" in advance of himself. Stanley had an equally good experience in this regard on his first expedition, not losing any goods from the small caravans sent ahead of his own party to Unyanyembe. "The Wanyamwezi as a rule are honest people they will not open a load & take anything out," wrote one missionary.[106] But the Nyamwezi were not the only porters to have a code of honor. One of Cameron's Waungwana went so far as to find a replacement to carry his load to Unyanyembe when he deserted in the Mgunda Mkali in July 1873.[107] Southon's Waungwana and coastal porters showed pride in their work on the journey upcountry in 1879 by taking extreme care of the goods entrusted to them, with not £1 in loss, damage, or theft by the midway point. The missionary wrote that "They are very faithful in all things & honest beyond measure, so that I never trouble about locking things up." During 1879 and 1880, Thomson had the same experience with his Zanzibaris, who "never once presumed to put forth their hands unlawfully to take what was not theirs."[108] Deserting porters did not always show such scruples, however. In April 1873 one of Cameron's Waungwana named Uledi disappeared with his load near the Mkata swamp. When returned by Chief Kisabengo, he was flogged "as an example." The porters "agreed that the punishment was well deserved, for on this part of the road, although it was not thought any disgrace to desert, yet it was considered a point of honour that a man should never run away with his load."[109] What is notable about this case is that collectively porters were just as interested in maintaining their reputations as employers were in enforcing discipline.

Collective pride was expressed in other ways. Porters insisted on being well dressed when departing on a long journey or arriving at major caravan termini. In contrast, while on the march, they often wore old rags.[110] Nyamwezi porters took pride in the tradition that once on the road from the last camp stop, they would not backtrack.[111] Besmirching the honor of porters could have serious consequences for employers. In one case in 1879 near Mahenge, mass desertion almost resulted from an unintentional smear by Joseph Thomson on his Waungwana porters' honor. Describing the incident, the youthful explorer wrote:

Seeing a porter offering beads of a kind suspiciously like my own to a woman to pound rice for him, I asked Chuma [his headman] where the man got them. The latter, who heard what I said, immediately went off among the men, telling them I was accusing them of stealing beads. A dreadful row was at once raised, the drums were beat frantically, and the horns blown to call all the men together. From all sides they came rushing, bringing their guns, etc. These they laid down at my feet with the air of injured innocence. They had never been accused of stealing before! "Here are our parcels," cried they; "look and see if we have anything belonging to you. Now give us our tickets of discharge, that we may go back to the coast, for we cannot go with you to be looked upon as thieves!" Every one was in the utmost excitement. Personal articles were packed, and preparation for a general return made, as if an unpardonable aspersion had been cast upon their unsullied honour, which as immaculate men they were bound to resent.

Thomson was forced to back down and apologize.[112]

Finally, specialist porters can be compared with amateurs. Often the sources express such differences between professional and amateur porters in ethnocentric terms: Nyamwezi or Zanzibari professionals, with their highly developed labor culture, are compared with amateur (or perhaps unwilling) porters of some other ethnicity. We must resist the temptation to essentialize the characteristics of specialist versus nonspecialist porters as a product of ethnicity. The key difference is that the professionalism of caravan labor emerged from experience and integration into a specific labor culture. Many Africans no doubt had other perceptions of work and perhaps masculinity that did not necessarily coincide with those held by specialist porters.

Amateurs had less discipline and motivation, could not or would not carry heavy loads, had no pride (often considering carrying the work of slaves or women), marched erratically, and would not travel far.[113] In contrast, explorer Frederick Elton was struck by the prodigious strength of professional porters working the central routes in comparison with his earlier experience of porters in Usangu, Ubena, and Uhehe:

> After our experiences of Wasango and Wachungu carriers, the immense loads undertaken by these . . . porters of Zanzibar and Uniamwesi [Unyamwezi] astonished us. Some of these fellows are magnificent developments of the human animal, with herculean frames; but even the smaller . . . possess a capacity for endurance, as well as a muscular strength, that makes us Europeans feel very poor creatures. I have seen them slide and stagger along a path, which a diminutive torrent has worn into a narrow deep winding groove, with slippery sides, or over a marsh, ankle-deep and knee-deep in black tenacious mud, for six and eight hours at a time, without once taking their loads off their heads.[114]

Experienced carriers themselves differentiated between their own abilities and those of amateurs. In 1883 Johnson traveled to the north end of Lake Nyassa and reported his porters' view of its Konde inhabitants:

> They have, I have been told, the poorest reputation as carriers, and I have heard my own porters compare a caravan of them to a string of ants, each ant carrying a very tiny bit. Any little joke like this is kept up and rubbed in, as it helps the carriers of larger loads to forget the strain on their own muscles.[115]

In addition to easing the daily workload, customary regulation and the code of honor of professional porters assisted them to manipulate the developing labor market, as we shall see. There were good practical reasons for regular porters to take pride in their work!

THE LABOR MARKET AND RECRUITMENT

Commodification of caravan labor and the emergence of a labor market epitomized the spread of market relations along the central routes. As we have seen, professional caravan porters who traveled year in and year out, working for wages and rations as well as occasional trading opportunities, increasingly met labor requirements as demand rapidly expanded from midcentury.[116] The continuing vitality of the Nyamwezi *vbandevba* and the extension of their operations throughout East and Central Africa contributed to the expansion of the labor market, while coastal Muslims and European missionaries and travelers also employed tens of thousands of porters. For many Nyamwezi, the caravan trade continued to be lucrative until after the imposition of colonial rule. Indeed, in 1894 a knowledgeable German observer wrote, "This tribe have been porters for a long time, through porterage reached a certain prosperity, and can be described accurately as a trading people."[117] The continuing high demand for Nyamwezi porters can be seen in the numerous contemporary accounts of Nyamwezi trading activities and caravans on the road, as well as reports of labor shortages at the main termini.

Many Nyamwezi, attracted to the traveling life and a steady income, joined the caravans of coastal traders. Even before the founding of Tabora by entrepreneurs from the coast in 1852, their Nyamwezi counterparts traveled "in large numbers" to the Arab depot of Isanga in Ukimbu to do business. Nyamwezi youths followed them there and offered to work for the Arabs and carry loads to the coast or to Unyanyembe. They thus replaced the "servile gangs" formerly employed by coastal traders but still utilized along the northern routes to Maasailand and the southern routes to Lake Malawi and beyond.[118] In September 1857, Burton and Speke met a large caravan of 400 Nyamwezi porters, apparently employees of four Arabs. They encountered another in October about 1,000 strong, under the command of slaves of Salim bin Rashid, an Arab trader based at Unyanyembe.[119] Fifteen years later, when Tippu Tip traveled to Urua (the Luba kingdom) in the eastern Congo, he took with him about 800 Nyamwezi porters, and Nyamwezi continued to work for him along the Lualaba River. Other coastal traders operating west of Lake Tanganyika in the 1870s, such as Jumah Merikani, also employed Nyamwezi gangs on a permanent basis.[120]

The trend toward labor commoditization accelerated during the 1860s. This was the decade during which massive ivory exports to Great Britain from East Africa began, in addition to the existing large trade in Indian reexports from East Africa, and exports to the United States and elsewhere.[121] Given the established and rising demand for cloth, guns, and other goods in the interior, more Nyamwezi took up regular wage work as hired caravan porters, both for coastal traders and the Nyamwezi *vbandevba*.

Despite the increasing activities of coastal traders, is clear that Nyamwezi caravan operators remained competitive. Burton believed that a "far greater" number of caravans of upcountry traders than Arabs plied the central routes. During a visit to Bagamoyo in 1866, a French missionary noted that Nyamwezi porters worked both for coastal traders and organized their own caravans.[122] Nyamwezi caravans were probably more numerous than those of coastal traders until at least 1880, later than has been realized. In June and July 1876, when missionary Roger Price traveled from Saadani to Mpwapwa, his party met almost daily "a goodly number" of ivory caravans bound for Winde and Bagamoyo and, presumably, Saadani. He emphasized the dominance of Nyamwezi and other caravans from the interior: "These were all purely native caravans." In 1878 another missionary encountered numerous Nyamwezi caravans over a two-month period. In the same period he noted just one large Arab-led caravan, and its porters were also Nyamwezi.[123]

There is no evidence for this period that either subsistence or commercial agricultural production in Unyamwezi was undermined by labor migration, although conflict and environmental change in some areas negatively affected farmers.[124] The agricultural labor force in Unyamwezi does not appear to have been diminished by the absence of large numbers of porters. On the contrary, porterage and trade helped mobilize and sustain a large backup labor force of women, slaves, and immigrant Tutsi cattle herders in precisely the most commercialized regions of Unyamwezi from which a high proportion of Nyamwezi males migrated along the caravan routes.[125]

The Nyamwezi elite and smaller traders continued to provide employment in their caravans well into the 1890s, while many young Nyamwezi men worked for coastal traders and Europeans. In 1888, at the start of the uprising against the Germans, Nyamwezi caravans were in Bagamoyo, and another "large Nyamwezi caravan" was diverted to Dar es Salaam with its ivory. Even during the fighting, a large Sukuma caravan with great quantities of ivory, cattle, and goats entered Bagamoyo.[126] In October 1889, the survivors of Stanley's Emin Pasha expedition met a Nyamwezi caravan 1,500 strong on the eastern edge of Unyamwezi. In June 1890, a German traveler returning to the coast encountered a large Nyamwezi caravan numbering about 1,200 in Ugogo, then another "great Wanjamwesi caravan" under the German flag, followed by several others in the Marenga Mkali.[127] Another traveler wrote of the Nyamwezi from his experience in 1891–92:

> The energies of the people are . . . absorbed in travel, and they trade in ivory, copper wire, salt, honey, and so forth, over the whole of central Africa, frequently journeying in large caravans, and being absent from home for two years or more. These expeditions are generally commanded

by Arabs . . . But very frequently voluntary associations are formed every spring, a drummer beating up recruits from village to village, which journey down to the coast or into the interior.[128]

And in June 1893 a missionary met in the Mgunda Mkali wilderness "a huge native caravan—fully a thousand people . . . all carrying up to what seemed their utmost capacity." The description of their loads suggests a Nyamwezi or Sukuma caravan.[129] Hundreds of smaller Nyamwezi and Sukuma enterprises arrived at the coast during these years.[130]

Nyamwezi and Sukuma porters carried vast quantities of ivory during the first years of German expansion. Traveling upcountry from Bagamoyo in July 1891, Stairs recorded that "considerable quantities of very fine ivory tusks are now on their way towards the coast, coming from Unyamwezi . . . This morning, we saw almost fifteen hundred ivories file past which will net the Germans 14,200 dollars [Maria Theresa thaler] thanks to export duty." At Morogoro, 11 days later, he wrote: "A huge caravan overburdened with ivory passed through our camp." Earlier, when at Bagamoyo, Stairs had commented on the "numerous close columns of Wanyamwezi" that arrived virtually every day. The identification of the business interests being served was complicated, however, because by this time Nyamwezi caravans carried the German flag.[131]

The expansion of the labor market was driven by the high demand for labor, rather than surplus supply originating from impoverishment of interior peoples, as Sheriff suggests.[132] As trade boomed, there was a parallel massive increase through the century in the demand for carriers. As the ivory frontier was pushed back into the farthest parts of the interior, the routes lengthened, caravans spent more time on the march, and caravan journeys became more-protracted affairs. More and more regions and peoples were drawn into the orbit of the commercial system. In addition, the second half of the nineteenth century was the age of European expansion in East Africa. The demand for porters further increased from the early 1870s as expeditions and caravans of European explorers and missionaries competed with local traders and each other for labor.[133] During peak periods, experienced porters could pick and choose among the numerous caravans leaving the coast. In some years coastal and interior towns were almost cleared of porters as demand outstripped supply.

The high demand for labor at Bagamoyo in the dry season of 1882 was described by the agent for the trading house Boustead, Ridley and Company: "Although an immense number of Wanyamwezi have come to the coast this season, they have all been hired at high rates, some very large caravans of traders having been dispatched."[134] In Tabora also, porters were reported to be "scarce" because of the large number of caravans on the road.[135] In Zanzibar the situation was often the same. The drain of labor away from the island

caused considerable consternation among Arab plantation owners, who peti-
tioned the sultan to prevent European travelers from "inducing slaves to run
away" and shipping them clandestinely.[136] A European traveler describes the
state of the labor market as it was in early 1883:

> The African Association on the Congo had drained off the very best porters
> in the town. Several large caravans, missionary and otherwise, had just left
> for the interior, so that there was hardly a good porter to be had. . . . To cap
> the situation, two large caravans were about to be organized for the interior,
> one for Victoria Nyanza, and another for Karema.[137]

Again, in June 1891, Stairs heard "of a great dearth of men" in Zanzibar
resulting from the large number of caravans leaving for the interior. Around
the same time another traveler was told "there were no porters to be had,
even at Zanzibar, so many caravans had been equipped for the Germans as
well as for the Imperial British East Africa Company, and for some private
expeditions that had combined to drain the country of available porters."[138]
Thus, in many years, demand far outstripped supply. More rarely was there
a surplus of porters at Bagamoyo, as during the dry season of 1878. *Pagazi*
were unusually cheap and plentiful. "Some men," wrote a missionary, "have
even despaired of getting work and are building and planting and will stay
here till next season."[139]

Photo 3.3   The old Bagamoyo caravansary as seen in 2000. (Stephen J. Rockel.)

The rising demand for labor forced structural and institutional change in the caravan business, reflecting increased specialization and the elaboration of the division of labor during the second half of the nineteenth century. Recruitment became a business in its own right, and hiring practices at the main termini were increasingly regularized so that employers could find porters without a long search. Recruitment "agencies" emerged at the coast, especially at Bagamoyo. "The whole and sole occupation here is preparation for journeys to the interior," wrote a missionary in 1878. "Everywhere the signs of a large pagazi business are apparent."[140] Porters were able to find work easily, either individually or through a popular headman, by registering with recognized recruitment agents. In Unyamwezi the important chiefs regulated access to porters by outsiders. None of these patterns of recruitment displaced the old Nyamwezi style of mobilization described above.

By the late nineteenth century, the most notable feature of caravan labor recruitment was the role of Indian entrepreneurs in the coastal towns, especially Bagamoyo.[141] From the earliest journeys of Europeans into the interior, Indian merchants were involved in outfitting caravans and recruiting porters. Burton's headman, Said bin Salim, was assisted by the "Cutch banyan" Ramji when the first gang of porters was hired at Bagamoyo. Ladha Damji, the Zanzibar customs master, sent a caravan of Nyamwezi porters to Kazeh with Speke and Grant. *Jemadar* Isa bin Kunari of Bagamoyo, according to the historian of the town, "very quickly realized the monetary rewards of becoming involved in the caravan trade" and by the 1870s was closely concerned with the hiring of porters, making the most of the position of his headquarters just behind the customs house. In 1873 another Bagamoyo resident, the local customs master, "Soorghy," by hard bargaining frustrated the attempts of Murphy of Cameron's expedition to find porters.[142] Indian recruiters were active in other coastal towns. In Saadani in 1884, an Indian "merchant" found porters for LMS missionaries. The Indian trader, Hamis Tarrier of Zanzibar, is mentioned as being able to recruit porters, although he did not satisfy the CMS missionary requesting them. Recruitment of porters for the southern routes was also handled on occasion by Indian traders, as Livingstone found at Mikindani in 1866.[143]

All these traders and officials had significant business interests aside from enlisting and hiring out porters. It is only when we consider the well-organized recruiting methods of Sewa Haji Paroo of Bagamoyo that a fully developed system is apparent.[144] Starting off in his father's general store in Zanzibar in the 1860s, Sewa Haji moved to Bagamoyo and into the business of supplying caravans with their trading goods and purchasing the ivory, rhinoceros horn, and hippopotamus teeth that they carried down to the coast. At the same time he expanded into the recruitment and supply of *pagazi,* a role first apparent to Stanley in January 1871, as well as operating transportation services and financing caravans of Arab and Swahili traders.

As Walter Brown comments, he became involved "in virtually every phase of long distance trade."[145]

In 1880, Sewa Haji and the Frenchman Emile Segère attempted to establish a caravan support business, including transport services and supply depots, which would be utilized by travelers in the interior. The caravans were to be operated by a permanent carrier workforce. The partnership quickly folded, but Sewa Haji continued on his own.[146] By the early 1890s, according to Baumann, he was to be distinguished from wholesalers such as Taria Topan and had largely given up trading deals: "His firm is now a 'staff placement' bureau in the greatest style, he is a carrier and worker agent."[147] For example, in 1888 Sewa Haji supplied 500 to 600 slaves to a German tobacco planter in his capacity of labor broker.[148]

Some historians believe that Sewa Haji was frequently able to monopolize all the porters in Bagamoyo, so that caravan leaders had to accept his terms. Brown, the historian of Bagamoyo, disputes that he achieved this level of control.[149] Nevertheless, Sewa aimed at monopoly and was successful in manipulating debt:[150]

> Sewa Haji recruits porters for all, for Germans, British, French and for the Congo State. . . . Whereas he gives even to the coastman at the most 10 Rps. [rupees] per month, to the Mnyamwezi and Msango only a few yards of cloth, the European [employer] must pay 15–20 Rps. monthly. Through small sums which Sewa advances to the Blacks in their leisure time, and then extortionately charges interest on, he knows that there will always be people on hand. He wins influential caravan leaders by high payments, for which the others' hard earned wages are so much reduced. In addition to the advances, which increase with interest and compound interest to infinity, still more 'charges' are subtracted from them, particularly if it is a question of dealing with naive interior people.[151]

Thus, on the coast, new forms of labor extraction were developed to meet demand and impose exploitative working conditions. The situation described by Baumann and emphasized by Glassman represents a new period in labor relations, one in which the conditions of imperialism and early colonial rule played a part. Nevertheless, the level of exploitation described by Baumann is exaggerated. The contract between Sewa Haji and the German, Hans Meyer, in 1889, shows that Meyer paid Sewa Haji MT$11 per month for each porter, who in turn received wages of MT$6. These rates are rather above those cited by Baumann. Nyamwezi were not treated any differently from other porters. Sewa Haji absorbed the cost of any desertions.[152] Labor brokerages and agencies such as that established by Sewa Haji played an important role later in the German period when caravan porters were recruited for plantation labor.[153]

Sewa Haji was frequently criticized by European travelers, often unjustly.[154] In some respects his ethics were in advance of contemporary European opinion. A condition of the contract under which he supplied "good" porters to the German Friedrich Kallenberg in 1891 was that flogging of porters would be prohibited. Kallenberg was proud of his record in keeping to the agreement.[155] Sewa Haji established the first hospital in Bagamoyo and a hospice for sick porters, operated by the Holy Ghost Fathers, as well as making other major charitable contributions. Among these were donations for hospitals in Zanzibar and Dar es Salaam.[156] His continuing concern for Nyamwezi porters was reflected in his will, which provided for the future care of "sick Wanyamwezi and poor persons" in the Sewa Haji Hospital (Dar es Salaam).[157]

More generally, along the central and southern Mrima coast, recruitment for Swahili and Arab caravans was arranged locally through patron-client, slave, or pawnship relationships, or through recognized agents.[158] Mtoro bin Mwinyi Bakari tells us that "if an Indian or an Arab wanted porters, the person who supplied them . . . was given a rupee for each porter as the jumbe's due. This levy was not all sent to one jumbe, but to the jumbe to whom the caravan had come."[159] The suggestion is that anyone with sufficient contacts could collect porters as long as the local *jumbe* (headman) received the recruitment tax. In the middle decades of the century, especially, when demand for labor was increasing but coastal recruitment facilities were not yet well established, porters were hired directly from among the thousands of Nyamwezi and other upcountry porters who arrived each year. Even this was not enough to ensure sufficient porters for coastal entrepreneurs and *madiwan* seduced by the tempting opportunities in the far interior. The result was that procurers or "touts" were sent up to 160 miles or more inland to persuade downward Nyamwezi caravans to divert to their particular village, both to secure porters and to profit from the visitors' ivory sales and purchases of cloth, beads, and other goods. "When they [porters] are rare," Burton wrote, "quarrels take place among the several settlements, each attempting a monopoly of enlistment to the detriment of its neighbours, and a little blood is sometimes let."[160]

European employers at first contracted Indian agents but soon developed their own recruitment techniques. Some travelers relied on their headmen to enlist carriers. Southon believed that this was the best method because "he [the headman] will know the capacity of the men and their trustworthiness better than anyone else."[161] A list of 522 porters from 1888 indicates that some of the headmen (designated "munyapara," meaning *mnyampara*) provided gangs.[162] Sometimes in these cases an anonymous subcontracting system operated, perhaps a forerunner of the anonymous hiring of Mombasa dockworkers, described by Frederick Cooper, which lasted into the 1930s.[163] Europeans with considerable safari experience sometimes recruited their own porters. The best-known case is that of Stokes. Stokes also found porters for other European travelers, especially CMS missionaries.[164] In 1892 Baumann, after two previous safaris, preferred to find his own men in various coastal towns, making sure that each had a known guarantor who was contracted to pay back the porter's advance in the case of desertion. Slave porters were usually guaranteed by their master, free men by notable Arabs or Indians.[165]

In Zanzibar, increasing European interests led to the establishment of alternative recruitment services with greater European control. From the late 1870s trading firms such as Smith, Mackenzie and Company and Boustead, Ridley and Company were active in fitting out caravans and hiring porters on behalf of the British Protestant mission societies, the Congo Free State, the Imperial British East Africa Company, and others. In 1886, for instance, Smith, Mackenzie and Company recruited 620 porters for Stanley's Emin Pasha Relief Expedition. In June 1891 the company assisted in procuring porters for Stairs's expedition to Katanga.[166] Rashid bin Hassani, a slave of Bisa origins, tells how he was recruited by Smith, Mackenzie and Company and introduced to a porter's life:

> I saw one day an amazing sight. There were Goan shops that sold wines and cognac and this day I saw Swahilis spilling money and throwing about rupees. We asked where they got their money and were told "You are all fools here; you will only get women; go abroad and you will get money. We went with a European from Smith Mackenzie's. Have a drink first and then we will go along." We sat and drank two or three days and were given money; these men were like Europeans. Eventually we went and saw three Europeans at a table; one had no left hand. Some of us were written on for a safari to the mainland. We were to get 10 rupees a month; half we drew and half was paid to our masters.[167]

Much of this work was subcontracted out to Indian traders.[168]

The Zanzibari colonial state established its own bureau for the recruitment and registration of porters, responding to the high demand through the 1890s, and its desire to safeguard local labor supplies. A tax of 10 rupees for each porter, whether slave or free, was levied on the contracting employer. The official justification was "to cover the expenses incurred by the Zanzibar Government . . . for recruiting and registering porters." The bureau was "an institution established for the welfare of the porters themselves."[169] Unfortunately I have no further sources on this bureau. No doubt the formalization of recruitment practices during the early colonial period was also aimed at controlling labor and limiting opportunities for negotiation and desertion, that is, at controlling costs. This can be seen in the legislation regulating porterage that was decreed in most of the East African colonies in the first few years of colonial rule.[170]

In the interior the role of chiefs was paramount. In Unyanyembe, Tippu Tip's father married the daughter of Chief Fundikira sometime in the early 1850s and from then on was able to gain access to many Nyamwezi followers.[171] Under Chief Isike (1877–93) the position of the Arabs in Unyanyembe weakened, and Arab traders had to pay high recruiting fees and a tax on caravans. A new labor law aimed to protect porters, servants, and slaves from indiscriminate summary justice meted out by Arab and Nyamwezi masters and employers. Isike utilized this law when he imprisoned and heavily fined several Arabs when two Nyanyembe slave porters were murdered in 1884. He then suspended Arab recruitment of Nyamwezi porters to ensure compliance. Isike's power was such that again in 1887, 1889, and 1892 he was able to prevent the recruitment of porters by Arabs for months at a time and, therefore, the movement of many coast-bound caravans. The Arabs demurred because their business was reliant on the goodwill of the Nyamwezi. These conditions lasted until his death resisting the Germans in 1893. Unomah believes that Isike's commercial and labor policies were a significant part of his overall program of building up royal power and reigning in potential opposition forces in Unyanyembe, including the *vbandevba*.[172] From 1893, new realities intruded. The Germans were now the paramount power in Unyanyembe. Under the terms of a treaty of submission imposed by imperial

Photo 3.4 Chief Fundikira III (direct descendent of Chief Fundikira I of Unyanyembe), a relative, and the author at Itetemia, Tabora. (Joerg Gabriel, 2000.)

representatives, Nyaso, Isike's successor, was bound to "assist European caravans with agents, [and] assist them with porters."[173]

Elsewhere in Unyamwezi, important chiefs including Mirambo in Urambo
and Mtinginyi in Usongo played a similar role in porter recruitment.[174] In
other parts of the interior chiefs supplied porters to travelers, often for a fee.[175]
In at least one case, porters were supplied as part of tribute payments. The
southern Kimbu chiefs sent porters to Mnywa Sele of Unyanyembe from his
accession in 1859 until his deposition in 1861.[176] Thus, in the interior, existing
institutions were adapted to meet the labor demands of merchant capital, as
Coquery-Vidrovitch and Lovejoy note for sub-Sahara Africa generally.[177]

In Ujiji, recruitment was in the hands of the Arab and Swahili elite of the
town, who utilized various sources. These included their slave and client
retainers, Nyamwezi, local Jiji and Guha (Holoholo) and, increasingly during
the 1870s to 1890s, Manyema from the eastern Congo.[178] As at the coast and
Tabora, political conditions had a great impact on the availability of porters.
In June 1881 Hutley found it very difficult to find porters due to the war conducted by the coastal traders against neighboring Urundi and Uvira.[179] From
the 1870s the power of the greatest Arab traders, Tippu Tip and Rumaliza,
was such that European travelers frequently turned to them for help. Stanley
hired Nyamwezi and Waungwana porters from Tippu Tip for work in the
eastern Congo in October 1876, as did French missionary François Coulbois
when he left Zanzibar for Ujiji in July 1883. Porters for the Congo Free State
official Edvard Gleerup, traveling from Stanley Falls to Zanzibar in 1885–86,
were supplied by Tippu Tip and Rumaliza in turn, and in 1886 the explorer
Wilhelm Junker had to turn to Tippu Tip for very expensive carriers when the
trader was at Tabora with his ivory caravan.[180]

All along the central routes, specialization and a developing division of
labor marked the caravan system during the second half of the nineteenth
century. Professional porters satisfied the bulk of the labor requirements of
large entrepreneurs and foreign travelers, both at the coast and in Unyamwezi.
Caravan work became increasingly commoditized due to structural change
including the emergence of a labor market and the spread of new values and
demands into the interior. Yet Nyamwezi culture and customs provided the
abstract material, the conscious models, through which the caravan became
institutionalized and its working culture universalized. At the same time, caravan culture was forged out of the work process and regulated and modified by
custom and experience. This is the subject of the following two chapters.

4

ON SAFARI: THE CULTURE OF WORK

We have tired of the ocean, we want the safari:
Marching in the sun, sleeping when it rains.
Lift the loads, lift the loads!
Lift, lift, lift![1]

To sleep with women we ceased long ago
But the old men at home
At every hour ask the girls:
You so and so, lift up your apron,
The old men.[2]

Nyamwezi marching songs

This is the journey we took the year before last. And the trouble we had was considerable. Everywhere we went, when we fought we fought, when we paid tribute we paid tribute, when we built stockades we built them, when we cultivated the fields we cultivated them, when we died we died. Nor did we reach somewhere near, we went far away. A journey has trouble like sleeping on an empty stomach, or spending a day thirsty; there is no comfort not even once. And if a man has not yet journeyed up-country, he knows nothing of the trouble in the world. You will realize each day that comfort and peace are in your home, with good clothes, a good bed, and good food. You know nothing of the trouble people can have until you go up-country, then you will know for sure that there is trouble up-country. Does it not mean sleeping on the ground, and journeying the whole day long, with never any rest? That is the fact about up-country.[3]

A Swahili view of the tribulations and achievements of the safari

A traveler is poor, even if he be a sultan.[4]

Swahili saying

The dominant image in the above texts is one of hardship and suffering, of a relentless struggle for survival, of a constant battle to find food and water along the caravan routes, and of psychological stress. Caravan life was to a large extent unremitting toil. But there are also notes of optimism and a sense of achievement. Amidst the very real harshness of the life of the average Nyamwezi *pagazi* or Mwungwana there were opportunities to be grasped. Porters were at the forefront of change in nineteenth-century Tanzania and were exposed to new ideas about cultural and economic developments, including capitalist relations.[5] As Selemani bin Mwenye Chande put it from a coastal perspective, "if a man has not yet journeyed up-country, he knows nothing of the trouble of the world."[6]

In the same way, the work of porterage was not just endless marching, with little relief from boredom and monotony. A German traveler in the late 1890s found that the constant walking of the porters produced a mesmerizing effect:

> Head somewhat sunken, eyes on the ground, they pay attention to nothing but the legs of the man in front and the narrow path reflecting the glaring sun . . . they set one foot before the other so mechanically that eventually the path seems to slide backwards faster than they themselves move forwards.[7]

But this gives the wrong impression, as the first song above suggests. Rough conditions and opportunity went together, and the hard slogging must be seen in conjunction with a vigorous social life and considerable variety in work. There were good times to be had, adventures to be experienced. Porters relished these and individually and collectively lived life to its fullest. There were dangers to be faced and crises to resolve. Camp life developed a pattern of its own, with songs, dance, storytelling, and recreation with games, drugs, and sex. But always there were threats, especially from the "three horsemen" of hunger and thirst, pestilence, and war, which often arrived together.[8]

Collective experience was the key to both survival and the reaching of larger goals. It was experience of caravan life and the caravan routes when mixed with preexisting cultural norms that created the working culture of the caravans and ultimately contributed to the cultural cohesion of twentieth-century Tanzania. The roads followed by caravans were the skeleton around which formed the territory of modern Tanzania; the central route was the backbone. Caravan life, reoccurring across vast spaces, and the intermixing of peoples, combined with other associated changes—the spread of Islam and Swahili, the slave trade, the acceptance almost everywhere of *utani* relationships—created a complex network of linkages concentrated along the main trade routes.

This chapter and the next are about day-to-day patterns of work and leisure that helped forge caravan culture and the custom of the roads. Apart from the broad background of eastern African cultures of the late Iron Age, the first influence on caravan life was interaction with the physical environment, as people traveled to hunt, migrate, or trade. The second section introduces the basic work of long-distance porters—the carrying of loads—along with the various types of burdens. The rhythm of the daily march, with its associated rituals of departure and arrival, is described in the third section. The basic pattern emerged out of long experience and became established as a customary routine, akin to aspects of the crew culture of sailors and other mobile workers. The chapter ends with an analysis of the work of caravan women and their role as reproducers of labor power. Caravan women are also considered as early female migrant laborers, whose history is otherwise only known from the colonial period. Finally, the caravan is envisaged in terms of a community, with the participation of children, as well as men and women.

PORTERS, PATHS, AND NATURE

Caravan routes were ultimately selected according to their utility for trade and the ability of resident communities to produce a large enough surplus to feed the armies of porters that traveled them.[9] During all but the most difficult conditions, caravans continued to cross East Africa, and porters struggled to survive the elements. But individual paths went in and out of use and changed their shape as the forces of nature conspired against human activity.

We have been left with numerous descriptions of East African paths or roads. In 1857 Burton found that

> the most frequented routes are foot-tracks . . . one to two spans broad, trodden down during the travelling season by man and beast, and during the rains the path, in African parlance, 'dies,' that is to say, it is overgrown with vegetation. In open and desert places four or five lines often run parallel for short distances. In jungly countries they are mere tunnels in thorns and under branchy trees, which fatigue the porter by catching his load. Where fields and villages abound, they are closed with rough hedges, horizontal tree-trunks, and . . . rude stockades, to prevent trespassing and pilferage. Where the land is open, an allowance of one fifth must be made for winding: in closer countries this must be increased to two fifths or to one half.[10]

By the late 1880s the main caravan routes differed from paths connecting villages in that they were a little wider, much smoother, and less covered with vegetation.[11] The windy, sinuous nature of all paths arose from the peculiarities of the landscape, weathering—especially flooding—the very limited time spent on construction and maintenance, and obstacles such as fallen trees.[12] Eventually temporary detours became part of the permanent way. Diversions were also created by new patches of cultivation started by farmers, and by stretches of heavy mud during the rainy season.

Seasonal weather patterns had a marked impact on the condition of the paths—partly because of growth and decay of the surrounding vegetation—and hence on the working conditions faced by porters. During the rainy season most travel was suspended. Roads were flooded and huge expanses of country turned into swampland. Defying the elements, caravans struggling through the water and mud of river valleys and bogs had a particularly trying time. One missionary wrote of his porters' experience during the rainy season of 1878:

> Hours together we waded knee-deep—thigh deep—in mud and water, and in several places the whole caravan consisted for a time of a row of heads and shoulders above the surface of the slimy water. At a deep place in the centre of one of these morasses one fine tall man stood, and aided, by the support of his hands, each man to get across the gap.

Another missionary asserted that "sometimes I have been carried for the best part of an hour with the water up to the men's chins."[13] Even unflooded country was tough going: "The roads are very bad being very slippery from the late rains," a missionary wrote while traveling from Saadani to Mamboya, "and where it is not thus slippery generally there is a thick black mud which is very disagreeable to pass through." He added, "The long, strong grass is very trying to the men carrying loads—when standing upright [it] is . . . from 8 to 12 feet high . . . when this is broken down by wind & rain across the path it makes it very difficult for the men to get along. This is certainly the worst time of the year to make a journey." The high grass in this region was like a "dense screen," and porters had to contend with blows from the recoiling reeds and injuries to their feet from sharp broken stalks.[14]

The crossing of swamps and bogs was always a difficult undertaking for heavily laden porters. Apart from the Mkata swamp[15] in the east, some of the worst were in Uvinza and Buha. Burton described the paths of western Uvinza as "truly vile, combining all the disadvantages of bog and swamp, river and rivulet, thorn-bush and jungle, towering grasses, steep inclines, riddled surface and broken ground."[16] Another European traveler described how a bog extending from the banks of the Mogunja River in Buha presented a tough problem to porters:

> The natives have built a bridge over it, about 100 yards long, but it does not reach the dry ground on either side of the bog, so that to get to it is necessary to wade for a distance of nearly ten yards through liquid mud about three feet deep. It took my caravan three quarters of an hour to get across, but my donkey had now to be taken over. He could not pass over the bridge, consisting of a few logs of wood supported by piles, and he had therefore to be driven through the mud. Ten men had to work for three hours before they could succeed in landing him safely on the other side. Several times one or

Photo 4.1 Stanley's caravan crossing the Mkata flood plain, 1871. From H.M. Stanley, *How I Found Livingstone* (London, 1872), 114.

two of the men and the donkey disappeared entirely under the mud, and it took the united efforts of all the others to extricate them.[17]

When the Hores' caravan crossed the Luiche River valley near Ujiji, several miles wide, covered in bush, reeds, and thorns, and very swampy, porters were first knee-deep and then up to waist-deep in mud. One man, Uledi, on being asked what the swamp was like, replied, "Oh, it is all right, but . . . there is a big snake in the mud just here, and if you don't mind, you will fall over him as I did!"[18]

In some places, great rivers ran where none existed during the dry season. In Uzaramo in January 1878, LMS missionaries reached a river 100 yards wide where formerly there had only been a "dry ditch" in the midst of a desert waste. "To add to the horror," one among them wrote, "the people say that crocodiles have lately nabbed two Wanyamwezi here and our men are afraid." The porters refused to cross until a rope was secured to trees on either bank.[19] Caravan members assisted each other when crossing rivers, as Gleerup shows when the large caravan he accompanied forded the Ruchugi River in Uvinza: "It was a strange sight to see the carriers with their heavy loads, children and women supported by those who . . . had got their bundles across, goats with horns tied, naked babies clinging tightly to their likewise naked mothers, all splashing in the water and struggling to prevent themselves being carried away by the strong current."[20]

Photo 4.2   Emin Pasha's caravan crossing the Duki River, August 1890. From

Once the rainy season was over, floodplains and marshes dried up and were replaced by great expanses of dried mud. These deserts presented their own difficulties for caravans traversing them. During the rains the mud was cut up in many areas by the hooves of domestic animals and game so that the surface became extremely irregular. Then when the rains ceased, the sun baked the ground as hard as stone. Such rough surfaces were very hard on porters with their bare feet.[21] The porters of more than one caravan must have had an especially painful experience when the game in question had been elephants, which left footprints perhaps over a foot across and nearly as deep, which then might be covered over by vegetation, making it impossible to avoid falling in them.[22] Another hazard during the dry season was the great stretches of thorn jungle, particularly around Mpwapwa and through the Marenga Mkali and Ugogo. Annie Hore wrote of the approach to Mpwapwa late in the dry season of the famine year of 1884: "Towards noon the heat was terrible, the whole face of the country seemed scorched up, not a green leaf was to be seen for miles. We were shut in by thickets, and even in some places by trees, but no leaves, only bare thorns everywhere . . . and not a bit of shade to be had anywhere." Another missionary traveling through northern Ugogo complained of "the long terrible thorns [which] tore our clothes and bags, and ripped up the covers of our bales of cloth."[23] Thorn bushes were a particular trial for porters, dressed, as they were, minimally. Sometimes they made themselves hide sandals to protect their feet.[24] At any time of year jungle paths presented porters with another difficulty. Bushes and the boughs of trees growing close on either side of the path met just above head level. Porters who head loaded had to stoop to avoid the branches.[25] Nevertheless, the dry season presented more advantages than disadvantages in terms of road conditions. Most of the long grass, "such a terrible obstruction to progress," was burnt down, clearing the paths.[26] Bogs shrank, and rivers retreated to their natural courses or disappeared altogether.

The more-direct effects of the climate were just as ravaging. At night during the dry season, temperatures in the mountains and on the savanna plateau could feel extremely cold to scantily clad carriers. Porters climbing over the Usagara mountains in August 1857 were exposed to "thick vapours and spitting clouds." At night the temperature fell to 48 degrees Fahrenheit, "a killing temperature in these latitudes to half-naked and houseless men." In the same region in August 1891, porters of another expedition "suffered severely from the cold." In Ugogo the open expanses are swept by cold winds off the mountains after sunset, so that extreme changes of temperature were common. Porters exposed to sudden drops had to huddle around their fires, losing sleep, and caught chills or became sick from other causes.[27] Conversely, from September to April, temperatures are often very hot. The effect on porters of the hot sun in the mountains of Urungu, south of Lake Tanganyika, is described by Livingstone: "The sun makes the soil so hot that the radiation is as if it came from a furnace. It burns the feet of the people, and knocks them up. Subcutaneous inflammation is frequent in the legs, and makes some of my most hardy men useless. We have been compelled to slowness very much against my will." One remedy utilized by porters preparing for a lengthy exposure to the burning sun was to cover themselves with a layer of fat or oil. Other options were to make short marches early in the morning, or to travel at night.[28]

LOADS: THE BLACK MAN'S BURDEN

Porters used three different techniques to carry single loads, varying according to the kind of physical environment they were most familiar with, the customary methods that they learned from their elders, and the characteristics of the load. Nyamwezi and Sukuma porters typically carried about 70 pounds (two *frasila*) or more on their shoulders, a technique well suited for wooded or forested country. Cloth bales were specially packed for shoulder carriage so that they were about five feet long and between 14 and 24 inches across and wrapped in tough matting.[29] The bale was then bound to flexible sticks lashed in a roughly fork-shaped cradle about eight feet long (as depicted in figures 4.2, 4.6, and 5.1). This had several advantages for the porter. He could keep a good grip, the load was kept firm, and it could easily be set down by resting the long end against a tree or other support, so that the weight of the bale never had to be lifted from the ground. The cradle helped keep the load dry and, by keeping it above ground level, protected it from termites and ants.[30] Beads in sacks were tied to smaller cradles and carried in a similar fashion.[31] Another option was to suspend two half loads, such as coils of brass wire or small boxes or barrels of gunpowder, from each end of a pole, a contrivance known as a *madala*. This could then be supported on the shoulder, which was protected by a grass, leather, or rag pad.[32] Some Europeans, including Frederick Jackson, later governor of the Uganda Protectorate, were impressed by the way Nyamwezi and Sukuma carriers used verbal cues at the end of the chorus of a marching song to transfer in unison their heavy loads from one shoulder to the other by "simply ducking the head downwards and then, with a sideways sweep, upwards."[33]

Swahili and Waungwana, on the other hand, preferred to head load, the second technique. This was less efficient than carrying on the shoulder, but the difficulties were minimized by a good carrying technique, as described by French-Sheldon:

> The Zanzibaris carry their loads sometimes balanced with their hands extended overhead one either side of the load, but with their bodies and heads perfectly erect, never looking at the immediate footpath, avoiding with deftness the overhanging branches or side projections. They put one foot directly in line of the other, without turning the toes out, making a very narrow tread . . .
>
> They universally carry long stout staffs . . . which they thrust ahead of them, and bear upon when ascending or descending mountains, and employ to sound streams when fording.[34]

A head load had to be lighter, averaging about 62 pounds, was difficult to manage in forests, and much greater exertion was required to lift it from the ground. To protect themselves, porters made head pads from cloth or grass and rushes.[35] Despite the awkwardness of packing cases, many European travelers used them for their goods.[36] In both Nyamwezi and coastal caravans, headmen and merchants rarely carried a load but had to be ready to take over from sick porters, or when desertions threatened their property.[37]

The third carrying technique was that utilized by forest peoples such as the Manyema of the eastern Congo, who, in the last decades of the century, were frequently found in East African caravans. They carried loads either on their backs or shoulders, making it easier to pass through the tangles of creepers lying across forest paths. A member of the Emin Pasha Relief Expedition noted that caravans of Manyema slaves and followers of Arab traders in the Congo included numbers of women who carried baskets of food and other necessities: "These baskets are borne on the back, and suspended from the forehead . . . The carriers do not, like our [Zanzibari] porters, cut their way through the bush, but trail along the native tracks, stooping under the low natural archways."[38]

Exceptionally heavy or awkward loads that could not be divided, such as large tusks or boxes, often had to be carried by two porters. Heavy boxes were especially detested; tusks were easier to manage. Double loads were difficult to maneuver up and down hills and across swamps. The usual carrying technique was to lash the load to a pole supported by two men walking in single file. This device was known as a *mzigaziga*. Sometimes a strong porter would prefer to bear a very heavy load himself rather than have the extra problems of sharing it with another man. Men of Herculean strength were known to carry 120-pound tusks. But where double loads were unavoidable, Nyamwezi *pagazi* could carry heavier weights than coastal porters. Gleerup described "sweating figures struggling under the heavy burdens of ivory" weighing up to 160 pounds. A large cowbell, which rang continually during the march, was tied to the sharp end of the tusk, which faced forward, while the porters' personal property was attached to the bamboo pole of the *mzigaziga*.[39] Large tusks reaching Zanzibar averaged 80 to 85 pounds, and tusks weighing 140 to 150 pounds were common. Of the largest, the American consul in Zanzibar had seen several of 175 pounds and had one in his own house of 182.5 pounds. "Probably in the interior are many as large, perhaps larger," he wrote, "but the negroes will not bring them to the coast, owing to their great weight."[40]

Caravans led by missionaries and explorers differed considerably from those of traders in terms of the type of loads carried. Merchant caravans carried almost exclusively trade goods, whereas missionaries and other European travelers employed porters to carry personal possessions, provisions, and the equipment and tools necessary to construct and run mission stations, or survey and map territory, as well as the trade goods necessary for progress. The list of "all the property in and pertaining to the English Mission House at Ujiji" gives a good idea of the quantity and type of the very functional goods that porters employed by the London Missionary Society carried 940 miles to Lake Tanganyika. Included were large quantities of cloth, beads, and wire; a year's supply of European provisions; clothing; a huge variety of implements, machinery, and tools; furniture and household effects; kitchen equipment; an assortment of guns and ammunition; books; stationery; a medicine chest; a great variety of "miscellaneous stores" such as 26 panes of window glass, canvas, blankets, a saddle, a tent, and so on; and a set of marine and scientific equipment including an anchor and chains, life buoys, tar, ship's sheathing metal, nails, and navigation aids.[41] CMS missionaries in Buganda had three and a half tons of New Testaments carried to the kingdom in one caravan in 1894.[42] The porters of Johnston's Kilimanjaro expedition had to carry loads of the usual cloth, beads, and wire currency, plus other trade goods including

Photo 4.3   Ivory porters at Bagamoyo. From Jesper Kirknaes and John
Wembah-Rashid, *Bagamoyo, a Pictorial Essay from Tanzania* (Denmark,

sacks of cowry shells, barrels of gunpowder, percussion caps, mirrors, knives,
bells, mousetraps, and rough musical instruments. There were gifts for chiefs
such as musical boxes, accordions, good-quality guns, playing cards, "fine
snuff," and "gaudy picture books." European food supplies included loads of
potatoes, onions, preserved goods, and live fowl.[43] Among more-prosaic items,
the goods of Abbé Debaize borne to Ujiji included bizarre things such as
"twelve boxes of rockets and fireworks, which would require about forty-eight
men to carry them, several boxes of dynamite . . . two coats of armour, several
boxes of brandy, two loads of penny pop-guns . . . and even a hurdy-gurdy."[44]

In addition to the employer's load or, in the case of small traders, their
merchandise, porters carried numerous personal effects and weapons. The

necessities of life for a frugal African traveler might include a mat, an ax to cut firewood, a pipe, an earthen cooking pot, and a spear for defence.[45] In the case of Von der Decken's coastal porters, a kit for the road consisted of

> a kitoma or squash bottle filled with water, a pack with foodstuff, their bedding, and small reserves of stuff, 'kauris' and similar things for their own use or in order to acquire this or that, which happens to catch their eyes during the trip, a pair of leather sandals which they wear where thorns lie on the path, a heavy musket, if they have proven their authorization, and every fifth or sixth person a cooking pot: it is indeed difficult to find a little bit of room for something else on the head, back, shoulders and hips.[46]

Many of Hore's men took with them "a little sleeping mat, a best . . . shirt, and a tiny bag containing smaller properties." Additionally, "perhaps two to three yards of calico worn as a wrap, and a small sheath-knife stuck in his girdle, completes the outfit . . . of one of these hard-working adventurous men." A Nyamwezi porter working in British East Africa might carry "a thick pad of cloth . . . wrapped round his stomach, a couple of coils of brass wire dangling from his belt, and a neatly made and sausage-like bag of selected beads also to wrap around his waist, or in a leather bag to sling from his shoulders . . . to enable him to buy extra food."[47] Rashid bin Hassani carried two lengths of cloth, a cooking pot, a blanket and a short Snider rifle as well as his load to Uganda in the early 1890s.[48] Other weapons often carried included bows and arrows, small battle axes, and large knives, or *sime;* and various types of flintlocks and other obsolete muzzle loading firearms, the occasional pistol, and, toward the end of the century, modern breech loading rifles.[49] Provisions in areas where there was little food to buy added further weight. In 1857 each porter had to carry at least eight days' worth of food to cross the Mgunda Mkali, and it was the same in 1882. The Nyamwezi typically carried extra food in goatskin bags. Stokes's caravans habitually carried "enormous quantities" of millet in order to ensure adequate supplies for the porters and to forestall plundering.[50] Such accoutrements added 20 or 30 pounds to each carrier's burden. The result was that a porter's total load might be 90 to 100 pounds, or more.[51]

Increasing European interests in East Africa led to even greater demands on their carriers. In the 1870s porters transported the first of many disassembled steamships to the central African lakes. The imposition of this new burden began earlier, when well-equipped European travelers took collapsible boats as part of their outfit. In 1867 the Livingstone search expedition of the RGS took a steel boat for use on the Zambezi and Shire rivers and Lake Malawi that had to be disassembled and carried by Kololo porters up and around the Murchison cataracts on the Shire.[52]

In Tanzania, Stanley was the first to make use of porters in this way and, in 1874, took a collapsible boat, the *Lady Alice,* up the central routes, sailing her on Lakes Victoria and Tanganyika before abandoning her on the lower Congo. Each boat section was the responsibility of four "Herculean" porters, who alternated in pairs. They were paid higher wages than all the headmen, with the exception of Manua Sera, the "chief captain"; received double rations; and had "the privilege of taking their wives along with them." Nevertheless, this was a terribly arduous experience for the boat porters, as the occasional reference to their troubles keeping up with the rest of the caravan indicates. When in the Uregga forest on the bank of the Lualaba River, Stanley recorded in his diary: "Boat came today, people utterly fagged out and disheartened."[53] In 1878, Johnston and Thomson's porters had to manage the difficult load of "a long mahogany collapsable boat," which was carried by "two giants."[54] The 1882 CMS caravan to Buganda, managed by Stokes, included a heavy oak boat carried in sections. The loads gave the Nyamwezi and coastal porters great trouble, as some sections had to be carried by two or more men. The result was constant tension on the march. Stairs's expedition to Katanga also took dismantled boats. The carriers of the sections "had a most arduous experience" in the Usagara mountains, "as, in addition to the rocks, the road was frequently obstructed by fallen trees."[55]

In 1882 the LMS organized a large caravan with the aim of launching a 32-foot-long lifeboat, the steel-plated *Morning Star,* on Lake Tanganyika. Nearly 1,000 porters were required for the specially designed boat, its fittings, and the other more-usual loads. The six heaviest sections including the fore and stern compartments were pulled by porters on narrow carts, two men harnessed in tandem. But five other very heavy sections weighing 180, 171, 150, 121, and 110 pounds were carried in the customary manner, along with many loads of normal weight. Before departure the prevailing opinion in Zanzibar was that it would be "impossible" to get the sections to Ujiji. The difficulties encountered included dragging the carts over the steep paths of the Usagara mountains, during which one slipped over a steep precipice, dangling by its harness, thereby endangering the lives of the porters pulling it. By the time the caravan reached Uyui, the porters were "quite knocked up." On completion of the epic journey, Hore wrote, "We only want a newspaper reporter to make it the greatest work yet done in Central Africa."[56]

The first steamship carried up the central route to Lake Victoria was the CMS vessel, the *Daisy.* The Zanzibari and Sukuma porters engaged to carry her had great trouble, and the Sukuma demanded very favorable terms to complete the journey. The boilers and some of the machinery failed to reach the lake, and so the *Daisy* was launched as a sailboat. Most of the parts of another mission vessel, the *James Hannington,* reached the lake in 1889, but construction was never finished. In 1939, Chasama, the old chief of Uzilima, still remembered how the porters were struck by the weight of the loads of rivets, despite their small bulk. In 1896 the steamship *Ruwenzori* was launched at Mwanza after the CMS had handed over the project to Boustead, Ridley and Company due to the great cost of porterage from the coast.[57] The Germans had their own schemes for launching ships on Lake Victoria, and a small steamer was assembled at the lake in 1892.[58] Steamships were also carried to Lake Tanganyika. In 1880 and 1882, caravans of the Belgian branch of the AIA transported a small steamer, the *Cambier,* up the central route to Karema.[59] Taking a different route, the LMS steamer *Habari Ngema* (Good News) was carried in 1883 from the north end of Lake Malawi to the south end of Lake Tanganyika.[60]

The most unpopular burdens of all were of the human type. The use of the palanquin, or *machila,* in some parts of East Africa, particularly in Portuguese territory, has a long history.[61] But on the mainland of Tanzania they were unknown until the late nineteenth century. "The porters of East Africa do not carry persons, but only things," the pioneer CMS missionary Johann Rebmann wrote in 1850. "In these countries people know nothing of carrying persons, but everybody is required to move on his own feet."[62] This remained the pattern until the arrival of Europeans in the interior. Most preferred to walk or occasionally ride a donkey where conditions permitted. Livingstone was carried "in illness" in a bedlike frame for the first time in his life in January 1869, after a quarter century of African travel.[63] But frequent ill health encouraged many to rely at times on the strength of their porters for personal locomotion. Burton found that the six slave porters hired from a Tabora Arab were

> like all porters in this part of the world, unable to carry a palanquin. Two men, instead of four, insisted upon bearing the hammock; thus overburdened and wishing to get over the work, they hurried themselves till out of breath. When one was fagged, the man that should have relieved him was rarely to be found; consequently, two or three stiff trudges knocked them up and made them desert.

Another set of six hammock men were hired "with difficulty" at Usagozi, only to desert eight days later.[64] When a sick Englishman in another expedition had to be carried, "the Swahili men refused the laborious and what they considered menial task of carrying him in a hammock." Other porters had to be found.[65] These travelers' comments say more about the relative egalitarianism of precolonial Tanzanian society than anything else. Nowhere do we have reports of chiefs or African traders being carried by *machila.*

Apart from sick European men, the *machila* was particularly associated with European women, especially missionaries, who began to travel upcountry in the last two decades of the century. European men assumed that their women could not walk long distances, and the women accepted this view, although they were prepared to walk some of the time.[66] Annie Hore was

Photo 4.4 Mission caravan on the march, late 1880s. Note the *machila*, the variety of loads, and the presence of women and children. From Rachel Stuart Watt,

pushed, pulled, and carried in "one of Carter's wicker bath chairs, with a broad double wheel . . . and fitted with short poles for lifting the whole affair over difficult places." Sixteen men were allocated to carry it. French-Sheldon was often carried in a *machila*.[67] As the century progressed and the use of the *machila* by European administrators and others became commonplace, it was even more resented. Bibi Nelea Nicodemo Msogoti remembered stories from her grandparents and parents:

> They also carried the white men, my dears, Jesus Christ saved us in many ways, they carried the white men also. If a white man was tired, the Africans carried him, they made something like a sling and he sat there, they carried them on their shoulders. Four people used to carry only one man in a sling.[68]

Tony Woods writes of colonial Malawi, "Machilla travel was more than a psychological affront; it was also a symbol of colonial repression."[69] But for most porters the difficulties of coping with a human burden did not often arise. Into the 1890s and the new century, trade goods, export commodities, and the miscellaneous baggage of imperialism continued to make up the standard load.

THE DAILY ROUTINE

A safari was a serious business. Dangers lay ahead. A methodical order underlay the routine of travel to help ensure success. Over the decades a work regime was established that drew on experience and was regulated by custom familiar to professional porters. A set pattern of marching and rest stops emerged, with variations for special circumstances. These patterns, which ensured that a caravan of hundreds of porters reached its destination with adequate rest for the reproduction of labor power, were not always easy for foreigners to discern, let alone control. Misunderstandings and arrogance led to disputes, with sometimes serious consequences. When outsiders tried to alter by force the successful system of the past, the result was sometimes the death of hundreds or thousands. An infamous example is from the British East African Protectorate, where, in 1898, 5,000 Ganda and Soga porters, who rarely traveled outside the lake region, were conscripted and taken from their own countries as the transport corps for the Indian Regiment, which was being moved from Uganda to the coast. Unaccustomed to the labor regime of long-distance porterage, to the food and conditions of the high plateau, and infected at Kivi, the railhead, with a virulent form of dysentery, three-quarters of them sickened and died.[70] In contrast to this disastrous episode, imposed on Africans by imperialists ignorant of the consequences, the conclusion reached by the majority of foreigners was to adopt most aspects of the indigenous caravan systems of the Nyamwezi, Swahili, and Yao, including the timetables and daily rhythms of the march.

If the dominant theme while traveling was order, there was a subtheme of disorder, which was especially associated with departures and arrivals. But here too there were elements of ritual. For two or three days prior to departure from any of the main caravansaries, such as Bagamoyo, Tabora, or Ujiji, porters made the most of their remaining time. "The most prudent ask that their advance be given them in cloth," Stanley wrote in Bagamoyo. "Those who have money require three days to spend it in debauchery and rioting, in purchasing [i.e. paying bride price for] wives, while a few of the staid married men, who have children, will provide stores for their families."[71] Baumann wrote rather more explicitly of the wait in Tanga before the safari along the northern route to Maasailand. *Askari* and *pagazi* indulged in the usual drinking, carousing, brawling, and womanizing that preceded long and dangerous journeys. Baumann was in continual conflict with the local authorities over his men's behavior. The camp was frequently visited by women who had been "seduced," and old people, children, and others who had been beaten. All required "Bakschisch." The *liwali* of Tanga, an "Arab burgermaster," gravely insulted by a Manyema carrier, was compensated with a bottle of cognac. Nevertheless, up to this point all was going well, until a Manyema porter was beaten to death for assaulting a woman. This crewlike behavior of bouts of disorderliness before the regular regime of the march was noted also in the last days of the professional porters. In 1899 a German official complained that "the Wangwana [*sic*] have the old habit of squandering their advance pay . . . with their girls in Bagamoyo, and indulge in Pombe and Tambo [*tembo:* palm wine] in the camps of Shem-Shem and Sensala a few days before their departure."[72]

More-peaceful rituals also marked the beginning of a safari. The night before departure, Nyamwezi couples followed the ritual of *mapasa.* Plastering their faces with flour, the man and woman exchanged affronts with the aim of creating a symbolic break to make parting easier. An offering of flour and a pot was then made at a fork along the path, or near the point of departure. Here a porter might place a hand on the ground, throw some flour over it so as to leave the impression of his hand, and pray to his ancestral spirits for a safe journey.[73] The *kirangozi* of Giraud's caravan invoked the blessing of the moon and the stars some hours before sunrise the day before departure from Bagamoyo in order to ensure a safe journey. When setting out, LMS Waungwana sang a hymn, *Kwanza twomba Mungu*—"First let us pray to God." Other mission Waungwana setting off for Lake Tanganyika, with high spirits and enthusiasm, "shout out their determination to go to Ujiji without stopping; others dolefully express their belief that they shall die under their load; others seek to encourage themselves and their comrades by such cries as 'I am an ass,' 'I am an ox and want two loads,' 'I am a pagazi.'"[74] When departing the coast, Nyamwezi porters dressed with care to make the maximum impression, as a Swahili observer recorded:

> When (the caravan) is leaving the town they all get red straps to wear, and some wear bells on their legs, and as they go the bells jingle. The same goes for their leader, but he wears a plume made from the feathers of every kind of bird, they (the feathers) are collected and fastened together, and he wears it on his head.[75]

In contrast, when on the road the porters wore their "worst attire."

The selection of loads was a serious business, as an unusually heavy, hard, or awkward load could mean grave difficulties for a struggling porter in the interior. Such loads could cause sores on head or shoulders, or handicap the carrier so that he would be forced to lag behind his companions, exposing him to dangerous exhaustion or perhaps attacks from robbers. Making these calculations, porters competed for the cloth bales and other more-desirable burdens; at the beginning of a journey there was often a mad dash for the best loads, with the headmen struggling to keep order.[76] When all was ready, in the case of a caravan departing Dar es Salaam,

> the signal was at last given to start. The drum beat its monotonous tum-tee-tum. The plaintive pleasant notes of the barghumi echoed and

re-echoed from afar. Crack, crack, went gun after gun from porter or onlooker. The men with lusty shouts laid hold of their loads as if they were treasures, and then, with a sonorous recitative from the kirangosis, and answering chorus from the men, they commenced the long march.[77]

Caravans marched only a short distance the first day from the coast or upcountry trading centers "to deter to the last the evil days of long travel and short rations." There were always last minute difficulties. Porters could not be found or had deserted and had to be replaced, others delayed joining the main body due to conjugal obligations, some were sick, and often additional loads had to be packed. Everyone was out of condition and unused to their heavy loads.[78] After a few days, the regular routine of East African travel was established. Each day's march began at about six and generally lasted until late morning, with a short halt at about eight or nine. Seven to thirteen miles would be covered. The porters preferred an early start because during the middle hours of the day paths became extremely hot to bare feet.[79] A special strategy to cross waterless country necessitated an alteration of the marching pattern. A long and exhausting double march called a *terekeza* or *telekeza,* literally in Kiswahili "cause to put on the fire," took travelers on to the next water supply faster than any alternative, as Cameron explains:

> A terekesa is so arranged that by starting in the afternoon from a place where water is found and marching until some time after dark, leaving again as early as possible on the following morning for the watering-place in front, a caravan is only about twenty hours without water instead of over thirty as would be the case if the start were in the morning. And as the men cook their food before moving from the first camp and after arrival at the second, no water need be carried for that purpose.[80]

The normal marching order was the *kirangozi* at the head, followed by a winding column up to about two miles long in the case of large caravans. Porters carrying ivory, the load signifying the highest status, were in the vanguard. Then came carriers of cloth and beads, followed by those of miscellaneous trade goods such as rhinoceros teeth, hides, salt, tobacco, brass wire, iron hoes, and camping equipment of the merchants or caravan leaders. In separate groups interspersed with the porters marched the *askari,* women, and children, each with his or her baggage, and donkeys and other animals. In the rear were the merchants or other employers, partly to act as a deterrent against desertion.[81] Dodgshun describes the *pagazi* of an Arab trader whom he met traveling in the company of the Swiss trader Philippe Broyon:

> The first 50 or so [were] in bright new red cloths, carrying each two-half loads on a stick, the first plied a drum, the next two were fantastically got

up with feathers etc. and one carried the flag. Then came the ordinary rank
and file. After the red cloth men came 150 more pagazi carrying cloth bales,
and then the usual tailing of sick and weak, 4 being chained together for
desertion.[82]

Porters on the march, like Stairs's Zanzibaris, tramped "steadily forward,
their arms swinging like pendulums, except when a hand is raised to steady
the load for a moment or two."[83]

Whether on the road or in camp, music and song were essential components of caravan culture. Sonorous chanting and singing in call-and-response
patterns led by the *kirangozi* helped maintain marching rhythm.[84] Burdens felt
lighter, and aches and pains were relieved when porters joined in one of the
many work songs of their profession. Songs were also a vehicle to express
sorrow, excitement, frustrations, grievances, social comment, or protest.[85]
Most importantly, the performance helped create the boundaries of a work-
based community, defining membership. As Frank Gunderson says about
modern Sukuma peasants' music, itself derived from nineteenth-century antecedents including porters' songs:

> Music performance such as this not only lightens the work load and trans-
> forms work into something more playful, but also performs a role in creat-
> ing a dynamic and heightened group consciousness . . . Working together
> with music becomes more than simply a technical means of accomplishing
> agricultural tasks; it plays a crucial role in establishing closeness, mutual
> support, and community solidarity.[86]

To know porters' songs, along with other aspects of caravan culture, was to be
initiated into the profession. Departures and arrivals were marked by mass singing for maximum effect.[87] Hard repetitive work requiring coordination such as
cutting wood, or passing loads overhead across a deep river, was accompanied
by song.[88] The Nyamwezi were known for their precise timing and harmoni-
ous recitatives, which delighted foreign listeners.[89] Moloney was so impressed
by the beautiful tenor voice of a blind singer performing in Tabora before an
entranced crowd, that he wrote "the whole performance gave distinct pleasure,
and would not have disgraced a London concert-hall." The unnamed balladeer
was no doubt Mugonza, the legendary Kimbu singer and composer.[90] Many of
the lyrics of Nyamwezi songs were recorded by European travelers and missionaries.[91] According to Unomah, writing of early 1970s Unyanyembe, "The
great *safari* and war songs composed during the period [of nineteenth-century
Nyanyembe power], like *Manyumba Nazovba* (I have Travelled Far and Wide),
or *Vbavba vbalifuma Nhwani* (Father Is Returning from the Coast) are still
sung with great emotion and pride. They recall for the *vbanyanyembe* [the
people of Unyanyembe] the prosperity and glory of the days gone-bye."[92]

Among a caravan's personnel there was always room for at least one drummer. When two or more caravans combined, several drummers might precede the main body of porters, thumping the safari beat and creating a formidable impression.[93] The usual Nyamwezi safari beat became so well known along the routes that it quickly became the tattoo for the prayer drum at the Protestant church in Buganda.[94] In many caravans a small band of drummers and part-time instrumentalists, such as *zomari* and *barghumi* players, performed in camp, leading dances, as well as on other appropriate occasions.[95] In addition, many Nyamwezi porters carried a goat's horn, used something like a bugle.[96] Livingstone wrote of the emotional impact of the call of the safari drum and *barghumi* at the start of a march: "These sounds seem to awaken a sort of *esprit de corps* . . . My attendants now jumped up, and would scarcely allow me time to dress when they heard the sounds of their childhood, and all day they were among the foremost."[97] When a particularly difficult section of road was ahead, the vigorous pounding of the drums and calls of the *zomari* and *barghumi* from the van of the caravan, combined with much singing and shouting, helped encourage exhausted porters.[98] Gunderson describes the soundscape production of a caravan on the road or in camp as the music of *ngomas,* hummed tunes, marching rhythms, reveilles, and fanfares combined with a variety of noises such as gunshots and "the general clatter of bells, horns, shouts, and whistles."[99] The ambiance of caravan travel was thus found in music as well as in forms of attire, which together were social expressions of the custom and practice of the work process.

After months on the road, porters underwent an almost ritualistic transformation when near their goal, usually one of the major termini such as Tabora or Ujiji. Professional pride was at stake, and they had to look their best—the more imposing the better—as is clear in an account by Thomson of the approach to Kwihara, Tabora, of his caravan in March 1880. It is worth quoting at length:

> In front marched the giant, bully, and butcher of the East African Expedition, appropriately named Ngombe (the ox). He was dressed in the usual shirt-like garment of the Waswahili. Tied round his neck, and hanging loosely down his back, he had a large scarlet joho [cloak]. In front he wore a fine leopard-skin. His head was adorned with an immense feather headdress. In one hand he held a huge ox-hide Ubena shield, and in the other an immense Manyema spear. . . .
>
> Following him came the caravan band, the drummer, and the zomiri player, with their faces painted and bedaubed, wearing . . . headdresses, and black johos flowing to their heels, and also leopard skins.
>
> Next in order marched a boy, dressed also in a black joho, carrying the flag which had led us so many hundreds of miles. This was guarded by three

of my headmen, in European coats and jacket, with . . . bandera (red stuff) trousers, and voluminous turbans. These had guns slung on their backs, and spears in their hands. After these came about ten kiringosis, all dressed to some extent like our leader, Ngombe, but having various other fantastic appendages in place of the leopard-skins.

The main body of porters came next, attired as if they had newly left the coast.

The rear was brought up by myself . . . surrounded by a picturesquely clothed group of headmen, in snow-white shirts and wonderful turbans.[100]

Appearances were so important that traders took on the responsibility of making sure that their porters were correctly attired when entering their home-town. Selemani bin Mwenye Chande wrote in advance to his creditor request-ing clothes before his caravan entered Bagamoyo.[101] Before entering Ujiji, the Hores' mud-stained porters stopped to rest and refresh themselves, and "from carefully preserved little bundles, brought forth clean white garments, and various array, for the entry into the town." Even the "nearly naked, and starv-ing" followers of Livingstone, bearing his body, made an attempt to present themselves in the usual style of a caravan making a grand entry at the end of a journey when they reached Kwihara. On such occasions the townspeople gath-ered to welcome the newcomers and join in the celebrations, shouting and firing guns. "In the past people fired salutes all the way to the customs house," Mtoro bin Mwinyi Bakari wrote of the arrival of Swahili caravans back at the coast.

Very soon after entering a town many of the porters would be "under the influence of liquor" and enjoying themselves to the full, much like bingeing sailors on shore leave, or New Zealand's kauri bushmen hitting the big city for a weekend of drinking and gambling. Even Livingstone's "set of orderly followers was for several days converted into a drunk and riotous mob," when they reached the coast after months on the road.[102] Such rituals may indeed have become grounded in local community festivities as described by Glassman for Pangani.[103] Nevertheless, Pangani was not exceptional, and the particularity of rituals of journey's end should be placed within the larger patterns of crew culture, and especially East African caravan culture.

Not all orderly arrivals were celebrated in disorderly fashion. Nyamwezi women had a special welcome for their long departed menfolk: "When the wife hears that her husband is about to arrive from a journey to the coast, she dresses herself in a feathered cap and in the best costume she possesses, and proceeds with other women in ordinary dress to the sultana's, where they sing and dance at the door."[104] Bibi Kalunde Kongogo's mother performed one of these songs when her trader husband returned from the coast sometime around the turn of the century:

Traders who went to the coast where there is no hope
Traders who went to the coast where there is no hope

They went!
Should get in the house and explain
Brothers went to the coast where there is no hope.[105]

Given that loved ones on safari literally disappeared for many months or even years, it is hardly surprising that relatives might assume that they would never return, either dying on the way or perhaps being sold into slavery.[106]

CARAVAN WOMEN: 'WICKED' WOMEN OR ENTERPRISING PARTNERS?[107]

Nyamwezi women generated enough agricultural production to support the caravan system, with additional household labor coming from their menfolk, children, slaves, and, perhaps, Tutsi clients.[108] But they were also present in most caravans, contributing their share of the labor burden. Caravan women, hitherto hidden from history,[109] were the first female migrant laborers in East Africa, following on from older traditions of Nyamwezi and Sukuma regional trade. Caravan women shared the daily workload with male porters according to a distinct gender division of labor. In addition, they frequently traveled with their children.

The gendered nature of labor migration in East and southern Africa is well documented. Africanist scholars have developed an influential model of female migration, although with little reference to precolonial history. As colonial capitalism became securely established, a pattern of female migration emerged that has been noted in studies of marriage policy, "runaway wives," and the patriarchal alliance between African indirect rule authorities and the colonial state. Both groups of senior males wished to stabilize rural society for political and economic reasons and, hence, control female independence. Young women, however, frequently resisted family, kin, and official controls, evading attempts by male elders and colonial officials to immobilize them through the invention and recognition in law of neotraditional marriage customs. The result was increased movements of women to mission stations and urban centers.[110]

The model has its limits, however. In parts of East and Central Africa there was no sudden break after the imposition of colonial rule. Female migration during the early years of colonialism was the culmination of earlier patterns established during the nineteenth-century caravan trade. In the corridor region between Lakes Tanganyika and Malawi, chiefs had built up large female households (a form of capital) during the slave-trading era. Around the turn of the century, conditions of colonial peace and economic change created new opportunities for women. Women devised strategies to improve their lot and found sexual and social relationships beyond the chiefly compounds. Groups of them seized opportunities to run away.[111] It is likely that similar patterns emerged in other regions, including Unyamwezi. In central Kenya, prostitution and the migration of women were encouraged by the environmental, economic, and political catastrophes of the 1890s and early 1900s, predating the patriarchal alliance of the colonial era.[112]

As Sharon Stichter notes for the colonial period, there was a difference between "specifically labor migration" and a search for "self-employment or support in the form of a husband or other male" as a result of the shortage of wage work for women, the latter being the most prevalent.[113] The distinction helps highlight the specific experience of female migrants, which was very different from that of men. Late precolonial female migration included elements of voluntary or coerced labor migration, self-employment, participation in family or kin trading concerns, and movements in search of security through attachment to a male protector. For both married and unmarried women, "pull" factors included possible freedom for fugitive slaves or wages for the few paid female porters. During the late nineteenth century, the impact of the various wars in Tanzania pushed out mobile refugee populations. The slave trade made women especially vulnerable and forced lone women to find protectors.[114] Slave concubines (*masuria*) from the coast traveled with their Muslim masters to all parts of Central and East Africa, including as far as the Congo.[115] Women also left unhappy marriages.[116] The variability in the "pull" and "push" factors was therefore similar but rather more complex than in the colonial period. Whatever the case, and allowing for the limited evidence, caravan women made the most of limited opportunities and contributed to the commercial expansion driven by the caravan trade.

Much of what we know about women in nineteenth-century East Africa derives from studies emphasizing female vulnerability in relation to the slave trade. Despite the dangers, women contributed a number of services of great value to caravan leaders and their porters. For example, they provided households for men, whether on the road or in semipermanent camps. Women resident in the capitals of chiefs who did business with visiting traders provided provisions, entertainment, food, and sexual services. Numbers of these women joined caravans or, in the case of slave women or pawns, found themselves part of a caravan entourage. Marcia Wright writes:

> In this environment, acquisition of women, as pawns, whether as "wives" of chiefs, or as slave dependents of traders made very little functional difference since normative distinctions were easily breached when it suited the masters' convenience. Women moved into and out of these latent or active conditions of servility as their asset-value figured in disputes and in the extraction of fines from men.[117]

And again, in a much-quoted passage, Wright asserts, "To be born a woman and to be dislodged from a conventional social setting in the late nineteenth century was to be exposed to the raw fact of negotiability. Hence the quest for protectors."[118] Vulnerable women might find themselves transferred through a chain of transactions from their homes to the entourage of a trader or end up as a porter's investment. The process might start with the pawning of a girl in lieu of a debt. At the creditor's household, she would be detached from her own kin, and thus without protectors and dependent, but neither slave nor free. Thus a pool of "expendable persons" emerged whose status was unclear, as they were not quite full lineage members and not quite slaves. Such marginal women and girls might nevertheless have a degree of freedom to exploit their unclear status.[119] Many, no doubt, joined caravans of their own free will, utilizing the relative lack of concern of putative male relatives.

The existing literature is important but has, in some respects, obscured our understanding of precolonial migrant women. Caravan women were not necessarily runaways, "wicked women," or slaves.[120] Slavery was not the major form of labor mobilization for caravans along the central routes, and this fact must have implications for the degree of coercion or subordination of caravan women. The corridor region between Lakes Tanganyika and Malawi that Wright concentrates on was a particularly disturbed and fragmented one during the nineteenth century. Emphasizing links between women and slavery and other marginal conditions overshadows other possible trajectories for women's lives.

In many parts of East Africa, women dominated local and regional trade, and large numbers of women traveled with their menfolk and families as partners in enterprise. In his study of Kamba porters, Robert Cummings has shown that from the second half of the eighteenth century, women partnered men in the kinship bodies that organized local trade. In this early stage, family groups traveled about with trade goods or acquired foodstuffs, the wives being the carriers. Sometimes the senior wife was the head of the small caravan. Later, control over long-distance trade fell to warriors and hunters, who utilized institutions that crosscut society beyond clan confines to provide labor and supervision and took more tightly organized caravans to the coast and elsewhere.[121] Women accompanied such caravans. They had various motivations for leaving home, and they filled several roles. The more privileged went either as small traders with their own goods or as seers or diviners. Others, taking their children, went with their husbands to assist in carrying either family or an employer's trade goods. It also seems that barren women joined caravans because of community hostility to their presence at home.[122] In another case, Mang'anja women of the Shire Valley were just as engaged as their husbands in local and regional trade, carrying bags of salt into the highlands. The numerous wives of Chief Kimsusa of the Mang'anga, for example, carried Livingstone's loads and provisions for several days in return for payment.[123] In these examples, we see caravan women as traders, porters, and partners of men.

Nyamwezi and Sukuma women also had a long history of involvement in regional and long-distance trade. Sukuma salt caravans to Lake Eyasi, for instance, consisted largely of unmarried young women. In Uvinza, the major source of salt in western Tanzania, women probably did not play a direct role in salt production, but, according to a Vinza elder, they came to the salt camps and cooked for the men. Many women must have taken part in salt caravans, judging by the quantity of Nyamwezi cooking vessels found at the springs.[124] No doubt the women worked as carriers as well. These examples were precursors to female participation in long-distance porterage, beginning early in the second half of the eighteenth century. There is also evidence from early regional trade that Nyamwezi women worked on their own account, and in Unyamwezi some women could accumulate property.[125] Nevertheless, men dominated larger commercial enterprises, and ivory was a male monopoly. It was as partners in enterprise in the broadest sense, as participants in the caravan system, and as kin of male traders and porters, that the labor of women provided hidden capital invested directly in an increasingly market-oriented system.

As early as 1799, a British naval officer pointed to the presence of women in long-distance caravans. Nyamwezi trade was "carried on by small groups of professional traders who transported their goods on donkeys and took their families with them to the coast." These pioneers sometimes stayed at the coast for a year or two, living in huts that they constructed.[126] We saw in chapter 2 how in 1850 missionary Krapf encountered a Kimbu caravan including women and children at Mtotana, on the coast south of the Pangani River. Nyamwezi women in the late 1850s and early 1860s continued to travel to the coast, taking their infants with them, and occasionally hiring themselves out as porters.[127] These examples and others from later times point to the survival of small-scale family- and kin-based trading concerns that should not be confused with the large undertakings of the commercial elite of Unyamwezi and the coast.

The tradition of Nyamwezi female travel continued into the first years of the twentieth century, the end of the era of the long-distance caravan trade. The documentary sources are usually silent on whether women were coerced, voluntarily accompanied family members, or otherwise found their way to the caravansary. Cameron's caravan included "women and slaves" of some of the porters. In Stokes's great caravan of some 2,500 porters in 1890, there were many women "who cooked and carried the cooking utensils and food." The CMS caravan of 1891 to Buganda included female porters. A couple was among travelers who joined another CMS caravan for protection. The woman carried her baby and a small load of camp paraphernalia, while her husband carried her regular load along with his own. In the 1890s, Mtoro bin Mwinyi Bakari stated that "both men and women carry loads" in Nyamwezi caravans visiting the coast, while August Leue was impressed by women keeping up with tough male porters.[128] Large numbers of Sukuma women walked to the coast with ivory caravans or gangs seeking hire for the return journey. "The women generally carry the cooking pots, corn, and apparatus of the camp," wrote a missionary, "but it is no uncommon thing to see women carrying a load of cloth or beads nearly as large as the men . . . carry." Many of Carl Peters's Sukuma porters had their wives, who were responsible for their private baggage, with them.[129] At the end of the period, when the construction of the central railway line eroded the importance of the caravan routes, and caravan traffic fell, many Nyamwezi men turned to railway construction. Nyamwezi women went independently or with their men to the construction camps and to plantations as they had earlier to the caravans.[130]

Beyond the family groups hinted at above, women entered into relationships with professional porters and traders as "caravan wives," often exploiting the relative autonomy of women outside the bounds of settled society. Indeed, virtually all caravan women were attached to men on a temporary or more-permanent basis. No bridewealth or in-law obligations resulted from caravan "marriages," and relationships were often short.[131] Given that women always had other prospective partners, they were able to achieve some negotiated advantage by attaching themselves to the higher-status males, such as headmen and *askari*.[132] Occasionally disputes between aspiring "husbands" were the result.[133]

Speke wrote of "marriages" between Waungwana porters and women in his caravan: "Many of my men had by this time been married, notwithstanding my prohibition. Baraka, for instance, had with him the daughter of Ungurue, chief of Phunze; Wadimoyo, a woman called Manamaka, Sangizo, his wife and sister." Later, Manamaka was described as the "head Myamuezi [*sic*] woman" of the caravan.[134] High-status women such as Manamaka influenced caravan management through their relationships with headmen and others. When Burton and Speke were traveling coastward from Unyanyembe, the caravan *mganga*'s unnamed sister-in-law, "cook and concubine to Seedy Bombay," the headman, played a role in the negotiations between Burton and the *kirangozi* Twanigana over the route.[135] Such women were not mere playthings at the whim of men, and their influence extended beyond that of an informal support corps. More-prosaic circumstances can also be illuminating, as shown in the patronizing comments of a European traveler concerning an argument between a Nyamwezi caravan woman and her man: "The scene was amusingly reminiscent of an East End row; the same gestures, the same shrill invective on the part of the female, the same surly and brief rejoinders from the superior sex."[136] Despite the tone of chauvinism and condescension, the comparison with the London working class is perhaps not out of place.

Some travelers showed genuine sympathy. Livingstone's attention was drawn to a "poor woman" from Ujiji who had gone with one of Stanley's porters to the coast, only to be "cast off" along the way, and then "taken by another." But this woman was no subservient dependent. She had an "excitable" temper, was "a tall, strapping young woman," and "must have been the pride of her parents."[137] A more-sardonic account of female independence in which the spirit of rebellion is apparent comes from Burton:

> At Inenge another female slave was added to the troop, in the person of the lady Sikujui, "Don't Know" . . . whose herculean person and virago manner raised her value to six cloths and a large coil of brass wire. . . . Don't Know's morals were frightful. She was duly espoused as the forlorn hope of making her an "honest woman" to Goha, the sturdiest of the Wak'hutu porters: after a week she treated him with a sublime contempt. She gave him first one, then a dozen rivals; she disordered the caravan by her irregularities; she broke every article intrusted to her charge, as the readiest way of lightening her burden, and . . . she deserted so shamelessly that at last Said bin Salim disposed of her at Unyanyembe, for a few measures of rice, to a travelling trader, who came the next morning to complain of a broken head.[138]

Sikujui clearly falls into the category of "wicked woman" despite her slave status. A few missionaries and other European travelers took a more-interventionist line and stated their moral objections to any such "doubtful feminine" forming liaisons with their porters.[139] Stanley, concerned not annoy

Photo 4.5 Caravan wives sporting new clothes, Simon's Town, 1877. From Henry M. Stanley, *Through the Dark Continent*, Vol. II (Toronto and London, 1988), opposite 360.

his Arab hosts in Zanzibar, expelled from his caravan 15 women—slaves and freed slaves—who had formed relationships with Waungwana porters and surreptitiously joined the caravan soon after departure from Bagamoyo.[140]

Clearly Nyamwezi and other women were an integral part of the nineteenth-century caravan system. The argument is strengthened by oral evidence, despite the denials of male informants. Nyamwezi men asked about female participation denied that it was possible, arguing that women were not strong enough, or that three months' walking was too much for a woman.[141] In contrast, Kalunde Kongogo, about 84 years old at the time of the interview, tells the following story.

> Yes, she traveled. My mother traveled with my father by foot, they went there to send the ivory and then they came back with hoes . . . My father took my mother but I was not yet born . . . Only my elder brother and sister were born. . . . They went here and there and then rested, so it was like this until they reached the coast. When they arrived at the coast they put down the loads of the Arabs and finished with their business of hoes.[142]

Bibi Dudu Rajabu Kheli gave similar evidence. Her mother's mother walked to Bagamoyo "many times" with the porters of her father's caravans when she was a young girl, meeting her eventual husband at the coast. Indeed, it was common practice for womenfolk of an *mtongi* to accompany him on his journeys.[143]

The wider significance of women's work has been obscured in documentary sources important for this study. One missionary even described women caravan members as "supernumeraries."[144] Fortunately, a few European travelers were not quite so obtuse. Grant thought that the wives of some of his and Speke's Nyamwezi porters were

> quiet, decent, well-conducted, tidy creatures, generally carrying a child each on their backs, a small stool and et ceteras on their heads, and inveterately smoking during the march. They would prepare some savoury dish of herbs for their men on getting into camp, where they lived in bell-shaped erections made with boughs of trees.[145]

Although there were rarely as many women as there were men in a single caravan, a kind of partnership is evident in the distribution of tasks. Men provided protection and access to food and clothing through their wages and *posho,* or trading profits. Women provided domestic and sexual services, as well as companionship, in addition to lightening men's burdens by carrying loads themselves. William Stairs, a careful observer of caravan life, had considerable insight into the valuable work of caravan women in European military expeditions:

> It is a great mistake to suppose that black women are a hindrance in any way to the rapid marching of a caravan in Africa, and that therefore they

should be forbidden to follow their husbands from the coast to the interior. On the contrary, women are of immense help to the men, and consequently to the leader of an expedition. The porter, loaded with his box or
bag of sixty pounds, his rifle and ammunition and mat, has quite enough
to carry through eight hours of marching, and is thoroughly fatigued at
the end of it. His wife then, if allowed to accompany him, carries for him
his cooking-pots, and food enough, perhaps, to last both of them six or
eight days.

   On arrival at camp she prepares his evening meal, gets the camp ready,
and, if necessary, washes his clothes for him, and helps in a hundred
ways her tired husband. Besides doing this, the women on the march
enliven everybody with their pleasant chatter and cheery singing. It adds
immensely to the comfort and happiness of the men if their wives are
allowed to follow them into the interior. It is only on very rare occasions
that a Zanzibar woman is not able to march just as far and just as fast as her
husband. . . . I have seen a woman carrying twelve days' rations for herself
and her husband, as well as the necessary cooking pots. Had this man been
single, he would probably have carried only three to five days' provisions,
and no pots or utensils to cook them in.[146]

Stairs went so far as to advocate that European travelers should register
women in their caravan books, pay them a monthly wage to act as a "small
provision-transport corps," and thus free male porters to carry their loads and
use their rifles.

Stairs was somewhat in advance of his time in recognizing the central
role of women in the reproduction of labor power,[147] but his observations
were shared by (or shared with) at least one other "man on the spot." In
February 1893, Emin Pasha was on the Lualaba River in the Congo with a
column of about 680 African soldiers and porters. In one of his last letters,
he wrote:

   The health of the men has been splendid. We have several of those who
   served with Stanley, Wissman, and Cameron. They are delighted, as there
   are very few ulcers and only five cases of smallpox. They cannot understand why we have not suffered; but I do. Every one of our men has at least
   one woman; every man builds a house every night on the road. The women
   carry all the food and prepare it, so the men are well housed and fed. On
   the road the men only carry a gun and 200 cartridges, and a long knife and
   a mat. If a man is sick, the women carry even these. In this way we made
   a march of seven days without seeing a living thing or a bit of food, and
   yet the men hardly suffered at all. Mons. Delcommene, who has just gone
   home from the Katanga, lost sixty-three men in five days' march without
   food, and the whole expedition lost eighty-seven per cent of their soldiers
   and men. They had no women.[148]

The same rule applied in a mixed Yao/Swahili caravan, where the ordinary male members had little to eat except maize. Those with wives seemed to fare somewhat better, as a missionary accompanying the caravan was offered several times some "delicacy," either flour or roasted sorghum, by one coast man from the large pot carried by his wife.[149] Clearly porters traveling with their women were much better equipped for the rigors of the road.

Women were also present in the caravans of coastal traders. The bigger Arab traders traveled with their wives and female slaves, who walked the full distance in bare feet or sandals, often 12 to 18 miles a day, "without appearing bothered." Some carried commercial loads such as beads. When he was at rest, the trader's tent was pitched behind a fence, so that a primitive harem was constructed to seclude his wives and concubines.[150] The manager of Burton and Speke's caravan, the Omani Arab Said bin Salim, had a personal retinue of 12, including his concubines Halimah and Zawada, "five children,"[151] and "five fresh captures male and female."[152] A description of the households of a big coastal trader, Said bin Mahammed of Mbwamaji (Tippu Tip's father), and of those of his followers while on the road, shows how well the domestic arrangements were taken care of, as well as the style of the women's traveling comportment:

> All the chiefs of the caravan carried with them wives and female slaves . . . tall, bulky, and "plenty of them," attired in tulip-hues, cochineal and gamboge, who walked the whole way, and who when we passed them displayed an exotic modesty by drawing their head-cloths over cheeks. . . . They had a multitude of fundi, or managing men, and male slaves, who bore their personal bag and baggage, scrip and scrippage, drugs and comforts, stores and provisions, and who were always early at the ground to pitch, to surround with a "pai," or dwarf drain, and to bush for privacy, with green boughs, their neat and light ridge-tents of American domestics. Their bedding was as heavy as ours, and even their poultry traveled in wicker cages.[153]

Females, mostly domestic slaves, made up about 16 percent, or 200, out of the 1,300 personnel of Arab caravans encountered by a European traveler one day in August 1891. He described them as "plump and glossy." They had small tents to sleep in and to protect themselves from the hot sun.[154]

Masuria certainly did not have the relative freedom that many Nyamwezi women had, but they were members of the caravan community and provided sexual and other domestic services to their masters. Some even traded on their own account, as the narrative from Kenya of Zaru binti Abdalla suggests. Zaru was of Maasai origin. As a young girl, she was taken to Mombasa, where she was eventually married to her second owner, a man from Muscat. In the early 1900s she traveled with him into the interior, where they traded, he in ivory, she in goatskins and other commodities. Her own accumulated wealth in jewelry was taken by her husband. At that point she ran away.[155] We can imagine similar stories playing themselves out along the central routes.

The scattered sources pointing to these intrepid women leave us with little more than snapshots. We do not know whether the majority of them were married and returned home with their husbands, or whether they were caravan wives and led an independent life. Certainly, some were widows seeking protectors and new partners,[156] while others were slaves or freed slaves. Some were both. No doubt there were others—slave or free—who fled abusive husbands.[157] Abused women also ran away from caravans. At Mtowa, on the western shores of Lake Tanganyika, Hutley observed the flight of slave women from the caravan of a coastal trader, instigated by his senior wife, indicating a degree of female solidarity.[158]

As we have seen, caravan women were of "very mixed" origin, although there must have been large numbers of Nyamwezi. By the 1890s at the latest, many wore the Swahili *kanga,* ear ornaments, and hairstyle, as Swahili fashions spread along with coastal prestige,[159] partly driven by the aspirations of slaves and former slaves to be identified as free. Laura Fair has pointed to "the importance of dressing up to one's status—be it actual or aspirational," in turn-of-the-century Zanzibar.[160] Whether there were equivalent changes in social identity among caravan women is unknown, but changes in dress and

Photo 4.6 Tippu Tip's camp. Note the screened tents indicating the presence of wives and concubines. From Wilhelm Junker, *Travels in Africa during the Years*

decoration do tell us something of their assertiveness. Yet recent research shows that coastal influence in central and western regions should not be overdrawn. Consumption patterns of imported cloth in early colonial East Africa show that style was driven not by international trends, nor the preferences of foreign producers and colonial importers, nor traditional coastal values. The key was local and regional consumer tastes influenced by the culture of the nineteenth-century caravan trade, the colonial context, and symbols of modernity.[161]

This mélange was reflected in changing sexual behavior as well. O. F. Raum believes that caravan women gave up "the inland virtues of diligence and humility and the tribal ideal of child-bearing."[162] Such a comment reflects missionary disapproval and ideological preferences; equally, it points to the possibility of infertility and miscarriages, as well as infanticide, and the use of methods of birth control or abortion. Compare Raum's comment with another on the fertility of Nyamwezi women, many of who undertook long journeys, in 1893:

> Families are very small, males predominating; women with more than one child are the exception . . . Three children are the most I found belonging to one wife. Drugs are employed to produce sterility; this and the practice of abortion account largely for the small size of the usual family. The doctors administer drugs for this purpose, but they keep them secret.[163]

This is confirmed in the oral evidence. Traditional medicines called *wibheko,* which might involve wearing a "kind of stick," were used to prevent conception and, occasionally, although it was recognized as being dangerous, a pregnant woman might resort to stillbirth or abortion. This result would be obtained after consultation with an expert female elder who supplied the necessary drugs.[164] Nyamwezi women clearly limited their fertility, and perhaps we can see this practice as part of a strategy to ensure their relative autonomy and freedom of movement.

Through careful attention to the labor process, to the nature of relationships, and to the larger context of the region's history, an argument can be made that caravan women were partners in enterprise with their men. Caravan women had to be intrepid and enterprising to survive the harsh world of the caravan routes. More narrowly, their labor provided capital for the old tradition of small-scale, kin-based trading enterprises, which survived through the century, and from which they themselves could benefit. It also created hidden capital for the operators of large commercial caravans and imperial expeditions, as the conditions for professional male porters improved when women were present. Certainly, there was coerced female labor as well in the caravans, and many caravan women were survivors of the slave trade or runaways, "wayward wives," and "disobedient daughters."[165]

They were from a variety of backgrounds and joined caravans for a range of reasons. Moreover, given the limited use along the central routes of male slave porters, and the fact that the Nyamwezi and their neighbors such as the Gogo were net importers of slaves, it seems likely that many caravan women were not of slave status. Nyamwezi women, in particular, were able to draw on the relatively high status of women at home and their traditional domination of agricultural work, taking advantage of the influx onto the land of both female and male slave labor. Caravan women were pioneers who asserted a degree of female autonomy not available to most nineteenth-century East African women.

By drawing attention to social reproduction, we can also envisage caravans as mobile communities. Caravan culture and the horizontal links it embodied were reproduced within the community of the caravan, which might involve almost all the adults in a locale.[166] Cultural and social reproduction, as well as the reproduction of labor power, were possible in part because children, as well as women and men, were socialized by the experience of porterage. Thus, a traveler in Northern Rhodesia described his long column as "a twisting, travelling town . . . more than one hundred men, women and boys wriggling along through the tall grass."[167] The caravan community might exist on a much larger scale. When Tippu Tip returned to the coast in 1881 after a long stay in Manyema, he was accompanied by about 3,000 men carrying 2,000 tusks, and by women and children.[168]

Children are even more invisible than women in the sources. Yet many porters were scarcely adults. In the small Nyamwezi caravans organized typically at the *kaya* level, numbers of young boys, hardly in their teens, gained experience by participating in journeys to the coast. They carried loads such as cooking pots and took over the loads of tired porters for short periods. They learned to hunt and to use weapons.[169] "Boys," paid lower wages than adult porters, are mentioned in several porter lists of European travelers,[170] and the caravans of coastal traders no doubt included children and youths.

The work of caravan children, like that of women, was a form of hidden capital, contributing to the commercial success of traders, as well as reducing the workload of porters. Child slaves commonly assisted traders and porters, their masters, by carrying cooking equipment, sleeping mats, and other items. Burton mentions the purchase in Ujiji by some of his porters of slave children, including a boy who, "apparently under six years, trotted manfully alongside the porters, bearing his burden of hide-bed and water-gourd upon his tiny shoulder." There were 14 slave children in Decle's caravan. There were slave children, the property of porters, in the 1894 CMS caravan to Buganda.[171] A slave boy taken in by the UMCA mission school at Kiungani, Zanzibar, had traveled to Unyamwezi, his job being to carry calabashes, an iron cooking pot, and a bag.[172] Another, from Bunyoro, gave details of his life on the road from Buganda to Unyanyembe in the caravan of his Swahili owner:

> When we left Kiswele, and went to the country of Nyambo, I was badly treated, and made to carry a great many things. I carried my master's mats . . . an eight days' march. We stayed for a time, and then left, and I was very well treated then, and many others were treated well too, but some badly. From the time we left Nyambo to Sumbua [Sumbwa] I was sometimes treated well and sometimes badly, and it was the same with the others. But master and slave all fared alike as to food.[173]

Girls are less frequently mentioned. However, a little girl—it is not specified whether slave or free—carried a water container on her head in the caravan bearing Livingstone's remains to the coast.[174] More rarely, slave children fared better. Kalulu, Stanley's young companion for several years, was immortalized for Victorian readers in his fantasy tale, *My Kalulu, Prince, King and Slave.*[175]

The caravan as community did not exist only through the socialization of children and outsiders. Despite a low rate of reproduction, women sometimes gave birth on caravan journeys. Usually the mother would have to begin the march again in a weakened condition after just one day's rest. In one case a CMS caravan stopped for a day when the wife of a *mganga* had a son. The couple had joined the travelers for protection. Both the woman and the baby died the next day.[176] In another, casually described by a missionary, a woman marched right up until the time of delivery, gave birth to the baby, then was ready to go on after a delay of "an hour or two."[177] In much the same way in another caravan, a woman carried on until it was impossible to continue. The observer, Decle, recorded that "I left her in charge of another woman and an Arab: later in the evening she walked into camp carrying a newly-born baby, and looking very little the worse for it."[178] These accounts say more about European attitudes toward African women than anything else and recall the "children of nature" discourse. We should compare them with Kalunde Kongogo's narrative of her mother's return journey from the coast.

> On the way back my mother felt sick, she was very sick, she was sick enough to go to traditional doctors. When they went, one doctor told them that "this woman has a child in her womb, but she caused the child to stop coming out because of her words, the bad words. She said, "I don't want to bear a child, I don't want this, this is a lot of trouble—sometimes I travel to the coast." . . . she got a cure from the traditional doctor . . . Mwana Minuka. The Gogo were there with Mwana Minuka . . . they wanted to help my mother. So Mwana Minuka played his game and said, "This woman has a child in her womb, so the child hurts her, but when you reach home, kill a goat and put the blood of the goat in a hole and this woman has to cross that

hole that has blood in it." So they killed a goat in the hole and my mother crossed the hole, they did it at a junction . . . After crossing it my mother started to bear children.[179]

Here the customs and values of the caravan are revealed in gendered form: the desire to control pregnancy in order to maintain autonomy; the resort to traditional sacrificial practices in time of crisis; the symbolic meaning of the crossroad ritual; and the reliance on aid from strangers—almost certainly called upon through *utani* joking relations—when far from home.

5

On Safari:
The Culture
of Leisure and Food

I will die the death of the bell, I say goodbye in the morning
I cry, hunger is in my body, it hurts like a sickness
The *vbandevba* are on the way to the coast
I shall search for food, I set off, I will pray to the spirits of the dead
The singer, Mwanamumeta, I give out the fringed cloths to all.[1]

Nyamwezi marching song

In this chapter further questions related to everyday experience are introduced. Danger from robbers, wild animals, and insects, and from fire, was
always close by. Periods of political instability in certain regions added to
the danger. Attacks on caravans and the closing of routes against competitors
were part of the armory of chiefs and big men. But most contact between
porters and peoples along the routes occurred more or less peacefully at
road junctions, market centers, and caravan stops. Mpwapwa was one of
the most important of these centers. The second section briefly summarizes
its history and role for caravans and porters. Then follows a discussion of
camp stops, and the social and cultural life of porters in their more leisured
moments on the road. The fourth section turns to the theme of provisions,
to consider what porters ate and drank, and how they obtained food and
water. The dangers of the road included drought and famine, and porters
were particularly vulnerable given their reliance on the marketed surplus of
agricultural and pastoral communities for provisions. The 1884–85 famine
was a key event in the history of the central routes and had a devastating
impact, foreshadowing the environmental collapse of the 1890s in much of
East Africa.

EXCITEMENT AND DANGER

The pleasures of community life added variety but also a measure of security to the work of porters. But going on safari was always an uncertain and
hazardous undertaking. The routine of marching and setting up camp could

be suddenly broken. There were numerous sources of insecurity, and death was commonplace. Famine and disease were the big killers. Otherwise the biggest threat came from hostile strangers. Conflicts with villagers along the routes over *hongo,* food supplies, women, and other causes were common. In times of war, caravans were frequently threatened.[2] Beyond settled areas there were always robbers who lay in wait for the unwary. Periods of instability in regions straddling main routes gave them free reign.

Robber bands operated in three ways. Attacks most commonly came from small groups who watched caravans from a distance and, when the time was right, ambushed straggling porters who had become separated from the column, often killing them and stealing their loads. This could happen almost anywhere, but the greatest risk areas were Ugogo and the Mgunda Mkali. In these regions, travelers at all times up until the mid-1890s were in danger. According to Mzee Shabani Kapiga, when in Ugogo, porters closed ranks for protection: "When you go around Ugogo you walk step by step, all of you . . . but if you remained behind, you are finished."[3] The second strategy was a direct assault on a weak point of a caravan by bandit gangs. An alternative was theft by stealth. In Ugogo a game called *mgugumbaro* involved competition by young men who would enter the protective thorn fence of a caravan camp to steal cloth. The contest was won by whoever succeeded.[4]

Numerous travelers recorded ambushes by robbers who cut off stragglers. While marching through the forest between Kigwa and Unyanyembe, an old porter of Burton and Speke's caravan, lagging in the rear, was beaten by three robbers who stole his load. One of the attackers was captured by Chief Kitambi of Uyui and executed. A straggling porter of a missionary caravan was attacked and robbed at Muhalala, just before entering the Mgunda Mkali. The local chief returned some of the lost goods to the missionaries.[5] Another case shows in more detail how many Nyamwezi chiefs tried to protect traders and caravan porters from bandits, applying severe penalties when culprits were found. A CMS missionary wrote of a successor of Kitambi:

> I don't think any one can accuse Magembe Gana of having a ravaging spirit. There are individuals who are thus disposed but they dare not carry out their pranks in his country or anywhere else. Only a few days ago some of his people knowing that some natives of Magingali had taken some Ivory to Tabora to sell, got to know when they would be returning and way-laid them in the Pori [the forest] and succeeded in getting over one hundred cloths. For this they suffered the extreme penalty of the Unyamwezi [*sic*] law, and I saw them being led by my place to execution. They are generally speared.[6]

As these examples show, local authorities struggled to maintain order,[7] and several other cases are noted of robbers who attacked porters being captured and executed or otherwise punished by chiefs, who also endeavored to return stolen goods and warn travelers of thieves.[8] But justice was often too late or not available. A porter from an Arab caravan was killed by a "Ruga-Ruga" a few days east of Tabora while walking with companions to a village to buy food with some hoes. In 1890 near Kisokwe a CMS porter was speared in the back and his load of cloth taken. During the same journey three more porters were attacked and robbed in the Mgunda Mkali. Two of these were killed by their assailants.[9]

Direct assaults by robbers on the main body of a caravan were almost as common, especially in times of endemic warfare. Large bands capable of frontal assaults operated throughout the central and western regions. A missionary describes an encounter with bandits in Ugogo in 1891:

> A number of these gentry suddenly rushed out upon the caravan from the thicket, on both sides of the path, uttering shrill war cries, and brandishing their spears in the faces of the frightened porters, some of whom were women. The boxes and bales went down . . . dropped in sudden panic by the terrified porters, who scattered right and left. The robbers whipped up four loads . . . and vanished with them . . . as quickly as they had come.

Strangely, given other recent attacks, the porters had not been issued ammunition and hence were relatively defenseless. But one porter sat on his load, determined to save it, and warded off his assailants with his empty gun.[10] In 1878 a caravan of the Catholic White Fathers was attacked in the Mgunda Mkali with the loss of two porters killed and 20 loads stolen. Selemani bin Mwenye Chande experienced numerous struggles during his travels, including a battle with robbers in the Mgunda Mkali in which three of his men were killed.[11]

Periods of instability, for instance the war between Tippu Tip and the Vinza during late 1881 and 1882, gave marauders carte blanche and made the paths between Urambo and Ujiji unsafe. As a result of the disturbances, other peoples in the region including the Tongwe, Karanga, and Ha were up in arms, attacking all who traveled along the main routes. For a time in 1882 it was unsafe to go far outside Ujiji unless with a well-armed escort because of the danger of being robbed or enslaved. Among other incidents, 20 of Mirambo's men were attacked on their way to Ujiji by Ha marauders, and ten loads were stolen. Some of the robbers were killed. Mission mailmen were at considerable risk, and several were killed or injured during this period.[12] One robber band, mostly Sagara, operated from Ikombo near Mpwapwa during the early 1880s. Although not especially powerful, they made numerous attacks on Arab caravans.[13] But resolute action by porters might frighten off assailants. When thieves tried to rob a Nyamwezi caravan at night east of Mpwapwa, the porters fired off their guns and forced a retreat.[14]

In Unyamwezi robber gangs were often referred to by European travelers as *rugaruga*.[15] This is a misnomer. More correctly, *rugaruga* were the standing armies of Nyamwezi chiefs, consisting of young, unmarried warriors.[16] A few legitimate chiefs resorted to highway robbery, but robber bands were usually under the control of aspiring "big men" out to increase their power by accumulating firearms, cloth, and other goods, which enabled them to attract followers.[17] They thrived during periods of instability and were sometimes strong enough to make direct assaults on caravans, often with great loss of life.

Even less predictable were encounters with wild animals, a staple of European travel accounts, yet no less real for all that. The possibility of experiencing the excitement and fear of meeting a rhinoceros, lion, or other beast on the road was part of the safari experience for porters and employers alike. Just a few days from Bagamoyo, lions killed two porters in one night during Selemani bin Mwenye Chande's journey to Manyema, despite the building of a stockade.[18] The threat was often present even if not realized, as Southon reported:

> One night a lion entered our camp near the Gombe River and after leisurely walking round my tent & pausing within six feet of where I was sleeping, he went off and at a distance . . . gave vent to his dissatisfaction [*sic*] in a few loud roars. This roused the men who put more wood on the fires and soon made everything light as day. Shortly after when the fires had burnt low, the lion came again and stood for a short time between my tent and the sleeping forms of the men who were a short distance away. I could distinctly hear his loud breathing but could not see the outline of his form nor could I fire at him for fear of injuring the men beyond. I, however, fired into the air which had the effect of causing him to give vent to a loud roar and to bound rapidly away.

The missionary asked his men why none of those sleeping in the open had been carried off. The answer was that all the porters slept in a row under a tarpaulin, and none was isolated from his companions.[19]

Hyenas and leopards were almost as dangerous as lions, especially at night, and were known to kill or maim. A porter was killed by a hyena at Dodoma in Ugogo. Another had his nose bitten off while he slept. A hyena, attracted by drying goat meat, penetrated into a campsite in the Pare mountains and bit a porter on the heel. A woman was carried off by a leopard from a campsite in the Kagera River valley.[20] Rhinoceroses were rare along the central routes but in the late nineteenth century were still common in the northern parts of Tanzania. The Swahili saying "Ukiona pera, ukiona mti— kwea [If you meet a rhino, and you see a tree—climb it]" governed the correct response to an encounter with a rhinoceros.[21] Crocodiles were an ever-present threat in the rivers, including several crossed along the central routes. Stanley's donkey was dragged under by Malagarasi River crocodiles.[22] Snakes were more rarely seen, but the deadly mamba certainly killed and, according to unnamed Arabs, was "known to oppose the passage of a caravan . . . Twisting its tail round a branch, it will strike one man after another in the head with fatal certainty."[23]

Perhaps more devastating in their effects on caravan members were insect swarms of various kinds, including tsetse flies, mosquitoes, ticks, fleas, bees, scorpions, termites, and ants. The most commented upon were biting ants of various species, including those known as *siafu* and *maji moto,* or "hot water." Ant invasions caused considerable consternation among porters. When swarming over campsites, they could only be deterred by fire or boiling water, and they frequently drove travelers to abandon their resting places.[24] Scorpions were a pest around campsites in Ugogo. A European traveler described them as "great black fellows, six inches in length. At night they swarm out of the ground, and flock to the camp-fires, or take refuge from the rain in one's tents and baggage."[25]

Campsites were dangerous places in another respect. Fires, once out of control, could quickly sweep through the concentrations of stick and grass huts erected by porters. The huts were especially susceptible to accidents of this kind, a missionary wrote after a fire destroyed his caravan's camp, "as the men sleep . . . with only a small hole to creep out of, making a roaring fire just near to it."[26] The danger came not just from the flames, but from the stores of gunpowder and ammunition usually placed at the center of the camp. When a fire broke out at a campsite at Misogwere during Thomson's first expedition, 12 kegs of gunpowder were inside the ring of burning huts, and explosions of porters' loaded muskets and powder horns threatened everyone trying to save the caravan's goods. In this case the gunpowder was quickly removed from the danger, and the bales of cloth and other goods were saved. The porters were lucky, as no deaths or serious injuries resulted, although many lost all their personal effects.[27] During the dry season, bush fires could cut routes, forcing caravans to take detours. Decle recorded an incident in July 1893 near the Muserere River east of Ujiji in which an Arab caravan 500 strong lost three men "burnt to death" in a bush fire.[28]

MPWAPWA: CARAVAN STOP AND MARKET TOWN

The best-known market and caravan towns of the central routes are Bagamoyo, Tabora, and Ujiji.[29] But there were numerous others. On the coast, Mbwamaji and Saadani were significant entrepôts and caravan termini.[30] In the east in Ukutu, there was Zungomero before its decline from the 1860s, although it was still on a route described to Livingstone by a coastal trader in 1870, and Beardall mentioned it in early 1881 as a place to buy food.[31] In the

far west in Burton's time Msene in southern Usumbwa had a market;[32] and in
the late 1880s and 1890s Usongo was an important caravan depot, particularly when Stokes was based there.[33] During the 1870s and 1880s, Mirambo's
capitals at Ikonongo and Iselamagazi were not only centers of political power,
but also hubs of the Nyamwezi caravan system.[34] During the second half of
the nineteenth century the most important caravan stop between the coast and
Tabora was Mpwapwa, "the great junction for the trade routes" where, by
the 1870s, almost all the roads from Winde, Saadani, Bagamoyo, and Dar es
Salaam merged.[35]

As Beverly and Walter Brown noted a generation ago, despite local and
regional characteristics that gave each of these towns its own special identity,
all the settlements along the central routes shared a common historical experience. They embraced many of the same immigrant groups; they developed an
economic interdependence that involved the same commodities, personnel,
and commercial practices; and they acquired a common cultural life derived
from the caravan system that was expressed linguistically, religiously, and
materially.[36] With a closer look, we can see these processes at work. For long-
distance traders and porters the pleasures of the major caravan termini and
trading towns helped to offset the harsh life of the road. Here caravan leaders,
traders, and porters had a chance to relax, refresh themselves, collect provisions, and meet old friends. Merchants could engage in trade or, if en route,
reorganize their goods and hire fresh porters. Male caravan personnel could
enjoy the pleasures of female companionship and let off steam, as do crews
in towns the world over. More broadly, travelers and permanent residents
engaged in a developing discourse that transcended cultural, ethnic, regional,
linguistic, and religious differences and helped spread a common way of life
along the central routes. Its features included an awareness of market relations, the reinforcement of familiar religious ideas and exposure to the perhaps
revelatory rites of Islam and Christianity, the use of trading lingua franca such
as Kinyamwezi and Kiswahili, and the easy recognition of customary caravan
labor culture. Despite the rough and tumble of caravan life and the potential
for misunderstandings during interactions between residents and strangers,
much potential friction was eased through recourse to *utani,* joking relationships initiated by ritual abuse between individual members of engaged and
recognized ethnic or cultural groups. These intersocietal relationships were
concentrated along the main trade routes, and at caravan stops and market
towns caravan personnel had extensive opportunities to engage in discourse
with local peasant and pastoralist communities. In the case of Mpwapwa, we
have sources that enable an insight into some of these economic, social, and
cultural relations between the settlement's inhabitants and the large migratory
population of caravan porters.

There is no mention of the district in the writings of Burton and Speke.
Farther south, Ugogi, "rich" in cattle and grain, partly fulfilled Mpwapwa's

role at that time.[37] But with the northward shift of the main caravan routes due to greater security and more reliable food supplies than the old Ruaha route could offer, Mpwapwa must have risen in significance. Its importance can be judged from several estimates of the number of caravan personnel passing through each year during the late 1880s and early 1890s, ranging from 100,000 to 160,000, counting return journeys.[38] Annie Hore, who passed through in 1884, describes its role:

> Mpwapwa has always been a place of importance, although nothing much in itself. It is a . . . point where many roads meet, and a terminus of a stage on the road for all travellers, whether from the interior or the coast. To the first it is a welcome resting-place after the vexations of the tribute-demanding people of Ugogo, and the heat and hunger of the desert between that country and Mpwapwa; to the others it is a place to halt, consider, recruit, and prepare, before entering upon the desert and the anxieties of Ugogo.[39]

Like most towns in the Tanzanian interior, Mpwapwa was really a concentration of many villages, each one consisting of a large *tembe,* a low, flat-roofed quadrilateral structure, often containing many rooms in which domestic animals were kept and a number of families and their dependents lived. In 1878, White Father missionaries counted 57 *tembe* scattered across the Mpwapwa plain and reckoned the permanent population at 1,500.[40] In the late 1880s, Pruen, a resident missionary for several years, estimated its population at about 2,000. At this time Mpwapwa consisted of "a collection of about a hundred tembés, scattered over an area about two miles by one, each tembé sheltering three or four families, usually people related to one another."[41] Given that the number of inhabitants of each *tembe* in Mpwapwa more realistically averaged about 40, Pruen's figure is probably much too low.[42] But the very much larger (in total) shifting population of mobile and constantly rotating caravan personnel gives a truer indication of the perpetual remaking of social, economic, and cultural boundaries and identities at the various nodes along the central routes, including Mpwapwa.

For caravans, Mpwapwa was far more important than its modest size suggests, as it was the last place to buy provisions and replenish water supplies before entering the Marenga Mkali, the nearly waterless waste taking three days' journey, including a *terekeza,* to cross. Just as significant, the Mpamvwa River cutting across the plain was as near to a perennial stream as exists in central Tanzania and thus a reliable source of water for parched porters. Along its banks were fine tamarind, sycamore, cottonwood, and baobab trees that provided welcome shade.[43] In May 1871, Stanley and Arab traders such as Sheikh Thani and Abdullah bin Nasib found food cheap and plentiful, including eggs, milk, honey, mutton, beef, ghee, *matama* (sorghum), *mawele* (millet), sweet potatoes, nuts, and beans. When Cameron's caravan entered

Mpwapwa in June 1873 at the end of a scorching *terekeza,* it was like arriving at a desert oasis: "The sight of fresh green trees and fields of maize, matama and sweet potatoes, and streams of beautiful crystal water running in threads through a broad sandy course . . . gladdened our eyes."[44] However, travelers arriving later in the dry season, toward the end of July or August, would find that provisions were expensive and sometimes in short supply, with little grain available for sale except for *matama* and a little maize.[45]

Mpwapwa is situated in a region of cultural intermixing and overlapping where people of Gogo, Sagara, Kaguru, Maasai, and Hehe origins, among others, intermarried and lived alongside one another.[46] In 1878, CMS missionary Last recognized Mpwapwa as "an intermediate place between at least 5 places, or districts, and to belong to none of them. The people pride themselves on the name Wagogo, but very few indeed are really Wagogo. There is here a mixture of all the tribes round about & also a number from very distant places."[47] In this respect Mpwapwa fits the model of an African frontier community assembled from "bits and pieces" of established societies.[48] But Mpwapwa's status as a frontier town was perhaps apparent mostly to the older communities on whose borders it was located. Its mixed population represented the reality of the central routes. Commercialization in nineteenth-century Tanzania had the effect of rearranging older relationships, utilizing them as the raw material—the "grammar," so to speak—of new linkages and processes that were to dominate Tanzania's future. New urban centers, sometimes themselves representing the "frontier," were no longer on the periphery, as relationships along the central routes increasingly rested on the market, and on the power of wealth and the gun, power that accumulated in and was directed toward places like Tabora, Ujiji, and, in a more-prosaic way, Mpwapwa. Given Mpwapwa's location on the marches of the territories of several peoples, its nearness to the different ecological zones of plain and mountain, and its status as a junction town on East Africa's most important caravan routes, it is not surprising that the population was very mixed and that new alliances and allegiances could be made and unmade there.[49]

The great number of caravans passing through Mpwapwa contributed to the heterogeneous character of the town, a characteristic that lasted well into the twentieth century. The "all-pervading Wanyamwezi" were present "in considerable numbers" in 1876.[50] Almost 80 years later the community was described as

> of diverse stock, which includes clans from other areas of Ugogo as well as people who are, by origin, Kuguru, Tumba, Sagara and "wetiliko" (half-bred Hehe-Gogo), to say nothing of little pockets of aliens such as the descendants of Nyamwezi porters and of the "wanyekulu," runaways from the Arab caravans who sought protection at the courts of the Gogo chiefs.[51]

During the 1870s ivory traders from the coast were resident, and the Swiss Phillipe Broyon lived there for some time, undercutting the Swahili and Arabs through his access to cheap imported cloth.[52] Recognizing the importance of the location, in 1876 the CMS established temporary quarters near Chief Lukole's residence, and then a permanent station at Kisimando, on the slopes east of Mpwapwa.[53] In 1887 the Gesellschaft für deutsche Kolonisation set up a station in the town that, after being sacked during Bushiri's rebellion, was converted to a military post for imperial troops. By August 1891, the district was in a state of temporary decline due to rinderpest—which had virtually wiped out the local herd of 6,000 cattle—the consequent poverty of its people, and the effects of continual German raiding in the area.[54]

Despite the historic events taking place in and around Mpwapwa, its function for porters remained much the same until the construction of the central railway beginning in 1905. An account of the arrival and stay of a two-mile-long column of porters in the late 1880s would equally apply to earlier decades:

> The large caravan . . . had arrived; and . . . it had taken up its quarters down by the river bed, amongst the shade of the stately fig-sycamores. The leaders . . . were contemplating a prolonged stay of two days, for the purpose of drying their bales of calico, which had been soaked by the unexpectedly heavy rains of the previous few days. Two or three miles of this material lay on the bushes around, drying in the tropical sun, giving the camp the appearance of an enormous laundry establishment.
>
> During the afternoon the porters . . . came up into the village to barter their goods for fowls and grain. For this purpose they brought with them cloth, wire, tobacco, and little supplies of gunpowder, perhaps half an ounce, wrapped up in dirty pieces of rag. With these they purchased the fowls and grain they required, pounded the latter in the mortar, lent by the seller, some of the more energetic also grinding it on his stones.[55]

The next day a cow was slaughtered to be sold in small pieces to some of the porters, for which the owner received calico, colored cloths, gunpowder, percussion caps, tobacco, beads, wire, cheap knives, and hoes.[56] This description suggests some of the processes of commercialization taking place along the central caravan routes.

Relationships between porters and the local people were not always so mutually beneficial, and, as elsewhere along the main routes, disputes were common or at least have been given more attention in the sources than the usual low-key interchanges. The great volume of traffic placed pressure on limited resources, both in the case of foodstuffs in lean years and the goodwill of Mpwapwa's inhabitants. Even in normal times, prices of basic provisions were comparatively high. Local men and boys always went about armed, even when attending to everyday activities such as grazing their herds, working in their fields, or visiting a neighboring *tembe*.[57] When numerous caravans descended on the district, draining food supplies and leading to high prices, tempers were often short. Fights between porters and residents commonly broke out over food supplies, thefts, women, and the abuse of local people.[58] A resident missionary reported an incident in which some Nyamwezi porters "stole wood from [a] tembe and began pulling down [the] chief's house." The inevitable consequence was that the local people sounded the war cry and gathered in large numbers but did not commence hostilities because of encroaching darkness, and perhaps because of the good relationship between the CMS missionaries and Chief Lukole.[59] Perhaps, too, chiefs such as Lukole no longer had the standing or resources to impose their will in places such as Mpwapwa, given the power of other residents such as coastal traders and Christian missionaries, as well as passing caravans.[60] This was the conclusion of the White Fathers, whose porters had been accused of the crime.[61] In October 1876, there was an unusual incident. The CMS caravan of Clark and O'Neill had been joined by that of Wilson and Robertson. The porters had in the meantime been employed building a mission house. On 5 October, according to Clark's journal,

> all the men some 240 marched out of camp without their loads intending to desert—the people of Mpwapwa thinking of this, went after them and a great fight took place on the great plain below us lasting some hours . . . In the end the Mpwa got them so that they could not proceed, and the fight ended.

The casualties were not high. The next day the *pagazi* left without their loads again but were persuaded to return.[62] One could speculate on the causes of this fracas. Was it really that the people of Mpwapwa were concerned for CMS interests, or was there some feud between the two sides? There was conflict on another occasion when Arab caravans, robbed by the bandits of Ikombo, retaliated by attacking their tormentors.[63] Environmental degradation was another cause for complaint. By the 1880s, the great fig sycamores along the river where porters camped were gradually being destroyed by the fires built at their base, and this alarmed residents, fostering resentment.[64]

As the Browns point out, there was a degree of inevitability to social unrest in caravan towns such as Bagamoyo, Tabora, and Ujiji: "The flood of immigrant settlers and transient porters . . . created explosive pressures that could not be contained by political deals between a new and old elite."[65] This was partly true for Mpwapwa as well. If the pressures of congestion were not such a factor as in the major entrepôts, there was still the continual rub of Nyamwezi and coastal porters against local tolerance, which was complicated by a heavy intake of *pombe* and *bangi* as well as a general competition for resources. Over time this dialectic contributed to and was mediated by aspects of caravan culture including *utani* and the spread of the Swahili language. From the porters' point of view, leisure in the towns and camp stops became inseparable from work life. Each was part of the whole of the safari experience.

"LIKE SCHEHERAZADE'S SISTER": CAMP AND SOCIAL LIFE

Nothing was more central to the working lives of caravan porters, and to the shaping and expression of caravan culture, than the collective familiarity of the camp stops, or *makambi*.[66] If no accommodation was available in villages along the way, and it was often not for security reasons,[67] each march would end at a recognized camping site, or a new *kambi* would quickly be erected by the porters out of materials at hand. At the same time, food was bought from local peasants, and meals were prepared. When food was plentiful, feasting could last for hours. The late afternoon and evening were available for rest and recreation, a temporary respite before the labors of the next morning. A vigorous social life revolved around music, song, and dance. Smaller groups engaged in games sometimes involving gambling; some consumed intoxicating beverages, or *bangi*. Sexual activity was another way to relax, and it is most likely that both heterosexual and homosexual

Photo 5.1   Porters encamped at Bagamoyo. Note the loads of cloth stacked against the coconut palms. From Alexandre Le Roy, *Au Kilima Ndjaro* (Paris, 1893), 85.

relationships were engaged in, although the sources are almost silent on this aspect of caravan life.[68] During the hours of darkness, porters huddled around campfires and swapped stories. Although camp life was organized around small groups of five or six porters—also called *makambi*[69]—who supported each other by dividing their labor when carrying out chores, and who shared a campfire, it was a collective experience and bonded people from different ethnicities and regions, aiding the creation of a horizontal consciousness. This collective consciousness could then be mobilized when disputes arose with caravan leaders.

The essential factors governing the site of a *kambi* were, first, that it was as near as possible to a normal day's march beyond the previous camping site; second, if near some obstacle such as a river or mountain pass or occupied clearing, it was on the far side according to the direction of march; and third, that it had water. Thus, most *makambi* were on or near riverbanks, lakeshores, or wells and, if at an obstacle such as a river, were situated so that porters did not have to begin the next day's march with the hard labor of a river crossing, which may become more difficult if rain fell over night. In such places, campsites were in pairs on either side of the obstruction.[70]

When leaving the coast, beyond Bagamoyo's sphere of influence, caravans utilized large *makambi* constructed by porters. "In this region," Burton wrote,

> they assumed the form of round huts and long sheds or boothies of straw or grass, supported by a framework of rough sticks firmly planted in the ground and lashed together with bark strips. The whole was surrounded with a deep circle of thorns which—the entrance or entrances being carefully closed at nightfall, not to reopen until dawn—formed a complete defense against bare feet and naked legs.[71]

Swahili porters erected long huts, Nyamwezi *pagazi* round-peaked ones. Several European travelers noted the "good taste" or "good thatch-work" shown in hut construction, even though they were built in very short time, and materials sometimes had to be collected from a distance.[72] Such huts gave reasonable protection from the rain and often lasted for months, so that the porters of many caravans in succession could benefit from them.[73] Where good building material was absent, as in the Mgunda Mkali, rough lean-tos were made of dry stalks and grass. In heavily treed regions during the rainy season, for instance in Uvinza, the best huts were made of bark sheets. Where there was no cleared space for hut building, porters might cut out the heart of a bush, making a kind of nest for protection from the elements.[74] By the 1890s many porters slept in small tents, and there were other indications of a slight improvement in material well-being for some. "These people travel very peacefully and comfortably. All the elders [*wanyampara*] have their tents, their wives, and their cooks," Stairs wrote of the 500 Nyamwezi porters traveling with his caravan for protection.[75] Swahili and Waungwana made light tents utilizing their cloth head pads. But the traditional *boothy,* a simple, quickly built hut, remained popular. Toward the end of the German period, tents were to be provided by law, but compliance was patchy.[76] Always, campsites were spatially ordered. In the middle were the tents of the caravan leaders, merchants or European travelers. Beside them were stacked the loads in huge piles. The porters erected their huts or arranged existing ones around the tents and goods. Beyond the huts, when thieves or wild animals were a danger, a thorn or brush *boma* fence ringed all.[77]

Although porters were experts at efficient camp construction, sanitary facilities were nonexistent, and at regularly used *makambi,* where up to 2,000 or more people might be crowded together at one time,[78] conditions quickly deteriorated. The heavily used campsite at Mvumi in Ugogo was, wrote Hore, "not unlike a dirty bare common in England" and was "horrible with the filth and refuse and ashes of many caravans." Stairs described the Mpwapwa campsite as "dirty and nauseating."[79] Accumulated excrement and garbage in old camps contributed to outbreaks of disease such as smallpox, dysentery, cholera, and tick-born fever. The threat of disease as well as the general filth and smell led some European caravan leaders to avoid them or to minimize their stay to 24 hours or less.[80] When conditions became intolerable after a few months of use, the remedy was to destroy the camps by fire. Travelers noted the charred remains of huts and *boma* fences at campsites along the roads, although often this was the unintentional consequence of fires left burning after a caravan's departure, or perhaps accidents.[81]

Porters organized themselves so that an efficient division of labor minimized the time and effort required for camp chores. Thomson's Waungwana quickly established order at campsites where no huts were available:

> In half an hour an entire village was run up with surprising dexterity. The men had already separated themselves into messes, for mutual convenience and comfort, and by the division and organization of their labours the most remarkable results were achieved. On arriving in camp each man in a particular mess or "khambi" knew exactly what to do. One as cook got out his pot, made a fire, and commenced boiling water for the rice or other cereal; a second went foraging for the food; others, again . . . commenced building a hut or shed. Of these, one man would prepare the ground; a second bring poles; a third grass for thatching; while numbers four and five would do the building. The grass for beds would then be laid in. By the time this was finished the mess meal was ready, and they could sit down under cover and enjoy it in defiance of wind and rain. The rapidity with which a whole camp was run up was really marvellous.[82]

A further advantage of such cooperation was that each *kambi* (or mess) had access to a greater variety of foodstuffs shared among its members than if each individual porter, perhaps with his wife, were responsible for his own purchasing and cooking arrangements.[83] Another account of the cooperative division of labor, from the northern route, highlights advantages for cooking:

> After a suitable place has been found for the night . . . the porters put their msigo [loads] down in the middle of it and go out, some to find firewood, others to get water in pots and pails and some to prepare for cooking, i.e. three stones are put together for a hearth on to which is put a thick-walled earthen cooking pot. After the others group themselves around a fire the five to six man strong cooking club receives their rations communally. While the food is cooking, a banana is eaten, a piece of sugar-cane is chewed . . . or a cob of corn is roasted in the fire.[84]

When women were present, they carried out much of this labor. They pounded or ground grain, cooked meals, cut wood, and attended to numerous other camp chores such as washing clothes, while their tired men recovered from the march and the weight of their heavy loads.[85]

The common small-group experience of work and play, eating and sleeping, and sometimes strikes and desertions made for very close bonds among porters in a *kambi*. It is likely that in each group porters were tied by family relationships, origin in the same village, or prior experience traveling together. Speke came to this conclusion when he tried to integrate Sultan Majid's slave gardeners (supplied as porters) with his professional Waungwana by rearranging the various *kambi* of his caravan. The effort was a failure. The Waungwana insisted on keeping the *makambi* intact.[86] Just as important as preexisting relationships were the experience and camaraderie of the safari, a point noted by Keletso Atkins for the very different context of the "kitchen associations" of Zulu migrant workers in Natal.[87] Real obligations to work-mates and deep friendships resulted from shared cooking, eating, and socializing in the fireside circle of the *kambi*. Only in the most desperate circumstances would *kambi* bonds be voluntarily broken. When porters faced starvation, such as at the base camps of the Emin Pasha Relief Expedition in the eastern Congo, an incapacitated porter might be removed from the close circle in order to reduce the vulnerability of his comrades.[88]

The work culture of the central routes was reinforced across the numerous ethnic groups involved in porterage by observance of and participation in artistic performance. Music and dance were central to camp life and, along with story-telling, expressed and transmitted the experiences and interests of porters. The history of music and dance in Tanzania, Iliffe writes, "illustrates . . . the mingling of peoples."[89] For porters the *kambi* was the focus of social life and cultural life. "When camp is reached, not the public shelter, not the chief's compound, not

Photo 5.2   Sukuma porters' *kambi* in the Kirunga forest. From G. A. Graf Von Götzen, *Durch Afrika von Ost Nach West* (Berlin, 1895), opposite 204.

the white man's tent, but the campfire becomes the point toward which all converge."[90] In the evening, small groups of porters sat around their fires, conversing, singing, and telling tales. A few had simple stringed instruments with which they accompanied themselves in song. Moloney even heard some of his porters singing tunes such as "The Bay of Biscay," "Home, Sweet Home," and "God Save the Queen," which they had picked up while serving on British ships in the Indian Ocean.[91] Examples such as this show how porous cultural boundaries were. Games were popular. Many Nyamwezi were avid gamblers, either playing *bao* or "heads and tails." Zanzibaris on Stanley's Emin Pasha expedition played a game "very like draughts," no doubt *bao*. In another caravan some porters even played cards.[92] When the camp was situated in the wilderness, with just a roughly built thorn or log enclosure to keep wild animals out, few moved away from the fire. "The more timid become like Scheherazade's sister in *The Arabian Nights.* They keep asking for stories and more stories to take their minds from the howling and whining shapes that flit through the darkness outside," Fortie wrote. Johnson described his porters as "interminable story-tellers." The performance involved audience participation, with the listeners helping out the less gifted. The subjects might include earlier safaris, perilous adventures with wild animals or hostile villagers, the fate of old comrades, or accounts of the character and mannerisms of employers. One missionary found that a good way to please his men was to read them a Swahili tale.[93]

Always, porters found extra energy, "the astonishing resilience of Africans," and held vigorous dances, sometimes in larger groups.[94] On the bigger occasions, young men and women from nearby villages might attend. When caravans passed through Ugogo, Unyamwezi, and other territories, it was quite common for local women to visit the camps and hold dances for themselves, which were "highly relished" by the porters.[95] It is not difficult to envisage porters and willing women entering into relationships on these occasions, as well as during longer stops at Bagamoyo, Tabora, Ujiji, and other towns.[96] The Waungwana of one RGS expedition were dedicated dancers and "danced themselves to sleep" most nights.[97] Nyamwezi *pagazi,* after long and exhausting marches, revived themselves and danced into the night, keeping the rhythm by drumbeat, clapping and stamping.[98] The catharsis of dance, along with song, was central to the celebration of important occasions, such as arrival at a long-sought destination, or the farewell of a caravan on a long wilderness journey.[99] Minstrels and itinerant dancers sometimes visited caravan campsites, providing high-caliber entertainment for delighted porters.[100]

The other major social activity was the consumption of psychoactive substances, or drugs.[101] These included tobacco, alcohol, cannabis, and, more rarely, datura.[102] The use of the first three was widespread in many Tanzanian societies during the nineteenth century. Tobacco was traded along the central routes, the major region of production being Ukutu.[103] In the interior, alcohol usually came in the form of *pombe,* which was locally produced.[104]

Here I will discuss cannabis (*bangi*) only.[105] During the nineteenth century, cannabis was part of the *materia medica* of many East African societies. Burton wrote that "in the low lands . . . it grows before every cottage door."[106] Like tobacco, it was traded over long distances. In the south, cannabis grown in Ngoni country was taken to Kilwa. During the German period, and no doubt much earlier, small-scale Nyamwezi traders carried it from Unyamwezi to the coast and to Zanzibar.[107] Arabs and Africans smoked it in large water pipes, the former with tobacco, and the latter without.[108] Interestingly, other traveling peoples such as the Kololo of the Zambezi region and the Bashilange of the Congo were confirmed users.[109]

In Nyamwezi society, *bangi* use was a significant part of male bonding, and for the same reason porters regularly smoked together. The warriors of *rugaruga* regiments smoked *bangi* to enhance combativeness and ferocity in battle.[110] Ordinary Nyamwezi men smoked *bangi* in their village *iwanza* or men's club, while women were so fond of their tobacco pipes that they took them to the fields while cultivating.[111] There is ample evidence, often expressed by foreign travelers in terms of moral condemnation, that porters used *bangi* while on safari. Burton noted they might smoke *bangi* or tobacco when having breaks during the march and between meals when in camp.

Stanley wrote of his porters on the 1874–76 expedition, "They smoke *banghy* until they literally fall down half smothered." Such escape was hardly surprising given the terrible conditions his style of travel exposed them to. During the return of Stanley's Emin Pasha Relief Expedition, Nyamwezi porters ground cannabis to a powder and then took it as a snuff or chewed it "half roasted," as well as smoking the leaf in large pipes. Casati believed that the Nyamwezi learned the use of "the fatal hasheesh" from Zanzibar Arabs. This is almost certainly incorrect. Stokes's great caravan in 1890 included many "wretched bhang smoker[s]" among the porters. Stairs believed the "craze for smoking hemp" contributed to illness among his porters during the first weeks of travel before they became conditioned.[112] Clearly cannabis use seen in this light diverted attention from the real causes of illness.

The German explorer Reichard was at first surprised by the cries of ecstatic smokers:

> The smoker quickly draws three to four puffs one after the other through the gurgling water and, when he has expelled the . . . smoke with raw . . . coughs, he begins to utter his own special cry in the strangest falsetto tone: one a cry like a child, another sings a phrase such as "njamera matimanumda timonumda njemu," which means roughly, "hemp smoking is beautiful." The third barks in falsetto like a jackal "woä' woä,'" another utters his war or travel name, always in falsetto.[113]

When a missionary commented to a Nyamwezi smoker that he was "making a great noise over it," the reply included a cultural defense: "God told them to smoke Bhang." An old Sukuma song asserts the superiority of *bangi* over tobacco, and regular *bangi* users over casual smokers:

> I put *bangi* in my pipe,
> Because I like to smoke it.
> Tobacco is not to be compared with it.
> My friends, mix it with the crust
> Inside the cooking pot and we will smoke.
> The tobacco smokers will fall down.
> If you tell them before, "It is strong,"
> They do not listen.
> They smoke and sleep with open eyes.[114]

It is unclear if the regular use of cannabis by porters arose specifically out of the conditions of the caravan system or was part of preexisting norms. Not only was it an escape from hard labor, but it offered a ritual of comfort and friendship among strangers. If it was a response to modernity, as the widespread consumption by migratory peoples and porters in particular suggests, then it is not a surprising one. This is the view of Johannes Fabian, who devotes a lengthy chapter in his exciting study of explorers, the Africans they met, and early anthropology—*Out of Our Minds: Reason and Madness in the Exploration of Central Africa*—to the "children of hemp," the Bashilange of the Lulua River region in the Congo:

> I cannot help but think of the children of hemp, whose story constitutes a pivotal chapter not only in the organization of this study. For there, local-ized and limited in time, a movement of modernization, inspired ritually, ideologically, and physically by a consciousness-altering drug, met an exploratory expedition representing the *oeuvre civilisatrice.* That expedi-tion was in desperate shape—out of control owing to desertion, illness, and lack of means. Pogge's and Wissmann's incorporation in the hemp cult and their obviously genuine friendship with Mukenge and Meta involved an exchange of minds beyond the call of needs and interests. In my view it was a paradigmatic event, expressive of the potential of ecstatic experiences, and a glimpse at a utopian meeting of the West and Africa on equal terms. Of course, eventually control took over.[115]

If strangers of the type represented by Pogge and Wissmann found acceptance and friendship in Central Africa among practitioners of a cannabis cult, then we can see that social use of *bangi* offered caravan porters access to similar cultural resources vital to survival, the massive confrontation with their work, and the challenge of modernity.

"UNTIL ALL LOVE OF MEAT AND DRINK IS LOST"

That most basic of human concerns—how to ensure some degree of food security, and how to obtain adequate provisions and water in the short term, was a central question for both caravan leaders and porters. A careful selec-tion of routes and the management of provisioning ensured in normal years basic rations for caravan personnel over the course of a journey. Even when localized famine prevailed, porters, being mobile, were usually able to march on to a district with a surplus. The same applied for water shortages. In October 1876, there was no food for sale in Mpwapwa "except at very great distances and at extraordinary prices." The demand of porters, therefore, was to move on. In October 1880, when Hore's caravan ran into difficulties in the Mgunda Mkali because two water holes had unexpectedly dried up, they were able to survive by making a series of forced marches.[116] During the infrequent years of major famine these strategies were not enough to meet the food needs of porters, who were therefore forced to resort to extreme measures or starve. And starve they sometimes did. Porters on the road were among the most vul-nerable when famine struck, because as strangers they lacked deep access to local resources. Their support networks such as *utani* were not strong enough to guarantee aid when people along the routes were themselves starving. This was the case during the 1884–85 famine in Usagara and Ugogo. An obvious option was to not travel at such times. When famine was widespread, caravan traffic was considerably reduced. But traveling was often necessary if famine conditions prevailed over a large region. Traveling could not be avoided when a caravan might be two or more years away from home. This was the Achilles' heel of the long-distance caravan system.

Even in normal times a porter's diet was monotonous, although there were occasional treats. Despite preferences according to region of origin, religion, and customary taboos, survival and health depended on adaptability. Preferences and taboos were ignored when necessary. When marching, porters ate only one or two meals per day, but on rest days they ate as frequently and as much as possible. Porters arriving at a well-stocked village after a march through desert or famine-stricken country were able to consume enormous quantities of grain, vegetables, meat, honey, and other foodstuffs.[117] As we have seen, the meal was prepared and eaten in a *kambi* of five to ten porters. If basic rations were provided by the caravan leader, the normal daily ration was one *kibaba* (about 1.5 pounds) of grain. The staple food for most was *ugali,* a stiff porridge of flour and water, with a little salt added. Meat, fish, or vegetables supplemented it if available. When porters were too exhausted or hungry to pound or grind grain, they boiled it whole. This filled the stomach but was difficult to digest, and perhaps limited in nutritional value.[118] The Nyamwezi preferred *ugali* made with sorghum flour, although millet or maize were acceptable, and sometimes they ate rice.[119] Swahili porters ate a basic diet of maize and beans, bean stew with meat once or twice a week, or rice. Waungwana ate mostly rice, with meat or dried fish when possible.[120] Rice for a whole caravan was packed in 60-pound *makanda,* long matting bags. In French-Sheldon's caravan, enough for the first eight or nine days was carried. In Burton's time, Zungomero was the last place before Unyamwezi where rice could be purchased.[121] This evidence agrees with Christopher Ehret's conclusion, based on the linguistic context of the introduction of rice into the East African interior, that it must have been "a very important element in caravan provisioning."[122] Porters also consumed grain in the form of *pombe* when this was available at camp stops and in the towns, according to the common practice in the interior.[123]

The other basic food was cassava. However, the root had a major disadvantage for travelers. Several references to cassava poisoning in the nineteenth century show that some porters were unfamiliar with preparation of the more-toxic bitter varieties or took chances with their lives due to lack of time for the long soaking process necessary to make toxic bitter cassava safe. The result was cyanide poisoning, which caused attacks of the epidemic paralytic disease known as *konzo.*[124] If properly prepared, cassava was safe. Decle's porters bought cassava flour en route between Ujiji and Tabora, which they ate without ill effects.[125] But around 1870, the 4,000-strong combined caravan of Tippu Tip and his associates was devastated by the effects of cassava poisoning after passing through mountainous and famine-stricken Urungu at the south end of Lake Tanganyika. This variety required soaking for six or seven days before fermentation, and then drying, after which the cassava could be safely consumed. But starving Nyamwezi and slave porters chewed the roots raw or roasted them unsoaked. The next morning hundreds of porters were stricken with vomiting and diarrhea. Forty porters died. Many others were saved, Tippu Tip believed, by eating a broth of peppers, ginger, and goat meat. A second reported case occurred when the survivors of the Emin Pasha expedition were in Karagwe in August 1889. Two young porters, ravenous and impatient, died in agony after eating raw roots purchased locally, despite several earlier warnings from their more-experienced comrades. Waungwana porters of the same expedition had earlier become ill with cassava poisoning when traveling up the Congo River. In a third case, in one day in December 1894, eight starving porters of the CMS Uganda caravan died in Iramba country after eating "a poisonous root," almost certainly bitter cassava. Numerous others were very sick. All these cases occurred in contexts of hunger and almost certainly a low protein intake, both associated with *konzo*.[126]

Porters added whatever vegetables, sweet potatoes, nuts, and other foods they could obtain to the high-bulk staple. *Posho* went further with the addition of edible herbs and roots collected in the vicinity of camps. During the rainy season travelers could collect mushrooms in the *pori,* or bush country. When locust swarms appeared, Nyamwezi and Sukuma porters ate the insects. Hungry porters ate wild fruits and termites as famine food.[127] But the most sought-after addition to the pot was meat. For some people the opportunities for meat consumption along the road were better than at home, according to Burton, and this was one inducement to work as a porter.[128] There were two sources: domestic and wild animals. From the first category, goat meat was popular. Although normally too expensive for the average carrier, headmen occasionally bought a goat and divided it. Herds of goats accompanied Stokes's caravans, a valuable addition to the staple millet.[129] Fowl were considered taboo by the Nyamwezi, but they were known to break the custom and eat them on journeys. Waungwana ate them regularly.[130] On special occasions, such as the day before departure or on arrival at a destination, and after especially hard marches, the caravan leader would slaughter an ox and distribute the meat among the porters. At market towns, porters might be able to buy pieces of beef from a local herder. When Baumann's caravan defeated the Mbugwe in March 1892, the 250 captured cattle kept his porters and *askari* in meat for months.[131] Elton's companion Cotterill captures the seriousness with which hard-working porters dealt with the carcass of a young bullock:

> Nothing could better describe than certain well-known passages in Homer the busy scene of slaughter and skinning and cutting up, and roasting

entrails and titbits, strung upon spits with alternate layers of fat. Libations
and meat offerings are wanting in the African ceremony. The final scene
is alike in both cases. Until 'all love of meat and drink is lost' they feast
and make merry through the livelong night, cramming down their throats
huge lumps of half-baked flesh, until the whole beast—be it cow, or zebra,
or rhinoceros—has vanished, except a few cracked, marrowless, blackened
bones.[132]

Success in hunting led to the same activities.[133] When Gleerup shot a
giraffe near Kondoa in Usagara toward the end of a long journey to the coast,
"all the carriers came running with their knives ready and shouting their
gratitude." Hundreds of porters quickly gathered around to compete for
pieces of meat. The Watts' porters devoured a zebra in an evening after a
series of hard marches on short rations. A successful buffalo hunt in Ugalla
by some of Cameron's porters forced a delay to the journey until all the
meat was brought to camp and divided.[134] The shooting of an elephant might
mean two or three days and nights spent drying the meat in hot ashes, or
smoking it on a platform over a slow fire. Three of four pounds of smoked
meat, an unobjectionable addition to the load, would then be carried on long
sticks "like gigantic kababs."[135] When Stanley shot successively a giraffe,
an antelope, five zebra, a buffalo, and a wildebeest after a period of short
rations, some of his Nyamwezi porters added nearly 35 pounds of dried
meat to their loads.[136] Less commonly, river pools provided fish, which were
smoked in large quantities to provide food for the road. The Sukuma made
full use of this option, many living close to Lake Victoria and thus being
used to a fish diet. Up caravans from the coast sometimes carried dried
shark into the interior for use as a side dish.[137]

For the Muslim Swahili and Waungwana, certain game presented religious difficulties. Wild boar, warthogs, and hippopotamuses were considered unclean, and so were normally left to Nyamwezi caravan members.
None of Cameron's men would bring in a wild boar shot near the Ugalla
River. "Only the faithful are down on their luck," Elton wrote after a successful buffalo hunt. Despite "almost starving," the Muslim porters would
not eat the meat because "no true believer was present to 'halal' either
beast. They are afraid of each other's tongues."[138] But during hard times on
the road, principles of pollution were often suspended out of necessity.[139]
The same applied to the eating of carrion. The Nyamwezi were known to
eat lion kills and putrid meat others would not touch, despite the possible
consequences. Reichard considered the practice the enjoyment of "racy"
behavior. More likely it was a cultural adaptation to decades of safari
experience.[140]

Although gathering, hunting, and fishing met some food needs,[141] porters
relied heavily on the purchase of foodstuffs from peasants along the routes.

The marketing system in nineteenth-century Tanganyika was relatively undeveloped compared with that in much of North or West Africa. Nevertheless, most peoples were familiar with permanent or temporary markets, especially in the northeast region and along the established caravan routes.[142] This was where commercial activities were most pronounced, and market values were relatively standardized, although subject to great variations according to supply and demand.[143] Porters found markets of some sort where foodstuffs were available at most of the bigger villages and towns along the central routes. In these places, such as Zungomero, Malolo, Mpwapwa, Tura, Tabora, Msene, Ujiji, and many other places, there was little problem obtaining food during normal times, except perhaps at the end of the dry season. Much of this is known in outline to historians, although no serious study of nineteenth-century markets or market response exists for the central routes, with the exception of Carol Sissons's unpublished work on the Gogo and Beverly Brown's on Ujiji.[144]

Elsewhere in populated districts, peasants commonly brought their surplus produce to the campsites to sell to caravan members. In 1857 the thriving peasant economy of Rumuma and other places in the Usagara and Rubeho mountains supplied caravans with their needs after leaner days on the march from the coast. "Here, for the first time," Burton wrote, "the country people descended in crowds from the hills, bringing fowls, hauling along small . . . goats, lank sheep, and fine bullocks—the latter worth twelve cloths—and carrying on their heads basket-platters full of voiandzeia, bajri, beans, and the *Arachis hypogoea.*"[145] The same applied in much of Ugogo. At Ziwa, the oasis on the eastern fringe and the first major provisioning place after the Marenga Mkali, porters could buy bullocks, sheep, goats, poultry, watermelons, pumpkins, honey, buttermilk, whey, curded milk, and flour.[146] Twenty years later, Hutley wrote of Mvumi, "We had not arrived in camp long before it was thronged with people anxious to sell food, some with meal others with nuts, goats, sheep, fat, etc.," and soon after, in Mstumbuyu: "The camp at an early hour was thronged by the natives anxious to sell their goods, of which they brought a great variety."[147] In some places, especially to the west of Tabora, peasants continued to respond in the same way during the early years of colonial rule. In 1893 near the village of Unyonga, in southwest Buha, villagers approached Decle's caravan to sell potatoes and cassava flour. Nearby, in the Muserere River valley, a market was held on the path, with salted meat, potatoes, millet, bananas, and other produce for sale to passing porters.[148]

When peasants did not bring their surplus to the porters, and in times of shortage, porters had to tramp around villages, hamlets and homesteads in the neighborhood of campsites to find food to buy,[149] or forage across the countryside and along the margins of fields, collecting edibles or stealing whatever they could get away with. If there had been earlier altercations

Photo 5.3 Speke and Grant's camp in the Uthungu Valley, southwest of Lake Victoria. Peasants bring provisions to sell to the travelers. From John Hanning Speke, *Journal of the Discovery of the Source of the Nile* (Toronto and London, 1996), 185.

between porters and peasants, then a chief might forbid his or her people to visit campsites, forcing porters to "send about the country" to obtain provisions.[150] In any case, porters visited villagers who provided services, such as grinding grain, for a small fee. Inevitably there were disagreements, and sometimes violence, when hungry porters plundered local food supplies or carried a high hand or were themselves abused or insulted. Caravan personnel, scattered across the countryside in small groups, were vulnerable in these circumstances.[151]

The potential for serious conflict is evident, such as when Tippu Tip's immense caravan, 3,000 strong, reached the village of Mtowa in December 1881. A missionary observed

> Of course in such a collection . . . there are a great many ruffians & plundering of the natives consequently is very common, in which matter the Arabs themselves are not blame-less for the rations they distribute to their men are far from being sufficient. On account of this they have very nearly come in collision with the Waguha & should it occur it would be a terrible disaster. The whole of the country would rise against their oppressors like one man.[152]

The following example from Tippu Tip's third great journey to the eastern Congo, circa 1870, shows how a relatively trivial incident could precipitate a serious conflict. When in Ugalla, the Nyamwezi and Waungwana carriers in his small advance caravan spread out to get their millet pounded in preparation for the seven-day trek across the uninhabited country stretching to Simba's in Ukonongo. One man, a slave from the coast, complained of being attacked without provocation in Riova's village after some grain was spilled. A confrontation resulted, with numerous deaths on both sides. It appeared that Tippu Tip and his people would all be killed. Then another of his caravans arrived, and the village was captured. But at least seven more porters were killed in the nearest villages, and 60 Nyamwezi porters and some of the trader's slaves, hearing of the fight, deserted and returned to Unyanyembe. After a few days the remaining members of the two caravans were attacked by a large force of Galla and Konongo warriors under Chief Taka, brother of Riova. This time the victory of the traders with their slaves and porters was complete.[153] The outcome of such incidents very much depended on the diplomatic skills of caravan leaders and local chiefs,[154] and on the balance of power, which—with the exception of very well-armed and -led caravans—usually lay with the peoples of the interior.

When negotiations broke down, death stared porters in the face. Belligerency on both sides, or failure to compensate villagers for thefts by porters, could lead to the partial or complete destruction of a caravan and the massacre of its workforce. A large Arab caravan from Tanga, trading in the region east of Lake Victoria and armed with 400 to 500 guns, was devastated by the Maasai in the early 1850s—the consequence of a dispute over the burning over of some grazing land.[155] Twenty-two members of Stanley's caravan were killed in running battles in Ituru, northeast of Unyamwezi. The dispute ostensibly arose over starving porters' thefts of milk and grain.[156] In 1890 the Gogo "almost utterly destroyed" an Arab caravan numbering about 500 porters—men, women, and children. The cause of the bloodshed is not stated, but it must have been related to a dispute over food or water.[157] As late as 1891, Chief Makangi of Kilimandini (Kilimatinde?) in Ugogo was strong enough to harass a strong Belgian expedition and overwhelm an ivory caravan.[158] According to a vague report current in 1890–91, the members of a Swahili caravan had earlier been massacred in Umbugwe, near Lake Manyara, turning this region into a virtual no-go area. Less-catastrophic but still-fatal collisions were common. During Baumann's visit to Umbugwe in March 1892, eight of his porters were killed while out buying provisions.[159] Toward the end of 1894, 22 porters of a CMS caravan were killed in Irangi when they plundered villages for food.[160]

"And in the vast bush while the sun burns down there is much trouble about water," Mtoro bin Myinyi Bakari wrote of the safari experience.[161] Water, or lack of it, was indeed a source of great difficulty during the dry season, when caravan traffic was at its peak. In regions such as Ugogo the wells consisted of pits 15 to 30 feet deep, which gave poor, slimy water, or shafts, which could be covered over with brush by their owners to prevent unwanted use and evaporation. In the Usagara mountains, deep pits were dug in streambeds and gave good water.[162] Control over wells in the dry center of Tanzania was the source of Gogo power that all caravans had to come to terms with.[163] There were numerous tales of caravans led to destruction over water disputes. The case of Kafuku's death in Ugogo has been recounted.[164] Burton also mentions a (different?) Nyamwezi caravan that was wiped out by the Gogo as a result of a dispute over access to water.[165] Pruen tells the story of how an Arab caravan refused to pay *hongo* when passing through Ugogo to the coast, trusting and relying on their strength. The Gogo did not respond with force of arms but closed all the wells along the route, using others unknown to the travelers. Except for a handful of survivors who reached the coast, all caravan members died of thirst.[166] In 1886 an Arab trader known as Kambi Mbaya (Bad Camp) was killed in Usukuma with all his slaves and porters. According to one account the dispute arose when his men tried to take water for themselves ahead of Sukuma herders who wished to water their cattle. "Angry words arose, blows were struck, the natives collected in force, and in vain the Arab endeavoured to restrain his followers." Another version had it that his men had thrown the corpse of a porter into a well used by the Sukuma.[167] Smaller-scale but nevertheless still lethal consequences of disputes over water were common.[168]

Even when general access to wells was assured, the huge numbers of people traveling in combined caravans sometimes led to struggles as individuals competed for the scarce liquid. The strongest came first. To ensure that his porters were not denied water by the more than 1,700 members of two Nyamwezi caravans accompanying his expedition, Stairs had his *askari* stationed around one water hole in Ugogo.[169] The Tuturu wells in the middle of the Mgunda Mkali were the site of tragic events on more than one occasion. In late September, 1890, Stokes's huge caravan arrived at the site. Tucker describes the scene:

> These wells are narrow and the shafts deep—some seventy feet. According to our custom, we [the missionaries] arrived first at the camping-ground, and were able, with the assistance of our tent-ropes, to get sufficient water for our use before the arrival of the huge caravan itself. The scene on its arrival is one that will never fade from my memory. There were three wells to supply 2,500 men [and women].
>
> The struggle for the water was terrible, not that the men fought—they did not do that. But the crowding the well-tops and the eager pressing into vacant places almost amounted to a fierce struggle, terrible to witness. In the course of the day three lives were lost by men losing their foothold, and falling headlong down the well. All night long the crowding continued, and when morning dawned there were yet men with their thirst unquenched.[170]

When strategic water sources such as the brackish springs of the Marenga Mkali dried up, as they sometimes did at the height of the hot season, then thirst resulted in death for careless porters.[171] In the dry season of 1891 the shortage of water along this stretch of the route made for particularly hard marching and caused great worry to travelers. Stairs's diary records that at one camp there was no water "except what the Europeans had." Later, he wrote, "I doubt whether one can find a gloomier, more desolate spot than the Marenga Kali or 'bitter waters' this month, seeing that for the last forty-two days no rain has fallen and that, curiously enough, even dew does not settle overnight." One of his porters died of "thirst and fatigue" in this desert.[172]

Options did exist to deal with water shortages. The *terekeza* march was a strategic response.[173] When marches were unexpectedly tough and long, and foot-sore stragglers remained behind without food or water, the first to reach new supplies might return with aid for their comrades. As an alternative, when the pace was forced to reach emergency supplies, loads could be abandoned along the road, to be retrieved the following day. This option was forced on Swann's LMS caravan during a severe eight-day march through the Mgunda Mkali. A third possibility was to march at night, carrying as much water as possible, during the period of great heat before the rainy season.[174] When all else failed, sick and exhausted porters were known to offer a month's pay for a gourd of water, and on at least one occasion a porter offered himself as a slave to a headman in exchange for water.[175]

Much drinking water was barely fit for human consumption. Traversing Buzinza in late August 1889, the height of the dry season, the Emin Pasha expedition were forced to make do with water from stagnant pools frequented by cattle and other animals, or liquid of "porridgy consistence," due to suspended mud and organic matter, obtained from swamps and their outlets. Hannington wrote that drinking water found along the road "when not absent altogether . . . was often so thick and black that it is scarce an exaggeration to say that one looked at it and wondered whether it came under the category of meat or drink." Cameron's porters' thoughts ran in the same direction. During the crossing of the Mgunda Mkali in late July 1873, the drinking water was so thick with suspended matter that the *pagazi* scornfully called it *pombe*. Another missionary provides further local color on East African water supplies. Drinking water was "at best, muddy and disagreeable in flavour, and of all shades of colour, from the light brown of weak tea to the deeper shades of coffee or chocolate, while in a few cases one meets with it white and milky."[176]

DROUGHT AND FAMINE: 1884–85

Widespread famine in eastern and central Tanzania occurred much less often during the 41 years from 1850 to 1891 than in the five decades from

1891 to 1941 coinciding with the early colonial period. In her analysis of famine in central Tanzania between the years 1860 and 1890, Sissons identifies only two periods, 1860–61 and 1884–85, in which there was much loss of life among farmers.[177] But famines or even shortages could be much more devastating for caravan porters, who, as short-term visitors and marginal outsiders with little claim on extremely scarce local resources, and often having only their *posho* disbursements to pay for food selling at prices beyond their means, were the first to starve.[178] The great famine of 1884–85, one of the worst on record, was caused by drought.[179] Several countries straddling the central routes, including Uzaramo, Uzigua, Ukaguru, Usagara, and Ugogo, were especially hard hit. By 1884 the CMS mission stations at Mpwapwa and Mamboya in Ukaguru were well established, and in that year several Europeans were traveling to other parts of the interior, passing through the affected regions. The documentary record allows, therefore, a discussion of the impact of the famine on porters.

The rains were late in the growing season of 1883–84, and the crops failed. By February 1884, the shortage of rain in the Mpwapwa area portended the approach of famine. By July and early August, famine conditions were apparent along central and eastern sections of the caravan routes. Ugogo was struck early. In the east, at Mpwapwa and in Usagara, there was still a little food, and many Gogo left their homes for these places. This is consistent with the Gogo name for the famine, *Chilemu,* meaning migration. But by November most people in Mamboya were "on the verge of starvation, and some were dying. A little to the north in the Nguru mountains, in Uzaramo, and in outlying areas of Uzigua nearer the coast, many poor farmers were forced to turn as supplicants to big men and chiefs and lost their independence. Others had no choice but to pawn or enslave themselves or family members. Everywhere Maasai, Baraguyu, and Gogo herders had great trouble finding pasturage and water for their cattle. In the west, Unyamwezi was less affected, and when famine conditions continued into 1885, some Gogo went to Unyanyembe for relief. The harvest was good, and small groups of Nyamwezi carried surplus grain through the Mgunda Mkali to sell in famine-stricken Ugogo and to caravans.[180] At the coast, porters from Unyamwezi and Usukuma arrived on their last legs. In July 1884, Stokes was in Saadani and then Bagamoyo, organizing his caravan to Uyui. He had to feed his upcountry porters for 15 days before they were fit to carry loads. "A more miserable set of skeletons you could not see," he wrote. At Bagamoyo the death rate was enormous; porters who arrived from the interior in bad condition were left to starve. Missionaries of the Holy Ghost Fathers did what they could, "having something like 200 at a time in a dying state." A few porters recovered, but most were too far gone.[181]

The scarcity of food earlier in the year and the impossibility of obtaining adequate provisions affected the labor supply at the coast. Few porters were available compared with normal years. Thousands of Nyamwezi and Sukuma on their way to Bagamoyo and other towns turned back. Stokes believed thousands died along the roads. The Indian touts who normally found men for travelers "had not a man to sell." The most powerful merchants of the interior, such as Chief Mirambo, had to leave large quantities of goods at the coast because there was no one to carry them.[182] Stokes eventually found enough porters, partly because he was able to get all the surviving Nyamwezi from Uyui and most of the Sukuma to come to him, as they had traveled down to the coast with his headmen, and partly by hiring Waungwana from Zanzibar. The labor crisis also affected Zanzibar slave owners. Acting through the European consuls, Sultan Barghash ensured that caravan leaders did not hire slave porters without their master's consent.[183]

In late July, Stokes's caravan left for Uyui. Only one of the Ugogo routes was passable and had food for sale. The journey was marked by extreme hunger and many cases of dysentery among his porters. Forty to fifty sick porters had to be left at various points along the road. Many others died, and others again deserted. At Mvumi the caravan was attacked in its camp by robbers in collusion with the chief, whose defense was that "the devil had entered his people." Two porters were killed, and others wounded. The consequences would have been much worse but for Stokes's mild response and payment of a large *hongo*.[184] In early October the LMS caravan of the Hores set off from Saadani for Ujiji. At Kondoa, near the eastern entrance to the Mukondokwa valley, the porters were able to buy food. They reached Kirasa in the Usagara mountains toward the end of the month. There they heard of hard times ahead in Ugogo, and of caravans broken up or forced to return due to the grim conditions.[185] Marching on, the caravan passed through the arid region on the east side of Mpwapwa. Lake Gombo was a dry basin. Annie Hore, on her second attempt to reach Ujiji with her husband, wrote:

> Every now and then I saw curious dark objects lying on, or beside the path, and shortly afterwards became aware that they were the dead bodies of helpless laggards from the various hungry caravans that had passed that way. The heat and drought had been so great, that these bodies were perfectly hardened and preserved. It was a terrible sight.[186]

In Ugogo the famine was at its height. At Msanga and elsewhere the people were eating husks and, in a reversal of normal conditions, came to the camp to try to purchase food from the caravan. By the time the caravan reached Mpara, many of the porters had finished their rations and were in despair on being told that there was no water. Some were obviously starving and sick. Others, perhaps more careful, or with private resources, were able to manage with less hardship. A little muddy water would be bought with tobacco and cloth.[187] The condition of the porters deteriorated the rest of the way through

Ugogo, despite their having been issued with extra cloth. The only food pro-
curable was sheep and goat meat, which caused dysentery for the weakest.
Some had to be left behind with a little cloth for maintenance.[188] One wonders
what became of them in their extremity. During this journey the Hores lost 80
porters out of 200, 50 by desertion, and there were several deaths.[189]

There was virtually nothing for travelers to eat along the 160-mile route
between Kwamamba, near Morogoro, and Bagamoyo. In Mamboya between
December 1884 and March 1885, hunger killed many of the resident poor and
elderly, who could not survive on a diet of grasses and wild fruits. In January
1885, a European traveler reported that the people between the coast and
Mpwapwa existed on "poisonous roots," probably toxic varieties of cassava,
"for which they scour the jungles." The porters of one missionary searched
the countryside for food for up to two days at a time, sometimes returning to
camp empty handed. They survived by buying plantain trees, "which they cut
down and ate for lack of anything better."[190] In this region famine strengthened
slavery; a reversal seen by a missionary "as though satan was making another
struggle against the kingdom of God." People were "carried off by night,"
women disappeared while working their fields, and clients' children were
sold by their chiefly patrons.[191] In parts of Ugogo famine conditions prevailed
through much of 1885, not so much from continuing lack of rain, but because
of the earlier consumption of seed, and debility. In the dry season of that year
most Gogo seemed to be able to survive, partly due to migration to more
favorable areas, although they had very little to sell to caravans.[192]

Fortunately, these were extraordinary times, even if in the longer perspective the experience of 1884–85 foreshadowed the German conquest of
the 1890s, which ravaged communities along the central routes, set loose
environmental catastrophe, and ultimately destroyed the caravan system.[193]
Customary defenses against exploitation and forms of protest were clearly
inadequate in such extreme contexts. Yet they were central to the labor culture
of the caravans and in normal times protected porters, as we will see in the
next chapter.

PART III

"HOME IS NEAR!"

6

CONTESTING POWER
ON SAFARI

Long-distance caravan porters created their own work culture in the unique context of nineteenth-century East African commerce. But this does not mean that they were substantially different from other migrant workers or crews. Like workers in other times and places, they acted to defend their interests and protect their independence. Like contemporary workers in Africa, Asia, and elsewhere, they were increasingly exposed to capitalist concepts of work, authority, and discipline. This chapter is about the contestation of power, the frequently arbitrary character of discipline, and the evolution of customary forms of protest in the nineteenth-century caravan system. We have little direct evidence from African enterprises, yet much can be surmised from patterns of resistance and the way conflicts played out in foreign-led caravans. Disputes arose when outsiders violated longstanding customs embedded in the labor culture of long-distance porterage. Misunderstandings and clashes over the meaning and practice of work laid custom bare, bringing into relief what for insiders was assumed.

The concept of legal pluralism—the existence of competing legal institutions or practices—helps crystallize in many cases the nature of authority and protest.[1] Conflicts over discipline and order were subject not just to opposing interpretations but were expressed in different "languages." Foreign caravan leaders, including Arabs and Europeans, used the languages of Islamic and Western notions of contract, and the prerogatives of legally constituted authority. In one of Speke's many disputes with his porters, he invoked the contract established at the British consulate: "There all their engagements were written down in the office-book, and the consul was our judge."[2] European travelers also utilized a spoken language of command, a simple lexicon derived from Kiswahili.[3] In contrast, porters saw their rights and the normal expression of authority in terms of the custom of caravan culture. In this sense we are reminded of E. P. Thompson's definition of custom as the "habitual usages of the country" that equate to rules and precedents.[4] Porters invoked long-standing work practices, the principle of equality with their work-mates and their right to work or not to work. Again, custom can be compared with the early development of the union rules, or "legislation" of early industrial workers in North America.[5] But porters were also quick to cite a breach of contract when it suited them.[6]

Foreign attitudes toward East African laborers were frequently expressed in the class and racial biases of Western societies. Indeed, in Victorian Britain, social investigators such as Henry Mayhew and George Sims drew direct connections between the British urban poor and African primitives, nudging their readers toward the appropriate response with catchphrases such as "wandering tribes in civilized society" and the "dark continent" around the corner from the general post office.[7] It is not surprising that European travelers in Africa utilized similar language. Occasionally we find direct comparisons between what were believed to be characteristics of porters and those of the Victorian working class. One explorer wrote of the typical porter that "despite his best interests, he will indulge the mania for desertion caused by that mischievous love of change and whimsical desire for novelty that characterize the European sailor."[8] Here we have a stereotype of crew culture, writ large. Yet the flippancy of the observation has a foundation in fact. Janet Ewald has recently written of the overlapping worlds of labor on land and at sea in the maritime Indian Ocean.[9] Nyamwezi porters and their womenfolk were also compared with London's East Enders, as we saw in a previous chapter.[10] A variety of stock images of the working classes were available for deployment.

Yet similarities to sailors and European workers go beyond such comparisons. Travelers' accounts are full of reports of porter resistance and protest, some forms of which were "hidden," while others were more open or collective, such as strikes and slowdowns.[11] The most commonly mentioned protest action was desertion, a powerful weapon because it took advantage of the porter's mobility, a great source of strength.[12] Desertion was almost universal, and few caravans were unaffected. It could range from the secretive disappearance of one or two individuals to the open desertion of a whole workforce, perhaps hundreds of porters. Desertion was the response to a whole range of threats and problems—from low wages and poor conditions to fear of known or unknown dangers ahead. Strikes were also frequent occurrences and often occurred in conjunction with mass desertions. Porters had considerable leverage over employers and if united could effectively defend their freedom of mobility and customary standards of work, remuneration, and discipline.

LANGUAGES OF AUTHORITY, DISCIPLINE, AND PUNISHMENT

The language of authority and the practice of discipline on safari reveal tensions between authoritarian and paternalist approaches, partially representing different interpretations of the imperial mission.[13] The issues dividing authoritarians and paternalists included the kind of disciplinary regime preferred, the level of consultation with headmen and guides, the system of rationing chosen, and the degree to which ethnic and cultural divisions were manipulated as part of caravan management. Authoritarians preferred to keep a wide social distance from their African employees, while paternalists sometimes shared in the rituals and leisure activities of the caravan while on the road. This kind of social gap was also evident in the caravans of some Arab traders, although the justification was expressed less in racial terms than in differences of culture, religion, and experience.[14] If there was any dividing line between the two approaches, one might expect that it would fall somewhere between the practice of missionaries and that of state-sponsored explorers and imperial agents. This was, however, not the case. There were brutal missionaries and sensitive explorers. The categorization suggested by John Comaroff does not neatly fit here.[15] Many Europeans straddled both camps. Almost without exception, caravan leaders—African, Arab, and European—used violence to a greater or lesser extent.

Routinely, paternalists were more prepared to negotiate with their porters and often took advice from those especially trusted. The more humane among the European missionaries and travelers preferred lighter punishments than was normal in the caravan system. They fumbled their way through difficult situations, cajoled and persuaded, and frequently gave in to their porters' demands when faced with collective action. The alternative was mass desertion and the potential collapse of the venture. Nearly always, the gap between caravan crew culture and European expectations remained wide. A tiny minority—Stokes was one, Last of the CMS another—treated Africans more or less as equals and fully adapted to the custom of the road. Stokes, as a consequence, became renowned as a caravan leader and employer.

Authoritarians attempted to impose order arbitrarily and with great violence. At the extreme, custom was forcefully subordinated to military-style discipline.[16] The consequences were sometimes devastating for porters and caravan leaders alike. Stanley cultivated an image of concern for his porters, nevertheless in many instances he sacrificed their lives without compunction. His instructions to the European officers in the Emin Pasha Relief Expedition express this contradiction. These emphasize the hardships that porters endured, with due allowance to be made for them, but at the same time prescribe "for trivial offences a slight corporal punishment."[17] Despite a show of adherence to customary values in Stanley's caravans evidenced, for instance, by the theater of *shauri* (a meeting or formal consultation), of which Stanley was very fond,[18] there was little precedent for the extreme brutality that he introduced into labor relations. Even Tippu Tip was shocked by his methods. Nevertheless, militarists like Stanley and Peters in the end had to accept the realities of African travel, which usually meant accommodation to the caravan system.

Porters' protests can be viewed through a different lens, that of the struggles of crews to dominate the work process, in this case in order to defend the customs of caravan culture. Thus the programs, timetables, and pace of caravan travel had to remain theirs as much as possible.[19] The labor historian is reminded here of the way in which early industrial workers tried to control the rhythms of the workplace through the management of stints, or output quotas, set by themselves and resting on a moral code, in opposition to the employer's "incessant attacks" and imposition of clock time.[20] Keletso Atkins's study of labor in colonial Natal shows how in Africa as well much conflict between laborers and white employers derived from different cultural interpretations of time.[21] As Chris Lowe recently said, "These struggles [between peasant time and industrial time] were perhaps not so much [over] industrial time as capitalist time, a distinction that may be worth reflecting upon, as it illustrates how the intrusion of industrial concepts of time into capitalist culture gradually came to affect realms of life and activity that were not strictly 'industrial.'"[22]

In small Nyamwezi caravans, the control of labor largely rested on the hierarchies of domestic or kin relationships, with due deference given to age, experience, and social position. This equated to the situation elsewhere in sub-Saharan Africa, where typically sons, daughters, nephews, and other dependents, enlisted by their elders and relatives for trading journeys, had to give up to them a proportion of the profits and goods received in exchange. The young were aware of this exploitation, nevertheless "social constraints and the obligation of submission counted for a lot."[23] In larger Nyamwezi caravans, discipline was maintained in part by the authority and status of the *mtongi,* the *wanyampara,* and other officials.[24] Famous headmen and caravan leaders such as K'shimba, one of Stokes's right-hand men, commanded obedience through great personal prestige. K'shimba was known as a fearless *msafari* and an autocratic caravan manager who led caravans many times between Lake Victoria and the coast.[25] In 1894 the missionary Albert Lloyd traveled with a large caravan commanded by the Mnyamwezi to Lake Victoria. His authority and the respect that porters accorded him were clearly evident when he addressed the caravan on the first night of the journey:

> As we looked on . . . a sudden hush falls upon the men, and silence reigns as K'shimba mounts a little rising in the middle of the camp, and, stretching out his hands, begins to deliver a great oration. His eloquence is wonderful, judging from his gesture and rapid flow of language. We, of course, could not understand his words, as he spoke in the Wanyamwezi lingo; but our cooks told us that he was exhorting his men to be faithful to him as chief, and to the Europeans as "great white masters"; bidding them neither to steal their loads, nor raid any of the villages through which they might pass. After he had continued some time in this strain, he changed his tone a little, and to a kind of chant he said, "Will you obey K'shimba," and then all the

men replied in the same tone, "We obey you Kshimba." This was repeated
over and over again, and then suddenly K'shimba stepped down from his
elevated position, and walked with great state into his tent.[26]

European travelers and traders relied on an experienced, efficient, and cooperative headman to control and discipline their porters. Headmen such as the
Zanzibari Omari bin Omari made names for themselves during the years of
colonial conquest:

> In Zanzibar he was a person of some importance; the men respected his
> direct speech and his big imposing form, and I never saw a porter or any
> of the men disobey or question an order from him . . . in the more remote
> interior, African travel depends as largely upon the head man as does an
> army upon its sargeants. It is the native head man, and the native head man
> only, who can tell you the real condition of the porters . . . whether they
> have food and shelter, and anything else it may be necessary to know. It is
> the head man who can work the whole caravan into good humour towards
> the European leaders . . . it is only the head man who can explain the neces-
> sities of the case from a native point of view, and get the natives themselves
> to believe that the Europeans are neither fools nor playthings.[27]

Porters had ideas of their own about matters of authority, discipline, and
justice. "They have a keen sense of unjust chastisement and strongly resent
it," wrote a missionary.[28] If a porter's behavior was a significant transgression
of the code of honor and customs of professional carriers, then independent
collective action might be taken by his fellows to rectify the matter. Theft
of property from either a work-mate or employer could result in punishment and the restitution of the stolen goods. In one case, the *kirangozi* and
the cook of an LMS caravan informed one of the missionaries that a porter,
Nasibu, had stolen some tobacco belonging to the mission: "They said he
ought to be flogged. So the fellow was tied up and thrashed." Not only was
such a theft contrary to caravan ethics, but it could cast suspicion on all
caravan members if the perpetrator were not detected and punished. Later in
the journey, a young porter removed a piece of *merikani* from his load. On
being discovered, he claimed that the load was too heavy. Despite this, he
was "rather severely handled" by his comrades, to the point that he agreed
to divulge where the cloth was hidden.[29] A missionary describes a similar
incident in another caravan of 150 Nyamwezi porters:

> One night I heard a noise in the camp & I jumped up to see what was the
> matter. I saw about 50 men surrounding one, & on enquiry I found he had
> been caught in the act of taking away one of the loads of cloth. They asked
> me what the[y] should do with him, (he was a Swahili & not of the porters).

I told them to tie him & watch him during the night. Next morning as we
were about to start I told another Swahili to give him a few lashes. This is
a lesson to all in the caravan.[30]

Rivalries between the Swahili and Nyamwezi may have contributed to this
incident.

Porter justice could be rough and ready. When the cook in Cameron's
caravan was accidentally shot and slightly wounded by the explorer's servant
Mohammed Malim, a number of porters demanded that he be put in chains,
"otherwise they would shoot him." Cameron's reaction to "this gross piece
of impertinence" was to instead chain "the insolent ruffians."[31] Such mutual
miscomprehension must have contributed to the constant disputes between
the explorer and his porters, and desertions from the caravan. Annie Hore
believed punishments approved by porters to be harsher than those preferred
by her husband in their LMS caravan. "The porters always unanimously
adjudge more punishment than Edward would be satisfied with, so that by
simply taking no part, but to lessen it on the plea of mercy, or the weakness
of the culprit, the community is satisfied by being permitted to carry out
their own customs."[32] In the following case it is unclear whether a collective
or authoritarian form of justice prevailed: "Some Unyamwezi [sic] men who
had been in the same part of the camp as I, but who had started earlier in the
morning, had flogged or choked a big, strong man to death. The naked corpse
lay just beside the footpath tied to a tree with a bark rope around the neck."
The nature of the man's offense is unknown.[33] Indeed, the *vbandevba* had the
legal power of life and death over porters until sometime in the early 1880s.
It was only then that Chief Isike forbade the execution of servants, slaves,
and deserting porters by members of the elite.[34] It is not clear how often this
practice took place, although confiscation of property was an alternative.
During journeys such punishments more often came after a *shauri* including
the interested parties and senior caravan members had heard from witnesses,
talked the matter over, and decided on a penalty, rather than instantaneously
in the heat of the moment.[35]

How did paternalists and authoritarians try to set the tone on their
caravans? What were their views on the question of disciplining porters?[36]
The paternalistic approach is exemplified in the writings of E.C. Hore
and other LMS missionaries. Responding to the opinion of one "African
authority" that porters were "black villains" and "the despair of every
traveller," Hore wrote:

[I] had already learnt so to depend upon and love some of our much-abused
followers as to be confident in undertaking an enterprise on which even
the safety of my wife and child would depend, in great measure, on their
kindness and faithfulness . . . and was not disappointed.[37]

He was referring to the carrying of his wife, Annie, and their young child the 950 miles from Saadani to Lake Tanganyika.[38] However, Hore's good relations with his porters were colored by his general views on Africans. Writing of the "various interior natives" of the Lake Tanganyika region, he described them as "infantile": "They are adult neither in wisdom nor in wickedness, *but will become so as they are trained.*"[39] Dodgshun held similar views, although his experience in Africa was to be much shorter than Hore's.[40] Early in his journey he recorded that the Africans of his caravan—coastal porters and South African teamsters—were "all more or less out of sorts," as were the Europeans. By adopting a better attitude, they would be less affected and therefore less "lazy." Thus, when the next day, "Mr. Price conducted the p.m. and gave the Kafirs a rousing address on the subject of their neglect of their health in yielding to every feeling of lassitude," the South Africans "took the hint and greatly improved in buoyancy and liveliness." With more experience, he found that the porters and teamsters managing the few remaining oxcarts were best managed by a readiness "to help them in bad places and to treat them kindly [which] makes them willing to try and try again."[41] Southon found that a caravan leader could make himself popular with his porters by knowing each one's name, and by paying attention to each individual, "perhaps making a joke at his expense—jokes are generally well received and Wangwana [*sic*] rather like being made the subject of one—or inquiry as to his health &c."[42] In Southon's view, the "the facetious Leader will always be popular even though he be a strict disciplinarian." The best way to deal with Swahili porters was with kindness: "If you punish, they will run away if they can, but be careful to cultivate every means for their comfort and you are their friends for ever."[43]

These three LMS missionaries took a relatively humane approach to caravan discipline, despite the paternalistic language, condescension, and stereotyping.[44] Such ethical paternalism derived from the conversionist outlook strongly represented in the LMS, a philosophy in opposition to the idea of trusteeship, in which Africans, under colonial conditions, were to be stripped of any rights.[45] It also rested on the common endeavor shared by Europeans and Africans on long journeys, as others, including Livingstone, recognized: "Our sympathies are drawn out toward our humble hardy companions by a community of interests, and it may be perils, which make us all friends." But like other paternalists, Livingstone did not admit any real equality between Europeans and Africans and spoke of the "inferiority" of his porters. He later wrote, "It is immense conceit in mere boys to equal themselves to me."[46] Another missionary, highly experienced, held similar views on the treatment of porters:

> The stories one so often hears of African travellers having perpetual rows with their caravan, of the carriers throwing down their loads and deserting,

are probably in most cases due to the inexperience or fault of the traveller himself. If you treat your men like human beings, and not like beasts of burden, show a little tact in dealing with them, asserting your authority when there is really need of doing so, and using common sense when difficulties do arise, you can get on quite well even in long journeys of hundreds of miles.[47]

Many European travelers found that by following Hine's advice, they received service above the ordinary, as well as respect, from their porters. In 1876 when Wilson of the CMS discharged his Nyamwezi porters, they bid the missionaries a "most affectionate adieux." Later, some of the same porters were met in a grain caravan going to the coast and "stopped and shook hands with us, and seemed much pleased to see us." Even when the work was of the toughest kind, a little respect went a long way. Of the brave "human donkeys" who pulled the carts loaded with steel boat sections to Lake Tanganyika for the LMS, not one had deserted when the caravan finally arrived at Ujiji. CMS missionary Mrs. Watt, who was both paternalist and authoritarian in her views, tells more than one story of how her husband's life was saved by their porters, and how she wept over the death of one of their men.[48]

A harsher attitude, evident in both words and action, was more typical of European caravan leaders, including many missionaries. When new to East Africa in 1876, A. M. Mackay wrote, "To be every day at the mercy of a few hundred half savage porters, who are absolutely self willed, and whom one can control in no other way except occasionally through their stomachs—is the real difficulty of African travel." Eleven years later his approach had not changed much. When departing Bagamoyo in 1887, he dealt with demands for more pay from his porters by making "violent threats."[49] Those who professed a preference for more-gentle methods still frequently resorted to violence. Even the comparatively gentle Dodgshun was not exempt. At Kirasa in September 1878, he used his stick and shot through the roof of a hut to get his men out to work. From then on he found himself in disputes with the *pagazi* "almost daily." Swann of the LMS assaulted a drunk porter whom he believed had insulted his wife, the justification being that an example had to be made for its deterrence effect. More generally he favored such methods to control porters who were insufficiently respectful toward Europeans.[50] French-Sheldon acted the "master" with her porters after an early "mutiny" was suppressed at gunpoint. Standing on a box, she heard cases from porters who brought up grievances. But flogging was still imposed as she thought necessary.[51]

A lengthy analysis of the correct method for dealing with porters, in which violence had its place, is given by Mrs. Watt.[52] It is valuable because it highlights the contradictions evident in the paternalism of the late nineteenth century, when the conversionist position had weakened. It was Mrs. Watt's opinion that very few European travelers who journeyed into the interior of Africa with "a native caravan" were not "greatly tried, at times by the insubordination of their porters." The question of how to deal with their "aggressive spirit of dis-obedience" was therefore an important matter. Effective discipline could, she felt, be established only through the use of measures that would, in the event of the likelihood of rebellion, "nip it in the bud." One example of a mission-ary caravan leader who adopted an entirely reasonable standard in this matter was Bishop Hannington, who "found it necessary . . . to snatch firebrands from the camp fire and hurl them at the recalcitrant porters, who obstinately refused to take up their loads and move out of camp." Another example was the (unnamed) missionary, "much liked by the porters," who "often raised his toe to propel a native towards the task which he had refused to perform." Mrs. Watt believed, after witnessing one such incident, that the two porters involved "evidently considered that the chastisement was just, and the admin-istration of it . . . quite natural."[53]

She then quotes an interesting (uncited) document to support her case that the occasional use of violence against porters was perfectly acceptable. This was "a printed leaflet of recommendations to Missionaries" distributed by the CMS in the early 1880s to those about to work in Africa, which contained sug-gestions on how to act toward "the natives" in different circumstances. In the section headed "Punishments" was written: "Stopping men's pay is not much good as the negro does not look forward. Stopping their 'posho' . . . when not actually on the march, and flogging in extreme cases are best."[54] According to Mrs. Watt these recommendations were only "temporarily adopted." As an old African hand of 25 years, she realized that you could not stop rations for the porters on whom your own life and property depended.[55] Besides, it was a "heartless and cruel" suggestion. Nor was flogging recommended by her, despite its popularity among many Europeans in East Africa. Mrs. Watt believed that flogging had "an obdurating and degrading effect upon the character of the native, making him more sullen, revengeful and treacherous." Instead, she recommended, "the short, sharp, though somewhat blustering punishment . . . which comes momentarily and expectedly in the very nick of time." Such a punishment had "a telling effect upon the offender," whereas flogging would destroy the traveler's reputation among the Africans and not improve them, either.[56] It was Mrs. Watt's belief that "the man who can administer a brisk and righteous reprimand to a native one minute, and be just the same cheery, joyful master, father and friend the next, is the man who has an ever open door into the heart of the African savage."[57]

No doubt Mrs. Watt would have supported Thomson, who, in an account that reads like a G.A. Henty story, in which the great white explorer single-handedly suppresses a potential rebellion, describes his "conquest" of his Waungwana porters. This story should be seen in the context of the conditioning of European readers of African travel accounts to "accept a particular kind of relationship between the two sets of peoples," meaning Africans and Europeans.[58] Distortions in such accounts were attempts to meet the prevailing patriotic, racial, and class attitudes of the nineteenth-century readership. For the labor historian, the play to such attitudes seriously misrepresents power relationships between European travelers and their porters.

When in Manda, Uguha, in January 1880, Thomson was faced with a strike organized the previous night by all 29 porters over his decision to travel into what they believed was cannibal country near the Lualaba River. According to Thomson, he unbuckled his belt and, without warning, struck left, right, and center at the sleeping men and drove them out of camp with their loads.[59] A few days later, at Makalumbi, six days down the Lukuga River, there were more protests. The explorer wrote, "My men came in a body, headed by Makatubu [a headman], and declared that they were determined not to go any further—that I was just forcing them along like donkeys to the Manyema, who would murder and eat them. In this determination they were firm, and neither threats not promises could move them from the position they had taken up." After a series of quarrels, a compromise was reached in which the explorer gave up his plan to reach the Lualaba, and the porters agreed to take a shorter route through Urua and then southeast to Iendwe on the southwest side of Lake Tanganyika to rejoin the main body of the expedition. When the local chief placed obstacles in the way of departure and failed to provide a guide, the porters again protested.[60] Thomson refused to listen:

> I was now roused to such as state of excitement that I vowed I would compel them to march though I had to shoot one of them as an example. I therefore ordered the men out, and told them to pick up their loads. No one stirred. I unbuckled my belt, and walking up to one I pointed to his load. Nobody spoke, and he did not move. With all the strength in me I brought the belt down upon his bare back. This made him wince, but it required another of the same before he obeyed me. I did not require to repeat the cure with the others. They shouldered their burdens, and in a sullen procession moved off towards the river.[61]

Thomson's resort to the formulaic language of control in retelling this incident makes it read like many others. His reliance on "the short, sharp, though some-what blustering punishment" recommended by Mrs. Watt says more about mid-Victorian expectations of proper interactions between European employers and African laborers than it does about the realities of caravan safaris.[62] Nevertheless, Thomson was one of the more humane European caravan leaders in East Africa and was most critical of those who used excessive force.[63] He was successful in preventing desertions throughout the RGS expedition, and there was only one death of a porter, a remarkably low figure.

Mrs. Watt tells us quite a lot about the attitudes of the paternalists on the question of discipline. Weule, the anthropologist, would probably have agreed with her, although in 1905 he started off holding different views. "One thing . . . which I absolutely fail to understand is the furious fits of rage to which every white man who has lived long in the country appears to be subject," he wrote soon after arriving in German East Africa. Then followed a qualification: "I cannot judge for the present whether life is really impossible without thrashing people—but I hope it is not the case."[64] After some time in the colony he decided that a little corporal punishment was not necessarily such a bad thing. One of the white men prone to "furious fits of rage" was the Swede Edvard Gleerup. In April 1886, his small party was traveling from Urambo toward the coast. He ordered his porters to keep close together because of the danger from bandits. But his people ignored him, and some went ahead. He wrote:

> Sick and nervous as I was, I was seized by an uncontrollable anger. A big, unpleasant carrier . . . threw his load to the ground and fled. I seized a heavy club from one of the other carriers and threw it after him with all the power at my command, but he bent over; the club whistled just above his head and fortunately did not hit him.[65]

Judging from the words of Weule and Gleerup, there was often ambivalence over the use of violence to impose discipline. But those favoring an authoritarian approach had no qualms whatsoever. Decle wrote of his march from Ujiji to Tabora in mid-1893: "It is a pleasure to look back and remember that I was obeyed to the letter. My Wangwana [*sic*] soon learnt that they had to obey as well as the others. Of course I had to commence by using 'kiboko'; but after a short time this was unnecessary, and I had only to give an order for it to be obeyed at once."[66] More extreme were the views of Carl Peters, who aimed to "carry out a thorough physical authority over the porter element," using his Somali *askari* as his agents: "Such African masses of men can only be kept in control by a determination uncompromisingly to carry out one's will in the teeth of all opposition." [67] Ewart Grogan was of a similar mind. He declared himself "a great believer in the Germans' African methods," which were "not restricted by the ignorant babblings of the professional philanthropist," as he believed British officials in southern Africa were.[68] Like Peters, Grogan did not just theorize but put his beliefs into daily action. One example should suffice here. While near Rwanda in 1898, Grogan and Sharp's Manyema porters continued to resist, despite harsh punishments. After two of the men were flogged for a petty theft in the presence of some of the local Tutsi, about 30 of the porters attempted to desert. The response of the two Britons was to threaten them with loaded weapons, and then to attempt to murder the "ringleader" as he disappeared. The porters were then brought back to camp along with their leader, who was luckily unharmed, the bullet having gone through his hat.[69]

Such "furious fits of rage" and less-dramatic forms of violence have been analyzed by Fabian, who situates them in the larger patterns of behavior of European explorers in late nineteenth-century central Africa. Much violence took place without rational calculation when the travelers in question were literally "out of their minds" under the influence of illness, drugs, fatigue, stress, and fearful emotions.[70] The problem with this explanation is that it is too close to that accepted by Europeans themselves. As Rempel notes, moral responsibility for violent conduct was thus "displaced onto the fever, and indirectly onto the physical environment that caused the fever."[71] Other uses of violence for disciplinary purposes were more calculated for public effect and took on aspects of theater in which the "dignity" of the traveler was restored. A further factor was the desire to demonstrate power by sanctioning or imposing physical punishments, in this way perhaps taking on aspects of the authority of African chiefs. Frequently violence was mere bullying with the aim of intimidating caravan personnel and Africans in general.

Violence in the name of authority went further than threats, slaps, beatings, whippings, and blows with gun butts. The murder of resisting porters by European caravan leaders may have been more common than the evidence suggests. While in Usagara, Mackay shot at his porters, wounding four of them, as they were deserting after a protracted dispute. He then defended himself from a summons issued by Consul Kirk after the porters lodged a complaint in Zanzibar on the grounds that he had no choice given the "mutiny" of his men and the possible loss of CMS property, and that Kirk was overstepping his consular authority. The charges were eventually dropped on payment of MT$200 compensation to the wounded porters by the CMS agent in Zanzibar, Smith, MacKenzie and Company.[72] Stanley had two porters executed for desertion during the Emin Pasha expedition. Others were sentenced to death, but their lives were spared.[73] The British scientist J.E.S. Moore regarded desertion as a capital offense, and when some of his porters disappeared near Lake Kivu, he asked the local chief to "catch or kill" any of them found in the district. His writings suggest nothing unusual or extreme in this; he even found it hard to understand why the English were reputed in Ujiji to be *kali sana* (very fierce) employers, and why it was so difficult for them to recruit porters there.[74] As for Peters, on one occasion he ordered the murder of two deserters, whose bodies were to be thrown into the Tana River and, on another, abandoned a porter unable to carry his load because of tuberculosis. Writing afterward, the German commented that the unusually load roaring of lions on the night in question, "left no doubt as to the poor fellow's fate."[75]

In many European caravans the threat of violence against troublesome porters was underwritten by the hiring of *askari,* who, during the early colonial period, were sometimes supplied by the German authorities. This change in the use of *askari* from a defensive guard to a coercive police force paralleled the change in the balance of power between caravans and communities along the routes.[76] As we saw above, Peters relied on his Somali *askari* to discipline his porters. Grogan and Sharp, once at Ujiji, were provided with soldiers by the Germans "to avoid any trouble with the men." Authority in the caravan of Italian trader Fortie in 1902 was backed up by "guards armed with long muzzle-loaders." Their function was clearly demonstrated when one of them shot and killed a porter deserting with a box of copper coins. By this time most porters had been disarmed. Weule's caravan similarly included *askari,* although in this case protection from attack was a major consideration, as he was traveling in areas very recently disturbed during the Maji Maji Rebellion.[77]

Almost all European caravan leaders, whether paternalist or authoritarian in outlook, resorted to floggings or summary beatings of the "brisk and righteous" type.[78] Stokes was an exception. Burton "cooled" arguing porters with a "long pole" and on another occasion had "disorderly" porters "summarily flogged." Speke, on his second journey of exploration, wrote that "I often had occasion to award 100 and even 150 lashes to my men for stealing." Yet a subversive undercurrent of mockery intrudes into Grant's account of the same journey. Grant had been demonstrating swordsmanship to the expedition's Zanzibari porters. On one occasion he brought a cane for that purpose onto the "parade ground" only to be met with titters from the assembled porters. Grant interpreted the incident to mean that they thought he was going to use the cane to discipline them, rather than demonstrate sword strokes.[79] Other floggers included Bishop Steere of the UMCA. During a journey from the southern coastal town of Lindi to Masasi in 1876, a Zanzibari porter was convicted of stealing and sentenced to a flogging, "fastened to the wheel of the cart." Vice Consul Smith, traveling on the Kilwa route, punished a porter wishing to break his contract with "fifty blows with a stick" administered by Smith's cook. In 1878, LMS missionaries gave "the usual ten strokes" for petty thefts in their caravan. CMS missionaries in the 1894 caravan to Buganda resorted to public floggings to punish and prevent thefts. Meyer compared his porters to beasts of burden and found them "constantly in need of the whip" wielded by his Somali *askari.* "Ordinary offences" drew 10 to 20 lashes. Peters habitually had resisting porters chained and flogged. Grogan and Sharp imposed discipline with a hippo whip, while Fortie resorted to corporal punishment on occasion.[80]

Stanley was an ardent flogger, with ideas on discipline and punishment well beyond customary views and practice in East Africa, as well as contemporary European standards. He acted accordingly throughout his African career. In one incident in April 1871, he had his cook so severely flogged for pilfering that the man's companions, alarmed by the harshness of the punishment, aided his desertion. Years later, during the Emin Pasha Relief Expedition, porters

Photo 6.1 Flogging of runaway porter, Pangani. From Ludwig von Höhnel,
Discovery of Lakes Rudolph and Stefanie (London, 1968), 55.

responded to brutal punishments by concealing infractions and covering up
for their comrades so that the true culprit could not be identified by the
European officers.[81] In July 1875, during Stanley's second expedition, a
porter was murdered by a fellow, Fundi Rehani. Rather than have Fundi
Rehani executed according to the recommendation of the "court" set up to
judge the matter, Stanley decided that he should be given 200 lashes, then be
chained until he could be delivered to the sultan in Zanzibar. Others involved
in instigating the fight that led to the murder received 100 lashes each. After
their return to Zanzibar, some of his porters reported that Stanley himself had
kicked and beaten to death one of their comrades.[82] During the Emin Pasha
expedition's march from Matadi to Leopoldville in April 1887, "a few examples" were made "by whipping in incorrigible loiterers." This set the tone for
the next two years and eight months of the expedition, during which "whole-
sale flogging" was the norm. Examples are scattered throughout the accounts
of European expedition members. In one case starving porters received 180
lashes for being absent while searching for food. In another, personal servants were given up to 50 lashes for stealing maize from a tent. One man, the
Zanzibari John Henry Bishop, initially sentenced to death for desertion, died
a few days after the substitution of a "severe flogging." Although a Christian,
he had been defended by the Muslim Rear Column porters, who threatened

mass desertion, saying "flog him if you like but our people are never shot." At Fort Bodo, sentries caught sleeping were sentenced to 25 lashes. A second offence was punished with up to 50 lashes and extra duties, while fines of MT\$5 or MT\$10, in addition, were imposed for third offences.[83]

It is possible to compare European attitudes and willingness to flog in late precolonial and early colonial East Africa with contemporary standards in the British army and in colonial contexts elsewhere. In the British West Indies, a Colonial Office Order in Council of 1824 limited the number of lashes permitted in the slave law for workplace discipline to 39.[84] This was modeled on the "biblical limit" of 39 strokes,[85] which was also observed in British India. In Hong Kong the Magistrates Ordinance of 1862 gave magistrates the power to order up to two public or private whippings for male offenders. Each whipping was to be a maximum of 36 blows of the rattan cane. No racial distinction was made in the law, but in practice only Chinese and other Asians were flogged. Before the 1860s, sentences of up to 100 strokes were typical. At the supreme court level, an ordinance in 1865 gave the court the power to sentence persons convicted of crimes involving offensive weapons to up to three whippings (in addition to the prison sentence) of up to 50 strokes each. This was restricted to male offenders. There was no racial distinction in law, but when in 1866 the court started to sentence Europeans to whipping, there was an outcry in the colonial community. This was often compared with the practice in China, where people sometimes received up to 800 strokes.[86]

In the British army the number of lashes of the cat-o'-nine-tails was set at 50 in 1847 following the death of a private soldier after he received 150 lashes. In 1871 the maximum was reduced to 25, and in 1881 flogging was abolished in the army except in military prisons.[87] In African colonial armies, flogging was retained for much longer, was used frequently and harshly during the 1890s and early 1900s, and survived until the Second World War.[88] The number of lashes permitted by military regulation in the West Africa Frontier Force (WAFF) during the late 1890s was 36 for stealing and a lesser number for other offenses. The same maximum was legislated for the WAFF by an ordinance of the Gold Coast government in 1900. In practice, corporal punishment was meted out more often and more severely than mandated.[89] In British East African territories during the first years of colonial rule, floggings were meted out only to Africans, and most floggings of porters appear to have been in the order of 10 to 30 lashes, which would not have been considered excessive according to imperial standards. In Zanzibar, colonial legislation governing caravans limited the number of lashes to 30.[90] But brutality far beyond these standards was common, as we have seen. The Germans were noted for the frequency with which they resorted to corporal punishment, which was applied to Asian indentured laborers as well as Africans, and a legal limitation of 25 strokes given on one occasion was not introduced until 1896. As Koponen notes, "The expression *hamsa ihshirini,* meaning 'twenty five,' became a refrain which was still current at the end of the 1960s among Africans who had experienced German rule."[91] What Foucault refers to as "the age of sobriety in punishment" in which "the old partners of the spectacle . . . the body and blood, gave way"[92] might have dawned in the Western imperial centers, but relations of authority involving white men and Africans remained stuck in the patterns of the ancien régime.

More than one European traveler believed that porters themselves preferred flogging to other punishments, such as fines. Thomson tried to get fines substituted for flogging when misdemeanors occurred. His Waungwana argued against it, saying that fines were unknown to them. A flogging was over in a minute, but fines would mean they would travel for months only to return without wages, which would be fined away. A strike precipitated in part by fining, during which a mass desertion was planned and then rehearsed as a bargaining counter, caused Thomson to back down. It was only when he promised to drop his insistence on fines and reintroduce corporal punishment that the porters relented and returned to camp.[93] We see here the successful defense of customary working conditions and wages, both so central to professional porters.[94]

Other punishments were imposed by some. Smith preferred to humiliate rather than flog quarrelling porters by making one of them "sit close to myself till his temper was cooled." Sometimes offending porters were punished by being made to carry the heaviest load—Smith's tent.[95] Many travelers and traders, whether foreign or African, used slave chains to discipline and make examples of deserters and other objectors.[96] Stanley found the chaining of recalcitrant porters so effective during his first journey that he wrote that he would "never travel in Africa again without a good long chain." Indeed, a set of chains remained a standard tool throughout his African career.[97] In 1872, he also used one room of his house at Kwihara as a jail to which his "incorrigibles" were confined without food for 40 hours when he deemed it necessary.[98] Grogan and Sharp were particularly sadistic and continually had difficulties due to their porters' passive resistance. They often lagged behind, delaying their arrival at camp until hours after their employers had reached it, thereby, according to the two Britons, hoping to avoid campsite duties. The following punishment was devised to deal with such incidents:

> We allowed them half-an-hour's margin, and every one who arrived after that, without having obtained permission in the morning for sickness or some valid reason, was made to stand with his load on his head in the middle of the camp until sunset, or as long as was deemed sufficient for his particular case. We found this much more effectual as a punishment than flogging or fines.[99]

One needs only to remember that their porters' loads were at least 60 pounds, that they would be standing in the hot sun for several hours, and that they had already completed a long day's march. It is no wonder Grogan and Sharp found this torture effective.

It is not surprising that authority was imposed more ruthlessly during the early colonial period, if not more effectively, than before. In earlier decades, porters had more options, and the balance of power did not favor imperial interests. Whatever the case, porters as workers and then as colonized Africans resisted and used what power and opportunities they had.

"THROW DOWN THE WHITE MAN'S LOAD": DESERTION

The notion of resistance has received considerable scrutiny over recent decades, and a variety of conceptual interventions have been made.[100] The categories of domination and resistance, richly portrayed in the class analysis of British Marxist historians,[101] have been subjected to redefinition through the work of Michel Foucault, who dealt with "everyday forms of power," and James Scott, who furthered analysis of "everyday forms of resistance."[102] During the 1980s a number of authors, including Scott, attempted to understand questions of intent by asking whether acts such as theft from the rich by the poor are merely survival strategies, or forms of resistance against social and economic inequalities. Advances came from the recognition of the ambiguity of resistance, the evolution of actors' intentions through experience and practice (praxis), and the consequent change of meanings.[103] Despite this blurring of categories, I agree with Ortner in retaining the concept of resistance, as it interrogates the limitations of authority and power relations of various kinds. An adequate account must show that resistors have their own politics of division and exploitation, for instance, along gender lines.[104] Also essential is an appreciation of the deep cultural repositories from which resistance springs, of the language of protest as well as the language of authority, and of resistance as merely one facet of the lives of the dominated. The alternative is to see resistance as merely reactive:

> The only alternative to recognizing that subalterns have a certain prior and ongoing cultural authenticity, according to subalterns, is to view subaltern responses to domination as ad hoc and incoherent, springing not from their own sense of order, justice, meaning, and the like but only from some set of ideas called into being by the situation of domination itself.[105]

Along with Ortner, I reject such a view, finding justification in the culturally rich and politically complex studies of Thompson, Ranger, van Onselen, Rediker, Chakrabarty, Peires, Isaacman, Atkins, and others.[106]

Yet close comparison contains its own dangers. The degree of dominance could easily be exaggerated, and the power of subalterns underplayed. The determining power of British capitalism suggested in Thompson's work had no parallel in nineteenth-century East Africa, nor was there such a far-reaching legal apparatus as governed Jack Tar during the eighteenth century. The jute mills of colonial Bengal are not an apt comparison. The rural population of Mozambique under the brutal cotton regime of the Portuguese was closer spatially and culturally, yet according to Isaacman this was a system of forced cultivation by vulnerable peasant farmers using household labor on their own land, a far cry from the mobile proletarian lifestyle of crews.[107] Some types of porter resistance do equate to those described by van Onselen in his pioneering work on migrant laborers in early twentieth-century Rhodesian gold mines.[108] Van Onselen's migrants engaged in wide-ranging opposition to capitalist exploitation, including desertion, slowdowns, sabotage, strikes, and playing off different employers. Freund argues that such resistance reflects a kind of worker consciousness.[109] Yet nineteenth-century caravan porters were relatively more powerful in relation to their employers, certainly before the 1890s, and particularly when working the familiar paths of the central routes. In more-remote regions such as the eastern Congo, they had fewer options: desertion was more dangerous, and cultural resources were less useful.[110] Further, porters resisted by feigning illness to protest against impossible conditions, manipulating employer confusion over individual porter identities, stealing from the caravan, and using drugs and alcohol during collective leisure time. Porters struggled to maintain control over the work process and defended themselves against dangerous working conditions and abusive authority. Most importantly, professional porters identified with a labor culture that held up an alternative work ethic against Western norms and thus collectively defended the customs of their trade until the deskilling of the colonial period.

Desertion was by far the most common expression of protest and assertion, affecting equally Arab and European caravans. Tippu Tip, conversing with a missionary about porters, asked rhetorically, "Do they not desert from all Europeans, as well as from Arabs?"[111] Indeed, the caravan that arrived at its destination with the same porters that it left with was a very rare one. As did merchant sailors, porters used desertion "in complex and ingenious ways": to resist authority and protest poor conditions, to avoid dangerous or famine-stricken routes, and to assert their freedom and mobility.[112] Not only this, desertion was a form of intervention into the labor market and helped drive up wages. Sometimes the cause was the failure of the caravan leader to propitiate an important chief or local cult. Porters saw such insults as a direct threat to their own well-being farther down the road. Other cases resulted from obvious dangers ahead—perhaps war, famine, or disease. Desertion was one of the easiest ways for porters to protect themselves and at the same time force caravan leaders to meet customary standards of rationing, rest days, workload, payment, discipline, and other matters. Patrick Harries writes of nineteenth-century Mozambican migrant laborers in South Africa, "What was considered desertion by employers was a traditional mechanism of survival to men . . . brought up to see mobility as a traditional means of coping with adversity."[113] Porters in East Africa were even better equipped than Harries' Amatonga to use their mobility as a collective bargaining tool, as great mobility was the very essence of their work. Both porters and employers were well aware of their respective bargaining strengths, hence the mere threat of mass desertion, whether intended or not, could have the desired effect. Sharon Stichter has noted, "Entering or leaving the labor market can be in itself one of the main responses workers have to the terms and conditions of their employment."[114]

Desertion was usually a continuous trickle, especially in the vicinity of the porters' homes. Waungwana and Swahili porters were more likely to desert within easy range of the coast, so that caravan leaders had to be particularly vigilant during the first week or two on journeys inland.[115] Sore muscles and sometimes unaccustomed hard work were added incentives, as Stairs recorded after 16 desertions during the first week out of Bagamoyo:

> The most dangerous moment for a caravan is this: still unused to their loads, the men become stiff, their morale is affected, and they desert. It takes not less than a fortnight's march for the carriers' muscles to become supple while remaining firm. But it's a thankless task to draw this agility out of them. I exhaust every means in my power trying to coax things along. I've strictly forbidden that the men should be beaten, harsh words are prohibited, our stages are short, and I'm generous in the distribution of cloth. I hope, in this way, to advance slowly for ten more stages.[116]

If porters usually disappeared in ones, twos, and threes, there were nevertheless many cases of mass desertions of most or the whole of a caravan's labor force.

Tales of desertion occur in virtually all accounts of East African travel. Thomson's safari to Lake Tanganyika is a notable exception.[117] Burton wrote that on both expeditions from 1857 to 1859 "we found . . . an unmitigated evil in the universal practice of desertion." On the first expedition "there was not, in the party of 80, an individual who did not at some time or other desert or attempt to desert us." And on the second expedition, they "fared not a whit better: we find in it 123 desertions duly chronicled."[118] Coastal merchants also suffered: they "complain loudly of the 'Pagazi' . . . these porters are prepaid $10 for the trip, and the proprietor congratulates himself if, after payment, only 15 per cent abscond."[119] In Speke and Grant's caravan, porters were very quick to perceive the dangers in Ugogo during the famine year of 1860, and many decided that the effort of marching on short rations to Unyanyembe was too much. A large caravan traveling in their wake, being the combined entourages of the Arab Masudi and several others, had the same experience.[120] Stanley did not experience mass desertion during his first journey, but there was a steady loss of porters in Ugogo and between Kwihara and Ujiji. During his second journey, about 50 porters out of 347 deserted during the 25 days' march to Mpwapwa, and 89 by the time Urimi was reached a month later.[121] In April and May 1873, Cameron's caravan lost 38 porters during the first 160 miles' march from the coast, and there were more individual desertions while passing through Ugogo. Many more porters abandoned the caravan between Kwihara and Ujiji later that year. A large Arab caravan met a few days from the coast was having similar difficulties.[122] The caravan of the Société de géographie led by Victor Giraud had a similar record. On the fourth or fifth day of the journey in 1882, five Ganda porters deserted, taking with them their advance wages and their guns.[123] From then on, labor disputes recurred with regularity. Finally, in May 1884, after a long journey to Lakes Bangweulu and Mweru, the caravan's Zanzibari porters rebelled for the last time, leaving the Frenchman at Mpala on the west coast of Lake Tanganyika, and returned to Zanzibar.[124] During the first years of German rule, it was a standing joke amongst Europeans that any German-led caravan leaving for the interior would have to return to the coast the following day due to the disappearance of three-quarters of its porters.[125]

It is not always possible to ascertain the reasons for particular desertions. Frequently, however, they occurred because of porters' well-founded fears, which were based on experience. In July 1857, nine porters hired at Dutumi deserted Burton and Speke's caravan in dread of being carried into slavery, an idea sometimes propagated by Arab traders.[126] In 1861 Speke and Grant's "Wezee" (Nyamwezi) porters deserted in Ugogo because they feared being attacked, so Grant believed, after a Gogo chief made threats of consequences if he was not satisfied with *hongo* payments. This happened again in the country north of Ukune on the road to Karagwe:

> We no sooner heard . . . the war-drum to collect the natives, and to intimidate our party into the settlement of the tax, than our porters would desert; and when the drums beat a "receipt" . . . and we were free to move . . . our Wezee porters would get up a row with us, and demand more cloth.[127]

Sixty of Tippu Tip's Nyamwezi porters deserted and returned to Tabora when other porters of the caravan were attacked and killed at Chief Riova's, near Ukonongo.[128] In January 1879, Dodgshun and the trader Broyon hired porters to go to Mirambo's. The porters of both Europeans abandoned them before the destination was reached, perhaps out of fear of the warriors of the dreaded Nyamwezi chief, Nyungu ya Mawe, or because their preferred destination was Uyui.[129] According to the Swahili trader Selemani bin Mwenye Chande, seven Nyamwezi porters deserted from his caravan in Usauwira (Usawira) beyond Ugala country. The reason was that Simba, the powerful local chief, had played his drums as the caravan arrived, frightening the porters, who abandoned their loads.[130] In the north, porters were always terrified of marauding bands of Baraguyu (Humba) or Maasai warriors. Mrs. Watt reports one case in which her caravan came across the site of a Maasai attack on another caravan, the evidence being many human bones and the remains of the massacred travelers' weapons. The next night, 12 porters deserted with their rifles, although they were later brought back by Stuart Watt and six loyal men.[131]

The war between Mirambo and the Unyanyembe *vbandevba* caused many porters to fear for their security. In 1873 Cameron had difficulty persuading his porters to advance west of Unyanyembe into disputed territory. "The pagazi declare they are afraid," he wrote, and they "deserted at every opportunity." They had good reason. A Gandan caravan of 75 was blocked by Mirambo's forces as they tried to leave Unyanyembe along a northern route. Only one man escaped.[132] Waungwana porters, coreligionists with the Unyanyembe Arabs, and frequently their slaves or clients—which placed them in opposition to Mirambo—were often in an awkward position when their missionary employers visited his territory and consequently deserted in droves. "When my men heard I was going up Mirambos [*sic*] road to the lake [Lake Victoria], there was fear and trembling, for none of the men knew the road, and Mirambo is dreaded." Stokes wrote. "I however stuck to my purpose of trying the new road up through Msalala. I named my day for starting, and just as I thought the evening of starting, I found about sixty of my porters deserted."[133]

Desertions also occurred for the opposite reason, as many porters originated from Urambo or allied chiefdoms. Broyon's porters, "natives of Mirambo," deserted because the Swiss trader "would not pass through their country."[134] In another case, a mass desertion occurred because of a misunderstanding. In August 1878, the first White Fathers' caravan into the interior reached the eastern borders of Unyamwezi. In the evening, as was usual, the *kirangozi* addressed the assembled porters. He said (in Kinyamwezi): "Tomorrow, at Tura, we reach two roads: one goes to Tabora, the other to Uyui. The Wazungu wish to take the first; we shall take the second. [Loud cheers.] Each of you must throw down the white man's load and follow me." The next morning the porters took the wages owed to them and left the remaining goods—250 loads—beside the path. In their ignorance and inexperience, the missionaries had hired men from chiefdoms allied with Mirambo, which included Uyui, who thus could not safely enter Unyanyembe. Their employers were left stranded until new porters could be found.[135]

"Am I to receive only eight dollars for this journey?" a belligerent Swahili porter exclaimed in November 1849. So began the earliest-known wage dispute in East African travel, during Krapf's journey from the Rabai mission station near Mombasa to Ukambani. The conflict was precipitated by the arduous conditions experienced by the porters, their water supplies having run out. Two weeks later the missionary wrote:

> I passed a night of trouble. As my people knew that to-day we would reach Kivoi and that our journey was drawing to its close, they asked

with the greatest insolence for an increase of pay; and now demanded thirteen instead of the eight dollars which had been agreed upon at Rabbai. They said that three dollars had been already consumed by their wives and children, and had been received in advance before leaving Rabbai; and now they insisted on receiving ten dollars more. Besides this they demanded all the ivory which Kivoi might give me in return for my presents. Should I refuse compliance, they threatened to abandon me forthwith.

Krapf promised to yield to the porters "if the demand were recognized as a just one by the authorities at the coast," and so the porters continued the journey.[136]

Low wages or inadequate rations usually led to a steady stream of desertions. Such was the case of an Arab caravan led by Isa bin Hijji, who had insufficient cloth to buy food for porters and slaves.[137] In another case, all the porters and servants of the first White Fathers' expedition to reach Ujiji deserted in April 1879, because they were paid just five *doti* per month and no *posho*.[138] Another mass desertion hit the first East African expedition of the AIA, led by Lieutenant Cambier. Perpetual labor troubles beginning at Bagamoyo culminated when 300 porters deserted over an outstanding wage claim.[139] The 1877–79 LMS expedition to Ujiji lost its porters when they deserted en masse at Kirasa because their pay was to be docked for "losses and mutinies." As we have seen, the European concept of fining was an infringement of custom. The *pagazi* thus "took offence" and returned to Zanzibar without rations, with only 11 under one headman remaining to continue their employment. By quitting, the porters lost the wages owed to them. The alternative was to accept payroll deductions and diminished freedom of action.[140] Three months later the reconstituted caravan lost several more porters, whom Dodgshun described as "the laziest half dozen fellows we have experienced." However, the missionary was at a loss to explain the desertion of some "good and trusty fellows," except to mention the "difficult work," and "perhaps an inborn tendency to idleness." Racial stereotypes were always handy explanations for porter resistance. Porters continued to abscond as the expedition struggled on to Ujiji.[141] In 1898, the various gangs of porters employed by Grogan and Sharp showed their dislike of their employers' brutal methods by running away. On one occasion even the ten *askari* and cook disappeared, which gives some idea of the conditions on this expedition![142]

Clearly, as these examples show, porters acted collectively as well as individually. The work culture of the caravan routes bound them together in defense of their common interests. Carriers in many, perhaps most, caravans were of varying ethnic origins, spoke different languages—although

Kinyamwezi and Kiswahili served as lingua franca—came from far-flung regions, and had different cosmologies. The Waungwana, although converts to Islam and having adopted other aspects of coastal culture, came from varying backgrounds, and many were born as far away as the eastern Congo, the north of modern Zambia and Mozambique, or Malawi. Yet as in ships crews or in bush camps or construction gangs, the origins of individuals in most circumstances made little difference. The work experience and conformity to the customs of professional porters saw to that.

Individual deserters had several options open to them. Most probably returned home if it was not too far away. Others sought hire with caravans traveling in the region. Sometimes they joined armies such as the *rugaruga* of Nyungu ya Mawe, who had taken up the cause of Msabila, the deposed chief of Unyanyembe, after the latter's death in 1865.[143] In Ugogo, deserting porters were encouraged to remain in settlements to increase their population and augment their strength, although it is not clear how many did so or how they were assimilated. This could be a dangerous proposition, perhaps leading to enslavement. Many deserters no doubt hid in the bush for several days, existing on whatever food they could find, rather than risking capture when entering a Gogo village.[144]

Employers also had options and throughout the period used various methods to prevent desertions and to punish and at the same time make examples of those who were caught. As we have seen, a favorite device used to restrain recovered runaways in both African and European caravans was the slave chain. Referring to a Nyamwezi caravan, Dodgshun wrote: "There were many pagazi, the first 20 in red clothes—nearly all had guns. 8 runaways were in chains—serve them right."[145] Tippu Tip used similar methods, yoking together hundreds of Zaramo men who were rounded up after a mass desertion.[146] CMS missionary J. Morton, whose porters decamped before he arrived in Unyanyembe in mid-1877, wrote of an unusual variation: "Instead of my absconding porters having bolted with my goods— I got some cloth, guns etc. of theirs, and on coming here found 6 of the ringleaders and put them in chains for 3 days."[147] Another missionary wrote that he had "even known an Englishman send runaway porters up country in slave-chains; the only way to oblige them to work out the time of which they had defrauded him." The story goes that one gang of about 30 prepared their escape by investing in files in Zanzibar. One night, about 50 miles from the coast, they filed through their chains and had fled the caravan by morning.[148] In order to prevent desertions, Peters at one point chained his porters together, regardless of whether they had made the attempt or not.[149] Deserters arrested at the coast were often handed over to the sultan and imprisoned, or sentenced to labor on a chain gang for short periods and fined.[150] The establishment of German stations in the interior, with their local police forces, meant that European caravan leaders upcountry could now hand over deserters to colonial officials for three to six months of hard labor.[151] Thus, in 1898, Grogan and Sharp used the colonial police force to track down several deserters in the Ruzizi Valley who had taken a month's pay and two months' rations with them. The offenders were flogged and sentenced to three months on a chain gang.[152]

Some caravan leaders, Peters included, took even more-ruthless measures. At Ngao along the Tana River in 1889, seven porters hired at Dar es Salaam deserted, probably influenced by the news concerning famine in the country ahead. Peters's response was to send some of his Somali *askari* to hunt for them among the Gallas who had settled near Ngao. His message to the Gallas, stated in the hearing of his *pagazi*, was "simply to cut . . . down" any porters who would not return. Despite this unambiguous response, more coastal porters disappeared. Later, when some of his Manyema men deserted with their wives, two were killed by the *askari* and thrown into the river.[153] Stairs, determined to hunt down a deserter named Sudi in order to set an example as a deterrent to others, sent squads of men 30 miles across the countryside and along the main route and offered a reward of 50 dollars and five bales of cloth for his capture. Contemplating the death penalty, he decided against it because "in a country supposed, like this one, to have a good administration, it could be that I haven't the right over life and death."[154]

Brutal punishments were not necessarily the best way to prevent desertions. Many European employers preferred less-extreme measures, such as the one outlined by Southon: "The chief and best way to prevent desertions is to cultivate such an acquaintance with each individual pagazi that he shall have a personal liking for every member of the Expedition." If desertions occurred near the coast, before personal relationships could be cultivated, the caravan should halt for a day while the deserter's headman and others were sent to bring him back.[155] Other practical steps were taken by many caravan leaders. As we saw in chapter 3, Baumann found guarantors for each of his porters hired at the coast. In some caravans extra porters were taken from Bagamoyo or Zanzibar to allow for desertions. Occasionally, porters deserting near the coast were rounded up by local authorities and sent back to the departing caravan, as when the merchant Abdallah Dinah sent back to Murphy two men caught by *Jemadar* Saba of Kaole, near Bagamoyo.[156] Stanley, expecting desertions after leaving Bagamoyo on his second expedition, posted a "strong guard" at the Kingani River after the caravan had crossed to the far bank, as well as another between Bagamoyo and the river.[157] During the first nights of his Maasai expedition, Thomson chose camps free of bush so that anyone leaving camp could be seen. To drive home the message, "in the hearing of the men, bloodthirsty orders were given to the night-guard to shoot down without warning any one observed to go outside camp." The head men were instructed to take turns inspecting the camp and report to Thomson or his assistant Martin every two hours. Thomson believed such precautions were particularly necessary given

Zanzibari porters' fear of the Maasai.[158] Giraud's porters were also hired at Zanzibar, and he was worried from the outset about the possibility of desertions early in the journey. So after landing on the mainland at Dar es Salaam with his men, he spent only a day there, giving little time for the porters to abscond. The French ship that had transported the 120-strong caravan from Zanzibar remained at anchor in the harbor as a deterrent.[159]

The establishment of the early colonial state offered employers further possibilities. CMS missionary Roscoe disingenuously wrote that when his porters were given a month's pay in advance at Zanzibar,

> Crowds of people . . . awaited these men when they were being paid and made great demands upon the wages they received . . . The latter had therefore to be guarded and kept in a locked yard after they were paid, until they could be marched to the beach and shipped to the mainland . . . If these precautions were neglected, the unfortunate men were left without money to purchase the numerous small comforts which they wished to take with them on the journey.

Then comes the real point of this exercise: if the porters were not in this way controlled, it was feared that they would break their contract and slip away or stay with their friends, thus costing the expedition both money and porters.[160] A more-reckless method of preventing desertions in Zanzibar was described thus:

> The S.S. *Juba,* of the Imperial East Africa Company started for Mozambique with a caravan of one hundred and fifty bearers commanded by Lieutenant Sclater, R.E., and accompanied by Mr. Whyte, naturalist. When the ship prepared to weigh anchor, she was surrounded by a perfect flotilla of shore boats, hovering around to pick up any double-dealing porter who thought to jump overboard with his three month's pay. Fortunately a steam launch of H.M.S. *Conquest* came to the rescue, and the officer, after due warning given, charged the interlopers and sank some five of them. No loss of life ensued, as the niggers can swim like fishes. Then the blue-jackets armed with single-sticks, dealt some shrewd blows to the right and left on the thick Zanzibari pates. After this gentle admonition the would-be rescue party sheered off, and the *Juba* steamed out of harbour.[161]

Clearly European employers found it much easier to utilize force (and racist stereotypes) during the 1890s than in the time of Burton, Speke, and Grant.

COLLECTIVE FORMS OF RESISTANCE: STRIKES AND SLOWDOWNS

Desertion could be either an individual or a mass form of protest, as well as a means to manipulate the labor market. But porters frequently engaged in collective actions of a less-ambiguous kind and more typical of labor regimes in the West and elsewhere, including strikes and slowdowns. Iliffe, writing of the caravan system, argues that

> a distinct pattern of labor relations grew up. The employer appointed the headmen and settled routine problems with them, but strikes were frequent and were conducted as collective actions to prevent the employer identifying ringleaders, a distinction between appointed spokesmen and anonymous action common in the early stages of labor organization and carried forward to colonial plantations.[162]

Yet "ringleaders" did step forward and present demands or negotiate grievances, and often headmen acted as spokesmen for the porters.[163] Strikes by caravan porters took place over the usual grievances: insufficient rations, low wages, too few rest days, overly long marches, brutal treatment, concern over dangerous conditions ahead, and in defense of advance wage payments.[164] In other cases insufficient details are available to ascertain the cause.[165] Slacking and slowdowns were part of the regulation of the work process, especially the length and pace of the daily march, as many travelers including Grant found:

> When the captain put down his load for as many minutes as he thought necessary, the rest . . . would also stop and refresh themselves with pipes, snuff, grain, dancing, and singing choruses. Generally there was an argument to settle how long the march should continue; and many were the excuses found for a halt, no water ahead being a common one.[166]

A day's delay at the last village of a settled district before entering a less secure region was also typical, and porters on occasion collectively enforced the option in order to rest and engage in petty trade.[167]

The issue of insufficient rations is one that crops up time after time in the sources. Porters frequently met their employers head on over this issue and showed a united front to many an impotent or insensitive caravan leader. When Speke and Grant's caravan ran short of food in Ugogo, "not a man would obey orders; they refused to march."[168] In 1873 Cameron's expedition had only reached the approaches of the Usagara mountains when the porters struck work, "claiming extravagant amounts of cloth in lieu of rations." Faced with Cameron's refusal to negotiate, the porters withdrew their demands (although many had already deserted). Months later in Ugunda, the porters refused to depart until they had finished processing their grain rations. This time they were supported by the headman, Sidi Bombay, and Cameron had no choice but to give way.[169] Disputes over halts to hunt for meat twice threatened Stanley's first expedition. In the first case, a confrontation ensued between the explorer and the guide, both threatening to shoot the other. Stanley was able to suppress the revolt only through the prompt action of the veteran Mabruki, who probably saved his life. In the second instance the porters approached him "in a body" to request a day to hunt and strengthen themselves for the remainder of the journey. Again Stanley turned them down, saying that they could halt on the banks of the Malagarasi River. The men agreed to pick up their loads and march, but with much grumbling.[170] A similar incident occurred during the march of one LMS caravan, although the outcome was different. The porters wanted to remain at the Lingerengere River for a day because of the plentiful food supplies there. The missionaries were forced to yield to them.[171] Food was also the issue at Uyui, in Nyamwezi territory, when 50 porters deserted Bishop Hannington's caravan in late 1882. The same evening the remaining porters refused to go any farther, being too tired and having no food or water at hand. Hannington does not indicate how discipline was restored, although he says that the next day was the same.[172]

Porters struck work when rations were stopped to punish them. In the case of a CMS caravan marching from Kagei on Lake Victoria to Msalala in Unyamwezi, the proximity of the caravan to the missionaries destination diminished the porters' bargaining power. One of the missionaries described the conflict:

> We resumed our march on Friday but the guide of the caravan purposely went to the wrong village where they were drinking beer. I was behind myself being unwell & Wise did not know the road, on arriving at the village I refused the men posho. They then struck work & refused to go on, & Saturday was spent in trying to bring them round, but being in Urima I did not mind, as we were only 2 days march from the port & I sent off 2 men to ask Mackay to send what Wangwana [*sic*] he c[ou]ld spare. More than half the Wasukuma porters came to terms & I paid the others off . . . The Wangwana arrived on Monday.[173]

The Waungwana based at the Msalala mission station effectively served as strike breakers.

Other strikes resulted from attacks on the principle of advance payment, customary ideas about rest days, and overwork. The right to advance payment was fundamental and had to be defended if porters were to retain their ability to influence the labor market. We see in the following account from Cameron a collective response to the explorer's threats. After the arrival of the expedition at Unyanyembe, the porters who had been hired to go only thus far were paid off. Others had been hired on monthly terms. These now went on strike, demanding two months' pay in advance to continue the journey. Cameron saw the wisdom of making some concession lest he be left with no porters at all—they had warned him that they would quit en masse. He therefore offered one month's pay in advance. This was still unacceptable to many of the men, and 60 of them quit.[174]

In 1861, Speke and Grant's Waungwana successfully struck work in Unyamwezi over the question of overwork. They "mutinied for a cloth apiece, saying they would not lift a load unless I gave it." Extra wages were demanded because of the shortage of porters—loads were being carried in relays.[175] The issue of rest days was also related to overwork but, more significantly, lay at the heart of control over the work process, especially the pace of the march. In 1882, after a difficult climb in the Usagara mountains, Giraud's men made it clear that they intended to have a substantial say in the progress of the caravan. They lined up in front of Giraud's tent "avec des visages de mélodrame" and through a spokesman explained that they were tired and did not intend to set off again the next day. They needed one more day to rest. They argued that normal caravan practice was to have one rest day every seven (a case of evolving custom?) and if it were necessary to march ten days straight, as they had just done, then they rested two days instead of one. At this point the porters retired en masse to the far end of the village to discuss the situation. After some time—we have only Giraud's version—they decided to give up the protest and continue the march the next day. The porters' argument was reasonable, but Giraud preferred to portray them as madmen and imbeciles, citing their protest as "a pretext in order to satisfy their tumultuous spirit."[176]

As with desertions, concern over the state of the country ahead led to strikes or attempted strikes. When Speke was at Chief Lumeresi's in Buzinza in August 1861, his Waungwana had second thoughts about continuing the journey:

> They swore it was no use my trying to go on to Karague; they would not go with me; they did not come here to be killed. If I chose to lose my life, it was no business of theirs, but they would not be witness to it. They all wanted their discharge at once; they would not run away, but must have a letter of satisfaction, and then they would go back to their homes at Zanzibar. But when they found they lost all their arguments and could not move me, they said they would go back for Grant, but when they had done that duty, then they would take their leave.[177]

In this case the porters appear to have backed down. But many strikes were more successful. Even Livingstone, who in Stanley's words received "universal respect" from all, both Arab and African, had to deal with a strike by his porters while traveling through Manyema early in 1871. They would go no farther and were persuaded to continue only by an increase of wages to MT$6 per month "if they behaved well."[178] On more than one occasion in 1877 and 1878, Dodgshun's *pagazi* "were rebellious and refused to go further," the missionaries being "helpless against them." Later he wrote: "The pagazi struck again and threatened to desert en masse but came round in time. They are afraid of the unknown country beyond. Thus we lost a day's march."[179]

Not all strikes were defensive. In the following case, porters struck work ostensibly to improve living conditions, although economic gain might have been a more-important motivation. In July 1858, just north of Unyanyembe, Speke's Nyamwezi porters refused to move unless they were given more cloth, arguing that they "were suffering from the chilling cold at night." The explorer's belief was that this was an "imposture," "a pretence too absurd to merit even a civil reply," and he told the headmen that such tricks should not be allowed to succeed, as advance wages had just been paid in cloth. The issue came to a head nearly three weeks later, in Urima, Usukuma. It was in fact cold at night, but the porters' real motive was to increase their stocks of cloth, as Speke wrote in his journal:

> Two days ago they broke ground with great difficulty, and only [continued] on my assuring them that I would wait at the place a day or two on my return from the Lake, as they expressed their desire to make a few halts there, and barter their hire of cloth for jembes (iron hoes), to exchange again at Unyanyembe, where those things fetch double the price they do in these especially iron regions. Now, to-day these dissembling creatures . . . stoutly refused to proceed until their business was completed,—suspecting I should break my word on returning, and would not then wait for them. They had come all this way especially for their own benefit, and now meant to profit by their trouble.

Speke got his way only through the support of the Beluch escort, who pointed out that the porters had been hired to carry out Speke's business, not their own, that it was his cloth that had gotten them so far, and that if they bought hoes on the outward journey, they would have to carry them all the way to Lake Victoria and then back to Unyanyembe. In addition, "other persuasive means" were adopted. The porters gave way and were able to buy their hoes on the return march.[180] A final example concerns a strike for higher wages, clearly planned in advance, in which porters took advantage of their strength as well as calculations of the employer's weakness and ability to pay. In September 1878, Cambier's AIA caravan was en route between Uyui and Unyambewa:

> On the morning of the 27th, when five leagues separated us from all habitation, the porters whom I had just engaged at Uyui refused to pick up their loads unless I consented to raise their wages which, however, had been agreed and paid in advance according to custom. It was again necessary to do it, for on the least threat on my part they would run away and abandon me in the wilderness with my merchandise.[181]

Here is evidence of a modern sensibility, in which collective action for increased wages determined what an employer would pay, with customary levels providing a minimum standard.

DAY-TO-DAY AND CLANDESTINE FORMS OF PROTEST

Desertion and to a lesser extent strikes and slowdowns, as well as the threat of stoppages and the withdrawal of labor, overshadowed the operations of the labor market and what can be called the collective bargaining process. In addition to deploying this arsenal, porters engaged in individual, clandestine, and everyday forms of protest—part of the continual struggle to assert autonomy against the will of the caravan leader. One should envisage this side of the contest not so much as an avoidance of direct confrontation, although it was partially that, but rather as a series of skirmishes on a different front. The key issues were the defense of custom and maintenance of control over the work process. Collective identification with caravan culture was a generalized form of resistance, yet the day-to-day activities and practices of porters, including individual protests, contributed to it.

Most studies of hidden, day-to day, or clandestine forms of resistance are concerned with peasants or agricultural laborers, for whom the immediate social context, the makeup of the household, and the nature of access to land and markets all impinge on strategies and therefore complicate the historian's reading of the meaning of subaltern behavior.[182] In contrast, the partly proletarianized labor force of the central routes was subject to a more-discernible set of pressures, making a reading of meaning less controversial. Nevertheless, it must not be forgotten that most porters retained links with their rural homes.

The appearance of such language as "lagging," "shirking," even "refusing" in travelers' reports is a clear indication of day-to-day resistance. Carriage of the odious human loads inevitably led to a concerted struggle over control of the work process, as Burton describes. Nyamwezi porters hired to carry his *machila* on the return journey from Ujiji to Unyanyembe at first "worked well, then . . . fell off." Asserting their independence and using a repertoire of tactics, they held the upper hand until the explorer threatened force:

> In the mornings when their names were called they hid themselves in the huts, or they squatted pertinaciously near the camp-fires, or they rushed ahead of the party. On the road they hurried forward, recklessly dashing the manchil, without pity or remorse, against stock and stone. A man allowed to lag behind never appeared again on that march, and more than once they attempted to place the hammock on the ground and to strike for increase of wages, till brought to a sense of their duty by a sword-point applied to their ribs. They would halt for an hour to boil their sweet potatoes, but if I required the delay of five minutes, or the advance of five yards, they became half mad with fidgetiness.[183]

Two years later Grant described his Nyamwezi porters (who eventually deserted) as frank and amiable on first acquaintance . . . but soon trying to get the upper hand, refusing to make the ring-fence round camp, showing sulks, making halts, or going short marches, treating with perfect contempt any message sent them even to sit apart from your tent.[184]

Missionary travelers had the same experience: Waunguana porters were "always trying to shirk their work" and "perpetually concocting dodges" to gain increased rations.[185] On Hore's journey to Mpwapwa in 1878, the 150 porters expressed their "discontent" several times with demands for more food and shorter marches. The missionary, however, was understanding of their protests, given "their endurance and wonderful spirits" and their "rough, faithfulness and loyalty to their work," and in consideration of the extremely difficult working conditions.[186]

In a later example, some of Peters's carriers, subjected to a particularly harsh regime, protested by disappearing at the beginning of the day and reappearing at the next camp without their loads. It was discovered that they had been left behind at the previous camp. These porters did not desert but refused to carry the loads allocated to them. Peters responded by chaining and flogging some of the offending porters, and putting into effect a scale of punishments for those caught deserting or throwing down their loads. He also instituted a system of discipline to ensure early starts each day and surveillance through record keeping to match men with their burdens.[187] Another form of protest was to feign illness. An example was noted by Grogan in 1898:

One of our boys . . . announced [on the march north of Ujiji] that he had smallpox; this was rather alarming, so I had him stripped, but could find no signs of the disease. As we did not want to give our boys any excuse for bolting or grumbling, a medical board of three headmen sat on the case, and having unanimously agreed that he was lying, we subjected him to the hippo-whip cure; next day he and his mate were not forthcoming.[188]

Here is a case of the punishment leading to the result that it was supposed to prevent.

More-fraudulent forms of deception occurred when Waungwana porters attempted to collect unearned wages at the coast. In October 1879, one Fundi Athman arrived, bearing a letter from CMS missionary Last, at the Zanzibar office of the agent for the LMS, Boustead, Ridley and Company. According to the letter, Fundi had informed Last that he had arrived in Mpwapwa after having been robbed while serving as a mailman for the LMS after earlier service in a caravan to Ujiji. His three companions were killed, and his package of letters and pay note had been lost, but he claimed 14 months' pay. While investigations were underway in Zanzibar, Fundi disappeared. It was discovered that he had never, in fact, been associated with the LMS.[189]

Another case was more easily detected by Boustead, Ridley and Company, as explained in a letter to Southon:

> We may mention that Swedi holds the pay tickets of several men who have apparently stayed at Urambo and elsewhere. It is however, said that the men were in Zanzibar, and as we always prefer to pay the men personally . . . we told him to produce the men, and as he brought two different sets of men who had probably never been out of Zanzibar and did not know the names on their tickets—we told him we should put him under the gun if he tried to cheat us again. He now waits until the right men arrive in Zanzibar.[190]

A more-sophisticated dodge was to claim a wage ticket from missionaries at two different stations, each missionary being unaware of the other's actions, then to give one of the tickets to another man, who would at the coast pretend to be the porter in question and with it claim outstanding wages. The ruse would succeed when the real porter subsequently appeared at the coast with his wage ticket. In the face of a genuine ticket and correct identity, the employer would have no choice but to pay up for a second time, unless a connection between the two men could be established.[191] Perhaps the most common method of false representation occurred before departure of a caravan, when porters presented themselves two or more times for their advance pay, playing on the naïveté of newly arrived Europeans. This was the experience of Moloney, who wrote: "Thanks to my ignorance of Suahili, several pagazi presented themselves at least twice for their pay, and when taxed for the offence, took refuge in a number of aliases that a London pickpocket would have envied."[192] The more-seasoned Stairs believed that "a great number of carriers have no other trade except to sign up in order to get their advance pay, then . . . go and hide in the swarming hovels of Bagamoyo."[193]

Fraud and theft can in certain circumstances be envisaged as forms of resistance deliberately opposed to the normative code of honor of professional porters.[194] Yet, if porters stole from their caravan, it was often because they were starving, as was the case when Speke and Grant's caravan crossed Ugogo. Food shortages caused the porters to complain and resist:

> The spirit of our men sank, and a deep, gloomy silence hung over camp, when we had no grain, and continuous days of bad sport with our rifles. Not a man would obey orders; they refused to march, and discipline had to be upheld in several instances by inflicting corporal punishment for the crime of stealing cloth to buy food.[195]

East African porters of the rear guard of Stanley's Emin Pasha Relief Expedition regularly stole food, as well as tools, guns, and trade goods in order to buy food. Expedition porters on the upper Congo received one-thirtieth of the ration entitlement that the white officers received, and many of them starved to death. Rempel believes that the porters regarded theft as legitimate or quasilegitimate and that they "shared a sense of entitlement," given Stanley's failure to provide adequate rations, or *posho*.[196] In East Africa, more-systematic pilfering occurred in some caravans, particularly of beads, which could be taken in quantities small enough to evade detection. One European traveler lost 16 loads of beads in this fashion, and another 2 loads out of 30.[197] Occasionally deserters stole entire loads. A porter deserted from a CMS caravan, taking a load of cloth and a gun, and escaping into grass almost 10 feet high. Mrs. Watt mentions the case of a Kamba porter who deserted after failing to break open a box. When 40 inexperienced Zanzibari porters deserted from another caravan, 17 loads were lost.[198] A variant was the propensity of some Manyema carriers "when in a country of thieves . . . to conceal a load of cloth during the night; in the morning they arrive in great distress and say that a load has been stolen."[199] Yet on the whole, theft by porters from caravans was surprisingly rare, except in cases of deprivation.

It is unsurprising that during the first years of the colonial period, open protests such as strikes were rarer and less effective than before. Desertion continued to be the main form of resistance. This does not mean that individual and hidden forms of resistance quickly superseded collective actions. During the 1890s desertion of dozens of porters at a time frustrated colonial caravan operators, who, in response, and to protect their property from theft, initiated the practice of packing loads in boxes and chaining them together.[200] In a rare depiction, a Nyamwezi-painted gourd from the German period shows porters carrying loads chained in series, while their European employers ride donkeys.[201] The gradual changes in patterns of authority and protest originating in increased commercialization and foreign interest in East Africa were substantially altered by the British and German invasions. African bargaining power diminished as most were disarmed, their caravans regulated, and their autonomy undermined. Increasingly the basic conflict between employer and employee became externalized. Porters relieved their privations and gave vent to their frustrations by helping themselves to food, livestock, shelter, and auxiliary labor as they passed along the main routes through communities weakened by conquest, famine, and environmental disaster. The pillage of peasants was easier than confronting racialized German military discipline. Such a breakdown of aspects of custom was inevitable given the changing conditions of the 1890s, including the deskilling associated with early colonialism.[202] Nevertheless, much of caravan culture survived into the colonial period, including the tools for mediating relationships across the ethnic and cultural mosaic of nineteenth-century Tanzania. This complex of practices and institutions, together making up a sociocultural grammar for forging networks and linkages, will be introduced in the next chapter.

7

CUSTOMS IN COMMON

The little claw of a dove,
The little claw of a dove,
Is the fighting of the Gogo, O father.
The little claw of a dove.

[Followed by] Are you there? Are you there?
[Response] Here we are, here we are.
[or] The coastal people are no men;
They have beaten Katate with chains.
All is gone in taxes and dues,

O father, all is gone.
Go away, you coastal people. Be my mother,
We have come to see you with our friends.
O mother of cowards, be my mother,
We have come to see you.[1]

Rising out of the Uthungu valley. . . . we passed cairns, to which every passer-by contributed a stone. Of the origin of the cairns I could not gain any information.[2]

Along the central routes, porters were central characters in a constantly rewritten drama of social and cultural interconnectedness, redefining, sometimes replacing, always recreating the manifold linkages of a vast and fluid network that included intergroup joking relations (*utani*), blood brotherhood, religious belief and ritual, the spread of trading lingua franca, caravan labor culture, and an increasingly common material culture, all of which worked through processes of trade and exchange, labor migration, slavery, and urbanization. This last chapter offers a glimpse of aspects of the grammar of the cultural networks emerging out of the caravan system that later shaped colonial and even postcolonial society. *Utani* in particular was a ready-made concept that porters, peasants, and newly urbanized townsmen and women eagerly took up and adapted in order to manage and make sense of rapid social change in the commercialized milieu of the caravan routes. Thus, we mark both an end and a beginning, as all safaris do.[3] The book closes, as it opened, with a discussion of one of the defining qualities of labor—the wage—in this context, a marker both of capitalist penetration and the alternative modernity of a transitional labor culture.

Given the diffuseness, ambiguity, and apparent opaqueness of some of the cultural phenomena discussed here, perhaps a conceptual way forward is suggested through sociological concepts developed by Anthony Giddens. Giddens writes in the context of a discussion of state formation, a topic beyond our immediate concerns. Yet he highlights crucial dimensions of the way that different societies are interconnected, reminding us that societies, including the kinds of societies found in precolonial Africa, do not have clearly demarcated boundaries, although they are usually associated with "definite forms of locale," which may or may not be fixed:

> Societal totalities are found only within the context of *intersocietal systems* distributed along time-space edges. All societies both are social systems and at the same time are constituted by the intersection of multiple social systems. Such multiple systems may be wholly "internal" to societies, or they may cross-cut the "inside" and the "outside," forming a diversity of possible modes of connection between societal totalities and intersocietal systems. Intersocietal systems are not cut of whole cloth and characteristically involve forms of relation between societies of differing types.[4]

To reconceptualize societies, Giddens uses a metaphor from art: "Societies" are "social systems which 'stand out' in bas-relief from a background of a range of other systemic relationships in which they are embedded." Here, it is the background of intersocietal systems—systemic intergroup relations—that concerns us, although it is important to remember that the way in which societies come to "stand out" in bas-relief is of course a historical process. Nineteenth-century Tanzania consisted of a range of social formations linked by such intersocietal systems.

UTANI: NETWORKING CULTURE

Utani (from the Kiswahili verb *–tania,* meaning to be familiar with, treat with familiarity, chaff[5]) refers to a complex sociocultural system of joking relationships that has operated historically in Tanzania in three contexts. Of oldest provenance is *utani* within kinship and affinal relationships, including between brothers-in-law, mother's brothers and sister's sons, and kin of alternating generations. Second, *utani* was adapted through historical processes to a great variety of nonkin, nonaffinal relationships between clan groups within a larger society as well as between particular clan groups across cultural or ethnic groups. There is reason to suggest that such clan-based *utani* relationships emerged at the same time as the emergence of clan identities.[6] Third, *utani* developed externally beyond kin, affinal, and clan relationships in new contexts often associated with commercialization and emerging modernity, between and among various types of sociocultural groups, often according to binary opposites.[7] Although losing some of its raison d'être in contemporary Tanzania, there is copious evidence that it was an important system for mediating relationships among the many ethnic and cultural groups of nineteenth- and twentieth-century Tanzania. As late as the 1940s, and increasingly in new contexts associated with the capitalist colonial economy, aspects of it were well understood by both Christians and Muslims.[8]

Utani is largely invisible in the historical record, the topic having been considered of relevance only to anthropologists. Only rarely have historians noted its existence.[9] Nevertheless, one would expect to find it discussed in accounts of "customary" law, in social histories, and in studies of intergroup relationships or labor migration. The first specific account of joking relationships in Tanzania, concentrating on the Bondei, was by Dora Abdy, in 1924.[10] In the late 1930s and 1940s, a number of colonial officials picked up the theme and wrote short accounts of joking relationships in a variety of contexts.[11] The most significant of these was by R. E. Moreau, who provided for the first time a rough comparative analysis of *utani* in 19 ethnic groups, specifying the duties of *watani* including ritual functions at weddings and funerals, sanitary tasks such as disposing of lepers and "unlucky children," and rights to hospitality and forfeits of property. In addition, Moreau reported his informants' accounts of the origin of *utani* relationships.[12] This functional approach to joking relationships is most famously associated with the name of A. R. Radcliffe-Brown,[13] who defines them as follows:

> The joking relationship is a peculiar combination of friendliness and antagonism. The behaviour is such that in any other social context it would express and arouse hostility; but it is not meant seriously and must not be taken seriously. To put it another way, the relationship is one of permitted disrespect.[14]

In this view the structured context in which the relationship takes place is key, because respect toward persons with particular status, as well as things, ideas, and symbols, is vital in the maintenance of social order. Joking relationships occur, therefore, in situations where there is "both attachment and separation, both conjunction and social disjunction," for example in the case of a marriage. In this example, the new relationship entered into by a man or a woman with their spouse's family results in a shift in the social structure. The new relationship takes the married man or woman outside their definite position within the lineage or clan, with its rights and obligations, into a field of social disjuncture and associated diverging interests, because before the marriage the spouse's relations were outsiders, and this outsider status survives the marriage. This structural disjuncture requires either continual extreme respect and the limitation of direct personal contact between the two sides or, alternatively, ritualized "mutual disrespect and license." This is the joking relationship. Any real antagonism is forestalled by reciprocal and regular teasing. In this way the disjuncture is both recognized and contained.[15] Further, a similar kind of disjuncture exists in relations between clans and even between ethnic groups:

> The general structural situation in these instances seems to be as follows. The individual is a member of a certain defined group, a clan, for example, within which his relations to others are defined by a complex set of rights and duties, referring to all the major aspects of social life, and supported by definite sanctions. There may be another group outside his own which is so linked with his as to be the field of extension of jural and moral relations of the same general kind. . . . But beyond the field within which social relations are thus defined there lie other groups with which, since they are outsiders to the individual's own group, the relation involves possible or actual hostility. . . . this separateness . . . is not merely recognised but emphasised when a joking relationship is established. The show of hostility, the perpetual disrespect, is a continual expression of the whole structural situation, but over which, without destroying or even weakening it, there is provided the social conjunction of friendliness and mutual aid.

Thus the kinds of alliances that are expressed through joking relationships, both internal and external, "are modes of organising a definite and stable system of social behaviour in which conjunctive and disjunctive components . . . are maintained and combined."[16] Joking relationships are therefore, according to Radcliffe-Brown, to be understood as part—often in combination—of a larger set of relationships of "alliance or consociation," which are established by intermarriage, by the exchange of goods or services, and by blood brotherhood.[17]

This analysis (which strongly influenced scholars of the Rhodes-Livingstone school, such as Gulliver and Mitchell) was subjected to the retort, from French anthropologist M. Griaule, that such a theoretical and comparative approach was not relevant or helpful, as dissimilar behaviors might be taken out of social context and wrongly compared.[18] He argued in his study of joking relationships amongst the West African Dogon that a better approach was to present the values and cosmology of the Dogon themselves; in other words, to show how the Dogon expressed their aims and beliefs through ritualized joking. Radcliffe-Brown defended his approach with the rejoinder that the debate was between two widely separated positions: Griaule's extreme cultural relativism and his own comparative social science. A way forward, and a compromise that suggests that the two approaches are not in fact incompatible, was offered by Peter Rigby.

> We may disagree with Radcliffe-Brown when he contends that certain kinds of social behaviour can simply be 'explained' if shown to have significant latent functions, and that the meaning of such behaviour in terms of the actor's values and cosmology is irrelevant. But it was his work on joking relationships and related patterns of behaviour which revealed their wide ramifications and theoretical importance.[19]

Nevertheless, to argue that joking relationships made sense only if it could be shown that they served to disarm potential antagonists who faced each other in contexts of "structural ambiguity" is inadequate. "The whole range of . . . concepts, values, categories, and cosmological ideas related to institutionalized joking behaviour must be taken into account." *Utani,* can best be understood not so much in a structural/functionalist sense, as argued by Radcliffe-Brown, but as an abstract idea or a "conscious model."[20] Here we have Rigby's major contribution to the debate. The implication that follows is that *utani* could be repackaged, remodeled, and reintroduced in changing historical circumstances, including in the new conditions associated with commercialization and the emergence of an alternative modernity.

Let's now consider *utani* amongst the Nyamwezi before considering its historical origins and intergroup joking between the Nyamwezi and other peoples. First, we must remind ourselves that the Nyamwezi in the nineteenth century were not an ethnic group, but rather a conglomeration of chiefdoms and clans of varying origins but with related cultural characteristics.[21] Given the large size of the Nyamwezi cultural region, differences emerged, for instance in patterns of speech, among inhabitants of widely separated localities. Neighboring cultures and groups exerted varying degrees of influence. The northern Nyamwezi of Nzega have been historically influenced by the Sukuma and Nyiramba, while the people of centrally located Unyanyembe have had close contacts with the Kimbu, Gogo, and Fipa. As a student of

Nyamwezi *utani* notes, "It is for this reason that you find a rather different outlook by the Nyamwezi regarding tribes which are not so geographically close to them, and hence the intensity of practices such as Utani varies."[22] At the same time, peoples of varying origins, such as the Tutsi, have been incorporated into Nyamwezi culture, bringing with them some of their own customs and beliefs.

Nyamwezi *bupogo, bupugu,* or *bumezi,* their counterpart of *utani,* included joking between in-laws and between grandparents and grandchildren. Beyond kin and affines, it was practiced among chiefdoms. The origins of inter-chiefdom *utani* appears to be conflict resulting from expansion of a neighboring chiefdom and, in the north, cattle raids. After the restoration of peace, subjects of losing chiefdoms were teased and reminded about their ruler's weakness. Intermarriages often occurred, restoring an element of reciprocity in which mutual joking could take place. Jokes highlighted minor local differences in foods, dances and songs, dialects, and fighting techniques. The development of *utani* across chiefdoms was cemented by gift exchanges between ruling clans as well as ordinary people. In time a sense of brotherhood developed.[23]

Intergroup joking partnerships were especially concentrated along the main trade routes, and the most commercially active peoples, especially the Nyamwezi, had a complex network of recognized joking partners, potentially including members of virtually all ethnic or other sociocultural groups they encountered while engaged in caravan travel. In 1975 Stephen Lucas, relying largely on his students' research, carried out a comparative analysis of Ngoni and Nyamwezi *utani* networks.[24] Comparing the findings of Shetto and Ntuli, he found that the Nyamwezi practiced *utani* with the following groups: in the west, the Tutsi, Ha, Nyaturu, Nyiramba, and Ngoni; and to the east, the Gogo, Hehe, Luguru, Bondei, Zigua, Digo, Shambaa, Zaramo, Pogoro, and Ndengereko. Lucas then consulted other sources in the "Utani Relationships in Tanzania" series in order to construct a table showing which peoples claimed to be *watani* of the Nyamwezi and the reasons given by informants for the origins of that relationship. He thus adds to Shetto's and Ntuli's lists the following peoples: Longo (Rongo), Lungu (Rungu), Fipa, Nyasa, Chagga, Meru, Mbunga, Ngindo, Rufiji, Doe, Kaguru, Kwere, Ngulu, and Rangi.[25] Elsewhere we find that the Sagara and the Kami are also *watani* of the Nyamwezi.[26] When we combine the various sources, the total number of joking partners of the Nyamwezi is at least 31. If we consult the map, we see that there is an astonishing correlation, first, with the regional neighbors of the Nyamwezi—examples include the Ha, Nyiramba, and Tutsi—but excluding those such as the Sumbwa and Konongo, whose cosmology and institutions are very similar, and, second, peoples lying astride the central trade routes (Gogo, Sagara, Luguru, Kaguru, Kwere, Zaramo) as well as routes leading to the sources of copper and ivory in the interior (Lungu and Fipa).

The conclusion that Lucas reaches is that the Nyamwezi caravan trade played a major role in the development of intergroup *utani* relations. *Utani* provided the modus vivendi by which the Nyamwezi and others could travel in peace through the territories of other peoples in order to reach market centers on the coast and elsewhere.[27] To build on Lucas's argument, *utani* lubricated relationships among porters of differing origins, and relationships between caravan personnel and host communities. *Utani* was perfectly suited as a readily available cultural concept for adaptation to the liminal situations regularly encountered by caravan porters. When porters were traveling, these relationships could be called into being by ritual abuse. Once the joking partnership was established, the traveler could call on the special hospitality of the joking partner, as well as aid in times of distress, for instance, with funerals. In turn, the host community might call on joking partners to play special roles in certain rituals, although such roles were usually reserved for interclan *watani*. *Utani* played, therefore, an ideological role in mediating access to resources.[28]

Utani, originating in domestic society but broadly familiar to most East African peoples, was consciously adapted to a new context associated with emerging East African modernity. It was reinvented as one of the customary "languages" that facilitated the work and survival of caravan porters, transmitted the working culture of the caravans, and more broadly encouraged intergroup and interethnic cooperation. *Watani* interrelated with each other as part of a wider social structure, in which caravan culture was central. Thus, to return to Lucas, it was "no accident that the historical 'next step' for Utani practices took place on the şisal and coffee plantations and in the rapidly growing urban centers of the early colonial period."[29] I agree. Indeed, it was these processes associated with one version of modernity—colonial capitalism—that sparked the interest of the British officials and anthropologists already cited.[30] Where I differ with Lucas is in my approach to East African modernity, which did not begin with the imposition of colonial administrative and economic categories, but with a positive response to the international capitalist economy, beginning in the late eighteenth century and reaching a peak in the middle to late nineteenth century. *Utani*, as it was reinvented by Nyamwezi and other porters, was as "modern" as any other indigenous cultural adaptation to the market and related social change.

Let's now consider oral traditions concerning the origins of *utani* between the Nyamwezi (in this case, more accurately the Sumbwa) and one of the peoples they regularly encountered during their caravan journeys, the Gogo. Most often informants give stereotypical accounts of conflict between the Nyamwezi and other groups—for example, the Fipa, Ngoni, Gogo, or Zaramo—after which peaceful relations are restored, and the former foes become *watani*. A minority also refer to intermarriage between groups as the origins of *utani*.[31] Occasionally more-detailed accounts are available. One of these is particularly interesting because we can compare a nineteenth-century version with traditions collected more recently. The starting place is Burton, who collected what we might call an *utani* founding charter, although he did not recognize it as such. I have already cited it in an earlier chapter.[32] A later version, collected in the 1970s, goes as follows:

> One day a Sumbwa chief named Kafuku passed through Gogoland with his caravan. He had already sold his ivory to the coast traders and was on his way home. The Gogo, as usual, attacked him and plundered all his property. Kafuku himself was killed but some of his people escaped peacefully to their homeland in Mbogwe (in Kahama district).
>
> Kafuku always travelled with a small horn packed with medicine in his pockets. The medicine in the horn protected Kafuku and his caravan from rain. It could not rain when Kafuku was on his way to the coast or back to his homeland. The tree from which this special medicine is extracted is known as "Mti gwe nsema" (tree of the *nsema* medicine) in the Sumbwa language. It is said or believed that when its medicine is exposed, no flies can land on it. Others believe that around such a tree no rain falls and that when one is uprooting it, one should not breathe, and if one wants to breathe one has to move away from the tree. . . .
>
> During the attacks, Kafuku dropped this horn. After his death, nobody could pick up the horn because of the magic power invested in it. It is said that in the daytime the horn used to cry and its tears were blood. At night the horn emitted fire. One thing which shocked the Gogo above all was the long period of shortage of rain that followed. The Gogo then went to the local medicine men and rain-makers so that they could know the reason why there was no rain. The reason given was the presence of Kafuku's horn which was preventing rain from falling. At first the Gogo did not . . . believe it, but when the dry period continued unending and was accompanied by famine, they sought a solution. They travelled to Kafuku's homeland in Mbogwe and met some [of] Kafuku's people. The Gogo were asked to pay 300 cattle if they wanted rain. The Gogo did not object to this. After paying the cattle to Kafuku's homeland [sic] they went to remove the horn from Gogoland and burned it in a dam. Rain began pouring in Gogoland.
>
> From then on, the Sumbwa began joking the Gogo that "Mwabona ihembe lye mwa Kafuku lyamala Bagogo?" (Have you seen Kafuku's horn which has killed many Gogo?) They tell them, "Never play with us Sumbwa. We are powerful!" Until today the Gogo are the watani of the Sumbwa.[33]

Both versions emphasize the magical powers of the Sumbwa, although Burton undercuts the verdict of the tradition by emphasizing Nyamwezi (Sumbwa) fear of the Gogo. Yet, later, he writes, "The Wagogo are not deficient in rude hospitality. A stranger is always greeted with the 'Yambo' salutation. He is not driven from their doors as among the Wazaramo and Wasagara; and he is readily taken into brotherhood." Caravan personnel were readily welcomed and plied with *pombe*.[34]

A variant semimythological account of the origins of Nyamwezi-Gogo *utani* goes as follows. A chiefly merchant named Lyobha sent his *pagazi* and slaves down to the coast to trade. As they returned, passing through Ugogo, the *pagazi* came across the large cattle herds of the inhabitants. To the travelers, the mooing of the cows sounded like an insult directed at their chief. When Lyobha heard this, he became angry and sent his warriors to attack the Gogo. In the fighting the Gogo held the advantage, because they wore shoes made of cattle hide, protecting them from the ubiquitous thorn bushes of Ugogo, whereas the Nyamwezi were barefoot. The Nyamwezi were forced to withdraw. Afterward, joking relations between the two sides began.[35] Clearly there is a southern flavor to this story. Cattle were rare in the tsetse-infested regions of southern Unyamwezi, and my source, Mzee Nkumbo, was born in Kiwele and grew up in Sikonge, to the south of Tabora.

In all three traditions, most noteworthy is the conflation of conflict and caravan travel as the origin of the relationship. The almost ritualized description of conflict is quite likely a rhetorical surrogate for the kind of managed relationship that *utani* embodies. Lucas points to such a possibility when he says, "I never really resolved the question about whether the conflict was real (actual warfare, etc) or virtual, i.e., that it may be constructed (or "reconstructed") historical reality using sets of complementary oppositions to define the actor/groups, or a combination of both!!! In any event, the caravans and establishment of long-distance trade certainly involved their share of conflictual situations."[36]

As for the Gogo, they have their own tradition, but once again it involves interaction with Nyamwezi travelers passing through Ugogo to the coast. Rigby writes:

> Gogo do not say that their *wutani* [Kigogo for *utani*] with the Nyamwezi arose out of warfare in the past. They have a legend that the Nyamwezi on their way to the coast had a stopping-place at Cigwe, in West-central Ugogo. There were a number of large logs (*matindi*) [Kigogo] lying about near the camp; so the Nyamwezi called the local people 'Wagogo,' because a 'log' in Kiswahili is *gogo* (pl. *magogo*). Thus the *wutani* arose out of name-giving, not out of previous . . . hostility.[37]

The Nyamwezi joked with the Gogo about their practice of circumcision, and especially clitoridectomy among Gogo women. The Gogo, in response, intruded upon the rituals and burials of Nyamwezi porters, even to the point of demanding some article in payment for desisting, and ridiculed the uncircumcised travelers.[38]

The reader will have noted that an appreciation of oral tradition is essential if the sociohistorical context of *utani* is to be understood. By and large, European observers were oblivious to the subtleties of such relationships amongst East Africans, but occasionally a glimpse of their complexity escapes into the early travelogues, against the grain. Burton, highly prejudiced but, in parts of his East African writings, astute, included the following passage in the concluding diatribe of his major work. The chapter, entitled "The Character and Religion of the East Africans; Their Government, and Slavery," begins with a discussion of the turbulent, argumentative nature and unstable temper of East Africans. Little did he realize he was describing, in his own sardonic way, a fundamental institution of East African life:

> Their squabbling and clamor pass description: they are never happy except when in dispute. After a rapid plunge into excitement, the brawlers alternately advance and recede, pointing the finger of threat, howling and screaming, cursing and using terms of insult . . . After abusing each other to their full, both "parties" usually burst into a loud laugh or a burst of sobs.[39]

More specifically, Speke reveals an *utani*-like relationship between the porters of different caravans, although the exact categories recognized by the participants are unclear.

> Towards the close of the journey a laughable scene took place between an ivory caravan of Wasukuma and my own. On nearing each other, the two kirangozis or leaders slowly advanced, marching in front of the single-file order in which caravans worm along these twisting narrow tracks, with heads awry, and eyes steadfastly fixed on one another, and with their bodies held motionless and strictly poised . . . rushed in with their heads down, and butted continuously till one gave way. The rest of the caravan then broke up their order of march, and commenced a general mêlée. In my ignorance . . . I hastened to the front with my knobbed stick . . . I [then] hesitated until they stopped to laugh at my excited state, and assured me that it was only the enactment of a common custom in the country when two strange caravan-leaders meet, and each doubts who should take the supremacy in choice of side. In two minutes more the antagonists broke into broad laughter, and each went on his way.[40]

Finally, and again from Speke, we have an unambiguous example of *utani* practiced by professional caravan porters of differing origins, Zanzibar and Unyamwezi:

At night I overheard a chat between Sangizo, a Myamuezi [Mnyamwezi], and Ntalo, a freed man of Zanzibar, *very characteristic of their way of chaffing.* Sangizo opened the battle by saying, "Ntalo, who are you?" N: "A Mguana" [Mwungwana] (freed man). S: "A mguana indeed! Then where is your mother?" N: "She died at Anguja" [Unguja: Zanzibar]. S: "Your mother died at Anguja! Then where is your father?" N: "He died at Anguja likewise." S: "Well, that is strange; and where are your brothers and sisters?" N: "They all died at Anguja." S: (then changing the word Anguja for Anguza, says to Ntalo), "I think you said your mother and father both died at Anguza, did you not?" N: "Yes, at Anguza." S: "Then you had two mothers and two fathers—one set died at Anguja, and the other set at Anguza; you are a humbug; I don't believe you; you are no mguana [*sic*], but a slave who has been snatched from his family, and does not know where any of his family are. Ah! ah! Ah!" And all the men of the camp laugh together at the wretched Ntalo's defeat; but Ntalo won't be done, so retorts by saying, "Sangizo, you may laugh at me because I am an orphan, but what are you? You are a savage—a mshenzi; you come from the Mashenzi, and you wear skins, not clothes, as men do; so hold your impudent tongue;" and the camp pealed with merry boisterous laughter again.[41]

Utani repackaged, revamped, and reinvented. A Mwungwana—a new man, bearing an identity forged in the slave workforce of the coastal plantation sector, the growing urban centers of the coast and interior, and in long distance caravans—jokes with a Mnyamwezi, a *pagazi,* a man of the far interior and the central routes. The caravan as an institution created a perfect context for the consolidation of *utani* and other relationships of consociation. We can imagine the same sorts of interactions taking place in villages along the main routes, places like Kashongwa, "a village situated on the verge of a trackless wild, peopled by a mixture of Wasukuma, Wangwana [*sic*] and Wanyamwezi."[42] Caravans, camping grounds, market centers, and junction towns, initially marginal to the communities and societies along the main routes, increasingly represented the mainstream as the caravan system matured. *Utani* itself, an expression of liminality, became indispensable, as part of the broader sociocultural networks of the caravan system.

Not only were the new sites of East African modernity ideally suited for the reinvention of *utani,* but culturally specific institutions—like *utani* itself—adapted themselves to the processes of network building associated with porterage. A good example is a characteristic of a typical Nyamwezi village, the *iwanza.* This facility, found, Burton says, almost only among the Nyamwezi,[43] consisted of two public buildings, one for each sex. The male version—the female was not open to men—was "a large hut, somewhat more substantial than those adjoining," containing "a huge standing bed-frame, formed, like the planked benches of a civilized guard-room, by sleepers lying upon horizontal crossbars" supported by sturdy forked legs. Also within was a hearth, grinding stone, bellows, weapons, "and similar articles." The doorways were guarded by various charms. "In this 'public,'" Burton continues, "the villagers spend their days, and often, even though married, their nights, gambling, eating, drinking pombe, smoking bhang and tobacco, chatting, and sleeping."[44] Travelers and strangers found a ready welcome in male *kwiwanza,* and it was no doubt there that much of the comraderie forged among porters on long caravan journeys was initiated or strengthened.

One such traveler was Grant, who also highlights the conviviality of the *iwanza:*

> Until lodging had been obtained, inside the village, we rested with our kit at the "iwansa"or club-house. It was a long room, 12 by 18 feet, with one door, a low flat roof, well blackened with smoke, and no chimney. Along its length there ran a high inclined bench, on which cow-skins were spread for men to take their siesta. Some huge drums were hung in one corner, and logs smouldered on the ground. The young men of the village gathered at the club-house to get the news.[45]

Twenty years after Grant, a missionary visitor found that *kwiwanza* offered ready opportunities to speak of "the most glorious of topics" amongst the Nyamwezi, given the ready welcome he always received. More importantly for us, he notes that *kwiwanza* were frequently used by coastal traders and Waungwana porters, as well as the Nyamwezi.[46] We can envisage that exchanges of all kinds, in Kinyamwezi and Kiswahili, involving ritual joking, blood brotherhood, religious debate, storytelling, the transmission of news, and the settlement of disputes must have occurred many thousands of times around the inviting fires and in the friendly society of the *iwanza.*

RITUALS OF THE ROAD

Passage and arrival, the crossing of space, the passing of time: caravan journeys were lived as personal and collective experience. Like Jack Tar in the maritime age of sail, porters saw their work as a test and thus partook of rituals of passage. Porters marked their physical progress with signs and rituals, much as sailors did when crossing the equator for the first time. Margaret S. Creighton sees the ceremony of King Neptune as a ritual of initiation that was central to the masculine world of communal dependency onboard ship.[47] Similarly, for porters, much ritual on safari symbolized personal achievement, marking a difficult section of the journey, expressing hope for the next stage.

Yet it also symbolized a collective identification with all who had preceded them, and those who would pass by in the future. There is something universal in this.

In August 1866, south of modern Tanzania in what is now Malawi, Livingstone began his approach to the lake:

> We passed two cairns this morning at the beginning of the very sensible descent to the Lake. They are very common in all this Southern Africa in the passes of the mountains, and are meant to mark divisions of countries, perhaps burial-places; but the Waiyau [Yao] who accompanied us thought that they were merely heaps of stone collected by some one making up a garden. The cairns were placed just about the spot where the blue waters of Nyassa first come fairly into view.[48]

Boundary markers, graves, debris from gardens, a lookout. Neither Livingstone nor his informants seemed to have a clear view of what the cairns represented. Trekking over the mountains near the shores of Lake Tanganyika, north of Kigoma, Hutley noticed something similar, except the mounds here consisted of grass and soil. After climbing uphill to the top of the ridge, at the point of descent, the local Jiji villagers plucked a handful of grass and added it to the heap. Hutley was not able to learn the meaning of this small ritual.[49] Several months later, four days east of Ujiji, he once again came across mounds, built up by passersby:

> At one place on the path . . . we came upon two heaps of grass which are called by the natives the residence of spirits. These especial two are said to be the boundary marks of the spirit of Kabogo's residence. The custom is to pluck a handful of grass and deposit it at this heap or to cast up dust with the feet, thus answering to a kind of propitiation of the *Muzimo.*[50]

Here is another possibility. The "spirit of Kabogo" was a nature spirit typical of the belief systems of the Ha and related peoples of western Tanzania. In the cults of such nature spirits, the earth priests performed rituals at auspicious locations by ceremonially offering scented grasses and leaves to the spirit.[51] When these places lay on caravan routes, porters, no doubt preferring not to anger local deities, added their own offerings, at the same time incorporating the local into the universal by adding their own interpretations. As Michele Wagner notes, the same sacred site could simultaneously serve multiple purposes, and meanings also changed over time, while the role of the earth priests, the *bateko,* also changed as they became intermediaries with outsiders and beneficiaries of commercialization.[52]

Another LMS missionary, Swann, traveling in the same region a few years later, noticed the little piles of stones and sticks at the end of wilderness tracts, in the outskirts of forests, and on hill tops. He asked several of the older porters for an explanation and was given some interesting answers. One typical response was that the stones and sticks represented a barrier to stop "a following devil." Another porter explained it this way: "The snake crawls around it and is delayed. The lion smells it and fears a trap. The traveller may rest his burden on it without stooping. An enemy fears medicine buried underneath."[53] One porter, a gun-bearer, was pressed for an answer as to why he added a stone to a cairn on a hilltop. He replied: "Was not the sun hot?—was not the hill steep? I was tired, but I had the strength to reach the top. I added the stone to the pile, at the same time saying to myself that trouble is over, and—may I reach the top of every hill I start to climb."[54] Local cosmologies, noted and respected, were nevertheless interrogated, as porters appropriated them and added their own meanings. Nolan, a historian of religion, has also studied this same episode: "The gun-bearer's action was not planned or purposive. . . . It was a ritual act marking the end of his climb. The displaced stone was a personal signature making a minute but permanent rearrangement on the hill's surface. . . . The gun-bearer did not express himself in words: the action conveyed what he had to say."[55] Thus some rituals of the road were an expression of individual achievement, but at the same time they became customary and were absorbed by the collectivity of caravan porters; the local, transformed by commercialization and the stirrings of modernity, becomes universal.

In other regions as well, such as Usui in the northwest, Ubena, and in Uguha across Lake Tanganyika, porters built up cairns of stones or placed small stones on specific rocks to propitiate nature spirits and *mizimu,* ancestral spirits. According to Thomson, the most common places for such monuments were at the borders of two districts or on the margins of wild and dangerous tracts. They consisted of piles of stones, rags, or sticks, or all three mixed together. All passersby would add to the cairns because they believed that if they did not, they would be struck down or die from disease. Even those porters who did not follow the custom in their own homelands were very careful to make the ritual offerings. Thomson's Waungwana did so, not surprisingly given their upcountry origins.[56]

Nyamwezi porters, keenly aware of the nuances of local spiritual practice, had their own rituals of the road.[57] Decle discusses some of them:

> On the march from time to time each of them will deposit in the same spot a twig of wood or a stone in such a way that a great heap gets collected. . . . If they halt in the midst of high grass each will plait a handful of grass, which they tie together so as to make a kind of bower. In the forest, if they are pressed for time, each will make a cut with a blow of a hatchet in a tree; but if they have time they will cut down trees, lop off the branches, and place these poles against a big tree; in certain places I have seen stacks of

hundreds of them round a single tree. Sometimes they will strip pieces of bark from the trees and stick them on the branches, and at others they will place a pole supported by two trees right over the path. On it they will hang up a broken gourd or an old box made of bark. . . . Near villages where two roads meet are usually found whole piles of old pots, gourds, and pieces of iron.[58]

Grant refers to "triumphal arches" erected either across the path or to one side. These were "ornamented" with horned antelope skulls, or elephant dung, bones, bows, and broken gourds. His explanation, although misplaced in its lack of understanding of Nyamwezi beliefs, resonates with some of the psychological meanings of a caravan journey as passage and experience:

One of the most pleasing sensations in going through an immense forest is suddenly to come upon the traces of man. The Wezee [Nyamwezi] experience this, for, in their forest south of Kazeh, they erect triumphal arches with poles. . . . It cheers the traveller, and gives fresh vigour to his weary limbs, for he knows that camp and water are never far distant, and that the trumpet of the caravan leader must soon sound the welcome "halt."[59]

Customs in common, aspects of caravan culture developing on the time-space edges of East African history. The background of intersocietal networks, institutions of consociation, and practices of the road moves increasingly into the foreground as porters do their work.

BARGAINING, CONTRACTS, AND WAGES

Paying close attention to the nuances of culture does not mean that we can afford to ignore vital issues related to economic change. I started off by arguing that the universal application of Enlightment and post-Enlightenment categories, and a belief that Africa was a continent of slavery in which the market principle was absent, has too often led to the assumption that free wage labor was nonexistent. Thomas Carlyle, representing the proslavery position of West Indian planters, argued that the black man was impervious to the logic of commerce and refused to work for wages: "Supply and demand, which, science says, should be brought to bear on him, have an uphill task of it with such a man," he wrote.[60] The nineteenth-century abolitionist and humanitarian lobby also had an interest in highlighting African slavery and, in its propaganda, played down or disparaged elements of emerging African modernity. Both views merged into the lineage of slavery that effectively obscured the variety of labor systems that existed simultaneously although unevenly in late precolonial Africa. Both views contributed as well to the persistent and pernicious notion of the "uneconomic African," an aspect of racial ideology that for decades infected much thinking about tropical development and, in the longer run, supposedly more-objective development theory.[61] Born in the era of the Atlantic slave trade, the "uneconomic African" owed much to eighteenth-century theories of tropical exuberance that had, by the late nineteenth century, became permanent features of a "racial endowment."[62] This legacy has distorted our understanding of nineteenth-century East Africa history. We must end, therefore, with a close analysis of the economic factor, in this case the wages earned by long-distance caravan porters.

The average porter, as a wage laborer, demanded and bargained for fair remuneration. Wages rose at crucial junctures during the second half of the century as porters pressed home their temporary advantage in the labor market. Porters were paid according to custom either for the anticipated journey or by the month. The Nyamwezi were relatively well placed within the labor market because of their good reputation and the structural advantages of their position within the caravan system.

"The porter will bargain over his engagement to the utmost bead, saying that all men are bound to make the best conditions for themselves." Burton, with typical jaundiced eye, was well aware of the realities of caravan travel.[63] In early 1861, Speke and Grant were in Unyamwezi, trying to recruit porters to continue their journey to Buganda:

> Men were in abundance in the country, and if a solitary one ran away, he could always be replaced. . . . But to collect one or two hundred we found a most difficult task: they are as fickle as the wind. . . . They higgle pertinaciously about their hire; and after they have been induced to accept double wages, they suddenly change their minds, think you've got the best of it, and ask for more, or more commonly disappear.[64]

This was a time of upheaval and disturbance in the western interior of Tanzania, with civil war in and around Unyanyembe. To the north, Mpangalala's Ngoni (Watuta) were "on the wing," and people were loath to leave home in the service of unknown *wazungu*. Even double wages might seem insufficient inducement to take the risk. Here the prime issue was security—an issue always at the forefront, given the high risks that caravan porters often faced— rather than wages. Some months later, when the *kirangozi* was asked why it was so difficult to persuade porters to join the expedition, the answer was that many were harvesting (it was late May—the end of the rainy season), while others were concerned about the Watuta menace.[65]

In September 1872, when near Simba's, 27 days from Tabora, Livingstone tersely recorded, "The pagazi, after demanding enormous pay, walked off." In 1873 Cameron found bargaining with his porters "most dreadful work."[66] The following year, Stanley found porters at the coast taking a tough negotiating position:

> In 1871 and 1872 I employed Wanyamwezi and Wanguana [*sic*] at the rate
> of $2.50 per month each man; the same class of persons now obtain $5 per
> month, and with some people I have had great difficulty to procure them at
> this pay, for they held out bravely for a week for $7 and $8 per month.

In addition, the porters, along with other caravan personnel including servants
and *askari,* demanded four months' pay in advance according to "custom."[67]
In early 1883, Thomson was looking for porters for his expedition to
Maasailand. "So great is the fear inspired by the Masai," he wrote, "that I was
not able to get a single man to volunteer to go for the customary #5 [*sic*] per
month and it was only when I promised a dollar extra per month to be given
as a present on their return if they proved good men that they began to turn
up."[68] One wonders whether the fear of the Maasai was exaggerated by the
porters to create an upward pressure on wages?

   Porters also bargained over their ration allowance. Dodgshun described a
dispute with his porters over the quantity of cloth issued to buy provisions:

> (28 Dec. 1877) At Pamagombe all day on account of the wet. The men refuse
> a shukka [a cloth two yards long] for 8 [porters] and want one for 6. All day
> the dispute goes on, but neither side gives way. We offered the medium 7, but
> they refused. (29 Dec. 1877) Up to 2 o'clock, in spite of various confabs, the
> revolt continued and we consequently lost the day's work. Then Waidingugu
> [a headman] came to say they agreed to a shukka a day for 7 men. So we
> served out the cloth and got all arranged in messes of 7.[69]

In this case the porters were clearly taking collective action forcing negotiations, with a strike the consequence of noncompliance. They had a spokesman
who represented their case to the missionaries. The end result was a partial victory for the porters, but to their employers this outcome was also acceptable. It
was a compromise that allowed the caravan to resume the journey to Ujiji.

   Apart from basic questions of wages and rations, porters were particularly
concerned to maintain control over both the pace of work and their mobility—
their freedom to move from one caravan to another if conditions so demanded.
This was reflected in their bargaining strategies. Up until colonial times, coast-
based porters were able to defend the twin principles of advance payment and
payment by the month. They had several motivations for retaining the custom
of advances. First, advance payment made it easier for them to secure their
wages than if the full amount were to be paid at the end of the journey. Second,
losses were minimized if desertion became preferable to tolerating unduly
arduous conditions. In fact, advance payment made desertion easier, as both
porters and caravan leaders well knew. If a porter successfully deserted during
the first months covered by an advance payment, then he might possibly end

up with a net gain. Third, if porters had to wait until the end of the journey for payment, they could be more easily coerced by the caravan leader.

The size of advance payments varied, but for journeys along the central routes, two or three months' pay was typical. In Zanzibar in June 1891 a missionary traveling to Uganda found that he had no choice but to accept taking men on with a three-month advance. When he objected to these terms, "they all simply walked off." He was forced to back down and hire "on their own terms" those who had not joined other caravans.[70] For unusually long journeys, or when the route was off the well-trodden roads, larger advances were demanded. Porters hired for the RGS expedition to Lakes Nyasa and Tanganyika in 1879 demanded four months' advance before agreeing terms, because the route was not well known. The men of Stairs's Katanga expedition also received four months' wages in advance.[71]

Many porters preferred a month-by-month arrangement to a fixed payment for a whole journey that would take an unspecified period of time. Under the "piece work" system, whereby they were paid per journey or to go a particular distance, porters were subject to a faster pace of work, meaning that they had to walk farther with fewer stops. This was because if they went at a more leisurely pace, they would be spending more time on the road for the same wage. Payment by the month removed this possibility and allowed more leisurely journeys. "Porters were never in a hurry to accomplish a journey," a missionary observed. "They received their daily rations, and were happy to remain on the road as long as possible, because they were paid by the month. Hence their wages accumulated."[72] Nyamwezi porters returning from the coast to their homeland had a different perspective. They had less reason to dawdle on the way and hence preferred payment for the whole journey when hired by travelers and traders bound for the interior.

Payment by the month was considered so important to porters that they bargained hard to retain it, even at the cost of a reduction in overall wages. This is the logic of another dispute, this time in Zanzibar, recorded by Dodgshun: "Early today a number of pagazi came for engagement, but we could not come to terms. We wished to give so much for the whole journey; they can't understand it and want to be hired by the month." The next day the porters returned and agreed to the rate of MT\$5 per month, "less than we really offered at first," wrote the bemused Dodgshun. Once the deal was struck, more porters made themselves available.[73]

Since porters were the first group of East African laborers encountered by missionaries, explorers, and imperial representatives, and for many years the most important, it was logical that they should be the target of attempts to reform African labor practices. One weapon was the negotiation or imposition of contracts and, later, decrees and ordinances backed up by the force of the incipient colonial state. This can be seen as part of the process of developing—as imperialists saw it—a more-efficient exploitation of labor, with the aim of securing African resources.[74] By the 1890s, labor contracts had become an important tool of the state in its goal of imposing the rule of law in the interests of colonial capitalism.[75] Yet, for a time, negotiated contracts brought African and European concepts of wage labor closer together. Usually contracts were agreed upon with the porters, and registered with the appropriate consul, and so were potentially enforceable at the coast. Reality quickly intruded, however, and caravans subject to coastal authority, whether of the sultan, consular officials, or the early colonial state, were often far removed from officialdom when in the interior.

There may have been precedents. There is reason to suggest that written contracts or at least records of employment terms were kept by Arab, Indian, and Swahili traders and merchants as well. Some business documents written in Arabic, Gujarati, and Swahili have survived from the nineteenth century.[76] Coastal traders were usually brought up in the Koranic tradition and were literate. Many coastal (and Yao) caravans employed a secretary, nominally a Muslim missionary, during the last decades of the nineteenth century.[77]

The earliest surviving contract is from Speke and Grant's expedition to Lake Victoria, Buganda and, ultimately, Egypt.[78] Its terms were formalized by Speke and the permanent employees of the expedition on the 8 September 1860, at the British consulate in Zanzibar. The purpose of the presence of the consul in this and other cases was to bring dignity and formality to the proceedings and impress the porters, creating an element of theater, and more practically, to act as a deterrent against desertion. It reads as follows:

> These men all severally agreed, before Colonel Rigby, Sheikh Said, Bombay, and myself, to serve as my servants on the following terms, as registered in the office-books at the British Consulate, Zanzibar, on the 8th of September, 1860: Supposing I gave Sheikh Said [MT]$500—Bombay, Baraka, and Rahan $60 each—the Wanguana [*sic*] $25 each—and Sultan Majid's Watuma [slave] gardeners $7 each, in ready money down, and promised to give them as much more on arrival in Egypt, as well as free clothes and rations on the journey, and a free passage back from Egypt to Zanzibar, then they bound themselves to follow me wherever I chose to lead them in Africa, and do any kind of duty, without hesitation, that men in such positions, while traveling with caravans, might reasonably be expected to do.

Then follows a "List of men engaged at Zanzibar—their pay, their appointments, and how disposed of."[79]

Another early survival is from Livingstone's last journey. The British consul in the Comoros Islands, William Sunley, recruited on 9 March 1866 ten "Johanna men," who were to "serve . . . as porters, boatmen or in any other capacity." They were to serve 20 months at MT$7 per month and received two months' advance pay. Musa, their headman, was paid MT$10 per month.[80]

A third example, from Stanley's second expedition of 1874–76, was made with 237 Waungwana, Nyamwezi, and coastal *pagazi* and *askari* in the presence of their friends and relatives, and witnessed and registered by the American consul:

> The undersigned, natives of Zanzibar, hearby [*sic*] pledge themselves to serve Henry Morton Stanley, Special Commissioner of the London Daily Telegraph and the New York Herald in the capacity of porters, servants, and Soldiers faithfully and loyally for two years, or until such time as he may require them for wages as maybe placed opposite their name below. They promise to accompany him to any part of Africa he may require to do his bidding cheerfully and promptly, failing which they agree to abide the consequences, forfeit their pay, and such other punishment he may inflict on them. Their employment is to begin from this day, at the rate of Five dollars per month dependent on good behaviour. November 15th 1874.[81]

Then follows a list of porters, the name of their "referee," the monthly wage to be paid to each, and their advance. Stanley elaborated further terms and conditions in his account of the expedition.[82] Whether these were mutually agreed upon with the porters and *askari* is not clear. According to Stanley, the porters and escort promised "that they would do their duty like men, would honour and respect my instructions, giving me their united support and endeavouring to the best of their ability to be faithful servants, and would never desert me in the hour of need." Wages varied from MT$2 to MT$10 per month. Adult porters received MT$5, and youths MT$2.50 per month, with four months in advance. Stanley promised to supply them cloths for clothing "at reasonable prices"; to "treat them kindly, and be patient with them"; to provide medicine and the best rations available, and if patients could not walk, to ensure that they would be left at a safe and convenient place with adequate cloth or beads to pay for support and a "native practitioner"; to ensure impartial justice in the case of disputes among the men and prevent bullying; to act as "father and mother" to them; and to do his best to protect them from "savage natives" and "lawless banditti."

In contrast to the last example, the contract made between Keith Johnston, leader of the RGS expedition of 1879–80, and the expedition's porters includes a promise by Johnston to supply rations and arms. The "Draft of agreement with porters at Zanzibar—April 17th," made before Dr. Kirk, the British consul, reads:

> I, Keith Johnston representing the Royal Geographical Society, on the one part, and the under named men in the other part hereby agree as follows:—

I, Keith Johnston will pay the undernamed men wages at the rates herein-
after noted, and will provide them with daily rations, and arms for defence,
during the journey which it is proposed to make from Dar-es-Salaam to
Lakes Nyassa & Tanganyika & other parts of the interior of Africa.

The under named men, in consideration of the above payments will
follow Mr. Keith Johnston, or other leader appointed in his place, during
the journey indicated above, and will serve him faithfully and remain with
him till such time as the journey shall have been completed.

Then follows a list of 138 porters, detailing names, ethnicity, previous
experience, wage per month, and the total advanced. The wage rates varied
from MT$4 to MT$10, MT$5 being the standard rate, and all the men
received four month's pay in advance.[83]

It is clear from these contracts and descriptive sources that porters successfully defended the principles of advance payment and monthly wages.

The willingness of porters to defend their prerogatives and the intrusive
power in labor matters of the British consul, John Kirk, are both clearly seen
in a dispute in June 1876 between LMS missionary Roger Price and his porters. Price believed that he had contracted to give his men one month's pay
in advance the day before departure from Zanzibar. This was a much smaller
advance than was usually given.

When the time came, only a few of the men would adhere to this arrangement, most of them demanding two months' and some even three months'
advance. I thought that possibly they might be brought to their senses if
I took them to the British Consulate; this I did, and Dr. Kirk was kind
enough personally to interrogate them on the subject. Finding that they
still held out for two months' advance, contrary to the original agreement,
he at once ordered one of his soldiers to take away the spokesman of the
party to the Fort to be there imprisoned.

The missionary went further:

Some days previous to this I had given, according to custom, to each man
four yards of calico as an outfit for the road. The agreement having now
been broken, I requested permission from Dr. Kirk, and the service of a soldier, to deprive all the men of the cloth which I had thus supplied to them,
and which they had had made up at their own expense. This was very summarily done at the Fort, where I found them in [the] charge of the soldier,
and bemoaning the ill fate of their comrade. I had now fairly the upper hand
of them, and they came one after the other to beg themselves back into my
service, willing enough to submit to any terms I liked to propose. I took
most of them back, rejecting only a few whom I considered to be the ring-

leaders. Having, by their own obstinate and unreasonable conduct, broken their engagement with me, I felt I had a perfect right to draw out a fresh one, which I did, dating from that day; and thus they deprived themselves of about a fortnight's pay.[84]

In its description of the porters' solidarity, their sense of grievance, Price's response and his appeal to the consular authorities, and the ready involvement of the representative of imperial power and capital, this account reads like dozens of other labor disputes. Clearly the porters felt that the contract violated custom, the time-honored and hard-won right to two to four months' advance payment, and that they could negotiate a compromise. Their mistake was to attempt to do so while still on the island of Zanzibar. They would have held considerably more negotiating power on the mainland. Just as clearly, the newcomer was prepared to ride roughshod over custom in defense of a dubious agreement.[85]

The terms of the above contracts may be compared with the first regulations concerning caravans and porters proclaimed by the government of the new Zanzibar Protectorate in October 1894. The regulations were aimed at protecting Zanzibar's labor supply and ameliorating the often harsh conditions on safari.[86] According to the "Regulations to be observed by caravan leaders and others in the engagement and treatment of Porters"[87] employers had to register details of the intended journey and the number of porters required with the government "registrar of porters" and pay a fee of ten rupees for each porter.[88] Clearly, official registration had a further purpose, as in earlier decades: to increase surveillance and aid the detection and punishment of deserters. Written contracts had to include identifying details of each porter, information as to the caravan's destination and length of absence from Zanzibar, an agreement that the hirer would pay two months' advance wages and passage to and from the mainland, and an agreement that the porters and caravan leader would abide by these regulations. Before departure of the porters from Zanzibar, a deposit was to be lodged at the British consulate as a guarantee for claims against the expedition. A suit of clothing was to be provided to porters before they left Zanzibar and, "when practicable," replaced every six months. Porters were also to be issued by the government a blanket and sheet every twelve months. Each porter had to be given a water bottle, and every six porters a cooking pot. Medicines were to be taken on the journey for the porters' use.

Some of the most important sections regulated rations supplied to porters. These were to include a *kibaba* of grain and vegetables plus four ounces of meat or fish daily per man, and "a sufficient quantity" of salt. Maximum loads including everything a porter had to carry were set at 75 pounds. Given the sometimes extreme punishments meted out to porters, there were provisions to curb exceptional brutality by caravan leaders. Lloyd Mathews, the first minister of the Zanzibar government, and formerly commander of the sultan's army, a man of lengthy experience in East Africa, had heard of cases of caravan leaders ordering 150 lashes for rebellious porters and considered this extreme.[89] Corporal punishment was therefore limited to 30 strokes and was to be carried out only after proper investigation. Only in "grave emergency" was any punishment other than flogging, chaining, or a fine to be awarded. In such a case, the caravan leader was to form a court of not fewer than two Europeans or Americans to try and sentence the offender. Finally, records were to be maintained of distances marched each day; offences by porters and subsequent punishments, as well as deaths, desertions, and discharges of porters; and disbursements of cloth and other materials supplied to porters.

The regulations contained several sections of benefit to porters, specifically the recognition of advance and monthly payments (although two months in advance was probably the minimum they would accept) and limits on punishment. But given the colonial context in 1894, porters were gradually losing the struggle over control of crucial aspects of caravan work, including bargaining, control over their own arms, and petty trading, and were increasingly subject to foreign ideas about work and justice.

There was no similar code governing the recruitment and treatment of porters in German territory on the mainland at this time, probably because there was no tradition in Germany like the master and servant legislation that was utilized by governments in most parts of the British Empire.[90] The character of German colonial labor legislation came from the institution of *Gesindewesen* in the homeland, which was a patriarchal and paternal relationship between masters and servants in the rural economy, the latter typically being single young men and women employed as herders, ploughmen, or domestic servants. In East Africa, *Gesindewesen* was adapted to provide a legal framework for the regulation of slave emancipation in order that settlers as well as indigenous slave owners could control the movements, potential for desertion, and contractual obligations of their laborers.[91] As such, it did not provide such a useful framework for the control of existing mobile or migrant wage labor. Regulations issued by the Germans in respect to caravans had different aims. In the early years of German colonization, "excesses" committed against peoples along the main routes by personnel of European caravans often led to revenge attacks on other caravans. To help prevent such attacks, Governor von Soden in 1892 decreed that foreign caravans could not travel through German East Africa without permission from the colonial authorities and, with exceptions, payment of a deposit, which would be used as security for indemnification of African claims against caravan leaders.[92] A second decree issued by Governor von Schele in November 1893 had the very limited aim of ensuring government access to porters and gave the administration the power to intervene into private agreements and divert porters hired by a private employer to government service. There was to be compensation for the employer but none for the porters.[93] It was only in 1896 that decrees setting standards for labor contracts and the punishment and discipline of Africans were issued. But much of this legislation was very short lived; the law governing contracts was amended in 1897 and abolished in 1899.[94]

As we have seen, two key conditions that had to be met before coast-based porters would work were advance payment and payment by the month. In large measure the aim was to buttress bargaining strength and ensure maximum mobility, but porters also strove to defend and improve wages per se. Porterage, Burton wrote, "knows but two limits: the interest of the employer to disburse as little as possible by taking every advantage of the necessities of his employé, and the desire of the employé to extract as much as he can by presuming upon the wants of his employer."[95]

One of the difficulties of attempting to measure the outcome of this clash of interests is the extreme complexity of the currency system that remained in use until the colonial conquest, and the fluctuations in the value of its main components: the Maria Theresa thaler, which was widely used in Zanzibar and on the coast,[96] the Indian rupee, and the *doti merikani*.[97] The thaler and the rupee were related in a direct way in that the subunits of both were annas and pice, but the number of pice to the thaler varied according to the supply of the former.[98] In addition, the value of the thaler against the rupee fluctuated, moving between 2.14 and 2.23 rupees between 1800 and 1850, and between 2.13 and 2.15 rupees in the single year of 1857. There were also obvious variations in cloth currency, which, along with beads[99] and other forms of currency such as brass wire or *masongo*,[100] was preferred in the interior. *Merikani* could be from 32 to 38 inches in width. To further complicate the issue, there were other cloths of lower quality, such as *kaniki* and *satini,* and expensive colored cloths, or "cloths with names," the forerunners of the *kanga,* which were also used as currency.[101] But the standard remained the *doti merikani.*

Despite these complications, there is evidence to suggest that actions by porters mediated through custom, as well as changes in the labor market, led to increased wages and better rations up until the colonial period, when progress ceased beginning in the early 1890s.[102] In purely cash terms, wages of porters hired at the coast increased in leaps at crucial junctures. Otherwise they tended to remain steady, with short-term fluctuations. A graph of the cash value of wages over time would show long plateaus separated by steps. This applies particularly when we consider wages paid by the month, but there is also evidence for increases in the 1850s and the late 1880s in wages paid per journey, as in the case of Nyamwezi porters returning to their homes. See graph 7.1 below. Burton noted in 1860 that

> When the Wanyamwezi began to carry, they demanded for a journey from
> the coast to their own country six to nine dollars' worth of domestics, col-

ored cloths, brass wires, and the pigeon's-egg bead called *sungomaji*. The rate of porterage then declined; the increase of traffic, however, has of late years greatly increased it. In 1857 it was 10 dollars, and it afterward rose to 12 dollars per porter.[103]

In the late 1880s, there was a further increase to about MT$15, then stagnation and even decline, as colonial conditions changed market conditions.

During the 1890s and early 1900s, structural shifts in the political economy of the region and restrictive colonial regulations resulted in the gradual deskilling of the caravan workforce and the suppression of wages.[104] Opportunities diminished as the ivory trade fell into European hands, and larger African entrepreneurs were eventually shut out of the caravan business. German control of the main market towns and caravansary reduced competition, and African caravans came under colonial regulation. Despite a further increase in the demand for porters during the early colonial period as the economy expanded and the Germans established their administration, pacification resulted in a substitution of forced or convict labor for the semiprofessional or professional porter in some parts of the colony.[105] A significant proportion of the porter workforce was employed by the colonial government or private contractors, who paid no more than ten rupees a month, less than the previous standard of MT$5 when the exchange rate and price inflation are taken into account. Many other porters were paid a flat rate per journey, or even per day, and thus piecework tended to replace payment per month. The long-term effect of these processes, and the increasing reliance by colonial employers on peoples hitherto not exposed to wage work, is perhaps what Iliffe meant when he wrote that "wages for laborers hardly increased from Stanley's time to the 1930s."[106] Yet until the deskilling of the early 1900s, caravan culture continued to offer a degree of protection.

At the coast, monthly wages increased markedly during the early 1870s. "In consequence of the scarcity of porters wages are at the present moment excessively high," Consul Kirk noted in March 1873, and in 1874 Stanley complained that porters would not work for less than twice what he had paid in 1871 and 1872.[107] Compare with the similar situation in contemporary French West Africa, where the economic logic of French expansion pushed up wages in the 1880s. Manchuelle argues that the labor demands of explorers, imperial agents, and colonial armies "created a kind of 'economic revolution.'"[108] In East Africa porters were usually paid in *merikani* cloth measured in so many *doti,* according to the wage value in Maria Theresa thalers. For example, a porter paid MT$5 per month would receive MT$5 worth of cloth for a month's work. Prices at Zanzibar for *merikani* gradually decreased into the 1860s as Sheriff has shown.[109] But after the initial purchase, *merikani* was recognized to have a standard exchange value compared with the thaler.[110] This had a regulating effect when cloth wages were exchanged for goods in Zanzibar, where one *doti merikani* was purchased for approximately MT$0.25. But on the mainland, the fixed value of the cloth increased in stages. On the coast it was MT$0.50, and in Ugogo MT$1.00.[111] Hence a Nyamwezi porter paid a cloth advance at the coast might expect to receive double its value or more if he exchanged it in the interior. As late as 1899, Nyamwezi and Sukuma porters refused to accept cash wages, despite German efforts to encourage monetization. As a German official noted,

> The reason is that cloth has twice the value in Tabora or Muanza than at the coast. Thus, if a Wayamuesi [*sic*] receives cloth for 20 Rs in Bagamoyo, these goods have a value of 40 Rs in Tabora. He can, therefore, squander a bit on the way and will find himself still well paid in Tabora. To find other reasons is probably not necessary.[112]

These increases in value reflected in part the cost of porterage of cloth to upcountry destinations.

Whether during early colonial or precolonial times, it is clear that porters collectively aimed to maximize their pay. But through experience expressed as custom they also retained the idea of a fair wage. A wage was fair when it was seen to be the same for all in a particular caravan, with recognized exceptions for certain skills. When employers failed to pay equitably, porters made their feelings clear, even when wages may have been higher than usual, as in Speke and Grant's caravan in Buzinza in October 1861:

> With at last a sufficiency of porters, we all set out together. . . . Indeed, we ought all to have been happy together, for all my men were paid and rationed trebly—far better than they would have been if they had been traveling with any one else; but I had not paid all, as they thought, proportionably, and therefore there were constant heart-burnings, with strikes and rows every day. It was useless to tell them that they were all paid according to their own agreements—that all short-service men had a right to expect more in proportion to their work than long-service ones; they called it all love and partiality, and in their envy *would* think themselves ill used.[113]

The same violation of custom is apparent in an episode that occurred in Mvumi, Ugogo, in June 1873. Cameron's assistant Murphy had hired a gang of Nyamwezi porters in Bagamoyo, but payment of their wages was arranged with a Khoja trader, Abdullah Dina. The trader gave the porters "such villainous cloth" compared with the "superior material" that the other porters in the caravan had received that the gang finally deserted en masse in anger and stole a load of cloth from a small caravan accompanying the main party.[114]

Table 7.1
Wage Rates for Nyamwezi Porters per Journey 1850–1900: Coast to Unyamwezi

Year	Caravan/s	Rate per journey	Advance[1]
pre-1857	estimate	MT$6-9	
1857–58	estimate	MT$10-12	
1857–58	estimate	(MT$9-10) 9-10 *shuka mrkni*[2]	
1860	Speke and Grant	MT$9.25 (to Tabora)	
1871	estimate	(MT$7.5-12.5) 25 *doti kaniki?*	
1871	Stanley	(MT$12.5)	
1872	estimate	MT$10	
1873	Cameron (RGS)	MT$11	MT$5.5
1876	estimate	50 shillings	
1877	estimate	MT$13.5 (to Lake Victoria)	
1878	various caravans	MT$7.5-10	
1878	various caravans	MT$6.5-11	
1881	One of Mirambo's caravans	2 "pieces of Amerikani"[3]	
1882	Ulaya (LMS) to Uyui	MT$12	
1882	Ulaya (LMS) to Urambo	MT$10	
1887–89	estimate	MT$15	
1891	Selemani bin Mwenye	6 *gorah* calico and 5 coloured cloths[4]	
1897–99	Kandt	(MT$15) 30 rupees, no *posho*	
1899	estimate	(MT$13) 26 rupees, inc. *posho*	

[1] Burton, *Lake Regions,* 236; Speke, "On the Commerce," 142 (Speke's estimate is low and anomalous compared with other evidence.) Speke, 25 September 1860, in *Journal,* 41; Bennett, *Stanley's Despatches,* 10; Stanley, *How I Found Livingstone,* 49; Vienne, "De Zanzibar à l'Oukami," 359; Murphy to Kirk, Bagamoyo, 19 April 1873, VLC 3/4, RGS; Wilson and Felkin, *Uganda,* 1:43; Mackay to Wright, Zanzibar, 10 January 1877, CMS CA6/016; Dodgshun, 17 August 1878, in *From Zanzibar,* ed. Bennett, 79; Muxworthy to Thompson, Zanzibar, 19 October 1881, LMS 4/3/C; Muxworthy to Thompson, Zanzibar, 3 June 1882, LMS 4/5/D; Hore to Whitehouse, Zanzibar, 26 September 1882, LMS 4/5/A; Nolan, "Christianity in Unyamwezi," 209; Selemani bin Mwenye Chande, "Meine Reise," 1; Yeo, "Caput Nili," 208; Leue to Governor, Bagamoyo, 11 February 1899, TNA G1/35. Approximate MT$ equivalents are given in brackets.

[2] A *shuka* was two yards of cloth, the basic male attire worn around the waist.

[3] This must mean 2 *gorah merikani* or 15 *doti merikani,* thus cloth worth about MT$7.50 at the coast. For the *gorah,* see the next footnote. This was perhaps a discount rate. See Southon to Thompson, Urambo, 15 August 1881, LMS 4/2/D.

[4] The *gorah,* or "piece" of cloth, differed greatly depending whether the cloth in question was *merikani* or *kaniki.* If the former, then it was usually about 30 yards long, or about 7.5 *doti.* If the latter, then it was just 2 *doti,* or 8 yards in length. This suggests that the cloth in this case was *kaniki,* otherwise the wage would have been extremely high. Sissons estimates that in Ugogo, colored cloths were worth on average three times the *doti merikani.* If we give the plain cloth a value of MT$6 at the coast, then with the colored cloths the wage is still higher than in earlier years, and consistent with Nolan's estimate for the late 1880s. See Sissons, "Economic Prosperity," 44, 46, 49–52.

Figure 7.1
Wage rates for Nyamwezi porters per journey, 1850–1900: From the

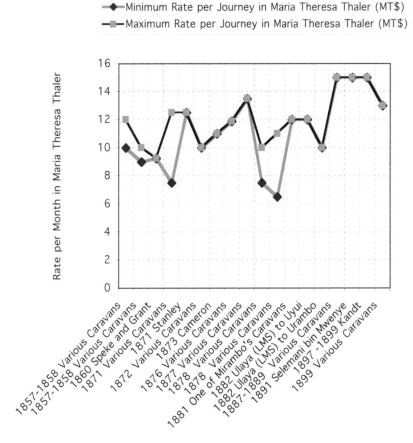

Custom also rewarded porters with particular skills, such as artisans (*mafundi*), personal servants, and *wanyampara,* who received higher wages than the average *pagazi.* Cameron paid his headman, Bombay, MT$12, and his porters MT$5 per month. The RGS expedition to Lakes Nyasa and Tanganyika paid the headman, Chuma, MT$10 per month, and MT$6 to a few particularly experienced porters. LMS missionaries paid headman Juma bin Nasibu MT$10 per month, and MT$6 for *mafundi,* while regular porters received MT$5. Other specialized caravan personnel such as guides and *askari* also received higher pay.[115] Boys, for example Pesa and Jacko in Cameron's caravan, were typically paid MT$1 to MT$3 less than adult porters.[116]

Table 7.1 and Figure 7.1 show wages paid to Nyamwezi porters for the journey from the coast to Unyamwezi. Most of my evidence comes from estimates, but wages paid for specific journeys are also indicated. Most porters traveling from the coast were Nyamwezi who had brought down ivory in their own or Arab caravans and were then employed by coastal merchants or others traveling upcountry. This was a continuation of the old pattern under which Nyamwezi porters earned their way back to their homeland. Given the paucity of information prior to 1857 for the central routes, a comparison with wages paid on the northern routes is useful. In 1848, Rebmann paid his coastal porters MT$7 for the return journey from Rabai, near Mombasa, to "Jagga," Chagga country on the slopes of Mt. Kilimanjaro. In the same year Krapf paid the same rate for a journey to Shambaai after a "boisterous demand" from his men to increase their wages from the original MT$5.[117] In 1850 Krapf learned that ivory porters employed by Tanga-based merchants were paid MT$10 for the journey to Mlozo in Maasailand. "For this, each bearer carries there and back again a heavy load of fifty-four pounds, and is often absent six months."[118] In 1857, porters were paid MT$10 for the return trip from Pangani or nearby towns to Maasailand, Nguru, or Chagga, and in 1861 MT$12, and even MT$14, half in advance, indicating a substantial increase in wages over 14 years.[119] On the central routes, in 1857 Burton hired porters at Zungomero for MT$15 for the return journey to Ujiji. The first leg implied a somewhat longer distance than that from the coast to Unyanyembe, indicating a wage well within the pre-1857 range. In this and the following year, the rate paid to Swahili porters for the outward journey to Unyamwezi was MT$10, half in advance, and therefore similar to that paid to Nyamwezi porters.[120] This rate, for a typical march of three to four months, indicates a rising trend.

Wage rates are known for numerous other destinations and journeys. In 1859, coastal porters in a trading caravan were paid for the long march to Ubena and back, half in advance, although porters also had opportunities to profit from slave trading. In 1860, Tippu Tip paid Zaramo carriers MT$10 for the similar round-trip to Urori (Usangu).[121] These figures are low, lower than Nyamwezi porters were getting at the same time for the march to Unyanyembe, when distance and journey time are compared. In many other cases it is difficult to make comparisons because arrangements were ad hoc and routes varied so greatly.

Table 7.2 shows wage rates for monthly paid porters, using samples from the hundreds of European caravans traveling the central routes. The paucity of information before the 1870s skews the representation toward the last third of the century and hence partially masks the significant jumps in earlier decades. As a baseline it is useful to compare the rates for caravan porters with wages for laborers in Zanzibar, who in 1856 were almost all slaves paid about 12 1/2 cents (pice) per day or MT$2.50 to MT$3 per month, half of which went to their owner. Overseers earned MT$7.5 to MT$10, and *mafundi* MT$5 to MT$7 per month. A contract from May 1865 between Messrs H.A. Fraser and Company and Zanzibari "Arab Contractors" for

Table 7.2
Monthly Wage Rates for Caravan Porters in Maria Theresa
(*Thalers,* 1860–1900)

Year	Caravan	Rate/month in MT$[1]	Advance[2]
1860–63	Speke and Grant	2.5	12 months
1866–74	Livingstone	(5-7) 10-14 rupees	2 months
1871–72	Stanley	2.5	
1873–74	Cameron (RGS)	5	4 months
1874–77	Stanley	5	4 months
1876	Price (LMS)	5	
1877–78	Elton	5	2 months
187?	Mwana Sera	5	2 months
1878	Cambier (AIA)	5	2 months
1879–80	Thomson (RGS)	5	4 months
1880	Stokes (CMS)	5	2 months
1880	Hore (LMS)	5	
1881	Johnson	4	1.5 months
1881	Juma bin Nasibu (LMS)		2 months
1883	Thomson	5 (plus bonus)	3 month
1883	Johnson	4	2 months
1884	H.H. Johnston (northern route)	5	
1884	Smith (southern route)	5	
1887–89	Stanley	5	4 months
1889	Meyer	6	3 months
1891	IBEAC	(5) 10 rupees	3 months
1892	Hore (LMS)	5	
1892–93	Baumann (northern route)	(5) 10 rupees	
1897–99	Kandt	(5) 10 rupees	
1899	Moore	(5) 10 rupees	1 month

[1] Where wages are given in rupees I have approximated the conversion to MT$ at a ratio of two to one. This overstates the true wage, which was suppressed under colonial conditions.

[2] Wage rates, central routes, with comparisons from the northern and southern routes. Speke, *Journal,* 552–53; Simpson, *Dark Companions,* 57; Livingstone, *Last Journals,* 51; Bennett, *Stanley's Despatches,* 160; Cameron, "Men's Accounts," RGS; Depage, "Note au sujet," 132; Price, *Report,* 65–66; agency and consular accounts 1873–81, consular records, ZNA AA9/10 (Elton); Hore, *Tanganyika,* 45; AIA, *Rapports sur les marches,* 50–51; agency and consular accounts 1873–81, consular records, ZNA AA9/10; Rotberg, *Joseph Thomson,* 307; O'Flaherty to Hutchinson, Ndumi, 9 August 1880, CMS G3A6/01; Hore to Whitehouse, Ujiji, 13 October 1880, LMS 3/3/B; mission diary, UMCA Zanzibar, 29 November 1881, ZNA CB1/5; Muxworthy to Thompson, Zanzibar, 26 July 1881, LMS 4/3/C; Thomson corr. RGS; mission diary, UMCA Zanzibar, 7 March 1883, ZNA CB1/5; Johnston, *Kilima-Njaro,* 60–63; Smith, "Explorations in Zanzibar Dominions," 106; memo by Herbert Ward, n.d., MP, box 94, file 56; Porter muster rolls headed "Revised List of Men Engaged for Mr. Montague Kerr" and "Men Engaged for Masai Caravan" in notebook "Stanley's Expedition," ZM; Meyer, *Across East African Glaciers,* 346; Rashid bin Hassani, "Story of Rashid bin Hassani," 99–100, 103; Hore, *Tanganyika,* 45; Baumann, *Durch Massailand,* 7; Yeo, "Caput Nili," 208; Moore, *To the Mountains,* 150.

the supply of sugar plantation workers on the island is even more revealing. According to Moses Nwulia's summary, the contractors agreed to supply

> one hundred, able-bodied male and female labourers and to place them at the sole disposal of the company for a period of five years. At the end of five years, the contractors were to guarantee "the freedom of all the said labourers, who shall be slaves." The Company agreed to pay to the contractors one year's wages at the rate of two dollars a month for every labourer delivered, and half a dollar a month for each labourer in the remaining four years; the balance of one dollar and fifty cents was to be paid to each labourer during each month of the four-year period.[122]

The specified wages were therefore well below the Zanzibar 1856 norm of MT$2.50 to MT$3 per month. However, it seems that this contract violated the practice of hiring laborers in Zanzibar, whether slave or free, according to normal market conditions, as well as the usual wage rates, given that Fraser advanced money to the Arabs so that they could buy slaves for his company's use. The British consul, Colonel Playfair, considered this objectionable.[123] In 1858–59, Burton and Speke's slave *askari,* always more highly paid than Waungwana or Nyamwezi porters, were paid MT$5 per month, half for themselves and half for their owner, with an advance of six months, the rest paid at the end of the journey. In 1878 laborers employed by the CMS on road construction from Saadani were paid MT$5 per month.[124]

A glance at the above tables and the graph should dispel the idea that Nyamwezi *pagazi* were somehow superexploited in comparison to coastal porters, a view that has recently found favor. Glassman writes that "Nyamwezi porters soon came to be regarded as cheap caravan labor, and their pay was regularly lower than that given to contracted slave porters from Zanzibar," and elsewhere that "Nyamwezi porters came to be regarded as the cheapest of caravan labor, more abject even than slave porters."[125] In fact, wages paid to Nyamwezi on a per-journey basis from the coast were more susceptible to the influence of the labor market and therefore fluctuated to a greater extent than wages paid on a monthly basis, which only rarely rose above the MT$5 mark. Sometimes the wages of Nyamwezi were below those of monthly paid porters, particularly for downward journeys which were paid at a lower rate, but at other times they were higher, given that the journey to Tabora took between two and three months. The Nyamwezi were recognized as the best porters in East Africa, and therefore when there was a labor shortage, their wages rose accordingly. But frequently the Nyamwezi *were* cheaper than coastal porters from the employer's point of view. There were several reasons apart from labor-market fluctuations. Firstly, they carried heavier loads than did coastal porters.[126] Secondly, they had a good reputation for honesty and professional pride.[127] Thirdly, they were famous for their endurance and usually made the journey from the coast to Unyamwezi in faster time than monthly paid and coastal porters for the reasons explained above. Christian converts sometimes employed by missionaries, such as the former slaves resident at the UMCA station at Mbweni, Zanzibar, were not paid any more than non-Christian porters, and often less.[128]

Apart from provisions and wages, porters were occasionally given gifts or bonuses for performance of special services, work well done, or as compensation for unusually arduous conditions. In many caravans, porters were given a cloth "outfit" of one *doti* before commencing a safari. Speke gave his men gifts "for the severe trials they had experienced in the wilderness once Tabora was reached" and when in Buganda arranged with *Kabaka* Mtesa for gifts of a small tusk for each of his Nyamwezi porters returning home. Livingstone gave each of his porters, except for "defaulters," a bonus of two *doti* and a handful of beads when in Urungu in 1872. The porters of another missionary traveler accepted extra payment in tobacco or salt for special care in carrying him across fast-flowing rivers, and for unusually long marches. Stairs gave a MT$2 bonus to porters who worked especially hard during the crossing of the Mkata River.[129] Such small gifts were customary for porters in Madagascar as well.[130] But overwhelmingly it was wages and perhaps profit from trade that were the tangible rewards for work.

A further factor giving flexibility to the wage system was money lending within the caravan. Those porters who had used up their *posho,* or who had no private trade goods to buy food or pay gambling debts, might borrow from their fellows or take an advance on their final pay. Influential caravan members such as Bombay and Bilal wadi Umani, headmen of Cameron's expedition, might act as banker, lending money to needy porters and receiving payment at the end of the journey.[131]

All too often scholars have underemphasized the material motivations of African workers. Beyond experience of the wider world and status at home, the reward was the wage. The very mobility of East African caravan porters made it possible for them to take advantage of variations in local markets and working conditions and, unlike most nineteenth-century Africans, they relied to a very great extent on purchases of food in order to survive. Partially proletarianized, the nature of their work pushed and pulled them to think in terms of the market, and wages earned on the labor market were central to this mentality. *Posho* and wages were controlled by custom; nevertheless, porters were alive to market opportunities when converting cloth or bead currencies, or negotiating wages with newcomers. *Posho,* or on downward journeys the sale of hoes, slaves, or other property, usually provided basic sustenance, but wages could be utilized for a variety of purposes and provided individual motivation. Porters occupied a unique structural position. Whatever the nature of their access to land in Unyamwezi or at the coast, while on safari they lost direct control over agricultural and pastoral surpluses. Although they made

8

CONCLUSION

Chapter 1 ended by noting that this book can be read on various levels. It is at one and the same time a journey, a labor history, a story of African initiative and adaptation to modernity, and a contribution to a history of Tanzania and East Africa that gives due attention to intersocietal linkages, networks, and cultures. These, in many cases stimulated by the caravan system, left an important legacy to later generations.

The journey began in Unyamwezi and surrounding countries. It took us first in the middle of the eighteenth century to the south and southwest, where early adventurers tapped the rich supplies of ivory, to the west of Lake Malawi, and to the east, where market centers on the Indian Ocean coast connected the far interior with the world market and sources of manufactured imports. As the caravan system matured into the mid-nineteenth century, we entered the middle stages of the journey, exploring multiple experiences of the safari along the length of the central routes and beyond Lake Tanganyika, with excursions along the branch routes to the north and the south, and a rest stop in Mpwapwa, one of the new multiethnic junction towns servicing the caravans. The safari experience became increasingly variable as many porters became wage-earning specialists, while others continued the old tradition of small-scale trading enterprise. Carriage of ivory and cloth remained the backbone of the porter's livelihood, but during the last quarter of the century, European intervention increasingly distorted the labor market and, by the mid-1890's, changed forever the safari experience. As we turned homeward, we encountered further aspects of porter labor culture including vigorous defences against sometimes abusive and arbitrary authority. Caravan culture, grounded in Nyamwezi cosmology and social norms, developed customary patterns born of long experience of the work process. If culture provided the adhesive fabric, economics provided the body, both figuratively and literally. Caravan porters, carriers of culture, were also buyers and sellers of goods and services, and bearers of market news along the length and breadth of East and Central Africa.

Ideological currents emanating from Europe were more disturbing. The legacy of post-Enlightenment thinking created an intellectual cloud of misunderstanding and misrepresentation, expressed in the uneasy juxtaposition of nineteenth- and twentieth-century racist assumptions and the often contradictory content of antislavery propaganda. What I have called a lineage of slavery represents various forms of imperialist and colonialist domination over at least 150 years, in which, sadly, the humanitarian lobby played its part. During the nineteenth century multiple expressions of positivist and dualist thinking unintentionally worked in tandem with more obviously racist ideas to create stereotypes of Africa as a continent of slavery, and Africans as incapable of achieving any degree of modernization on their own. The labor question was thus central to the partition of Africa. East African porters were clearly recognizable to humanitarian and imperial interests as laborers, but not in any modern sense. Wage labor, after all, could not exist except as a foreign import. Caravan porters were merely conveniently available (and irritatingly necessary) bodies on which the status of slaves could be hung. Being apparently slaves, they represented an obvious target for imperial reform, and with investment in modern transportation and infrastructure necessary for the colonial project, they could and ultimately would be done away with.

The exigencies of domination and liberation from slavery cast into the shadows the closely observed reports of knowledgeable travelers and missionaries, who described a complex reality. Many of the more acute European travelers in nineteenth-century East Africa—Krapf, Burton, Thomson, Hutley, the Hores, Stokes, Stairs, Baumann, Reichard, and others—were well aware of the conditions of travel and the organization of the caravan system. Yet the slave paradigm, with its prominent anti-Arab and anti-Muslim bias, frequently expressed in generalized, editorialized, and distorted renditions of antislavery propaganda based on Livingstone's writings, remained pervasive. It could not have been otherwise. How could a reasonably nuanced image of Africa—let alone one free of racism—take hold in a chauvinistic age during which some European countries continued to trade surreptitiously in African slaves, and others were happy to buy slave-produced commodities, while material progress was valued above all else?

As colonial rule became a reality, and with slavery abolished, metropolitan historians and missionary schoolteachers could safely, without fear of contradiction, and without any research available to point to different conclusions, write and teach a more or less standardized and erroneous version of late precolonial East African history in which the red ribbon of slavery was the dominant strand.[1] The complexity of economic and social change, if at all recognized, was presented as the work of foreigners, Arabs, and Indians. Over several decades, one unsatisfactory idealization after another took hold, justifying European domination and "explaining" African economic "backwardness," among them "tropical exuberance," vent-for-surplus theory, the backward-sloping labor supply curve, "arrested development," trusteeship, and development theory. It was only in the 1960s that scholars broke the mold and made a fresh start. Yet in some respects nineteenth-century East African history remained foggy. The slave paradigm continued to obscure other, often related, social and economic developments.[2] The uneconomic African lingered onstage, and the East African interior remained largely outside world history. A recognizable modernity, including social relations adapted to merchant capitalism, sophisticated patterns of consumer demand—especially for imported machine-made goods—entrepreneurship and the pursuit of profit, wage labor, a more secular conception of power, and new types of urban space, was discernable in only a few works.[3]

Reliance on inadequate conceptual tools and uncritical use of primary sources deterred analysis or even recognition of the great variety of labor systems coexisting in late precolonial Africa. I have argued that these systems, including wage labor, domestic and other types of slavery, corvée labor, and patron-client relationships, should not be seen merely as separate, disconnected relics or innovations representing different points of development. They overlapped and influenced each other, just as plantation slavery was part and parcel of capitalist relations in America. Various forms of labor supported waged caravan work in the most commercialized regions, including the Mrima coast and Unyamwezi. New accumulating protoclasses such as the Nyamwezi *vbandevba* were able to employ wage laborers as well as attract clients and buy slaves.

Yet it was preeminently waged caravan porters who developed a transitional form of labor that showed an African face to the modern world, and an African modernity to the peoples of the region. The virtual absence of industrial technology inherent in the porter's most basic function in no sense changes that. The caravan system invented itself as a response to the capitalist world market, yet it drew on precapitalist institutions. African caravan operators and long-distance porters reconceptualized older ideas and invented new customs in order to act as full participants in the international economy. As Sheriff and others have shown, rising demand for East African ivory in Europe and North America due to the rapid increase in middle-class purchases of cutlery, pianos, billiard sets, and other ivory products, and huge reductions in the price of imported cotton cloth as a consequence of the expansion of steam-powered mass production, drove much of East African trade and the caravan system.[4] In this context the emergence of wage labor along the central routes represents a modern response, as personal and patriarchal ties of family and lineage, clan, and chiefdom were increasingly undercut by the lure of market opportunity. Unomah describes a changing social structure in Unyamwezi, as rising entrepreneurial elephant hunters, traders, and caravan operators, the *vbandevba*, dominated society by the mid-nineteenth century, often under-mining the power base of the older *batemi*, traditional chiefs with their ritual powers.[5] The market brought other products of the industrializing world, both transported and utilized by porters: firearms, mass-produced metal goods, and cash. This incipient African modernity, strongest in the caravans and the new multicultural urban centers of the main routes, was displaced by imperial expansion, the ultimate expression of positivist forces.

Good labor history depends upon a clear understanding of the labor process—what workers do, how they do it, and what forms of social and cultural organization are utilized and changed in the process. This book has attempted to describe an African labor culture emerging on the frontiers of international capitalism. A fundamental problem arose in the writing: how to undertake the kind of "translation" argued for by Chakrabarty[6] in order to make sense of such a working culture? The concept of crew culture helps bridge the gap. Specialist caravan porters were much like crews or gang laborers in other late precolonial or early colonial contexts where market forces were beginning to bring about social and economic change, albeit with great regional variations, as in the settler colonies of southern Africa, North America, and Australasia; in the maritime world of sailors; and in other contexts—the Sherpas of the Himalayas come to mind—where migrant laborers maintained a consider-able degree of autonomy. A major difference between caravan porters and, for example, merchant mariners in the age of sail was a much greater degree of interaction for the former with communities beyond the workplace—with peas-ants and pastoralists along the trade routes. Clearly such differences grew out of the local economic and environmental context and the work process.

For porters, work and leisure revolved around patterns accepted throughout the region. An evolving custom governed caravan labor, handed down by the Nyamwezi pioneers of the central routes but also patterned on the work experience and timetables of the journey and the material needs of large caravans. The Nyamwezi drew first on their early familiarity with regional trade including travel to sources of iron, salt, cattle, and copper, as well as on their social and political institutions and cosmology. As they entered the ivory and cloth trades and undertook much longer journeys, a more systematic and specialized pattern of caravan organization emerged. Leading merchants organized large-scale enterprises and hired labor, while smaller community-based ventures mobilized family members, clients, and perhaps a handful of waged porters for safaris to the coast. In large caravans, special officials had clearly delineated responsibilities. Professional porters were noted for their readiness to undertake numerous long and difficult journeys, their knowledge of the roads and regional cultures, their understanding of caravan culture, their endurance and strength, and their survival skills. They took pride in their work and collectively regulated their own and their workmates' behavior according to a recognized code of honor.

Custom controlled not only work but also wages, which nevertheless rose in fits and starts until the early colonial period. Porters were quick to seize the initiative during periods of rapid labor-market expansion. Otherwise, they defended existing wage levels by collective refusal to work for less. At least two systems of wage payments coexisted. Nyamwezi porters often made their own way to the coast in order to engage in caravans heading upcountry. They preferred to be paid in cloth currency for a fixed journey to their homeland and, by relatively fast travel, aimed to maximize payment for time and ensure arrival in Unyamwezi for the agricultural season. Coast-based Waungwana and other porters hired for travel upcountry preferred payment by the month with a three-month advance. This ensured a regular income for long and less predictable journeys, which could then be undertaken at a relatively slow pace. Advance payment enabled intervention into the labor market, which could be manipulated through the threat and practice of desertion. The great mobility of porters meant that they could easily move from one caravan to another, pitting one employer against another in the process. From the employer's perspective desertion was a curse, yet the very freedom that porters exercised enabled caravan leaders to hire ready labor at short notice.

Contrary to some earlier accounts by historians, homeward-bound Nyamwezi were more successful than coast-based porters at regulating wages and occasionally forcing an increase. This bargaining power rested on a number of factors. First, the Nyamwezi held a strategic position as the principal caravan labor force. In purely numeric terms they dominated the central routes, as the rough counts and estimates of caravan departures and arrivals from the 1880s and 1890s indicate. Second, the influence of the Nyamwezi agricultural schedule had a profound impact on the timetables of all caravan operators relying on their labor or traveling to and beyond Tabora. Third, their homeland included the most commercialized chiefdoms astride the central routes, including Urambo, Unyanyembe, and Usongo. Fourth, they had a good reputation amongst coastal and foreign caravan operators, who, by employing them, were better able to manage their labor costs. Homeward-bound Nyamwezi porters traveled quickly. More generally they bore heavy loads because of their special carrying technique and their professional honor.

Although there are dangers in reifying the role of porters from one particular region,[7] the role and experience of the Nyamwezi in the pioneering days of the caravan system, their fundamental transformation of the labor process, and their continuing dominance of the central routes must be acknowledged.

From Nyamwezi social and political organization came many of the hierarchies, nomenclatures, and specialized functionaries of caravan organization. To these were added elements from coastal culture such as Islam (not especially strong amongst the Nyamwezi during the nineteenth century) and the Swahili language, as well as from the foreign world of industrial capitalism. Manufactured goods including cloth, guns, beads, and iron goods became part of the material culture of caravan life. Nyamwezi porters developed a sense of professional ethics noted by numerous contemporaries. The Nyamwezi, as well as the communities with whom they interacted, readily adapted familiar concepts such *utani* to caravan life. The emergence of a Nyamwezi diaspora across East Africa, and into modern Zambia and the Democratic Republic of the Congo, is further evidence of their influence.[8] The better-known Swahili diaspora largely overlapped the earlier Nyamwezi one. As Roberts notes, the Nyamwezi were seen by other East Africans to be at the forefront of change, and Nyamwezi travelers often acted as advisors to chiefs around the region.[9]

Allowing for the special position of the Nyamwezi, the world of caravan labor was a cosmopolitan one. Many if not most caravans heading upcountry included members from all over eastern and central Africa, as wage lists and muster rolls indicate. On more lengthy, porters from various parts of the interior were added to the original workforce to replace deserters, the sick, and those completing their contracts. In the second half of the nineteenth century, caravans arriving at Ujiji or Tabora from the Congo typically included large numbers of Manyema porters, slave or free. Swahili porters, including Zanzibaris and the Waungwana, were of extremely varied origins, as they or one or both parents were often of slave origins. They did not forget their ancestry even as they absorbed elements of coastal Muslim culture. As we have seen, there were some differences between Waungwana or Zanzibaris and Nyamwezi porters in terms of their experience of the caravan system. Yet they shared in the making of caravan culture, were comrades on long safaris, and together enjoyed the leisure pursuits of the *kambi* and the *iwanza*—music, song, storytelling, and the consumption of stimulants. This was the life of caravan professionals. Coastal slave porters were hired on the same terms as free men and sometimes wandered for years in the far interior, completely independent of their masters. Formal slave status made little or no difference in the end.[10] Like other porters, Zanzibaris and Waungwana identified with the collectivity of the caravan labor force, especially when issues of authority, discipline, and punishment threw into the open the competing or even contradictory interests of management and labor.

Power within a caravan in many respects lay with the porters. Once on the road, they set the pace of the march. They had a number of weapons at their disposal to enforce custom. The threat of desertion was the most potent, as employers stood to lose their goods and trading profits if abandoned by their porters. When professional porters deserted, they acted according to the expectations of a complex labor culture. The threat of desertion was a defence of customary standards for rest days, rations, workloads, payments, and discipline. The work ethic of professional porters implied a sense of honor, notions of resistance against injustice, assertions of freedom and independence from employers, and a practical understanding of dangerous conditions ahead. Collective forms of protest including strikes, slowdowns, and mass desertions were frequent occurrences, while disgruntled individuals resorted to various forms of subterfuge to express their displeasure with working conditions. Caravan labor culture included customary ideas about justice, and attempts by caravan leaders to override the collective will and impose unpopular punishments such as fines were frequently resisted. Headmen acted as spokesmen for their porter gangs when disputes broke out. The most famous caravan headmen commanded obedience through the immense respect that rank-and-file porters accorded them. Foreign employers at first had to accept or adjust to a peculiarly East African conception of wage labor. Yet the harshness of colonial conquest brought with it authoritarian and militarist conceptions of labor management in many European caravans, in which African laborers were treated as expendable, and the *kiboko* ruled supreme.

European intervention in the region brought further changes to the caravan system. Throughout the nineteenth century the balance of power between the caravan and agricultural or pastoral communities lay with the latter. As historians have long noted in the case of coastal traders traveling upcountry, necessity and good business sense encouraged the building of cultural, social, and economic ties with local elites and communities. The same applied even more so to porters as they moved across, into, and beyond caravans and communities of all types and widened the impact of caravan culture, as alliances, linkages, and networks were established. This widely understood pattern was broken in the 1890s, a consequence of European aggression. The caravan system as a whole became overburdened with the excessive demands of the new rulers, both on the labor market and on the ability of agricultural communities to feed the thousands of travelers. With colonial arrogance, porters were frequently given license to take what they needed from farmers along the main routes, which in turn became progressively depopulated as local people retreated miles into the bush, avoiding the depredations.[11] Here we see an undermining of the old ethics of the caravan system and a major shift in the balance of power between caravans and peasant communities.

Almost alone in the East African interior, the substantial Nyamwezi merchant elite continued to mount large-scale elephant hunting, ivory trading, and caravan operations into the 1890s, creating employment and stimulating labor-market participation in the early colonial economy. The *vbandevba* soon lost its strength, however, as a result of colonial regulation and discriminatory practices; the movement upcountry of European, Asian, and Swahili competitors; the expansion of the elephant frontier beyond German East Africa; and the closing of borders, as well as economic change in the international arena. The decline of the *vbandevba* probably led to a reduction in the demand from indigenous employers for professional porters. Nevertheless, porters continued to find employment in the caravans of government and other expeditions, private traders, the *Schutztruppe,* and the missions. There is also some evidence that despite the overall increase in the demand for labor, much porterage became short-term work, paid by the day or for a stage in a longer journey. Temporary labor could now be requisitioned from chiefs, or even supplied from amongst the prisoners held at German *bomas*.[12] By the turn of the century, the day of the specialist *mpagazi* or *msafari* was largely over.

Professional porters pioneered the first modern labor migrations in East Africa. They were migrant (really, itinerant) laborers par excellence. Although semiproletarian, they were largely dependent on the market for survival when traveling. At the same time, they utilized a variety of nonmarket cultural adaptations and concepts, such as *utani,* in order to ensure security and fulfill basic needs when visiting stranger communities and create cohesion within the mixed caravan workforce. Additionally, close attention to the experience of women shows that female and family labor contributed to the massive labor demands of the safari and to the health of male porters and profitability of caravan ventures. It is notable that in Unyamwezi the most commercialized chiefdoms contributing large numbers of porters increasingly relied on female agricultural labor as well as an influx of slaves and Tutsi immigrants in order to support the caravan system. This topic is dealt with elsewhere.

Yet the alternative modernity created by long-distance caravan porters had its own contradictions and limitations. Elephants were a wasting resource, and human porterage was clearly a dead end as a force for market transformation. Nevertheless, economic expansion in nineteenth-century East Africa was not merely extractive. A degree of added value and small-scale manufacturing accompanied the caravan trade.[13] This was a transitional period during which new ideas gained currency and old ones were reconceptualized. Within this context a wider African worldview found its place, perhaps the most lasting effect of the caravan system. The spread of joking relationships along the caravan routes, as well as Islam, Christianity, and the Swahili language, facilitated a complex series of crosscutting linkages and networks—the intersocietal systems that helped create social and cultural cohesion across what eventually became the nation state of the Republic of Tanzania. Innovative forms of knowledge, including caravan culture itself, combined with the old, creating something uniquely East African. The caravan took new ideas to remote peoples, mixing the local with the universal. Other associated social and cultural processes played a role: the emergence of the Nyamwezi and Swahili diasporas, the movement and mixing of peoples associated with the slave trade, new patterns of urbanization. Not negating existing identities,

NOTES

CHAPTER 1: TRANSITIONAL FORMS OF LABOR

1. Frederick Johnson, *A Standard Swahili-English Dictionary* (Nairobi, 1939), 36.

2. The twelfth-century Arab geographer Idrisi, quoted in Cyrus Townsend Brady, Jr., *Commerce and Conquest in East Africa with Particular Reference to the Salem Trade with Zanzibar* (Salem, MA, 1950), 28.

3. John Roscoe, *Twenty-five Years in East Africa* (Cambridge, 1921); S.C. Lamden, "Some Aspects of Porterage in East Africa," *TNR* 61 (1963):155.

4. I use the name Tanzania, although in precolonial times there was no such country. I do this because my subject concerns both what was called Tanganyika during the British colonial period and the island of Zanzibar (Unguja to its inhabitants).

5. Norman R. Bennett, ed., *Stanley's Despatches to the New York Herald* (Boston, 1970), 10.

6. Kenneth Iain Macdonald, "Push and Shove: Spatial History and the Construction of a Portering Economy in Northern Pakistan," *CSSH* 40 (1998): 287–317; Sherry Ortner, *Life and Death on Mt. Everest: Sherpas and Himalayan Mountaineering* (Princeton, NJ, 1999).

7. Peter Linebaugh and Marcus Rediker, "The Many-Headed Hydra: Sailors, Slaves and the Atlantic Working Class in the Eighteenth Century," in *Jack Tar in History: Essays in the History of Maritime Life and Labour,* ed. Colin Howell and Richard J. Twomey (Fredericton, New Brunswick, 1991), 22; Peter Linebaugh and Marcus Rediker, *The Many-Headed Hydra: Sailors, Slaves, Commoners, and the Hidden History of the Revolutionary Atlantic* (Boston, 2000). Some porters did in fact work as sailors. See White Fathers, *A l'assaut des pays nègres: Journal des missionaries d'Alger dans l'Afrique Equatoriale* (Paris, 1884), 55; J.A. Moloney, *With Captain Stairs to Katanga* (London, 1893), 105.

8. John Iliffe, "Wage Labour and Urbanisation," in *Tanzania under Colonial Rule,* ed. M.H.Y. Kaniki (London, 1980), 283. Thaddeus Sunseri, in his important critique of existing scholarship on Tanzanian labor migration, has reemphasized the influence of precolonial porterage on early colonial migrant labor. See "Labour Migration in Colonial Tanzania and the Hegemony of South African Historiography," *AA* 95 (1996): 589.

9. A partial list might include R. Bulliet, *The Camel and the Wheel* (Cambridge, 1975); E.W. Bovill, *The Golden Trade of the Moors* (London, 1970); Robin C.C. Law, *The Horse in West African History* (Oxford, 1980); Robin C. C. Law, "Wheeled Transport in Pre-colonial West Africa," *Africa* 50, no. 3 (1980): 249–62; Robert W. Harms, *River of Wealth, River of Sorrow: The Central Zaire Basin in the Era of the Slave and Ivory Trade,*

1500–1891 (New Haven, CT, 1981); J. W. King, "An Historical Note on Nile Transport," *UJ* 30, no. 2 (1966): 219–23; Jamie Monson, "Canoe-Building under Colonialism: Forestry and Food Policies in the Inner Kilombero Valley, 1920–1940," in *Custodians of the Land: Ecology and Culture in the History of Tanzania,* ed. Gregory Maddox, James L. Giblin, and Isaria N. Kimambo (London, 1996), 200–12; E. Gilbert, "The *Mtepe:* Regional Trade and the Late Survival of Sewn Ships in East African Waters," *International Journal of Nautical Archaeology* 27, no. 1 (1998): 43–50; J. Forbes Munro, "Shipping Subsidies and Railway Guarantees: William Mackinnon, Eastern Africa and the Indian Ocean, 1860–93," *JAH* 28 (1987): 209–30; Martin Lynn, "From Sail to Steam: The Impact of the Steamship Services on the British Palm Oil Trade with West Africa, 1850–1890," *JAH* 30 (1989); 227–45 Martin Lynn, "Technology, Trade and 'A Race of Native Capitalists': The Krio Diaspora of West Africa and the Steamship, 1852–95," *JAH* 33, no. 3 (1992): 421–40; Ayodeji Olukoju, "Elder Dempster and the Shipping Trade of Nigeria during the First World War," *JAH* 33, no. 2 (1992): 255–72; Mervyn F. Hill, *Permanent Way,* 2 vols. (Nairobi, 1950); David Killingray, "'A Swift Agent of Government': Air Power in British Colonial Africa, 1916–1939," *JAH* 25 (1984): 429–44.

10. E. P. Thompson, *The Making of the English Working Class* (Harmondsworth, UK, 1968), 12.

11. Cornelia Essner, "Some Aspects of German Travellers' Accounts from the Second Half of the 19th Century," *Paideuma* 33 (1987): 200. To be fair, there was often praise as well.

12. Mary Louise Pratt, "Fieldwork in Common Places," in *Writing Culture: The Poetics and Politics of Ethnography,* ed. James Clifford and George E. Marcus (Berkeley and Los Angeles, 1986), 39–40.

13. Gabriel Ogunremi has shown that porterage was often an "economically rational" form of transportation. See *Counting the Camels: The Economics of Transportation in Pre-industrial Nigeria* (New York, 1982), 81–94.

14. It was not so easy, as many colonial governments found, but that is another story.

15. Pioneers include Lamden, "Some Aspects of Porterage"; Robert J. Cummings, "A Note on the History of Caravan Porters in East Africa," *KHR* 2, no. 2 (1973); Robert J. Cummings, "Aspects of Human Porterage with Special Reference to the Akamba of Kenya: Towards an Economic History, 1820–1920" (PhD diss., University of California, Los Angeles, 1975); Donald Herbert Simpson, *Dark Companions: The African Contribution to the European Exploration of East Africa* (London, 1975); François Bontinck, "Voyageurs africains en Afrique Equatoriale," *Zaire Afrique* 107 (1976): 411–24.

16. Catherine Coquery-Vidrovitch and Paul E. Lovejoy, "The Workers of Trade in Precolonial Africa," in *The Workers of African Trade,* ed. Catherine Coquery-Vidrovitch and Paul E. Lovejoy (Beverley Hills, CA, 1985), 11. In Sharon Stichter, *Migrant Laborers* (Cambridge, 1985), only about 10 percent of the book is allocated to precolonial migrant labor. This reflects the limited research undertaken to that point. Tiyambe Zeleza, *A Modern Economic History of Africa,* vol. 1, *The Nineteenth Century* (Dakar, Senegal, 1993), 3, also notes the disparity.

17. An important study that considers the implications of African social dynamics for the emergence of a nonslave plantation work force in colonial East Africa is Frederick Cooper, *From Slaves to Squatters: Plantation Labor and Agriculture in Zanzibar and Coastal Kenya, 1890–1925* (New Haven, CT,1980).

18. Three very important studies have helped redress the balance: Keletso Atkins, *The Moon Is Dead! Give Us Our Money! The Cultural Origins of an African Work Ethic*

(Portsmouth, NH, 1993); Patrick Harries, *Work, Culture, and Identity: Migrant Laborers in Mozambique and South Africa, c. 1860–1910* (Portsmouth, NH, 1995); François Manchuelle, *Willing Migrants: Soninke Labor Diasporas, 1848–1960* (Athens, 1997).

19. Stichter, *Migrant Laborers,* 2.

20. Sunseri, "Labour Migration."

21. Frederick Cooper, "Work, Class and Empire: An African Historian's Retrospective on E. P. Thompson," *SH* 20, no. 2 (May 1995): 239.

22. Shahid Amin and Marcel van der Linden, eds., introduction to *"Peripheral" Labour? Studies in the History of Partial Proletarianization* (Cambridge, 1997), 2, quoting Robin Cohen.

23. Quoted in Terence O. Ranger, "African Reactions to the Imposition of Colonial Rule in East and Central Africa," in *Colonialism in Africa 1870–1960,* ed. L. H. Gann and Peter Duignan, vol. 1, *The History and Politics of Colonialism 1870–1914* (Cambridge, 1969), 1:307 (my italics).

24. Quoted in Patrick Brantlinger, "Victorians and Africans: The Genealogy of the Myth of the Dark Continent," *Critical Inquiry* 12 (Autumn 1985): 181, for discussion, 179–82.

25. In African history, scholars have increasingly opposed binary perspectives that suggest a clear contrast or stages between the "precolonial" and "colonial," "primitive" or "archaic" and "modern," "precapitalist" and "capitalist." See David Newbury, *Kings and Clans: Ijwi Island and the Lake Kivu Rift, 1780–1840* (Madison, WI, 1991), 11; Manchuelle, *Willing Migrants,* 63; Susan Keech McIntosh, ed., introduction to *Beyond Chiefdoms: Paths to Complexity in Africa* (Cambridge, 1999); Frederick Cooper, "Conflict and Connection: Rethinking Colonial African History," in *History after the Three Worlds: Post-Eurocentric Historiographies,* ed. Arif Dirlik, Vinay Bahl, and Peter Gran (Lanham, MD, 2000), 158.

26. This is why German Governor Count von Rechenberg put the Nyamwezi at the center of his economic development plans after the Maji Maji Rebellion, both for peasant production and labor. See John Iliffe, *Tanganyika under German Rule, 1905–1912* (Cambridge, 1969).

27. Coquery-Vidrovitch and Lovejoy, "Workers of Trade," 16–17.

28. Gyan Prakash, ed., "Introduction: After Colonialism," in *After Colonialism: Imperial Histories and Postcolonial Displacements* (Princeton, NJ, 1995), 4.

29. See Marcus Rediker's comment about "unity within diversity" in the broad plebeian culture in Britain and North America during the eighteenth century. *Between the Devil and the Deep Blue Sea: Merchant Seamen, Pirates, and the Anglo-American Maritime World, 1700–1750* (Cambridge, 1987), 202.

30. Foucault explicated the function of "genealogy" as a means to analyze "the various systems of subjection: not the anticipatory power of meaning, but the hazardous play of dominations." Here I use lineage as the analogy, which is perhaps more apt in the African context. See Brantlinger, "Victorians and Africans," 167.

31. E. A. Alpers, *The East African Slave Trade* (Nairobi, 1967), 3–4.

32. Georg Wilhelm Friedrich Hegel, *The Philosophy of History* (Toronto, 1956), 93, 96. For the complete discussion, see ibid, 91–99; also extracts from Hegel's *Lectures on the Philosophy of World History,* in *Race and the Enlightenment: A Reader,* ed. Emmanuel Chukwudi Eze (Cambridge, MA, 1975), 109–49.

33. Gyan Prakash, *Bonded Histories: Genealogies of Labour Servitude in Colonial India* (Cambridge, 1990); Gyan Prakash, "Colonialism, Capitalism and the Discourse of Freedom," in *"Peripheral" Labour?* ed. Amin and Van der Linden, 9–25.

34. Prakash, *Bonded Histories,* 3. For the broader issues of historicism—including the "first in Europe then, elsewhere" structure of time that this discussion raises—see Dipesh Chakrabarty, *Provincializing Europe: Postcolonial Thought and Historical Difference* (Princeton, NJ, 2000), 6–16.

35. Chakrabarty, *Provincializing Europe,* 19.

36. Chakrabarty, *Provincializing Europe,* 63, 67. Chakrabarty uses the term "Enlightenment." More correct in this context would be "post-Enlightenment" or "positivist."

37. Chakrabarty, *Provincializing Europe,* 71.

38. For discussion of similar ideas in the context of peasant politics in India, see Chakrabarty, *Provincializing Europe,* 12–14.

39. Ronald Robinson and John Gallagher, *Africa and the Victorians: The Climax of Imperialism* (New York, 1968), 308. For the relationship between the antislavery lobby and direct intervention, see Cooper; *From Slaves to Squatters,* 32, 34–35; Brantlinger, "Victorians and Africans," 166–203; Helmuth Stoecker, ed., *German Imperialism in Africa: From the Beginnings until the Second World War,* trans. Bernd Zöllner (Atlantic Highlands, NJ, 1986), 37, 98–99; Norman R. Bennett, introduction to *Arab versus European: Diplomacy and War in Nineteenth-Century East Central Africa* (New York, 1986); P.J. Cain and A.G. Hopkins, *British Imperialism: Innovation and Expansion 1688–1914* (London, 1993), 390–91; Zeleza, *Modern Economic History,* 418; Jonathon Glassman, *Feasts and Riot: Revelry, Rebellion, and Popular Consciousness on the Swahili Coast, 1856–1888* (Portsmouth, NH, 1995) 51–52; and most recently Andrew Porter, "Trusteeship, Anti-slavery and Humanitarianism," in *The Oxford History of the British Empire: The Nineteenth Century,* ed. Andrew Porter (Oxford, 1999), 198–221. For a contemporary example of such rhetoric, see Fred. L.M. Moir, *After Livingstone: An African Trade Romance* (London, 1924), 62.

40. Bennett, *Arab versus European,* is particularly good on European attitudes toward the East African Arabs.

41. See Tim Jeal, *Livingstone* (London, 1973); and especially Dorothy O. Helly, *Livingstone's Legacy: Horace Waller and Victorian Mythmaking* (Athens, 1987).

42. For example, Lieutenant-Colonel Wauwermans, "L'oeuvre africaine dans ses rapports avec les progrès du commerce et de l'industrie," *Bulletin de la Société de géographie d'Anvers* 3 (1878): 273–88. See Adam Hochschild, *King Leopold's Ghost: A Story of Greed, Terror, and Heroism in Colonial Africa* (New York, 1999), 28, 30, 38, 42, 57, 78, 92–93, 299.

43. Klaus J. Bade, "Imperial Germany and West Africa: Colonial Movement, Business Interests, and Bismarck's 'Colonial Policies,'" in *Bismarck, Europe and Africa: The Berlin Conference 1884–1885 and the Onset of Partition,* ed. Stig Förster, Wolfgang J. Mommsen, and Ronald Robinson (London, 1988), 121–47; Stoecker, *German Imperialism in Africa;* Juhani Koponen, *Development for Exploitation: German Colonial Policies in Mainland Tanzania, 1884–1914* (Helsinki, 1994), 82–84. For German cotton imperialism, see Thaddeus Sunseri, *Vilimani: Labor Migration and Rural Change in Early Colonial Tanzania* (Portsmouth, NH, 2002), chap. 1.

44. (Dresden, Germany, 1899).

45. See Friederike Eigler, "Engendering German Nationalism: Gender and Race in Frieda von Bülow's Colonial Writings," in *The Imperialist Imagination: German Colonialism and Its Legacy,* ed. Sara Friedrichsmeyer, Sara Lennox, and Susanne Zantop (Ann Arbor, 1998), 72.

46. Hochschild, *King Leopold's Ghost,* 28.

47. "How Is Africa to be Evangelized?" in Alexina Harrison Mackay, *A. M. Mackay, Pioneer Missionary of the Church Missionary Society to Uganda* (1890; repr., London, 1970), 453.

48. For racist European portrayals and other stereotypical views of East African Arabs, see Bennett, *Arab versus European,* 7–17; Christine Bolt, *Victorian Attitudes to Race* (London, 1971), 112–15.

49. A recent book on East Africa by an amateur historian states: "The great advantage of this secondary trade [i.e., the ivory trade] from the slaver's point of view was that transportation from Africa's interior was virtually free . . . the slaves being sent to market themselves were used to carry the tusks." Daniel Liebowitz, *The Physician and the Slave Trade: John Kirk, the Livingstone Expeditions, and the Crusade against Slavery in East Africa* (New York, 1999). The subtitle gives an indication of the author's perspective.

50. This point has been made by D. A. Washbrook in "Orients and Occidents: Colonial Discourse Theory and the Historiography of the British Empire," in *The Oxford History of the British Empire,* ed. Robin Winks, vol. 5, *Historiography* (Oxford, 1999), 603.

51. "A Visit to Zanzibar, 1844, Michael W. Shephard's Account," in *New England Merchants in Africa,* ed. Norman R. Bennett and George E. Brooks (Boston, 1965), 263; Ward to Clayton, Zanzibar, 20 July 1850, in ibid., 466.

52. David Livingstone, *Missionary Travels and Researches in South Africa* (London, 1857). For sales, see Helly, *Livingstone's Legacy,* 28, 55n7.

53. David and Charles Livingstone, *Narrative of an Expedition to the Zambesi and Its Tributaries; and the Discovery of the Lakes Shirwa and Nyassa, 1858–1864* (1865; repr., London, 2001); Helly, *Livingstone's Legacy,* 25.

54. Richard F. Burton, *The Lake Regions of Central Africa* (1860; repr., St. Clair Shores, MI, 1971).

55. Jeal, *Livingstone,* 299. Jeal does not give his source.

56. Livingstone and Livingstone, *Narrative,* 100; Reginald Coupland, *Kirk on the Zambesi: A Chapter of African History* (Oxford, 1928), 156–57.

57. David Livingstone, *The Last Journals of David Livingstone,* ed. H. Waller (New York, 1875), 441 (my italics).

58. This has been noted by Ogunremi for Nigeria. See *Counting the Camels,* 71. K. Y. Daaku writes of Akan trading caravans that "most of the people who were described as slaves by the European observers were those who had hired their services to some inland traders." Quoted in Zeleza, *Modern Economic History,* 289.

59. Edward Hutchinson, "The Best Trade Route to the Lake Regions of Central Africa," *JSA* 25 (30 March 1877): 430.

60. Samuel Baker, *The Albert N'yanza, Great Basin of the Nile, and Explorations of the Nile Sources,* 2 vols. (London, 1866).

61. Joseph Mullins, "A New Route and New Method of Travelling into Central Africa Adopted by the Rev. Robert Price in 1876," *PRGS* 21 (1877): 233–44.235. For similar missionary views, see S. T. Pruen, *The Arab and the African* (1891; repr., London, 1986), 214; Roscoe, *Twenty-five Years,* 12, 14.

62. "Zanzibar and East African Trade. Letter Addressed by Consul Holmwood to Mr. James F. Hutton, President of the Chamber of Commerce of Manchester," (printed circular), 10 April 1885, MP, box 66, IBEAC file 12.

63. Horace Waller, "The Two Ends of the Slave-Stick," *Contemporary Review* (April 1889): 532–33.

64. Moloney, *With Captain Stairs,* 118; Moir, *After Livingstone,* 4. See 132, 171 for similar statements; also T. M. Lindsay, introduction to *A Lady's Letters from Central Africa,* by Jane F. Moir (Glasgow, 1891), 7.

65. Moir, *After Livingstone,* 62. Lindsay made similar points, adding that the next steps were treaties and foreign office involvement: Lindsay in Moir, *Lady's Letters,* 7–8.

66. "Report by Sir A. Hardinge on the British East Africa Protectorate for the Year 1897–98," *HCPP,* C.9125, m.f. 105. 547–548.

67. Quoted in Cooper, *From Slaves to Squatters,* 41.

68. Livingstone and Livingstone, *Narrative,* 101–2 (see quote above); Coupland, *Kirk on the Zambesi,* 156–57; Roland A. Oliver, *The Missionary Factor in East Africa,* 2nd ed. (London, 1965), 11n2.

69. For example, Walter Hutley, "Central Africa—The Slave Trade," *Times,* 30 May 1882, 6, reprinted in the *A-SR* (June 1882) and in James B. Wolf, ed., *The Central African Diaries of Walter Hutley, 1877–1881* (Boston, 1976), 289–96.

70. Edwin W. Smith, "The Earliest Ox-Wagons in Tanganyika: An Experiment Which Failed," pts. 1 and 2, *TNR* 40 (September 1955): 1–14; 41 (December 1955): 1–15.

71. Wauwermans, "L'oeuvre africaine," 362–63.

72. L. K. Rankin, "The Elephant Experiment in Africa: A Brief Account of the Belgian Elephant Expedition on the March from Dar es Salaam to Mpwapwa," *PRGS,* n.s., 4 (1882): 273–88; Norman R. Bennett, *Mirambo of Tanzania 1840? –1884* (New York, 1971), 113–14.

73. Letter by James Bradshaw, published originally in the *African Times,* then in the *Manchester Courier,* and then in the *A-SR* 21, no. 5 (November 1878).

74. This aspect of my argument was anticipated in Brantlinger, "Victorians and Africans," 170 passim.

75. Livingstone and Livingstone, *Narrative,* 268. The load was meal, not ivory. The story of the arrival of the caravan and the freeing of the slaves is told most authentically in the unpublished papers of Horace Waller, who was present at the scene, and in John Kirk's diary, quoted in Coupland, *Kirk on the Zambesi,* 194. See the discussion in Landeg White, *Magomero: Portrait of an African Village* (Cambridge, 1987), 16–17. He writes "Repeated in mission journals, in published memoirs and official accounts, and in propaganda literature with dramatic illustrations, it became part of the iconography of colonialism in central Africa."

76. Livingstone to James Gordon Bennett Junior, Unyanyembe, 13 March 1872, in *Livingstone Letters, 1843–1872: David Livingstone Correspondence in the Brenthurst Library, Johannesburg,* ed. Maurice Boucher (Johannesburg, 1985), 209.

77. Frederick L. Maitland Moir, "Eastern Route to Central Africa," *SGM* 1, no. 4 (April 1885): 111, also quoted in James Stevenson, *The Arabs in Central Africa and at Lake Nyassa* (Glasgow, 1889), 10. A less-emotional account appears in Moir, *After Livingstone,* 82–83. See also A. J. Swann, *Fighting the Slave-Hunters in Central Africa* (1910; repr., London, 1969), 48–49; Brady, *Commerce and Conquest,* 149–50 (quoting Swann); Roscoe, *Twenty-five Years,* 12. An example from the southern Sudan (in this case the maltreatment of a pregnant slave porter) is in Baker, *Albert N'yanza,* 1:132. Another from Kenya in 1890 is in William Hoffman, *With Stanley in Africa* (London, 1938), 171.

78. *A-SR,* series 4; vol. 1, no. 7 (18 July 1881): 99.

79. The two versions are reproduced in Helly, *Livingstone's Legacy,* 148, 150.

80. For the Waungwana, see Jonathon Glassman, "Social Rebellion and Swahili Culture: The Response to German Conquest of the Northern Mrima" (PhD thesis,

University of Wisconsin–Madison, 1988), 97–101; Glassman, *Feasts and Riot,* 61–62. There is a similar contemporary explanation in C. T. Wilson and R. W. Felkin, *Uganda and the Egyptian Soudan* (London, 1882), 1:14.

81. Chief Abdallah Fundikira, interview, Tabora, 4 July 2000. Andrew Roberts, "Nyamwezi Trade," in *Pre-colonial African Trade,* ed. Richard Gray and David Birmingham (London, 1970), 61; Andrew Roberts, "The Nyamwezi," in *Tanzania Before 1900,* ed. Andrew Roberts (Nairobi, 1968), 128; Coquery-Vidrovitch and Lovejoy, "Workers of Trade," 15–16.

82. Edward Coode Hore, *Tanganyika: Eleven Years in Central Africa* (London, 1892), 235–36. For similar statements about Kabunda's use of captive porters, see Moir, "Eastern Route," also quoted in Stevenson, *Arabs in Central Africa,* 9–10; Moir, *After Livingstone,* 82–85; Swann, *Fighting the Slave-Hunters,* 192, 246 (also noted in the introduction by Norman Bennett, xii). The Kabunda case was played upon by numerous writers precisely because it was relatively unusual and at the same time could be employed to reinforce imperialist arguments about the slave trade.

83. Andrew Roberts, *A History of Zambia* (London, 1976), 123, 139–40.

84. Livingstone, *Last Journals,* 353n; Verney Lovett Cameron, *Across Africa* (London, 1877), 1:305; David Northrup, *Beyond the Bend in the River: African Labor in Eastern Zaire, 1865–1940* (Athens, 1988), 27–28. Compare with Burton's statement that "On the Uruwwa route caravans are composed wholly of private slaves." *Lake Regions,* 374. See also François Renault, "The Structures of the Slave Trade in Central Africa in the 19th Century," in *The Economics of the Indian Ocean Slave Trade,* ed. William Gervase Clarence-Smith (London, 1989), 152–53; Melvin E. Page, "The Manyema Hordes of Tippu Tip: A Case Study in Social Stratification and the Slave Trade in Eastern Africa," *IJAHS* 7, no. 1 (1974): 69–84.

85. Joseph Thomson, *To the Central African Lakes and Back* (1881; repr., London, 1968), 1:8–9, 73–75, 91, 274; Hutley, 26 April 1879, *Central African Diaries,* ed. Wolf, 105; Hore to Mullins, Ujiji, 16 April 1879, 31–32, LMS 2/1/B. For an imperialist view of the slave trade to Unyanyembe, see Hutley, "Central Africa—The Slave Trade."

86. J. L. Krapf, *Travels, Researches and Missionary Labours during an Eighteen Years Residence in Eastern Africa* (1860; repr., London, 1868), 423; William Percival Johnson, *My African Reminiscences 1875–1895* (1924; repr., Westport, CT, 1970), 74–75. See also Edward A. Alpers, "The Story of Swema: Female Vulnerability in Nineteenth-Century East Africa," in *Women and Slavery in Africa,* ed. Claire C. Robertson and Martin A. Klein (Madison, 1983), 185–99.

87. J. E. Hine, *Days Gone By: Being Some Account of Past Years Chiefly in Central Africa* (London, 1924), 136.

88. Lionel Decle, *Three Years in Savage Africa* (London, 1898), 316. Stanley reported meeting in Ukwere in 1871 a "chain slave-gang" carrying "nothing but themselves." See Henry Morton Stanley, *How I Found Livingstone* (London, 1872), 91–92.

89. Chap. 3 deals with professional porters.

90. Abdul M. H. Sheriff, "Localisation and Social Composition of the East African Slave Trade, 1858–1873," in *Economics of the Indian Ocean Slave Trade,* ed. William Gervase Clarence-Smith, 132 (map), 139, 143–44.

91. For a case from this period that makes clear the disadvantages for caravan operators of using "freshly trapped" captives as porters, see Burton, *Lake Regions,* 54–55.

92. The first steps were taken by Alpers in *East African Slave Trade.*

93. This is Sheriff's term.

94. This is not say that there had been no movement away from the overtly racial views of the late nineteenth-century writers on East Africa. As Washbrook points out, "colonialism had a pre- and a post-history, and reading such qualities ["the paradigmatic qualities imputed to the 'colonial' episteme," concentrated in the late nineteenth century] backwards and forwards across the entire colonial (and European) cultural experience leads to anachronism." See Washbrook, "Orients and Occidents," 603.

95. R. Coupland, *East Africa and Its Invaders: From the Earliest Times to the Death of Seyyid Said in 1856* (Oxford, 1938), 307.

96. Brady, *Commerce and Conquest,* 144. Brady also mentions hired porters.

97. Kenneth Ingham, *A History of East Africa* (London: 1962), 60.

98. H.A.C. Cairns, *Prelude to Imperialism: British Reactions to Central African Society 1840–1890* (London, 1965), 136; J.S. Galbraith, *Mackinnon and East Africa, 1878–1892: A Study in the "New Imperialism"* (Cambridge, 1972), 22. See also Bade, "Imperial Germany," 144.

99. R.W. Beachey, *The Slave Trade of Eastern Africa* (London,1976), 184n8 and n9, 289. The anti-imperialist scholar Moses D.E. Nwulia comes to the same conclusion, distinguishing between the carriage of trade goods along the "most important" central route and the Kilwa route: *Britain and Slavery in East Africa* (Washington, DC,1975), 102–3.

100. Alpers, *East African Slave Trade,* 26. A slightly different version, once again without supporting citations, states that there was an upsurge in the use of slave porters in the 1880s. See John Iliffe, *A Modern History of Tanganyika* (Cambridge, 1979), 44.

101. Baxter to Wright, Mpwapwa, 13 June 1878, CMS CA6/05; For a second case, see 26 August 1878, White Fathers, *A l'assaut des pays nègres,* 156. It is not clear whether the slaves carried ivory or perhaps foodstuffs.

102. *An Introduction to the History of East Africa,* 3rd ed. (Cambridge, 1965), 29. This inaccuracy is repeated on pp. 33 and 37.

103. Mohamed Mangiringiri, interview, Tabora, 20 July 2000. Other informants told that *pagazi* could be either slaves or free people working for wages.

104. In one textbook the chapter on nineteenth-century East Africa has much to say on slavery, the slave trade, and their impact on African societies, but little on other forms of economic organization. See Philip Curtin, Steven Feierman, Leonard Thompson, and Jan Vansina, *African History* (London, 1978), chap. 13. Compare with the suggestive discussion on emerging market relations in Gray and Birmingham, "Some Economic and Political Consequences of Trade in Central and Eastern Africa in the Pre-colonial Period," in *Pre-colonial African Trade,* ed. Gray and Birmingham, 3–5; also Roland A. Oliver and Anthony Atmore, *Africa Since 1800,* 3rd ed. (Cambridge, 1981), chap. 6; Bill Freund, *The Making of Contemporary Africa* (Bloomington, 1984), 68–69; Zeleza, *Modern Economic History,* 296–318; John Iliffe, *Africans: The History of a Continent* (Cambridge, 1995), 180–86.

105. Generally, O.F. Raum, "German East Africa: Changes in African Tribal Life Under German Administration, 1882–1914," in *History of East Africa,* ed. Vincent Harlow and E.M. Chilver (Oxford, 1965), 2:196–97. For northeast Tanzania and the northern route, see Helge Kjekshus, *Ecology Control and Economic Development in East African History* (London, 1977), 111–16; Juhani Koponen, *People and Production in Late Precolonial Tanzania: History and Structures* (Jyväskylä, Finland, 1988), 103–4, 118–19; Isaria N. Kimambo, "Environmental Control and Hunger in the Mountains and Plains of Nineteenth-Century Northeastern Tanzania," in *Custodians of the Land,* ed. Maddox, Giblin, and Kimambo, 71–95. Glassman, *Feasts and Riot,* chap. 1, explores some implica-

tions of the commoditization of material things but has much less to say about the commodification of labor power. For the central routes, see John Hanning Speke, *What Led to the Discovery of the Source of the Nile* (Edinburgh, 1864), 357; Alfred C. Unomah and J. B. Webster, "East Africa: The Expansion of Commerce," in *The Cambridge History of Africa,* ed. John E. Flint (London, 1976), 5:296.

106. These innovations were clearly limited in many respects and were hindered by the very existence of the transportation problem. For instance, it is impossible to imagine that a single grain market along the trade routes could have emerged without railways.

107. Glassman has dealt comprehensively with the northern route. See *Feasts and Riot,* 74–78.

108. Coquery-Vidrovitch and Lovejoy, "Workers of Trade," 17–18.

109. A porter list dated September 1888 includes details of wage rates and advance payments for a large caravan leaving Zanzibar. The identified slave porters were engaged according to the same terms as other porters. See "Men Engaged for Masai Caravan," notebook, "Stanley's Expedition," ZM.

110. Thomson, *To the Central African Lakes,* 1:67–68. For the porter list, see "Royal Geographical Society's East African Expedition 1879: Draft of Agreement with Porters at Zanzibar," Alexander Keith Johnston, Jr., Corr. 1870–80, RGS; copy of contract with a list of 128 names dated 17 May 1879 in AA9/10, consular records, Zanzibar National Archive; printed in Robert I. Rotberg, *Joseph Thomson and the Exploration of Africa* (London, 1971), 307. For slave porters handing over part of their wages (usually half) to their owner, see Muxworthy to Southon, Zanzibar, 28 June 1880, LMS 3/4/E; James T. Last, *Polyglotta Africana Orientalis* (London, n.d.), 14; Swann, *Fighting the Slave-Hunters,* 31; Rashid bin Hassani, "The Story of Rashid bin Hassani of the Bisa Tribe Northern Rhodesia," recorded by W. F. Baldock in *Ten Africans,* ed. Margery Perham (Evanston, IL, 1963), 99–100, 103. In some cases, however, the owner was less generous and seized a greater part of the slave's wages. See T. H. Parke, 18 October 1888, in *My Personal Experiences in Equatorial Africa as Medical Officer of the Emin Pasha Relief Expedition* (London, 1891), 285; O. L. McDermott to undersecretary of state, foreign office, 22 January 1890, MP, box 94, file 56. There are discussions of *vibarua,* or slave wage labor, in Jonathon Glassman, "The Bondsman's New Clothes: The Contradictory Consciousness of Slave Resistance on the Swahili Coast," *JAH* 32, no. 2 (1991): 291–93; Jonathon Glassman, *Feast and Riot;* Thaddeus Sunseri, "Slave Ransoming in German East Africa, 1885–1922," *IJAHS* 26, no. 3 (1993): 481–511; Sunseri, *Vilimani.* See also Frederick Cooper, *Plantation Slavery on the East Coast of Africa* (New Haven, CT, 1977).

111. Muxworthy to Wookey, Zanzibar, 28 June 1880, LMS 3/4/E. Dr. Kirk was the British consul in Zanzibar, and Captain Mathews was commander of the sultan's forces.

112. Dodgshun, 24 December 1877, in Norman R. Bennett, ed., *From Zanzibar to Ujiji: The Journal of Arthur W. Dodgshun 1877–1879* (Boston, 1969), 50.

113. Stokes to Lang, 26 July 1884, CMS G3A6/01; Annie Hore, *To Lake Tanganyika in a Bath Chair* (London, 1886), 60–63.

114. Cooper, *From Slaves to Squatters,* 34n29.

115. Stairs, 15 and 29 June 1891, in Janina M. Konczacki, ed., *Victorian Explorer: The African Diaries of Captain William G. Stairs 1887–1892* (Halifax, Nova Scotia, 1994), 188, 190; Moloney, *With Captain Stairs,* 22–23.

116. *ZEAG,* 26 April 1893, 10, reprinted from the *Times.*

117. Cooper, *From Slaves to Squatters,* 48–52.

118. Cairns, *Prelude to Imperialism,* 99.

119. Rediker, *Between the Devil,* 203–4. If we replace "plebeian" with "peasant," the comparison is apt.

120. E. P. Thompson, *Customs in Common* (London, 1991), 2.

121. Thompson, *Customs in Common,* 6–7.

122. Thompson, *Customs in Common,* 3–4.

123. James Belich, *Making Peoples: A History of the New Zealanders, from Polynesian Settlement to the End of the Nineteenth Century* (Auckland, 1996), 349–60.

124. Belich, *Making Peoples,* 424–25.

125. Belich, *Making Peoples,* 425–28.

126. Belich, *Making Peoples,* 435.

127. Belich, *Making Peoples,* 428.

128. This paragraph is based on Belich, *Making Peoples,* 428; and especially Duncan Mackay, "The Orderly Frontier: The World of the Kauri Bushmen, 1860–1925," in *The Shaping of History: Essays from the New Zealand Journal of History,* ed. Judith Binney (Wellington, 2001), 257–65.

129. For more on the ambiguous attitudes of mainstream colonial society to crews, as "both heroes and villains," and harbingers of "progress" but also as disorderly ruffians, see Belich, *Making Peoples,* 431–36. Similar themes are discussed with reference to Canadian woodsmen in Ian Radforth, "The Shantymen," in *Labouring Lives: Work and Workers in Nineteenth-Century Ontario,* ed. Paul Craven (Toronto, 1995), 204–77.

130. Belich, *Making Peoples,* 430–31.

131. One historian who has attempted to move beyond earlier assumptions is Janet J. Ewald in "Crossers of the Sea: Slaves, Freedmen, and Other Migrants in the Northwestern Indian Ocean, c. 1750–1914," *AHR* 105, no. 1 (February 2000): 69–91.

132. It is astonishing, for instance, that there are just seven or eight satisfactory histories in English of maritime labor in the age of sail. In India, the Banjari transport specialists of preindustrial times still await their historian, as has been noted by David Washbrook.

133. Viewpoints from various disciplines include Edward Said, *Orientalism* (London, 1978); Clifford and Marcus, *Writing Culture;* Mary Louise Pratt, *Imperial Eyes: Travel Writing and Transculturation* (London, 1992); Chakrabarty, *Provincializing Europe.* Ania Loomba, *Colonialism/Postcolonialism* (London, 1998), is a useful guide to the issues. Megan Vaughan discusses some of the implications for African history in "Colonial Discourse Theory and African History, or Has Postmodernism Passed Us By?" *Social Dynamics* 20, no. 2 (1994): 1–23.

134. Cooper, "Work, Class and Empire," 236. Successful examples include Harries, *Work, Culture, and Identity;* Atkins, *The Moon Is Dead!* Manchuelle, *Willing Migrants.* Anthropologist Sherry Ortner frames her study of Sherpa mountaineers in almost the same way. See *Life and Death,* 5.

135. James L. Giblin and Gregory Maddox, introduction to *Custodians of the Land,* ed. Maddox, Giblin, and Kimambo, 1–14.

136. See Stephen J. Rockel, "Safari! The East African Caravan System in the Nineteenth Century" (unpublished manuscript), chap. 4.

137. Stichter, *Migrant Laborers.*

138. See the discussions in Loomba, *Colonialism/Postcolonialism,* 231–45; Sherry B. Ortner, "Resistance and the Problem of Ethnographic Refusal," *CSSH* 37 (1995): 173–93; Ortner, *Life and Death,* 17–18.

139. Bethwell A. Ogot, Terence O. Ranger, and Allen F. Isaacman have been three of the most influential. Washbrook, "Orients and Occidents," 600–1, makes a similar point.

140. Vaughan, "Colonial Discourse Theory," 1; Steven Feierman, "African Histories and the Dissolution of World Histories," in *Africa and the Disciplines: The Contributions of Research in Africa to the Social Sciences and Humanities,* ed. Robert Bates, V.Y. Mudimbe, and Jean O'Barr (Chicago, 1993).

141. Henrietta Moore and Megan Vaughan, *Cutting down Trees: Gender, Nutrition, and Agricultural Change in the Northern Province of Zambia, 1890–1990* (London, 1994), xxiii. See also Geertz's ideas on the articulation of cultural forms through "social action." Clifford Geertz, "Thick Description: Toward an Interpretive Theory of Culture," in *The Interpretation of Cultures* (New York, 1973), 17.

142. Johannes Fabian, *Out of Our Minds: Reason and Madness in the Exploration of Central Africa* (Berkeley and Los Angeles, 2000), 1–9.

143. For the social background and worldview of London Missionary Society personnel, see John L. Comaroff, "Images of Empire, Contests of Conscience: Models of Colonial Domination in South Africa," in *Tensions of Empire: Colonial Cultures in a Bourgeois World,* ed. Frederick Cooper and Ann Laura Stoler (Berkeley and Los Angeles, 1997), 163–97; John de Gruchy, ed., *The London Missionary Society in Southern Africa, 1799–1999: Historical Essays in Celebration of the Bicentenary of the LMS in Southern Africa* (Athens, 2000).

144. Roy C. Bridges, "Nineteenth-Century East African Travel Records, with an Appendix on 'Armchair Geographers' and Cartography," *Paideuma* 33 (1987): 181.

145. Moore and Vaughan, *Cutting down Trees,* xxiii.

146. See Stephen J. Rockel, "Relocating Labor: Sources from the Nineteenth Century," *History in Africa* 22 (1995): 447–54, for further discussion.

147. See Rockel, "Safari!" chap. 5.

148. Hamid bin Muhammed (Tippu Tip), *Maisha ya Hamed bin Muhammed el Murjebi yaani Tippu Tip,* trans. and ed. W.H. Whitely (Nairobi, 1974); Rashid bin Hassani, "Story of Rashid bin Hassani," 81–119; Jacob Wainwright, "Tagebuch von Jacob Wainright über den Transport von Dr. Livingstones Leiche 4. Mai 1873–18 Februar 1874," *PM* 20 (1874): 187–93; James MacQueen, "The Visit of Lief Ben Saeid to the Great African Lake," *JRGS* 15 (1845): 371–376; Said bin Habeeb, "Narrative of Said bin Habeeb, an Arab Inhabitant of Zanzibar," *TBGS* 15 (1860): 146–48.

149. Mtoro bin Mwinyi Bakari, *The Customs of the Swahili People,* trans. and ed. J.W.T. Allen (Berkeley and Los Angeles, 1981); Carl Velten, ed., *Safari za Wasuaheli* (Göttingen, 1901); Carl Velten, ed., *Schilderungen der Suaheli* (Göttingen, 1901); Lyndon Harries, trans. and ed., *Swahili Prose Texts* (London, 1965).

150. A good example is A.C. Madan, trans. and ed., *Kiungani; or, Story and History from Central Africa* (London, 1887). Slave narratives of this type have been effectively analyzed by Marcia Wright in *Strategies of Slaves and Women: Life Stories from East/ Central Africa* (New York, 1993).

151. Marion Johnson, "Cloth as Money," *Textile History* 11 (1980): 193–202; Marion Johnson, "The Cowrie Currencies of West Africa," *JAH* 3 (1970): 17–49, 331–51; Jan Hogendorn and Marion Johnson, *The Shell Money of the Slave Trade* (Cambridge, 1986). In the Senegambia region, by the early nineteenth century cloth from French India known as *pièces de guinea,* or bafts, "had become for all practical purposes the currency." See Manchuelle, *Willing Migrants,* 46.

152. J. Clyde Mitchell, "The Causes of Labour Migration," in *Forced Labour and Migration: Patterns of Movement Within Africa,* ed. Abebe Zegeye and Shubi Ishemo (London, 1989) 28–29.

153. François Coulbois, *Dix années au Tanganyka* (Limoges, 1901), 41; Franz Stuhlmann, *Mit Emin Pascha ins Herz von Afrika* (Berlin, 1894), 89; Roberts, "Nyamwezi Trade," 66; Unomah and Webster, "East Africa," 284–85; Bennett, *Arab versus European,* 32.

154. Carol Jane Sissons, "Economic Prosperity in Ugogo, East Africa, 1860–1890" (PhD thesis, University of Toronto, 1984), 187, and analysis, 188–89; also Raum, "German East Africa," 170; Iliffe, *Modern History,* 129–30, for the early 1900s.

CHAPTER 2: PIONEERS: THE BIRTH OF A LABOR CULTURE

1. See among others Merrick Posnansky, "Connections between the Lacustrine Peoples and the Coast," in *East Africa and the Orient,* ed. H. Neville Chittick and Robert I. Rotberg (New York, 1975), 216–225; the various articles by J.M. Gray in *TNR* and *UJ;* Edward A. Alpers, "The Coast and the Development of the Caravan Trade," in *A History of Tanzania,* ed. Isaria N. Kimambo and A.J. Temu (Nairobi, 1969), 35–56; Edward A. Alpers, *Ivory and Slaves in East Central Africa* (Berkeley and Los Angeles, 1975); Gray and Birmingham, *Pre-colonial African Trade;* Owen J.M. Kalinga, "The Balowoka and the Establishment of States West of Lake Malawi," in *State Formation in Eastern Africa,* ed. Ahmed Idha Salim (Nairobi, 1984), 36–52; Alfred C. Unomah, "Economic Expansion and Political Change in Unyanyembe, c. 1840–1900" (PhD thesis, University of Ibadan, 1972); Unomah and Webster, "East Africa"; Aylward Shorter, *Chiefship in Western Tanzania: A Political History of the Kimbu* (Oxford, 1972); Buluda A. Itandala, "A History of the Babinza of Usukuma, Tanzania, to 1890" (PhD thesis, Dalhousie University, 1983); Abdul M.H. Sheriff, "Ivory and Commercial Expansion in East Africa in the Nineteenth Century," in *Figuring African Trade,* ed. S. Liesegang, H. Pasch, and A. Jones (Berlin, 1986), 415–49; Abdul M.H. Sheriff, *Slaves, Spices and Ivory in Zanzibar* (London, 1987); Koponen, *People and Production;* Clarence-Smith, *Economics of the Indian Ocean Slave Trade;* Rockel, "Safari!"

2. Roberts, "Nyamwezi Trade," 41.

3. See Sheriff, *Slaves, Spices and Ivory,* 89, graph 3.2.

4. Sharon Stichter argues that analysis can be made at both a structural and individual level. Both are useful. See "The Migration of Women in Colonial Central Africa: Some Notes Towards an Approach," in *Demography From Scanty Evidence: Central Africa in the Colonial Era,* ed. Bruce Fetter (Boulder, CO, 1990), 208.

5. Mitchell, "Causes of Labour Migration," 31–33, 40–44. Like Mitchell, François Manchuelle rejects explanations that assume that Africans were not economically rational. Manchuelle, *Willing Migrants,* 4–8. Individual motives will be dealt with in chap. 3.

6. Manchuelle, *Willing Migrants,* 12–13, 25, 26.

7. Manchuelle, *Willing Migrants,* 38–39. A similar argument is made for the Yao in Kings M. Phiri, "Political Change among the Chewa and Yao of the Lake Malawi Region, c. 1750–1900," in *State Formation,* ed. Salim, 53–69. For the Nyamwezi, see below.

8. Manchuelle, *Willing Migrants,* 39.

9. Paul E. Lovejoy, *Caravans of Kola: The Hausa Kola Trade 1700–1900* (Zaria, 1980), and *Salt of the Desert Sun: A History of Salt Production and Trade in the Central Sudan* (Cambridge, 1986).

10. Peter C.W. Gutkind, "The Boatmen of Ghana: The Possibilities of a Pre-colonial African Labor History," in *Confrontation, Class Consciousness, and the Labour Process: Studies in Proletarian Class Formation,* ed. Michael Hanagan and Charles Stephenson (New York, 1986), 123–66.

11. However, there are many examples in precolonial Africa of societies that have accumulated surpluses for the maintenance of an elite from a basis in agricultural and pastoral production rather than long-distance trade. Additional surplus from trade buttressed these foundations. This is argued by Graham Connah, *African Civilizations* (Cambridge, 1987).

12. Gutkind, "Boatmen of Ghana," 127–28.

13. For an earlier attempt to explain Nyamwezi wage labor using Gutkind's model, see Stephen J. Rockel, "Caravan Porters in Nineteenth-Century Tanzania: Traders, Slaves, or Workers?" (paper presented at the annual meeting of the Canadian Association of African Studies, York University, May 1991).

14. Gutkind, "Boatmen of Ghana," 128; Manchuelle, *Willing Migrants,* 63.

15. Gutkind, "Boatmen of Ghana," 144.

16. A major exception is the recent book by Allen F. and Barbara Isaacman, which includes a detailed account of Chikunda elephant hunters of the Zambezi valley: *Slavery and Beyond: The Making of Men and Chikunda Ethnic Identities in the Unstable World of South-Central Africa, 1750–1920* (Portsmouth, NH, 2004).

17. Alpers, "Coast," 43.

18. Alpers, "Coast," 43, Abdallah, *Yaos,* 26–28.

19. A. Bocarro, "Gaspar Bocarros's Journey from Tete to Kilwa in 1616," in *The East African Coast: Select Documents From the First to the Earlier Nineteenth Century,* ed. G.S.P. Freeman-Grenville (Oxford, 1962), 167.

20. Alpers, "Coast," 44; Abdallah, *Yaos,* 26–28.

21. Anon., "Some Notes on Kilwa," *TNR* 2 (1936): 94–95; Neville Chittick, "The Early History of Kilwa Kivinje," *Azania* 4 (1969): 153–59; David Lawrence Horne, "Mode of Production in the Social and Economic History of Kilwa to 1884" (PhD diss., University of California, Los Angeles, 1984), 138–140, 146–47.

22. Horne, "Mode of Production," 156; Sheriff, *Slaves, Spices and Ivory,* 162–63.

23. Ward to Shepard, Zanzibar, 26 January 1849, in *New England Merchants,* ed. Bennett and Brooks, 437. On the Bisa and their caravans, see also Burton, *Lake Regions,* 374–75; Livingstone, *Last Journals,* 101, 24 September 1866; E.D. Young, *The Search After Livingstone* (London, 1868), 184; Harry H. Johnston, *British Central Africa* (London, 1897), 62; P.A. Cole-King, "Transportation and Communication in Malawi to 1891, with a Summary to 1918," in *The Early History of Malawi,* ed. Bridglal Pachai (London, 1972), 73; Alpers, *Ivory and Slaves,* 178–79; Andrew D. Roberts, *A History of the Bemba* (London, 1973), 109–11, 120–21; Roland A. Oliver, *The African Experience* (London, 1991), 130.

24. One *frasila* is equivalent to 35 pounds in weight.

25. Alpers, *Ivory and Slaves,* 243–253; Roberts, *History of Zambia,* 120–121; Abdallah, *Yaos,* 30–34.

26. The phrase is quoted in Alpers, *Ivory and Slaves,* 22.

27. Both songs are quoted in Abdallah, *Yaos,* 28–29. For comments and another example, see Alpers, *Ivory and Slaves,* 22.

28. For the Mgunda Mkali, see Rockel, "Safari!" chap. 3. For Ugogo in the nineteenth century, see Sissons, "Economic Prosperity."

29. For the political history of the Nyamwezi, see R.G. Abrahams, *The Political Organization of Unyamwezi* (Cambridge, 1967); R.G. Abrahams, *The Peoples of Greater Unyamwezi, Tanzania* (London, 1967); Achim Gottberg, "On the Historical Importance of the Crisis of the Fundikira Empire," in *Afrika-Studien,* ed. W. Markov (Leipzig, 1967), 63–83; Roberts, "The Nyamwezi"; Bennett, *Mirambo;* Shorter, *Chiefship in Western Tanzania;*

Unomah, "Economic Expansion"; Alfred C. Unomah, *Mirambo of Tanzania* (London, 1977); J.B. Kabeya, *King Mirambo* (Nairobi, 1976).

30. Richard F. Burton, "The Lake Regions of Central Equatorial Africa," *JRGS* 29 (1859): 161; Shorter, *Chiefship in Western Tanzania*, 242–43; Mathias E. Mnyampala, *The Gogo: History, Customs and Traditions,* trans. Gregory Maddox (New York, 1995), 45; Peter Rigby, "Joking Relationships, Kin Categories, and Clanship among the Gogo," *Africa* 38, no. 2 (1968): 135n2.

31. See Shorter, *Chiefship in Western Tanzania;* Rockel, "Safari!" chap. 3.

32. Shorter, *Chiefship in Western Tanzania,* 225.

33. J.E.G. Sutton and Andrew D. Roberts, "Uvinza and Its Salt Industry," *Azania* 3 (1968): 45–86; Roberts, "Nyamwezi Trade," 44–47.

34. Sutton and Roberts, "Uvinza and Its Salt Industry"; Roberts, "Nyamwezi Trade"; Unomah and Webster, "East Africa," 273; Unomah, *Mirambo of Tanzania,* 7–8.

35. For Nyamwezi agriculture and forest pursuits, see Rockel, "Safari!" chap. 4.

36. For detailed discussion, see Rockel, "Safari!" chap. 4.

37. See Rockel, "Safari!" chap. 3, for the background to this historic reorientation.

38. This idea is borrowed from Unomah, *Mirambo of Tanzania,* 7.

39. Known as the Watuta. See Elzear Ebner, *The History of the Wangoni* (Peramiho, Tanzania, 1987), 59–61; Shorter, *Chiefship in Western Tanzania,* 255–61; Abdul M.H. Sheriff, "Tanzanian Societies at the Time of the Partition," in *Tanzania,* ed. Kaniki, 33.

40. Abrahams, *Political Organization,* 9–10; Bennett, *Mirambo,* 10. The phrase is Bennett's.

41. D.A. Low, "The Northern Interior, 1840–84," in *History of East Africa,* ed. Roland A. Oliver and Gervase Mathew (Oxford, 1963) 1:314; Cummings, "Aspects of Human Porterage," 48, 103–4, 108–9; Sheriff, *Slaves, Spices and Ivory,* 156; Report of Sir A. Hardinge for the year 1897–98, *HCPP,* C.9125, m.f. 105.547–548, 26.

42. Cameron, *Across Africa,* 1:191; also Burton, *Lake Regions,* 255.

43. Jacob Wainwright, "Tagebuch," 192. Wainwright was mission educated and was the first East African to author a safari journal.

44. Sissons tells us: "There was no way of integrating a traveling occupation, such as long-distance trade during dry season months, with the demands of the agricultural cycle." See "Economic Prosperity," 177.

45. Swann, *Fighting the Slave Hunters,* 58. Nyamwezi porters arriving at Zanzibar told Bishop Edward Steere that they regarded any of their compatriots who never undertook a journey to the coast as a "milksop." See Bennett, *Mirambo,* 12; also Burton, *Lake Regions,* 235; Roberts, "Nyamwezi Trade," 66.

46. Wilson and Felkin, *Uganda,* 1:43.

47. Paul Reichard, "Die Wanjamuesi," *ZGEB* 24 (1889): 259; Bennett, *Mirambo,* 12.

48. Ortner, *Life and Death,* 44.

49. Jonathon Glassman has recently written: "[Nyamwezi] caravan labour was seen not as a way to earn a living, but as a way to prove one's manhood." In *Feasts and Riot,* 59. See also Bennett, *Mirambo,* 12; Unomah and Webster, "East Africa," 284.

50. Mitchell, "Causes of Labour Migration"; Stichter, *Migrant Laborers,* 5–6.

51. As Helge Kjekshus points out, we must look to local factors as well as external forces when considering the expansion of the caravan trade and porterage. Kjekshus, *Ecology Control,* 111–25. See also Koponen, *People and Production,* 81; Rockel, "Safari!" chap. 4.

52. Kalinga, "Balowoka," 36.

53. Kalinga, "Balowoka," 38, 39–40.

54. Kalinga, "Balowoka," 45–46.

55. Kalinga, "Balowoka," 46, 49–50.

56. John M. Gray, "Trading Expeditions from the Coast to Lakes Tanganyika and Victoria before 1857," *TNR* 49 (1957): 227; G.S.P. Freeman-Grenville, "The Coast, 1498–1840," in *History of East Africa*, ed. Oliver and Mathew, 1:53; Roberts, "Nyamwezi Trade," 47–48; Bennett, *Mirambo,* 17.

57. Alpers, *Ivory and Slaves,* 180. Roberts is less convinced by the evidence. See "Nyamwezi Trade," 56. Given the history of the Balowoka, his view should be updated.

58. Henry Salt, *A Voyage to Abyssinia* (London, 1814), 32–33; also quoted in Alpers, *Ivory and Slaves,* 180.

59. Krapf, 13 February 1850, in *Travels,* 420.

60. Livingstone, *Last Journals,* 418. See Roberts, "Nyamwezi Trade," 54–57, for a discussion of the early Nyamwezi and Sumbwa copper trade with Katanga; also Unomah, "Economic Expansion," 47–48.

61. Charles Pickering, *The Races of Man and Their Geographical Distribution* (London, 1850), 202.

62. Captain T. Smee, "Observations during a Voyage of Research on the East Coast of Africa, from Cape Guardafui South to the Island of Zanzibar, in H.C.'s Cruisers Ternate (Capt. T. Smee), and Sylph Schooner (Lieutenant Hardy)," in Richard F. Burton, *Zanzibar, City, Island and Coast* (London, 1872), 2:510; also mentioned in Roberts, "Nyamwezi Trade," 49, and Alpers, *Ivory and Slaves,* 235.

63. Sheriff, *Slaves, Spices and Ivory,* 177. The Balowoka are exceptional in being remembered as state builders, not in Kimbu or Nyamwezi tradition, but in traditions collected in northern Malawi by Kalinga.

64. MacQueen, "Visit of Lief Ben Saeid," 371; Sheriff, *Slaves, Spices and Ivory,* 177.

65. Burton, "Lake Regions," 161; Burton, *Lake Regions,* 214. See also Shorter, *Chiefship in Western Tanzania,* 233; Sheriff, *Slaves, Spices and Ivory,* 177.

66. Discussed in Rockel, "Safari!" chap. 3.

67. Sheriff suggests that Kafuku's death was "probably not before 1830." Shorter suggests a date of approximately 1825, which seems too early. See "A Note by Dr. Aylward Shorter," in *Pre-colonial African Trade,* ed. Gray and Birmingham, 230.

68. Roberts, "Nyamwezi Trade," 49.

69. Shorter, *Chiefship in Western Tanzania,* 233–34.

70. For the tradition and a discussion, see Roberts, "Nyamwezi Trade," 48–49. See also Sheriff, *Slaves, Spices and Ivory,* 177.

71. See Rockel, "Safari!" chap. 3.

72. Burton, "Lake Regions," 126; Roberts, "Nyamwezi Trade," 67; Shorter, *Chiefship in Western Tanzania,* 235.

73. MacQueen, "Visit of Lief Ben Saeid," 372.

74. Shorter, *Chiefship in Western Tanzania,* 235–39.

75. John Studdy Leigh, 15 March 1839, in "The Zanzibar Diary of John Studdy Leigh," pt. 2, ed. James S. Kirkman, *IJAHS* 13, no. 3 (1980): 494.

76. Diary of Richard P. Waters, 18 October and 18 November 1842, in *New England Merchants,* ed. Bennett and Brooks, 253, 254.

77. Bennett and Brooks, *New England Merchants,* 254n5; Bennett, *Mirambo,* 26.

78. W.D. Cooley, "Geography of N'yassi," pt. 2, *JRGS* 15 (1845): 213; Charles Guillain, *Documents sur l'histoire, la géographie et le commerce de l'Afrique orientale* (Paris, 1856), 1:380; Burton, *Zanzibar,* 1:343.

79. J.A. Grant, "Summary of Observations on the Geography, Climate, and Natural History of the Lake Regions," *JRGS* 42 (1872): 251–52.

80. James Christie, *Cholera Epidemics in East Africa* (London, 1876), 427–28.

81. For a detailed account of the climate of Unyamwezi and rainfall statistics collected during 1879–80 at Urambo, see E. Southon, May 1880, in "The History, Country and People of Unyamwezi," pt. 2 (manuscript), LMS 3/4/C.

82. Burton, *Zanzibar,* 2:298. See also Roberts, "Nyamwezi Trade," 61, 65–66; Francis Patrick Nolan, "Christianity in Unyamwezi 1878–1928" (PhD diss., University of Cambridge, 1977), 36; Sissons, "Economic Prosperity," 187.

83. Ward to Webb, Zanzibar, 14 June 1849; also Ward to Shepard, Zanzibar, 2 May 1849, in *New England Merchants,* ed. Bennett and Brooks, 444, 441.

84. Burton, "Lake Regions," 181; *Lake Regions,* 423–24; Gray, "Trading Expeditions," 228; Sheriff, *Slaves, Spices and Ivory,* 175–77.

85. Edmund Roberts, quoted in Gray, "Trading Expeditions," 228.

86. MacQueen, "Visit of Lief Ben Saeid," 373.

87. Tippu Tip, *Maisha,* 99 § 130, 13 § 2; Roberts, "Nyamwezi Trade," 50.

88. Diary of Richard P. Waters, 24 June 1839, in *New England Merchants,* ed. Bennett and Brooks, 211; Guillain, *Documents,* 2:380. Waters also noted that he had met "a very respectable man who has been five times far into the interior," indicating that by this time there were professional caravan leaders among the coastal traders.

89. "A Visit to Zanzibar, 1844: Michael W. Shepard's Account," in *New England Merchants,* ed. Bennett and Brooks, 263.

90. Quoted in Walter Thaddeus Brown, "A Pre-colonial History of Bagamoyo: Aspects of the Growth of an East African Coastal Town" (PhD diss., Boston University, 1971), 115. Alpers believes Swahili traders had probably traversed the continent to reach Angola by the 1780s: *Ivory and Slaves,* 161–63.

91. Krapf, *Travels,* 430.

92. François Bontinck, "La double traversée de l'Afrique par trois 'arabes' de Zanzibar (1845–1860)," *EHA* 6 (1974): 8.

93. For the full story, see Bontinck, "Double traversée" and the sources mentioned there. There is a brief discussion in Sheriff, *Slaves, Spices and Ivory,* 186–87. Said bin Habib's own account is in "Narrative of Said bin Habeeb."

94. Freeman-Grenville, *East African Coast,* 231; Alpers, "Coast," 48–49 (my italics).

95. Roberts, "Nyamwezi Trade," 51.

96. John M. Gray, "Ahmed bin Ibrahim: The First Arab to Reach Buganda," *UJ* 11, no. 1 (1947): 80–97; Gray, "Trading Expeditions"; Sheriff, *Slaves, Spices and Ivory,* 183–190 and the sources listed there.

97. Glassman deals with the post-1850s period. See "Social Rebellion," 130–139.

98. "Questions Asked of Monsieur Morice about the East Coast of Africa," in *The French at Kilwa Island,* ed. G.S.P. Freeman-Grenville (Oxford, 1965), 118–19. Possibly it is the Bisa or Nyamwezi, rather than the Yaos, who are referred to. Burton notes the distinctive "crest of hair" as an identifying feature of the Bisa. See *Lake Regions,* 375.

99. Alpers, *Ivory and Slaves,* 19. Similar proscriptions and rituals were associated with elephant hunters.

100. Alpers, *Ivory and Slaves,* 230.

101. Krapf, 14 February 1850, in *Travels,* 421; Roberts, "Nyamwezi Trade," 52n1. An Arab trader returning to the coast from Unyamwezi sometime during the early 1840s traveled in a caravan 700 strong. See Pickering, *Races,* 201.

102. Krapf, 13 February 1850, in *Travels,* 420. A slightly different version is given by Colonel Sykes, quoting Krapf's journal, in "Notes on the Possessions of the Imaun of Muskat, on the Climate and Productions of Zanzibar, and on the Prospects of African Discovery from Mombas," *JRGS* 23 (1853): 117.

103. For example, Burton, "Lake Regions," 408–411; Burton, *Lake Regions,* 237–39. Caravan organization will be dealt with in more detail in chaps. 3, 4, and 5.

104. Burton, *Lake Regions,* 300. Also quoted in Roberts, "The Nyamwezi," 128. Fundikira's namesake, Abdallah Fundikira, heard of his ancestor's journeys from his own father. Chief Abdallah Fundikira, interview, Tabora, 4 July 2000.

105. Coulbois, *Dix années,* 50; Unomah, *Mirambo of Tanzania,* 13; Norman R. Bennett, "Mirambo of the Nyamwezi," in *Studies in East African History,* ed. Norman R. Bennett (Boston, 1963), 2. Manchuelle, *Willing Migrants,* 59–63, notes that similarly, there was no stigma attached to the sons of Soninke royal families working as *laptots* (boat crews on the Senegal River) during their youth, although there would have been if they worked as infantry soldiers or as stokers.

106. Unomah, *Mirambo of Tanzania,* 14.

107. Unomah, "Economic Expansion," 86–96, 104–16, 151, 155–79. See also Sheriff, *Slaves, Spices and Ivory,* 180–81, 193–94; Chief Abdallah Fundikira, interview, Tabora, 4 July 2000. Sometimes agricultural surpluses funded the purchase of ivory and slaves and other trading ventures.

108. Nolan, "Christianity in Unyamwezi," 34; MacQueen, "Visit of Lief Ben Saeid," 373; Cooley, "Geography of N'yassi," 213; also sources mentioned in Roberts, "Nyamwezi Trade," 58, and in Kjekshus, *Ecology Control,* 119. For the introduction of donkeys into western Tanzania, see Christopher Ehret, *An African Classical Age: Eastern and Southern Africa in World History, 1000* B.C. *to A.D. 400* (Charlottesville, 1998), 64, 66, 67, 86, 136–37, 179.

109. For the origins of this tax, see Walter T. Brown, "Bagamoyo: An Historical Introduction," *TNR* 61 (1970): 72; Walter T. Brown, "The Politics of Business: Relations between Zanzibar and Bagamoyo in the Late Nineteenth Century," *AHS* 4, no. 3 (1971): 635–36; David Henry Anthony, "Culture and Society in a Town in Transition: A People's History of Dar es Salaam, 1865–1939" (PhD diss., University of Wisconsin–Madison, 1983), 33–34. A slightly different version is given in Alpers, "Coast," 49–50. Unfortunately, its abolition cannot be securely dated.

110. Freeman-Grenville, *East African Coast,* 239.

111. Burton, "Lake Regions," 58. "Deceiving" caravans refers to extortionate business practices on the arrival of upcountry caravans at the coast.

112. Glassman, "Social Rebellion," chap. 2.

113. Roberts, "Nyamwezi Trade," 67.

114. This question will be dealt with in chap. 3.

115. Cummings, Iliffe, Sheriff, and Glassman all point to a process of proletarianization. Doubters include Nolan and Koponen.

116. Amongst the Kamba of Kenya, hunting for ivory is remembered as "real hunting," to be distinguished from hunting for meat. See Edward I. Steinhart, "Elephant Hunting in 19th-Century Kenya: Kamba Society and Ecology in Transformation," *IJAHS* 33, no. 2 (2001): 338.

117. Steinhart, "Elephant Hunting in 19th-Century Kenya," 340, makes this point for the Kamba.

118. Burton, "Lake Regions," 170; Burton, *Lake Regions,* 286; Unomah, "Economic Expansion," 2–8; Nolan, "Christianity in Unyamwezi," 24–25; Kjekshus, *Ecology Control,* 43.

119. Rockel, "Safari!" chap. 4.

120. Burton, *Lake Regions,* 473.

121. Burton, *Lake Regions,* 76 (Duthumi), 175 (Ugogi), 177, 180 (Marenga Mkali), 203 (Mgunda Mkali), 210 (Ugogo), 290 (Unyamwezi), 317 (Lake Tanganyika), 473, 538.

122. John Hanning Speke, 3 December 1859, in *Journal of the Discovery of the Source of the Nile* (New York, 1864), 79–80.

123. Paul Reichard, *Deutsch-Ostafrika: Das Land und seine Bewohner* (Leipzig, 1892), 422–23.

124. As much as 20 percent of late twentieth-century African ivory exports prior to the trade ban are thought to be found ivory. Roy Bridges, "Elephants, Ivory and the History of the Ivory Trade in East Africa," in *The Exploitation of Animals in Africa,* ed. Jeffrey C. Stone (Aberdeen, 1988), 202–5.

125. Quoted in Bridges, "Elephants, Ivory and the History of the Ivory Trade," 204. See also Unomah, "Economic Expansion," 85.

126. Burton, *Lake Regions,* 538, also 472. For further details on found ivory, see Reichard, *Deutsch-Ostafrika,* 423–24.

127. Bridges, "Elephants, Ivory and the History of the Ivory Trade," 209–10.

128. Reichard, *Deutsch-Ostafrika,* 425; Unomah, "Economic Expansion," 85.

129. Burton, *Lake Regions,* 473.

130. For prohibitions on wives, see Reichard, *Deutsch-Ostafrika,* 427; A.G.O. Hodgson, "Some Notes on the Hunting Customs of the Wandamba of the Ulanga Valley, Tanganyika Territory," *Journal of the Royal Anthropological Institute of Great Britain and Ireland* 56 (1926): 61–62; Isaacman and Isaacman, *Slavery and Beyond,* 89–90.

131. Burton, *Lake Regions,* 473–74. For more on ritualized drinking before the hunt, see Reichard, *Deutsch-Ostafrika,* 428.

132. Burton, *Lake Regions,* 474.

133. Burton probably means *fundi.* See below.

134. Burton, *Lake Regions,* 474. This is probably an imaginative construction of a hunt. It is not likely that Burton actually witnessed such an event.

135. See for example, Hodgson, "Some Notes on the Hunting Customs of the Wandamba," 59. "From North-Eastern Rhodesia across Nyasaland, the southern part of Tanganyika Territory and the north of Portuguese East Africa to the coast of the Indian Ocean, the older hunters may generally be recognized by a series of cicatrisations on hands and arms, the principle of which remains the same, though the number and extent may vary considerably . . . There is a certain similarity in many of the concomitant customs and observances." See ibid. for the case of the Ndamba, and Isaacman and Isaacman, *Slavery and Beyond,* for the Chikunda.

136. In Ukerewe there was rather different trajectory. According to oral traditions specialist elephant hunting was introduced by wandering Sukuma hunters and remained firmly under the control of the *omukama,* the king, who claimed both the tusks from each elephant. Successful hunters were rewarded with cattle. See Gerald W. Hartwig, *The Art of Survival in East Africa: The Kerebe and Long-Distance Trade, 1800–1895* (New York, 1976), 68–71.

137. Unomah, "Economic Expansion," 92–93; Isaacman and Isaacman, *Slavery and Beyond,* 111.

138. Mzee Shabani Kapiga, interview, Kakola, 25 July 2000.

139. Reichard, *Deutsch-Ostafrika,* 426; Hodgson, "Some Notes on the Hunting Customs," 60–64; Roberts, "Nyamwezi Trade," 68.

140. Reichard, *Deutsch-Ostafrika,* 426–27. There is no space here to discuss the cosmological and symbolic aspects of elephant hunters' medicine (*dawa*). For details, see Reichard, *Deutsch-Ostafrika;* Hodgson, "Some Notes on the Hunting Customs"; Steinhart, "Elephant Hunting in 19th-Century Kenya," 344–46; Isaacman and Isaacman, *Slavery and Beyond,* 83–124.

141. Kamba elephant hunters also had their hunting cult, the *Waathi* society, which controlled the spiritual power believed to be inherent in gifted hunters, but also the spoils of the hunt. Steinhart, "Elephant Hunting in 19th-Century Kenya," 340, 343–46. There is no mention of such a society amongst the Ndamba or Chikunda.

142. Roberts, "Nyamwezi Trade," 68; Unomah, "Economic Expansion," 88.

143. Unomah, "Economic Expansion," 88–89. The *Yeke,* the Nyamwezi who settled in Shaba province of the Democratic Republic of the Congo in the nineteenth century, clearly took their name from the *Vbayege.* See Roberts, "Nyamwezi Trade," 68n6.

144. Unomah, "Economic Expansion," 86–88.

145. Unomah, "Economic Expansion," 8, sung by the descendents of Kapigamiti. I have slightly changed Unomah's rendering.

146. Unomah, "Economic Expansion," 89.

147. Interestingly, a different process occurred amongst the Kamba. As they were squeezed out of the ivory trade by coastal competition in the mid-nineteenth century, Kamba elephant hunting also went into decline only to be revived in the 1890s under the pressure of famine and ecological crisis. See Steinhart, "Elephant Hunting in 19th-Century Kenya," 342–43, 347. In contrast, the Nyamwezi maintained a strong position in the ivory trade, and their hunters were guaranteed a market.

CHAPTER 3: THE RISE OF THE PROFESSIONALS

1. Hans Koritschoner, "Some East African Native Songs," *TNR* 4 (October 1937): 56.

2. Roscoe, *Twenty-five Years,* 54; Andrew Roberts, "Nyamwezi Trade," 64–65, 67, 71; Nolan, "Christianity in Unyamwezi," 26–28; Philip Stigger, "The Late 19th. Century Caravan Trade and Some of Its Modern Implications: The Shinyanga Example" (unpublished paper, Simon Fraser University, n.d.), 7–8, 9, 15–17.

3. Nolan, "Christianity in Unyamwezi," 27. For a stimulating discussion of the impact of consumer demand in nineteenth-century East Africa on global economic systems, including the production of imported cloth in Salem and Bombay, see Jeremy Prestholdt, "On the Global Repercussions of East African Consumerism," *AHR* 109, no. 3 (June 2004): 755–81.

4. John Hanning Speke, "On the Commerce of Central Africa," *TBGS* 15 (1860): 144; Speke, *Journal,* 99; Grant, "Summary of Observations," 250; Burton, *Lake Regions,* 242.

5. Walter Hutley, "Mohammadanism in Central Africa: Its Influence" (manuscript paper), in Hutley to Thompson, Urambo, August 1881, LMS 4/2/D; also quoted in Bennett, *Mirambo,* 32. In 1891, Nyamwezi women were noticeably better dressed than

their Gogo neighbors, "being clothed from the breast to below the knee." Moloney, *With Captain Stairs,* 56.

6. Shorter, *Chiefship in Western Tanzania,* 136–37.

7. Mackay to Hutchinson, Uyui, 11 June 1880; Mackay to Wright, Kagei, 23 August 1880, CMS CA6/016; Roberts, "Nyamwezi Trade," 51, 71; Bennett, *Mirambo,* 32; Stigger, "Late 19th. Century Caravan Trade," 5–8. For firearms in general, see R. W. Beachey, "The Arms Trade in East Africa," *JAH* 3, no. 3 (1962): 451–67; Iliffe, *Modern History,* 51–52.

8. Stigger, "Late 19th. Century Caravan Trade," 7–8; also Roscoe, *Twenty-five Years,* 54.

9. Mackay to Wright, Mpwapwa, 14 October 1876, CMS CA6/016; Roberts, "Nyamwezi Trade," 71; Nicholas Harman, *Bwana Stokesi and His African Conquests* (London, 1986), 190. Beachey in "Arms Trade," 467, suggests that one million firearms and four million pounds of powder were imported into German and British East Africa in the period from 1885 to 1902.

10. For an interesting discussion of the relative importance of manufactured textiles (woolen goods) and guns in the calculations of migrant laborers in nineteenth-century Lesotho, see William H. Worger, *South Africa's City of Diamonds: Mine Workers and Monopoly Capitalism in Kimberley, 1867–1895* (New Haven, CT, 1987): 73–76, 83.

11. Mathias Ntabo, interview, Mayombo, 26 July 2000.

12. Chief Abdallah Fundikira, interview, Tabora, 4 July 2000; Mahmood Mohamed Sheikh, interview, Kwihara, 24 July 2000; Wilson and Felkin, *Uganda,* 1:43; Stigger, "Late 19th. Century Caravan Trade," 27–28.

13. Stigger, "Late 19th. Century Caravan Trade," 13–14, 15–17; Itandala, "History of the Babinza," 229; Koponen, *People and Production,* 124–25; Hussen Ally Kalunga, interview, Tabora, 20 July 2000; Omari Musa Kagoda, interview, Kakola, 25 July 2000. In similar fashion, Sotho migrants working at Kimberly in the 1870s invested heavily in livestock and ploughs for their farms. Worger, *South Africa's City of Diamonds,* 76.

14. Chief Abdallah Fundikira, interview, Tabora, 4 July 2000; Unomah, "Economic Expansion," 89.

15. Mahmood Mohamed Sheikh, interview, Kwihara, 24 July 2000; Per Hassing and Norman Bennett, "A Journey across Tanganyika in 1886," translated and edited extracts from the journal of Edvard Gleerup, *TNR* 58 and 59 (1962): 133.

16. Hussen Ally Kalunga, interview, Tabora, 20 July 2000; Burton, *Lake Regions,* 326, 384; Decle, *Three Years,* 319. In the documented cases the slaves were bought in Ujiji, in 1858 and 1893 respectively, and taken eastward, probably into Unyamwezi.

17. Rashid bin Hassani, "Story of Rashid bin Hassani." See also Robert Cummings, "Note on the History of Caravan Porters," 112–13; T. O. Beidelman, "The Organization and Maintenance of Caravans by the Church Missionary Society in Tanzania in the Nineteenth Century," *IJAHS* 15, no. 4 (1982): 613. For a general discussion of porter motivations, see Coquery-Vidrovitch and Lovejoy, "Workers of Trade," 17–18.

18. Chief Abdallah Fundikira, interview, Tabora, 4 July 2000; Burton, *Lake Regions,* 237; Hutley, 22 June 1878, in *Central African Diaries,* ed. Wolf, 36; Abrahams, *Peoples of Greater Unyamwezi,* 38; Unomah and Webster, "East Africa," 285; Iliffe, *Modern History,* 44.

19. Cameron, *Across Africa,* 1:183; Wilson and Felkin, *Uganda,* 1:76–77. Similar comments are in Burton, *Zanzibar,* 2:298; François Coulbois, *Dix années,* 48; Mackay to

Wright, Uyui, 25 May 1878, CMS CA6/016; Broyon to McGregor, Zanzibar, 1 October 1879, LMS 2/3/D.

20. Nolan, "Christianity in Unyamwezi," 36, 201–2; Koponen, *People and Production,* 114, 116. Stigger, "Late 19th. Century Caravan Trade," 11–17, has accounts of small-scale trade in northern Unyamwezi and Usukuma leading to participation in caravans to the coast. The Nyamwezi and Sukuma share similar institutions and cultures.

21. Sheriff, *Slaves, Spices and Ivory,* 174; Glassman, "Social Rebellion,"104; Speke, *Journal,* 350. Mackay reported meeting "many small caravans" bound for the coast in mid-1876. Mackay to Wright, Zanzibar, 12 December 1876, CMS CA6/016.

22. Robert Pickering Ashe, *Chronicles of Uganda* (1894; repr., London, 1971), 22.

23. Berniger (?) to Governor, Mpwapwa, 1 June 1893, TNA G1/35.

24. Dodgshun, 2–8 May and 19 June 1878, in *From Zanzibar,* ed. Bennett, 64, 73; Wilson and Felkin, *Uganda,* 1:42; Graf von Schweinitz, "Das Trägerpersonal der Karawanen," *DK* 2 (1894): 19; Nolan, "Christianity in Unyamwezi," 36, 201–2.

25. Alfred R. Tucker, *Eighteen Years in Uganda and East Africa* (London, 1911), 57.

26. Burton, *Lake Regions,* 111–12; Burton, "Lake Regions," 411–12; Cummings, "Note on the History of Caravan Porters," 114.

27. Chief Abdallah Fundikira, interview, Tabora, 4 July 2000.

28. Southon to Thompson, Urambo, 17 April 1882, LMS 4/4/B; Griffith to Thompson, Uguha, 1 July 1882, LMS 4/4/C; Copplestone to Thompson, Uyui, 2 September 1882, LMS 4/5/A; Roberts, "Nyamwezi Trade," 65n5. Mwana Kapisi's caravan got only as far as Uyui. For more on Mwana Seria, see Stokes to Lang, Uyui, 18 December 1884, CMS G3A6/02.

29. Anne Luck, *Charles Stokes in Africa* (Nairobi, 1972), 59, 63–65, 68, 85, 157–58, 163, 203; Harman, *Bwana Stokesi,* 23, 34–47, 54–56; C.F. Holmes, "A History of the Bakwimba of Usukuma, Tanzania, from Earliest Times to 1945" (PhD diss., Boston University, 1969), 160–62; for "a land of porters," see Blackburn to Lang, Uyui, 2 July 1885, CMS G3A6/02. Stokes, thankful to be on safari, wrote soon after his first wife's death that he was "quite at home" with his "wild boys." Stokes to Lang, Kulehi camp, 26 July 1884, CMS G3A6/01; Luck, *Charles Stokes,* 59.

30. Tucker, *Eighteen Years,* 26–27. Tucker implies that it was Stokes who had created this system. In fact, this ordered arrangement was typical of most caravans, whether Nyamwezi, Sukuma, or coastal. The cloth noticed by Tucker was probably a portion of the porters' advance wages.

31. I use the Swahiliized *wanyampara.* In the original political context in Usukuma, for example, the correct term is *banamhala.*

32. C.T. Wilson, "A Journey from Kagei to Tabora and Back," *PRGS,* n.s., 2 (1880): 619; also quoted in Achim Gottberg, *Unyamwesi. Quellensammlung und Geschichte* (Berlin, 1971), 120.

33. C.F. Holmes and R.A. Austen, "The Pre-colonial Sukuma," *JWH,* 14, no. 2 (1972): 384, state that a *banamhala* was "an advisory council of village elders" subject to the authority of *ng'wanangwa,* who was subject to the *mtemi.*

34. Copplestone to Hutchinson, Uyui, 22 March 1881, CMS G3A6/01; Tabora Stationschef, "Beantwortung des Fragebogens" (1899), in Gottberg, *Unyamwesi,* 242–24. The author wrote that the position was only open to senior males, and that a *mnyampara* had "several villages under him." In Ukimbu, the elders making up the council of the chiefdoms were known as *ivanyaampala.* In Usumbwa, they were *banyampara.* See Shorter, *Chiefship in Western Tanzania,* 24, 120–22.

35. Hussen Ally Kalunga, interview, Tabora, 20 July 2000.

36. Raum, "German East Africa," 169. See a similar comment on famous Sherpa porters in Sheryl B. Ortner, *Life and Death on Mt. Everest: Sherpas and Himalayan Mountaineering* (Princeton, NJ, 1999), 14.

37. Speke, *Journal*, 125; Nolan, "Christianity in Unyamwezi,"53; Sheriff, *Slaves, Spices and Ivory*, 181. For an overview of Nyamwezi *waganga* and their work, see Wilhelm Blohm, *Die Nyamwezi* (Hamburg, 1931) 1:165–72.

38. F.J. Lake, "The Organisation of Ancestor Worship," 1–2, Nzega District Book, Tanzania National Archives, Dar es Salaam. For discussion of a decorated gourd, see chap. 6. For religious ritual on caravans working the northern routes, see Glassman, "Social Rebellion," 138.

39. Burton, *Lake Regions*, 509–10, 241. Rituals of the road are discussed further in chaps. 4 and 7.

40. Also *kilangozi* or *kiongozi*. Compare with *–ongoza*, the Kiswahili word meaning to drive forward, carry on vigorously, lead.

41. Juma S. Nkumbo, interview, Uyui Ward, 21 July 2000. One missionary, perhaps unaware of customary practices, described his *kirangozi* as a "Wanyamwezi chief," while another believed he was usually chosen from among the *wanyampara*. Southon to Whitehouse, Lagula, Ugogo, 6 August 1879, LMS 2/1/D; Wilson and Felkin, *Uganda*, 1:43.

42. Juma S. Nkumbo, interview, Uyui Ward, 21 July 2000.

43. Burton, *Lake Regions*, 112, 234; Livingstone, *Last Journals*, 135; J.F. Elton, *Travels and Researches among the Lakes and Mountains of Eastern and Central Africa*, ed. H.B. Cotterill (1879; repr., London, 1968), 372; Mtoro bin Mwinyi Bakari, *Customs of the Swahili*, 160; Mtoro bin Mwinyi Bakari in *Swahili Prose Texts*, Harries, 183.

44. Burton, *Lake Regions*, 112; Wilson and Felkin, *Uganda*, 1:43; A.J. Swann, *Fighting the Slave Hunters in Central Africa* (1910; repr., London, 1969), 41. For the election of a *kirangozi*, see Burton, *Lake Regions*, 431–32. For a somewhat different account of the functions of *virangozi* in coastal caravans, see Glassman, "Social Rebellion," 93.

45. Speke, *Journal*, 50.

46. Unomah, "Economic Expansion", 262–63.

47. Burton, *Lake Regions*, 240.

48. See "Note on the History," 113 and especially n24. John Iliffe takes a similar view: "Some porters were lifetime professionals, but most were occasional migrants." See "Wage Labour and Urbanisation," 279. Sheriff also uses the label "professional porters." Sheriff, *Slaves, Spices and Ivory*, 103.

49. Roberts, "Nyamwezi Trade," 65; Nolan, "Christianity in Unyamwezi," 72–73.

50. Koponen, *People and Production*, 113–14.

51. Iliffe, *Modern History*, 45, 77; Terence O. Ranger, "The Movement of Ideas, 1850–1939," in *History of Tanzania*, ed. Kimambo and Temu, 161–88.

52. Burton, *Lake Regions*, 299. Speke agreed, describing the Nyamwezi as "professionally voluntary porters." See James MacQueen, "Observations on the Geography of Central Africa," *PRGS* 3, no. 4 (1859): 210.

53. Swann, *Fighting the Slave Hunters*, 58; A.W. Dodgshun, "Central African Expedition: Rev. A.W. Dodgshun. Lists of Requirements" (manuscript), 11, LMS 2/1/B. Sometimes the merits of specialists were less directly stated. In 1861 Speke was told by Musa Mzuri, an Indian trader at Kazeh, that using his own slaves as porters was "more trouble than profit"; hired porters were "more safe." Speke, *Journal*, 108.

54. *ZEAG,* 26 April 1893, 10 (my italics), reprinted from the *Times.* Holmwood's assertion that slave status had little impact on the professionalism of caravan porters is borne out by the case of slave porters in the Merina kingdom. See Gwyn Campbell, "Labour and the Transport Problem in Imperial Madagascar, 1810–1895," *JAH* 21 (1980): 341–56.

55. Rediker, *Between the Devil,* 94, 11–12.

56. May French-Sheldon, *Sultan to Sultan* (London, 1892), 121; Karl Weule, *Native Life in East Africa,* trans. Alice Werner (1909; Westport, CT, 1970), 40. Compare with porters in the Merina Empire, who, according to Campbell, "developed a characteristic tumescent lump . . . across their shoulders. "Labour and the Transport Problem," 349.

57. C.W. Hobley, *Kenya: From Chartered Company to Crown Colony* (London, 1929), 200.

58. Speke, *Journal,* 128. *Nguruwe* means "pig" in Kiswahili and thus is a nickname.

59. Speke, *Journal,* 162–63.

60. Mackay to Wright, Zanzibar, 12 December 1876, CMS CA6/016.

61. Juma S. Nkumbo, interview, Uyui Ward, 21 July 2000.

62. Unomah, "Economic Expansion," 399. Unomah also gives another slightly different version of Mwana Kakulukulu's story, 89n23. See 386–89, 391, 399, for other examples.

63. Abrahams, *Peoples of Greater Unyamwezi,* 39.

64. Christie, *Cholera Epidemics,* 222; French-Sheldon, *Sultan to Sultan,* 105; Oscar Baumann, *Durch Massailand zur Nilquelle* (Berlin, 1894), 4–5.

65. Moloney, *With Captain Stairs,* 277.

66. A.B. Lloyd, *In Dwarf Land and Cannibal Country* (London, 1900), 35.

67. *Between the Devil,* 293–94 passim.

68. Sunseri, *Vilimani,* 59.

69. Beidelman, "Organization and Maintenance of Caravans," 611–12.

70. *Ulaya* means "Europe."

71. Wookey to Whitehouse, Maguhika, 23 June 1880; Southon to Whitehouse, Urambo, 6 July 1880, LMS 3/2/B. For short accounts of the careers of other caravan headmen in East Africa, see *Victorian Explorer,* ed. Konczacki, 192; Hobley, *Kenya,* 200–1; Luck, *Charles Stokes,* 157. There is a list of headmen who followed Stokes "every year" in Plunket to Salisbury, Brussels, 15 December 1895, enclosure no. 108, *HCPP,* C8276, "Africa" 8, mf.102.501.

72. Moloney, *With Captain Stairs,* 264. See the "Who's Who of Africans" in Simpson, *Dark Companions,* 191–98, for a list of many of the better-known porters and headmen who worked for European travelers in East Africa.

73. Burton, *Lake Regions,* 112; Cummings, "Note on the History of Caravan Porters," 113. Just as "old salts" were valued for their experience and as keepers of customary lore. Rediker, *Between the Devil,* 156–58.

74. W.G. Stairs, "Shut up in the African Forest," *NC* 29, no. 167 (1891): 55.

75. Stairs, 10 August 1891, in *Victorian Explorer,* ed. Konczacki, 206.

76. Roberts, "Nyamwezi Trade," 61; Koponen, *People and Production,* 113.

77. Pruen, *Arab and the African,* 175.

78. Weule, *Native Life,* 373–75; 9 (map).

79. For multilingualism at the commercial center of Mazinde in northeast Tanzania, see Steven Feierman, *The Shambaa Kingdom: A History* (Madison, 1974), 199–200.

80. Grant, an experienced hunter, admired the resourcefulness and hunting and survival skills of his and Speke's Nyamwezi porters. James Augustus Grant, *A Walk across Africa* (Edinburgh, 1864), 42–43; also Stanley, *How I Found Livingstone,* 261.

81. Very little has been published on the important topic of *utani,* but considerable research was carried out at the University of Dar es Salaam by Stephen A. Lucas and his students during the 1970s. See chap. 7.

82. Henry Morton Stanley, *Through the Dark Continent* (1899; repr., Toronto, 1988), 1:41; Weule, *Native Life,* 40.

83. Moloney, *With Captain Stairs,* 223. There is further praise of "the Zanzibari as a marvel of stamina," 263–64.

84. Thomson, *To the Central African Lakes,* 1:201–2.

85. Thomson quoted by W. P. Johnson in an extract from *The Nyasa News,* reprinted in the *ZEAG,* 31 January 1894, 9–10; Simpson, *Dark Companions,* 145; Johnson, *ZEAG,* 31 January 1894, 10.

86. Ortner, *Life and Death,* 42–44.

87. Moloney, *With Captain Stairs,* 159. See Parke, *My Personal Experiences,* 503, for similar comments.

88. Quoted in Ortner, *Life and Death,* 43.

89. Ortner, *Life and Death,* 44.

90. Southon to Whitehouse, Urambo, 24 December 1879, LMS 2/3/B.

91. Muxworthy, representing Boustead, Ridley and Company, to Thompson, Zanzibar, 5 April 1881, LMS 4/3/B; Muxworthy to Thompson, Zanzibar, 2 June 1881; Muxworthy to Thompson, Zanzibar, 22 September 1881; Muxworthy to Thompson, Zanzibar, 17 November 1881, all LMS 4/3/C; Hutley, 13 November 1880, in *Central African Diaries,* ed. Wolf, 226.

92. Southon, "History, Country and People of Unyamwezi," pt. 5, 10.

93. Hutley, 17 September 1881, in *Central African Diaries,* ed. Wolf, 282; Southon to Whitehouse, Ujiji, 29 September 1879, LMS 2/2/B.

94. Tucker, *Eighteen Years,* 134–35.

95. Hore to Thompson, SS *Java,* 20 January 1881, LMS 4/1/A; Beidelman, "Organization and Maintenance of Caravans," 610.

96. Livingstone, 10 December 1870, in *Last Journals,* 348; Harries, *Swahili Prose Texts,* 180; Roberts, "Nyamwezi Trade," 58 and sources there; Nolan, "Christianity in Unyamwezi," 201; Stigger, "Late 19th. Century Caravan Trade," 10.

97. Southon, "History, Country and People of Unyamwezi," pt. 5, 8. The eight tusks in question averaged 78 pounds in weight. Five were over 90 pounds, and the other three were below 60 pounds. There are many examples in the literature of porters making long journeys carrying such loads.

98. Livingstone, 23 April 1872, in *Last Journals,* 418.For other examples of porters of exceptional strength, see Burton, *Lake Regions,* 112; Lloyd, *In Dwarf Land,* 37; Marius Fortie, *Black and Beautiful* (London, 1938), 57–58.

99. Victor Giraud, *Les lacs de l'Afrique Equatoriale* (Paris, 1890), 43. For other headmen and porters with Congo experience, see Harry H. Johnston, *The Kilima-Njaro Expedition* (London, 1886), 60–63. Petro Kapunga of Ndono in Unyamwezi, one of Nolan's informants, who was interviewed in the 1970s, kept letters of recommendation from caravan leaders he had worked for at the turn of the century. Nolan, "Christianity in Unyamwezi,"15.

100. Pruen, *Arab and the African,* 192.

101. Rediker, *Between the Devil.*

102. Burton, *Lake Regions,* 198; also ibid., 236.

103. C. de Vienne, "De Zanzibar à l'Oukami," *BSG* 6, no. 4 (1872): 359.

104. Speke, *Journal,* 45, 64, 75. In contrast, the less-experienced Grant wrote that they "had no claim to honour or honesty—113 of them, although handsomely paid, deserted

us, carrying away a considerable quantity of property." Grant, *Walk across Africa,* 43. The large number of desertions was mainly due to the food shortage in Ugogo and Mgunda Mkali. See Speke, *Journal,* 73–95; Grant, *Walk across Africa,* 32.

105. Murphy to Kirk, Bagamoyo Camp, 19 April 1873, VLC 3/4 RGS; Decle, *Three Years,* 355. For other examples, see Burton, *Lake Regions,* 195–96, 384; Elton, 27 November 1877, in *Travels,* 370.

106. Livingstone to Lord Stanley, Bamberre, Manyema country, 15 November 1870, in *HCPP,* C.598, m.f. 78.621; Bennett, *Stanley's Despatches,* 5–6; Henry to Wright, Mpwapwa, 1 October 1878, CMS CA6/012. See also Stairs, 31 July 1891, in *Victorian Explorer,* ed. Konczacki, 201. Reichard generally belittled the Nyamwezi but in some respects praised their scrupulousness: "Porters use only the part of their wages advanced to them if they are completely sure that they are to go on the journey." Reichard, "Wanjamuesei," 308.

107. Cameron, *Across Africa,* 1:135.

108. Southon to Whitehouse, Lagula, Ugogo, 6 August 1879, LMS 2/1/D; Thomson, *To the Central African Lakes,* 2:205–6. See also Pruen, *Arab and the African,* 97–98, for a lengthy testimonial of the honesty of Zanzibari porters. Sir Philip Mitchell recorded similar experiences in British East Africa: of 10,000 odd loads carried each year from 1905 to 1908, including trade goods, such as cloth, beads, paraffin, and knives, virtually none were lost for any reason, and pilfering was hardly known. See Lamden, "Some Aspects of Porterage," 157. Hobley describes the code of honor of coast porters that he observed during the 1890s in terms of ethics: the porter "must never abandon his load . . . travellers of the older generation . . . could recall incidents in which an exhausted porter has stuck to his load even to the point of death, when he only had to abandon it to gain certain safety. It was considered a disgraceful thing to pilfer from a load during a march, and it rarely occurred. No mean virtues these! As all over Africa, food and water must, if need arose, be shared with a comrade." Hobley, *Kenya,* 199.

109. Cameron, *Across Africa,* 1:59–60. This raises the question of the extension of a code of honor to ideas about justice. This will be examined in chap. 6.

110. For discussion, see chap. 4.

111. Burton, *Lake Regions,* 157, 450–51.

112. Thomson, *To the Central African Lakes,* 1:195–96.

113. See for examples, Elton, *Travels,* 324–25, 331 (Chungu or Bena, north of Lake Malawi); Moir, "Eastern Route," 107 (Lake Malawi-Tanganyika corridor); Johnston, *Kilima-Njaro,* 42–43, 51–52 (Nyika and Rabai); Last, *Polyglotta Africana Orientalis,* 18 (Sangu); Alison Redmayne, "Mkwawa and the Hehe Wars," *JAH* 9, no. 3 (1968): 428 (Hehe); Konczacki, *Victorian Explorer,* 201 (Sagara); Moloney, *With Captain Stairs,* 131–32 (Tabwa?).

114. Elton, *Travels,* 396.

115. Johnson, *My African Reminiscences,* 100; also Weule, *Native Life,* 393, for the difference between Yao and Makonde carriers. For comments on the aid to morale and discipline provided by shared jokes, see Hore, *Tanganyika,* 35.

116. For a fuller discussion of the labor market in the context of the fortunes of the Nyamwezi *vbandevba,* in which issue is taken with Sheriff's characterization of Unyamwezi as a labor reserve, "a foretaste of the colonial situation," see Stephen J. Rockel, "'A Nation of Porters': The Nyamwezi and the Labour Market in Nineteenth-Century Tanzania," *JAH* 41, no. 2 (2000): 185–94.

117. Schweinitz, "Trägerpersonal," 19.

118. Burton, *Lake Regions,* 235; Unomah, "Economic Expansion," 77.

119. Burton, *Lake Regions,* 153, 186. No doubt many members of these caravans were independent traders who had joined the larger group for security.

120. Tippu Tip, *Maisha,* 53 § 68, 75 § 100, 77 § 103; Stanley, *Through the Dark Continent,* 2:100 passim; Cameron, *Across Africa,* 1:299. In this region the opportunities for plunder and trade probably outweighed wage incentives.

121. Sheriff, *Slaves, Spices and Ivory,* Appendix C, "Ivory Imports into the United Kingdom, 1792–1875," 257–58.

122. Burton, *Lake Regions,* 237; Glassman, "Social Rebellion," 92–93.

123. Roger Price, *Report of the Rev. R. Price of His Visit to Zanzibar and the Coast of Eastern Africa* (London, 1876), 23, 39; Hutley, 5 and 30 May, and 16, 17, 18, and 24 June, in *Central African Diaries,* ed. Wolf, 25–26, 30, 34, 35, 37. The first of these was not an ivory caravan but one of work seekers. In another entry, Hutley notes that near Mpwapwa, "several caravans . . . passed during the day, some going in and others coming out." There is no indication whether these were Nyamwezi or Swahili/Arab caravans. Hutley, 7 April 1878, in *Central African Diaries,* ed. Wolf, 19–20. See also Nolan, "Christianity in Unyamwezi," 59.

124. In 1884–85 during the severe famine in eastern and central regions of Tanzania (Unguru, Uzigua, Ukaguru, Usagara, and Ugogo), parties of Nyamwezi carried surplus grain to Ugogo, hundreds of miles to the east through the Mgunda Mkali, while Gogo traveled in the opposite direction to seek relief in Unyanyembe. See Hore, *To Lake Tanganyika,* 120, 125, 127.

125. For detailed discussion see Stephen J. Rockel, "Safari! The East African Caravan Trade in the Nineteenth Century" (unpublished manuscript), chap. 4.

126. Rochus Schmidt, *Geschichte de Araberaufstandes in Ost-Afrika* (Frankfurt an der Oder, 1892), 29, 78; Brown, "Pre-colonial History," 282; Brown, "Bagamoyo: An Historical Introduction," 82. Brown's source is H. F. von Behr, *Kriegsbilder aus dem Araberaufstand in Deutsch Ostafrika* (Leipzig, 1891), 138. See also Glassman, *Feasts and Riot,* 203, 213–14.

127. A. J. Mounteney Jephson, 17 October 1889, in *The Diary of A. J. Mounteney Jephson: Emin Pasha Relief Expedition 1887–1889,* ed. Dorothy Middleton (Cambridge, 1969), 409, Carl Peters, *New Light on Dark Africa,* trans. H. W. Dulcken (London, 1891) 531, 533, 535.

128. Moloney, *With Captain Stairs,* 57.

129. Ashe, *Chronicles,* 439. See also Stuhlmann, *Mit Emin Pascha,* 758, for an account of a large Sukuma caravan taking many cattle and "thousands of goats" to the coast.

130. William G. Stairs, 29 July 1891, in "De Zanzibar au Katanga: Journal de Capitaine Stairs (1890–1891)," *CI* 2 (1893): 47; Stairs, 31 July 1891, in *Victorian Explorer,* ed. Konczacki, 201–2; Schweinitz, "Trägerpersonal," 19; and the discussion in Brown, "Pre-colonial History," 282–86; Brown, "Bagamoyo: An Historical Introduction," 82.

131. See Stairs, 2 July, 8 July, 9 July, and 1 August 1891, in *Victorian Explorer,* ed. Konczacki, 193, 197, 190, 202; Moloney, *With Captain Stairs,* 36. For the thaler, see chap. 7.

132. Sheriff, *Slaves, Spices and Ivory,* 247, 182.

133. Bennett, *From Zanzibar,* 57n; Cooper, *From Slaves to Squatters,* 52.

134. Muxworthy to Thompson, Zanzibar, 14 July 1882, LMS 4/5/D.

135. Hutley, 7 March 1879, in *Central African Diaries,* ed. Wolf, 86.

136. White Fathers, *A l'assaut des pays nègres,* 52–53; Dodgshun, 26 January 1878, in *From Zanzibar,* ed. Bennett, 56–57,

137. Joseph Thomson, *Through Masai Land* (1885; repr., London, 1968), 23. See also Stokes to Lang, Zanzibar, 1 March 1883, CMS G3A6/01; Hore to Thompson, Ujiji, 10 February 1885, LMS 6/1/A; Kathryn Barrett-Gaines, "Travel Writing, Experiences, and Silences: What Is Left out of European Travelers' Accounts: The Case of Richard D. Mohun," *HIA* 24 (1997): 58. For similar comments referring to various recruitment centers, see Stanley, *How I Found Livingstone,* 49; Dodgshun, 13 May 1878, in *From Zanzibar,* ed. Bennett, 67–68; Mackay to Wright (?), Uzigua, 9 December 1877, CMS CA6/016; O'Flaherty to Hutchinson, Mpwapwa, 20 October 1880, CMS G3A6/01; Hore to Thompson, Zanzibar, 23 June 1882, LMS 4/4/C; Hore to Thompson, LMS Camp, Makwui, 17 July 1882, LMS 4/4/D; Hutley, 21 June 1881, in *Central African Diaries,* ed. Wolf, 270.

138. See Stairs, 13 June 1891, in *Victorian Explorer,* ed. Konczacki, 188; French-Sheldon, *Sultan to Sultan,* 85. The shortage of porters at Zanzibar reflects the general labor market for porters at the coast, and the demand for both Waungwana and Nyamwezi.

139. Dodgshun, 17 August 1878, in *From Zanzibar,* ed. Bennett, 79. See also Parke, 23 February 1887, in *My Personal Experiences,* 18, for Zanzibar: "The place swarms with enormous numbers of loafers who are anxious to find employment as carriers, &c."

140. Dodgshun, 11 August 1878, in *From Zanzibar,* ed. Bennett, 77, Beidelman, "Organization and Maintenance of Caravans," 610.

141. There is still no detailed account of Indian capital on the coast during the nineteenth century. For an introduction, see Gervase Clarence-Smith, "Indian Business Communities in the Western Indian Ocean in the Nineteenth Century," *The Indian Ocean Review* 2, no. 4 (1989): 18–21. For earlier times, see Edward A. Alpers, "Gujarat and the Trade of East Africa c. 1500–1800," *IJAHS* 9, no. 1 (1976): 22–44. For Zanzibar, see Sheriff, *Slaves, Spices and Ivory,* 82–87; 202–8. Martha Spencer Honey, "A History of Indian Merchant Capital and Class Formation in Tanganyika c. 1840–1940" (PhD thesis, University of Dar es Salaam, 1982) is disappointing on this period, but see 5, 102–4; also Robert G. Gregory, *South Asians in East Africa: An Economic and Social History 1890–1980* (Boulder, CO, 1993), 44–45; D.A. Seidenberg, *Merchant Adventurers: The World of East African Asians 1750–1985* (New Delhi, 1996).

142. Burton, *Lake Regions,* 26; Speke, *Journal,* 41; Brown, "Pre-colonial History," 262–63, 158; Cameron to Frere (?) Shamaba Gonera, 18 March 1873, VLC /2/14; Murphy to Kirk, Bagamoyo, 19 April 1873, VLC 3/4, RGS.

143. Hore, *To Lake Tanganyika,* 63–64; Henry to Wright, Zanzibar, 25 July 1878, CMS CA6/012; Livingstone, 25 March 1866, in *Last Journals,* 26. See Wilson and Felkin, *Uganda,* 1:29–30, for an unnamed "Hindu" recruiter at Bagamoyo, and A.M. Mackay, 3 January 1877, in diary, CMS CA6/016 (unnamed "Hindi" in Tanga).

144. Short accounts are John A.P. Kieran, "The Holy Ghost Fathers in East Africa 1863–1914" (PhD thesis, University of London, 1966), 355–56; A.T. Matson, "Sewa Haji: A Note," *TNR* 65 (March 1966): 91–94. A more-detailed biography is in Brown, "Pre-colonial History," 185–99.

145. Stanley, *How I Found Livingstone,* 49, 51–55; Bennett, *Stanley's Despatches,* 11–12; Simpson, *Dark Companions,* 76; Muxworthy to Hore, Zanzibar, 17 November 1879, LMS 2/3/D; Muxworthy to Southon, Zanzibar, 10 December 1879, LMS 2/3/D; Muxworthy to Hore, Zanzibar, 13 October 1880, LMS 3/4/E; Muxworthy to Thompson, Zanzibar, 14 July 1882, LMS 4/5/D; Hore to Thompson, LMS Camp, Makwui, 17 July 1882, LMS 4/4/D; Brown, "Pre-colonial History," 186.

146. Bennett, *Mirambo,* 150; Bennett, *Arab versus European,* 110–11.

147. Baumann, *Durch Massailand,* 3. There is evidence, however, that Sewa was still heavily involved in trade in the Lake Victoria region. See Brown, "Pre-colonial History," 190–91.

148. Sunseri, *Vilimani,* 32.

149. Kieran, "Holy Ghost Fathers," 355; Glassman, "Social Rebellion," 95; Glassman, *Feasts and Riot,* 60; Brown, "Pre-colonial History," 189.

150. See Glassman, "Social Rebellion," 94–97, for debt relations at Bagamoyo. Glassman states that by the late 1880s, Sewa Haji was "skimming off half the cash advance typically given to Nyamwezi porters." He also suggests that "free Nyamwezi porters thus gave up to Sewa Haji the same proportion of their wages as slave-porters gave to their masters." But the wage subject to deduction was only the advance wage in the case of free Nyamwezi porters, not all as it was for slave porters' wages. For the latter case, see Rashid bin Hassani, "Story of Rashid bin Hassani," 100, and for the northern routes, Glassman, "Social Rebellion," 132.

151. Baumann, *Durch Massailand,* 3–4. The difference between the two rates represents Sewa Haji's costs and profit. For rupees and other currencies, see chap. 7.

152. "Copy of the Agreement between the Indian Merchant Siwa Haji and Dr. Hans Meyer [concerning] the Engagement of a Caravan," in *Across East African Glaciers: An Account of the First Ascent of Kilimanjaro,* by Hans Meyer, trans. E.H.S. Calder (London, 1891), 345–46. In 1878 Indian recruiters charged between MT$8 and MT$12 per porter supplied. See AIA, *Rapports sur les marches de la première expédition* (Brussels-Etterbeek, Belgium, 1879), 51–52, where Cambier outlines a contract similar to that made between Meyer and Sewa Haji.

153. Sunseri, *Vilimani,* 56.

154. Brown, "Pre-colonial History," 186–87. Stokes accused him of cheating his porters. Stokes to Lang, Uyui, 18 December 1884, CMS G3A6/02. But a few years later, Stokes himself was making business deals with Sewa Haji. See Matson, "Sewa Haji," 91.

155. Friedrich Kallenberg, *Auf dem Kriegspfad gegen die Massai: Eine Frühlings-Fahrt nach Deutsch-Ostafrika* (Munich, 1892), 45. Thanks to Harald Sippel for the reference. There was no such provision in the contract with Meyer, who routinely had his porters whipped.

156. Kieran, "Holy Ghost Fathers," 356; Brown, "Pre-colonial History," 193.

157. Quoted in Brown, "Pre-colonial History," 197.

158. For a fictional account in which pawnship serves as a "recruitment" mechanism, see Abdulrazak Gurnah, *Paradise* (London, 1994).

159. Mtoro bin Mwinyi Bakari, *Customs of the Swahili,* 154. For customary dues (*ada*) paid to *majumbe,* see Glassman, *Feasts and Riot,* 57, 60, 63–64, 149, 155, 193.

160. Speke, "On the Commerce," 141; Speke, 23 October 1860, in *Journal,* 62; Burton, "Lake Regions," 57, 80; *Lake Regions,* 82, 119–20, 236. For activities of couriers in the Kilwa Kivinje area and touts in Uzigua, see Horne, "Mode of Production," 156; James L. Giblin, *The Politics of Environmental Control in Northeastern Tanzania, 1840–1940* (Philadelphia, 1992), 46–48.

161. Southon to Whitehouse, Urambo, 18 December 1879, LMS 2/3/A. See also Cameron, *Across Africa,* 1:11; Bennett, *Stanley's Despatches,* 158–59; Last to Whiting, Mamboya, 4 October 1881, Ashe to Lang, Msalala, 10 February 1883, CMS G3A6/01; Muxworthy to Thompson, Zanzibar, 24 May 1882, LMS 4/5/D; Beidelman, "Organization and Maintenance of Caravans," 610; Sunseri, *Vilimani,* 59. From his experience in the

1890s, Hobley wrote: "Having selected his principal *Mniapara* [*mnyampara*], the leader, if wise, left the selection of the junior headman in his hands, and each of the juniors then collected his own squad of porters, subject to the approval of his chief." Hobley, *Kenya,* 198. A similar system operated for the recruitment of Sherpa porters during the early days of European mountaineering in Nepal. See Ortner, *Life and Death,* 13.

162. "Men Engaged for Masai Caravan," September 1888, notebook entitled "Stanley's Expedition," ZM.

163. Frederick Cooper, *On the African Waterfront* (New Haven, CT, 1987), 30, 36–40. A porter list including only the headman's name plus the number of men in his gang is in MacKenzie to Jackson, 10 November 1888, MP, box 63, IBEAC file 1A, 1888–89. See also Rockel, "Relocating Labor," 448. Sunseri discusses other recruitment mechanisms during the German period in *Vilimani,* 60.

164. Tucker, *Eighteen Years,* 26–27; Lloyd, *In Dwarf Land,* 34.

165. Baumann, *Durch Massailand,* 7; Schweinitz, "Trägerpersonal," 19.

166. Smith, Mackenzie and Company. *The History of Smith, Mackenzie and Company, Ltd.* (London, 1938), 27; Stephanie Jones, *Two Centuries of Overseas Trading: The Origins and Growth of the Inchcape Group* (Basingstoke, UK, 1986), 113, 128; Moloney, *With Captain Stairs,* 22. For Boustead, Ridley and Company, see Hore to Thompson, Zanzibar, 23 June 1882, LMS 4/4/C.

167. Rashid bin Hassani, "Story of Rashid bin Hassani," 99–100.

168. Especially at Bagamoyo and Saadani, for example, Baxter to Lang, Zanzibar, 4 August 1884, CMS G3A6/O1.

169. The editors of the *Zanzibar Gazette* included the information in the edition of 21 November 1894 as part of a rebuttal to criticism from the London paper the *Freeman* on the handling of the slave trade by the protectorate government.

170. See pages 218–19, below.

171. Burton, *Lake Regions,* 184; François Bontinck, trans. and ed., *L'autobiographie de Hamed ben Mohammed el-Murjebi Tippo Tip (ca. 1840–1905)* (Brussels, 1974), 22, 41. Tippu Tip said, "Whatever he [his father] wanted in and around Tabora he got . . . at this time he was as though chief in the Nyamwezi manner, having much property and many followers." Tippu Tip, *Maisha,* 13 § 2.

172. Norman R. Bennett, "The Arab Impact," in *Zamani: A Survey of East African History,* ed. Bethwell A. Ogot (Nairobi, 1973), 218; Norman R. Bennett, "Isike, *Ntemi* of Unyanyembe," in *African Dimensions,* ed. Mark Karp (Boston, 1975), 61; Unomah, "Economic Expansion," chap. 6, esp. 286–88; Nolan, "Christianity in Unyamwezi," 58–59; A.J. Temu, "Tanzanian Societies and Colonial Invasion 1875–1907," in *Tanzania,* ed. Kaniki, 105.

173. A translation of the "contract" is in Unomah, "Economic Expansion," 357. In an earlier treaty signed on 2 October 1892, Isike committed himself to cancelling the ban on Nyanyembe porters joining German caravans. The text is in Gottberg, *Unyamwesi,* 351. See also Raum, "German East Africa," 176–77; Temu, "Tanzanian Societies," 107.

174. Bennett, *Mirambo,* 83, 87, 152; White Fathers, *A l'assaut des pays nègres,* 206; Jephson, September 1889, in *Diary,* 399–400, 406.

175. Livingstone, 7 July 1866, in *Last Journals,* 69 (Yao); Elton, *Travels,* 320, 323–24 ("Wachungu," north end of Lake Malawi), 326–28, 355 (Chief Merere of the Sangu); Selim bin Abakari, "Meine Reise nach dem Nyassa," in *Schilderungen der Suaheli,* ed. Velten, 91 (Merere); Fortie, *Black and Beautiful,* 65, 100 (Chief Masanja of the Sukuma).

176. Aylward Shorter, "The Kimbu," in *Tanzania Before 1900,* ed. Roberts, 109.

177. Coquery-Vidrovitch and Lovejoy, "Workers of Trade," 12.

178. Hutley, 28 June 1881, in *Central African Diaries,* ed. Wolf, 272; Decle, *Three Years,* 309.

179. Hutley, 21 June 1881, in *Central African Diaries,* ed. Wolf, 270.

180. Stanley, *Through the Dark Continent,* 2:88–89; Coulbois, *Dix années,* 15; Hassing and Bennett, "Journey across Tanganyika,"129, 132; Wilhelm Junker, *Travels in Africa during the Years 1882–1886* (1892; repr., London, 1971), 559–62.

CHAPTER 4: ON SAFARI: THE CULTURE OF WORK

1. Fortie, *Black and Beautiful,* 29.

2. "Song of Porters," file 2, African songs, Hans Cory Collection, Africana Library, University of Dar es Salaam.

3. Selemani bin Mwenye Chande on his journey in 1891, in Harries, *Swahili Prose Texts,* 259. The Swahili and German versions are in "Safari Yangu Ya Barra Afrika," in *Safari za Wasuaheli,* ed. Velten, 49; "Meine Reise ins innere Ostafrikas bis zum Tanganyika," in *Schilderungen der Suaheli,* ed. and trans. Velten, 54–55.

4. W. E. Taylor, *African Aphorisms or Saws from Swahili-Land* (1891; repr., London, 1924), 70.

5. Ranger, "Movement of Ideas," 161–88; Iliffe, *Modern History,* 45.

6. See note 3.

7. Richard Kandt, *Caput Nili,* 2nd ed. (Berlin, 1905), 108, quoted in Iliffe, *Modern History,* 45–46.

8. See Rockel, "Safari!" chap. 3; Koponen, *People and Production,* chap. 4.

9. Rockel, "Safari!" chap. 3.

10. Burton, *Lake Regions,* 233; also Burton, "Lake Regions," 28–29; Dutrieux in AIA, *Rapports sur les marches,* 59. One colonial official reckoned that transportation by porterage involved walking along paths winding four times the distance of a straight line between the departure point and the destination. Iliffe, *Africans,* 118. But these would not have been main caravan routes.

11. Pruen, *Arab and the African,* 175.

12. Pruen, *Arab and the African,* 175–76; also Moloney, *With Captain Stairs,* 31.

13. Hore, *Tanganyika,* 33–34; James Hannington, *Peril and Adventure in Central Africa* (London, 1886), 85.

14. Last to Wright, Mamboya, 16 April 1879, CMS CA6/014 (quote); Last to Lang, Mamboya, 19 February 1883, CMS G3A6/01; Burton, *Lake Regions,* 86.

15. Discussed in Rockel, "Safari!" chap. 3.

16. Burton, *Lake Regions,* 234.

17. Decle, *Three Years,* 328.

18. Hore, *To Lake Tanganyika,* 148–49.

19. Bennett, *From Zanzibar,* 53–54.

20. Hassing and Bennett, "Journey across Tanganyika," 133. For another vivid account of a river crossing see Fortie, *Black and Beautiful,* 92–93. For various techniques for crossing flooded rivers, see Roscoe, *Twenty-five Years,* 8–9. Occasionally rivers were bridged by trees.

21. Thomson, *To the Central African Lakes,* 1:127; Hore, *To Lake Tanganyika,* 104–5.

22. For example, Beardall to Waller, Dar es Salaam, 27 April 1879, MP, box 77, IBEAC file 61.

23. Hore, *To Lake Tanganyika,* 82; O'Flaherty to Hutchinson, Uyui, 29 November 1880, CMS G3A6/01. Burton wrote of thorns that "tenacious as fish-hooks, tore without difficulty the strongest clothing." *Lake Regions,* 177.

24. Thomson, *To the Central African Lakes,* 1:128; Krapf, *Travels,* 269; Carl Claus von der Decken, *Reisen in Ost-Afrika in den Jahren 1859 bis 1865,* ed. Otto Kersten (1869–79; repr., Graz, Austria, 1978), 1:232. French-Sheldon, *Sultan to Sultan,* 162–63.

25. Swann, *Fighting the Slave Hunters,* 53; Stairs, 14 August 1891, in *Victorian Explorer,* ed. Konczacki, 209; Rhodes to Portal, Kampala, 2 April 1893, enclosure, reports relating to Uganda by Sir Gerald Portal, *HCPP,* C.7303, m.f. 100.506.

26. Hore, *To Lake Tanganyika,* 64.

27. Burton, "Lake Regions," 116; Moloney, *With Captain Stairs,* 43; Thomson, *To the Central African Lakes,* 2:261–62; Stairs, 28 July 1891, in "De Zanzibar au Katanga," 46; Stairs, 18 August 1891, in *Victorian Explorer,* ed. Konczacki, 211.

28. Livingstone, 8 November 1872 and 20 September 1866, in *Last Journals,* 466, 97–100; Parke, *My Personal Experiences,* 199; Charles New, *Life, Wanderings, and Labours in Eastern Africa* (1873; repr., London, 1971), 481.

29. The packing process was often carried out by specialist packers at the warehouses of Indian merchants in Zanzibar or on the coast. See Stanley, *How I Found Livingstone,* 46–47; Bennett, *Stanley's Despatches,* 10–11; Wilson and Felkin, *Uganda,* 1:24–25; Thomson, *To the Central African Lakes,* 1:37.

30. Burton, *Lake Regions,* 112–13, 241; Vienne, "De Zanzibar à l'Oukami," 360; "Central African Expedition: Rev. A.W. Dodgshun. List of Requirements," LMS 2/1/B; Southon, "History, Country and People of Unyamwezi," pt. 5; Hore, *To Lake Tanganyika,* 23–24; Lloyd, *In Dwarf Land,* 37; Bennett, *Stanley's Despatches,* 10–11; Paul Reichard, "Vorschläge zu einer Reiseaurüstung für Ost- und Centralafrika," *ZGEB* 24 (1889): 55; Junker, *Travels,* 567 (illustration); French-Sheldon, *Sultan to Sultan,* 123; Mtoro bin Mwinyi Bakari, *Customs of the Swahili,* 164; Mtoro bin Mwinyi Bakari in Harries, *Swahili Prose Texts,* 181; Weule, *Native Life,* 104 (illustration).

31. Burton, *Lake Regions,* 113, 115–16; Bennett, *Stanley's Despatches,* 10–11.

32. Burton, *Lake Regions,* 113, 531; Vienne, "De Zanzibar à l'Oukami," 360; Bennett, *Stanley's Despatches,* 10–11; Mackay to Hutchinson, Zanzibar, 5 March 1877, CMS CA6/016; Henry to Wright, Mpwapwa, 1 October 1878, CMS CA6/012; Thomson, *To the Central African Lakes,* 1:38; Reichard, "Vorschläge," 56; Pruen, *Arab and the African,* 179; Fortie, *Black and Beautiful,* 100. See the illustration in Speke, *Journal,* 103. In the Merina Empire porters also carried loads suspended from bamboo poles on their shoulders, as was the norm in East Asia. See Campbell, "Labour and the Transport Problem," 349. Campbell is incorrect, however, when he contrasts this technique with that of porters on the mainland.

33. Frederick J. Jackson, *Early Days in East Africa* (1930; repr., London, 1969), 80; Lamden, "Some Aspects of Porterage," 156.

34. French-Sheldon, *Sultan to Sultan,* 122.

35. Von der Decken, *Reisen in Ost-Afrika,* 1:232; Dodgshun, "List of requirements," LMS 2/1/B; Hore, *To Lake Tanganyika,* 23–24; Lloyd, *In Dwarf Land,* 37; Southon to Whitehouse, 29 November 1880, LMS 3/3/D.

36. Tate's sugar cube boxes were of such convenient size that large numbers of them were carried upcountry and converted into beehives. Pruen, *Arab and the African,* 58.

37. Burton, *Lake Regions,* 113; Von der Decken, *Reisen in Ost-Afrika,* 1:232; Weule, *Native Life,* 80.

38. Parke, *My Personal Experiences* 73, 187. On Manyema women, see also Hutley, 8 July 1881, in *Central African Diaries,* ed. Wolf, 276; Livingstone, 24 May 1871, in *Last Journals,* 377 (on the market women of Nyangwe); Jephson, *Diary,* 178–79; Alfred Sharpe, *The Backbone of Africa* (London, 1921), 94, 96–97; Northrup, *Beyond the Bend,* 18; Ruth Rempel, "Exploration, Knowledge, and Empire in Africa: The Emin Pasha Relief Expedition, 1886–1892" (PhD thesis, University of Toronto, 2000), 252.

39. Burton, *Lake Regions,* 112, 237, 241; Wilson and Felkin, *Uganda,* 1:44 Dodgshun, 30 May 1878, in *From Zanzibar,* ed. Bennett, 69; Cameron, *Across Africa,* 1:124; W. Robert Foran, *African Odyssey: The Life of Verney Lovett-Cameron* (London, 1937), 65; Pruen, *Arab and the African,* 179; Jackson, *Early Days,* 80; Lamden, "Some Aspects of Porterage," 157; Hassing and Bennett, "Journey across Tanganyika," 141. See also chap. 3.

40. Hines to Seward, Zanzibar, 25 October 1864, in *New England Merchants,* ed. Bennett and Brooks, 529. On large tusks, Burton writes in *Lake Regions,* 540, "The tusk is larger at Zanzibar than elsewhere. At Mozambique, for instance, 60 lbs. would be considered a good average for a lot. Monster tusks are spoken of. Specimens of 5 farasilah [*sic*] are not very rare, and the people have traditions that these wonderful armatures have extended to 227 lbs., and even to 280 lbs. each."

41. The full list is in Hore to Whitehouse, Ujiji, 8 January 1880, LMS 3/1/A. See Hore, *Tanganyika,* 45–46, for the loads of another LMS caravan.

42. C. F. Harford-Battersy, *Pilkington of Uganda* (London, 1899), 231–32.

43. Sissons, "Economic Prosperity," 115; Johnston, *Kilima-Njaro,* 44–46.

44. Thomson, *To the Central African Lakes,* 2:96.

45. Coulbois, *Dix années,* 202. This was almost identical to the 10 pounds of personal baggage allowed to Fortie's porters. Fortie, *Black and Beautiful,* 101.

46. Von der Decken, *Reisen in Ost-Afrika,* 1:232.

47. Hore, *Tanganyika,* 45; Jackson, *Early Days,* 80; Lamden, "Some Aspects of Porterage," 158. See also Burton, *Lake Regions,* 237 for a similar list for Nyamwezi porters, this one including a three-legged stool.

48. Rashid bin Hassani, "Story of Rashid bin Hassani," 103. See also Parke, *My Personal Experiences,* 102; Meyer, *Across East African Glaciers,* 49, for outfits of Zanzibari porters.

49. Burton, *Lake Regions,* 242, 295, 479; Cameron, *Across Africa,* 1:73; Foran, *African Odyssey,* 59; Last to Wright, Mpwapwa, 1 September 1879, CMS CA6/014; Thomson, *To the Central African Lakes,* 1:81, 84; Hore, *Tanganyika,* 87; Muxworthy to Thompson, Zanzibar, 3 June 1882, LMS 4/5/D; Peters, *New Light,* 75.

50. Burton, *Lake Regions,* 242; Sissons, "Economic Prosperity," 182–83; Rachel Stuart Watt, *In the Heart of Savagedom* (London, n.d., ca. 1912), 25; Tucker, *Eighteen Years,* 32; Burton, "Lake Regions," 155; Copplestone to Lang, Uyui, 4 March 1882, CMS G3A6/01; Lamden, "Some Aspects of Porterage," 157; Mtoro bin Mwinyi Bakari, *Customs of the Swahili,* 161; Luck, *Charles Stokes,* 157. Porters' food will be discussed in chap. 5.

51. Wilson and Felkin, *Uganda,* 1:44 Dodgshun, "List of Requirements," LMS 2/1/B; Pilkington to ?, Saadani, 14 July 1890, in *Pilkington,* by Harford-Battersby, 83; Watt, *In the Heart,* 157.

52. Simpson, *Dark Companions,* 62–63. Porterage of the various steamers placed on Lake Malawi is beyond this book's scope. But see, among other sources, Moir, "Eastern Route," 95; Moir, *After Livingstone,* 37; Johnson, *My African Reminiscences,* 205, 211; Selim bin Abakari, "Safari Yangu Ya Nyassa Waqati Bwana Major von Wissman

Alipopeleka Stima Katika Juto la Nyassa," in *Safari za Wasuaheli,* ed. Velten, 50–105; Selim bin Abakari, "Meine Reise nach dem Nyassa mit der Dampferexpedition des Herrn Major von Wissman," in *Schilderungen der Suaheli,* ed. Velten, 56–115; M. Prager, *Die Wissman-Expedition* (Leipzig, 1901); "British Central Africa," *ZEAG,* 22 November 1893; Cole-King, "Transportation and Communication," 77–84; Oliver, *Missionary Factor,* 36–37.

53. Bennett, *Stanley's Despatches,* 188–89; Simpson, *Dark Companions,* 114, 116, 118–19, 124, 128; Stanley, *Through the Dark Continent,* 1:64–65; Stanley, 12 November 1876, in *The Exploration Diaries of H. M. Stanley,* ed. R. Stanley and A. Neame (London, 1961), 136. Stanley's Emin Pasha Relief Expedition also had a steel boat, the *Advance,* carried in 12 sections. See Simpson, *Dark Companions,* 179.

54. Thomson, *To the Central African Lakes,* 1:87; Simpson, *Dark Companions,* 146, 147, 150.

55. Harman, *Bwana Stokesi,* 45; H. B. Thomas, "Church Missionary Society Boats in East Africa," *UJ* 25, no. 1 (1961): 47: Moloney, *With Captain Stairs,* 32; Stairs, 1 August 1891, in *Victoria Explorer,* ed. Konczacki, 202. The boat porters received extra rations. In 1889 Stokes's porters carried a sailing vessel, the *Limi,* to Lake Victoria. Harman, *Bwana Stokesi,* 100.

56. Hore, *Tanganyika,* 182–91, 199–220, 204–5; Swann, *Fighting the Slave Hunters,* xi, 25; Hore to Whitehouse, Zanzibar, 26 September 1882, LMS 4/5/A; Hore to Whitehouse, Zanzibar, 27 September 1882, LMS 4/5/A; Hore to Thompson, Kisokwe, 3 December 1882, LMS 4/5/C; Hore to Whitehouse, Urambo, 22 January 1883, LMS 5/1/A; Hore quoted in Hassing and Bennett, "Journey across Tanganyika," 130n9; Bennett, *From Zanzibar,* xxiii.

57. Thomas, "Church Missionary Society Boats," 44–53; Simpson, *Dark Companion,* 138–39; Wolf, *Central African Diaries,* 76n15; MacKay, 21 March 1889, in *A. M. Mackay,* by Mackay, 391–92; S. Napier Bax, "The Early Church Missionary Society Missions of Buzilima and Usambiro in the Mwanza District," *TNR* 7 (1939): 46.

58. "Wissman Dampfers—Bericht uber Victoria Nyanza," 1891, G6/21, TNA. Stokes arranged transportation. Thanks to Laird Jones for the reference.

59. Hutley, 7 May 1881, in *Central African Diaries,* ed. Wolf, 262; Norman R. Bennett, "Captain Storms in Tanganyika: 1882–1885," *TNR* 54 (1960): 59.

60. Moir, *After Livingstone,* 76–81. For background, see James B. Wolf, "Commerce, Christianity, and the Creation of the Stevenson Road," *AHS* 4, no. 2 (1971): 363–71; Hore to Whitehouse, Zanzibar, 27 September 1882, LMS 4/5/A; Hore to LMS, Mkange, 11 November 1882, LMS 4/5/B.

61. See the detailed description of palanquins and their bearers in Mesuril, near Mozambique island, in 1809, in Salt, *Voyage to Abyssinia,* 28–29; also Cole-King, "Transportation and Communication," 76.

62. J. Rebmann, "Narrative of a Journey to Madjame, in Kirima, during April, May, and June, 1849," *CMI* 1, no. 14/16 (1850): 381.

63. Livingstone, 8 and 9 January 1869, in *Last Journals,* 286.

64. Burton, *Lake Regions,* 240, 264, 266, 275, also 384–85. Compare with attitudes in early nineteenth-century Yorubaland. Ogunremi writes, "When Clapperton reached Ijanna and asked for some hammock-men to carry the invalids in the party, he was promptly told that the Oyo people 'could not and would not carry a hammock—that a man was not a horse.'" See *Counting the Camels,* 74. For another example, see Gabriel Ogundeji Ogunremi, "Human Porterage in Nigeria in the Nineteenth Century: A Pillar in the Indigenous Economy," *Journal of the Historical Society of Nigeria* 8, no. 1 (December 1975): 42n9. Of course horses could not be used for Tanzanian travel.

65. Elton, 15 December 1877, in *Travels,* 388. It was wishful thinking for French-Sheldon to write that "They [her porters] have no objections to carrying a *mzunga* [*sic*] (white man), but they very much object to carrying a fellow pagazi (porter)." *Sultan to Sultan,* 117. See also Southon to Whitehouse, Mpwapwa, 16 July 1879, LMS 2/1/D.

66. Griffith to Whitehouse, Ujiji, ? October 1879, LMS 2/2/B. In Nyasaland, missionary M.A. Pringle left a sympathetic account of the *machila* men who carried her to Blantyre, and their sufferings. *A Journey in East Africa towards the Mountains of the Moon* (Edinburgh, 1886), 180–81.

67. Hore, *To Lake Tanganyika,* 8; French-Sheldon, *Sultan to Sultan,* 16, 103, 121, 245.

68. Bibi Nelea Nicodemo Msogoti, interview, Tabora, 8 August 2000.

69. Tony Woods, "Capitaos and Chiefs: Oral Tradition and Colonial Society," *IJAHS* 23, no. 2 (1990): 260–61. Woods cites the case of a megalomaniac colonial official who had his dogs carried in a *machila.* See also Cole-King, "Transportation and Communication," 82.

70. Hobley, *Kenya,* 103–4.

71. Bennett, *Stanley's Despatches,* 160–61.

72. Baumann, *Durch Massailand,* 7–8; Leue to Governor, Bagamoyo, 11 February 1899, TNA G1/35. For similar scenes, see Stanley, *Through the Dark Continent,* 1:57–59; Giraud, *Lacs,* 45.

73. Mtoro bin Mwinyi Bakari, *Customs of the Swahili,* 165, 297n18; Decle, *Three Years,* 345–46; M.H. Löbner, Usoke, Bezirk, Tabora, 1 March 1910, in "Fragebogen-Beantwortung für ganz Wanyamuezi durch Missionar M.H. Löbner," in Gottberg, *Unyamwesi,* 138; Puder, Hauptmann, and Stationschef von Tabora, "Beantwortung des Fragebogens," in *Unyamwesi,* by Gottberg, 245.

74. Giraud, *Lacs,* 45; Hutley, 22 October 1879, in *Central African Diaries,* ed. Wolf, 133; Hore, *Tanganyika,* 47–48. For similar jokes and boasts, see Burton, *Lake Regions,* 240; Hore, *Tanganyika,* 35–36.

75. Mtoro bin Mwinyi Bakari in Harries, *Swahili Prose Texts,* 181.

76. Thomson, *To the Central African Lakes,* 1:81–82; Swann, *Fighting the Slave Hunters,* 35–36.

77. Thomson, *To the Central African Lakes,* 1:88. For similar accounts, see Livingstone, 2 November 1867, in *Last Journals,* 196; Fortie, *Black and Beautiful,* 29; Weule, *Native Life,* 80–81. A *barghumi* is made from a kudu horn, and its sound resembles the "sad, sweet music" of a French horn. See Burton, *Lake Regions,* 470.

78. Burton, *Lake Regions,* 53–54; Murphy to Kirk, "shamba," 3 miles from Bagamoyo, 21 April 1873; Cameron, 28 March 1873, in journal, VLC 3/1, RGS; Cameron, *Across Africa,* 1:156–62, 171–77; Last to Whiting, Mamboya, 4 October 1881, CMS G3A6/01.

79. Omari Musa Kagoda, interview, Kakola, 25 July 2000; Burton, *Lake Regions,* 239–44; Vienne, "De Zanzibar à l'Oukami," 359–60; Last to Whiting, Mamboya, 4 October 1881, CMS G3A6/01; Roscoe, *Twenty-five Years,* 8; Moloney, *With Captain Stairs,* 32; Swann, *Fighting the Slave Hunters,* 36. Von der Decken describes a different routine along the northern route of marching with numerous short breaks until an hour or two before sunset. *Reisen in Ost-Afrika,* 1:232.

80. Cameron, *Across Africa,* 1:83; also Burton, "Lake Regions," 118n; Burton, *Lake Regions,* 150–51. Waller and Wolf incorrectly describe a *terekeza* as a "midday halt." See Livingstone, *Last Journals,* 457n; Wolf, *Central African Diaries,* 37fn.

81. Burton, *Lake Regions,* 241; also W.G. Stairs, "From the Albert Nyanza to the Indian Ocean," *NC* 29, no. 172 (1891): 955–58. Cameron, *Across Africa,* 1:75. Cameron

believed that struggles for the best loads had more to do with obtaining "a dignified position in the caravan" than a light load.

82. Dodgshun, 19 June 1878, in *From Zanzibar,* ed. Bennett, 73.

83. Moloney, *With Captain Stairs,* 32.

84. Dodgshun, 2–8 May 1878, in *From Zanzibar,* ed. Bennett, 64; Thomson, *To the Central African Lakes,* 1:88, 201–2; French-Sheldon, *Sultan to Sultan,* 120; Jackson, *Early Days,* 80; Lamden, "Some Aspects of Porterage," 159–60.

85. An excellent history of a work song is Leroy Vail and Landeg White, "'Paiva': The History of a Song," in *Power and the Praise Poem: Southern African Voices in History* (Charlottesville, 1991), 198–230. See also Atkins, *The Moon Is Dead!* 73–74.

86. Raum, "German East Africa," 169; Frank Gunderson, "From 'Dancing with Porcupines' to 'Twirling a Hoe': Musical Labour Transformed in Sukumaland, Tanzania," *Africa Today* 48, no. 4 (2001): 4. See Rediker, *Between the Devil,* 90, 189–90, for similar comments about sailors' shanties, which he says in their pattern of call and response were probably derived from African culture.

87. Stanley, *Through the Dark Continent,* 1:112–13; Frank McLynn, *Stanley: The Making of an African Explorer* (Chelsea, MI, 1990), 306; Thomson, *To the Central African Lakes,* 1:88; Hutley, 3 August 1878, in *Central African Diaries,* ed. Wolf, 45; Gillman, 25 October 1905, in diaries, RH MSS. Afr.s.1175(1).

88. Thomson, *To the Central African Lakes,* 1:97; Jephson, 2 June 1887, in *Diary,* 103; Gillman, 25 October 1905, in diaries.

89. Grant, *Walk across Africa,* 42; Stanley, *Through the Dark Continent,* 1:112–13, 2:154; McLynn, *Stanley,* 306; Hutley, 3 August 1878, in *Central African Diaries,* ed. Wolf, 45; White Fathers, *A l'assaut des pays nègres,* 19; Richard Böhm, *Von Sansibar zum Tanganjika* (Leipzig, 1888), 19; Roscoe, *Twenty-five Years,* 55; Robert Pickering Ashe, *Two Kings of Uganda or, Life by the Shores of the Victoria Nyanza* (1889; repr., London, 1970), 329; Coulbois, *Dix années,* 19–20; Mackay, 11 September 1883, in diary, CMS G3A6/01. Johannes Fabian is especially perceptive on European encounters with African music, and how appreciation grew with exposure. See *Out of Our Minds,* 114–20.

90. Moloney, *With Captain Stairs,* 79; Iliffe, *Modern History,* 80. Other famous singers and composers included Sembeiwe and Iguwa.

91. Some are discussed in this book. Others are in Stanley, *How I Found Livingstone;* Stanley, *Through the Dark Continent,* 1:112–13; Pruen, *Arab and the African,* 101–3; Mtoro bin Mwinyi Bakari, *Customs of the Swahili,* 165–66; Seminar für Orientalische Sprachen, "Lieder und Sangesweisen und Geschichten der Wanyamwezi," *MSOSB* 4, no. 3 (1901): 45–62; Weule, *Native Life,* 264–65, 388–92; Fortie, *Black and Beautiful,* 29. A useful introduction to Nyamwezi and Sukuma songs is Koritschoner, "Some East African Native Songs," 51–64, but see especially Gunderson, "From 'Dancing with Porcupines.'" Songs of Sukuma and Swahili porters are in Paul Kollmann, *The Victoria Nyanza,* trans. H.A. Nesbitt (London, 1899), 164; Brown, "Bagamoyo: An Historical Introduction," 69–70. See also Mackay, *A.M. Mackay,* 57.

92. Unomah, "Economic Expansion," 115.

93. Dodgshun, 19 June 1878, in *From Zanzibar,* ed. Bennett, 73, Thomson, *To the Central African Lakes,* 1:87; Hutley, 18 June 1878, in *Central African Diaries,* ed. Wolf, 35; Weule, *Native Life,* 80–81

94. Ashe, *Chronicles of Uganda,* 344n.

95. Thomson, *To the Central African Lakes,* 1:91, 306–8. A *zomari* is a wind instrument in the shape of a clarinet but sounding something like bagpipes. See ibid., 50.

96. Burton, *Lake Regions,* 294.

97. Livingstone, 2 November 1867, in *Last Journals,* 196.

98. Thomson, *To the Central African Lakes,* 1:201–2.

99. Gunderson, "From 'Dancing with Porcupines,'" 8. For an entertaining description, see Burton, *Lake Regions,* 242.

100. Thomson, *To the Central African Lakes,* 2:247–48. Toyin Falola notes the same care given to appearances when travelers entered towns in Yorubaland. "The Yoruba Caravan System of the Nineteenth Century," *IJAHS* 24, no. 1 (1991): 121–22.

101. Selemani bin Mwenye Chande, "Meine Reise," 48; Selemani bin Mwenye Chande, "Safari yangu," 54; Geider, "Early Swahili Travelogues," 48.

102. Hore, *To Lake Tanganyika,* 152–53; Murphy to Sir B. Frere, Zanzibar, 7 March 1874, VLC 3/4, RGS; Mtoro bin Mwinyi Bakari, *Customs of the Swahili,* 162. For similar accounts, see Burton, *Lake Regions,* 225–26; Stanley, 27 February 1875, in *Exploration Diaries,* ed. Stanley and Neame, 59–60; Hutley, 19–21 and 27 July 1878, in *Central African Diaries,* ed. Wolf, 42, 43–44; Thomson, *To the Central African Lakes,* 2:204–5; Hore, *Tanganyika,* 62–63; Brown, "Pre-colonial History," 2.

103. Glassman, *Feasts and Riot,* 172–73.

104. Grant, *Walk across Africa,* 99. Chiefs were sometimes referred to as "sultans" by travelers. Sukuma women had a variant welcome ritual. See Kollmann, *Victoria Nyanza,* 164.

105. Kalunde Kongogo, interview, Usele, 29 July 2000.

106. Shabani Kapiga, interview, Kakola, 25 July 2000.

107. This section is based on Stephen J. Rockel, "Enterprising Partners: Caravan Women in Nineteenth Century Tanzania," *CJAS* 34, no. 3 (2000): 748–78.

108. Rockel, "Safari!" chap. 4.

109. The rich European sources on porterage are frequently silent on the subject of women because of the prejudices of Victorian times, the circumspection of male missionaries, and the concern of male travelers to censor their accounts of details regarding relationships with African women. See Cairns, *Prelude to Imperialism,* 53–57; Fabian, *Out of Our Minds,* 79–86, which emphasize European anxieties as well as the intimacy of many relationships. For the reticence of one traveler, see Barrett-Gaines, "Travel Writing, Experiences, and Silences," 53–70. Compare with recent work on women at sea in Howell and Twomey, *Jack Tar in History.*

110. Among others, Martin Channock, *Law, Custom and Social Order: The Colonial Experience in Malawi and Zambia* (Cambridge, 1985); Marjorie Mbilinyi, "Women's Resistance in 'Customary' Marriage: Tanzania's Runaway Wives," in *Forced Labour and Migration,* ed. Zegeye and Ishemo, 211–54; Moore and Vaughan, *Cutting down Trees;* Jane Parpart, "Sexuality and Power on the Zambian Copperbelt: 1926–1964," in *Patriarchy and Class: African Women in the Home and the Workforce,* ed. Sharon B. Stichter and Jane L. Parpart (Boulder, CO,1988), 115–38; Dorothy Hodgson and Sheryl McCurdy, "Wayward Wives, Misfit Mothers, and Disobedient Daughters: 'Wicked' Women and the Reconfiguration of Gender in Africa," *CJAS* 30, no. 1 (1996): 1–9.

111. Wright, *Strategies of Slaves and Women,* 129–37.

112. Janet Bujra, "Women 'Entrepreneurs' of Early Nairobi," in *Crime, Justice and Underdevelopment,* ed. Colin Sumner (London, 1982), 122–61; Luise White, *The Comforts of Home: Prostitution in Colonial Nairobi* (Chicago,1990), chap. 2.

113. Stichter "Migration of Women," 215; Moore and Vaughan, *Cutting down Trees,* 155.

114. Wright, *Strategies of Slaves and Women;* Alpers, "Story of Swema," 185–99.

115. Wright, *Strategies of Slaves and Women,* 219n17.

116. Jane I. Guyer, "Household and Community in African Studies," *ASR* 24, no. 2/3 (1981); Stichter, "Migration of Women."

117. Wright, *Strategies of Slaves and Women,* 9.

118. Wright, *Strategies of Slaves and Women,* 43.

119. Wright, *Strategies of Slaves and Women,* 29.

120. Hodgson and McCurdy, "Wayward Wives"; Wright, *Strategies of Slaves and Women.*

121. Cummings, "Aspects of Human Porterage," 58–75; Charles H. Ambler, *Kenyan Communities in the Age of Imperialism* (New Haven, CT, 1988); Claire C. Robertson, "Gender and Trade Relations in Central Kenya in the Late Nineteenth Century," *IJAHS* 30, no. 1 (1997).

122. Cummings, "Aspects of Human Porterage," 192, 194; Robertson, "Gender."

123. Livingstone, 5 and 8 October 1866, in *Last Journals,* 106–9; Elias C. Mandala, *Work and Control in a Peasant Economy: A History of the Lower Tchiri Valley in Malawi 1859–1960* (Madison,1990), 49.

124. H. S. Senior, "Sukuma Salt Caravans to Lake Eyasi," *TNR* 6 (1938): 87; Sutton and Roberts, "Uvinza and Its Salt Industry," 60–61.

125. Rockel, "Safari!" chap. 4.

126. Nolan, "Christianity in Unyamwezi," 33–34.

127. Speke, 26 October 1861 and 14 April 1862, in *Journal,* 181, 356; Burton, *Lake Regions,* 204, 241, 246; Grant, *Walk across Africa,* 98; Grant, "Summary of Observations," 250.

128. Cameron, *Across Africa,* 1:72; Tucker, *Eighteen Years,* 26; Ashe, *Chronicles of Uganda,* 26; Mtoro bin Mwinyi Bakari, *Customs of the Swahili,* 164; John Salaita, "Colonialism and Underdevelopment in Unyanyembe ca. 1900–1960" (MA thesis, University of Dar es Salaam, 1975), 11.

129. Last, *Polyglotta Africana Orientalis,* 21–22; Peters, *New Light,* 64, 71. See Hannington, *Peril and Adventure,* 96, sketch; Hassing and Bennett, "Journey across Tanganyika," 141; P. H. Yeo, "Caput-Nili: The Travels of Richard Kandt in German East Africa," *TNR* 63 (September 1964): 208; J.E.S. Moore, *To the Mountains of the Moon* (London, 1901), 152; Randabel to Superior General, Karema, 2 August 1885, quoted in "Extracts from a History of Karema Mission 1885–1935," by P. Majerus, in Mpanda District Book, TNA, Dar es Salaam.

130. Thaddeus Sunseri, "'Dispersing the Fields': Railway Labor and Rural Change in Early Colonial Tanzania," *CJAS* 32, no. 3 (1998).

131. Raum, "German East Africa," 169; Cummings, "Aspects of Human Porterage," 3. Compare with the temporary marriages arranged by Muslim Hausa traders for the duration of their journey. See M. B. Duffill and Paul E. Lovejoy, "Merchants, Porters, and Teamsters in the Nineteenth-Century Central Sudan," in *Workers of African Trade,* ed. Coquery-Vidrovitch and Lovejoy, 163, 164n1.

132. Like women in the Zambian Copperbelt during the colonial period, caravan women could often manipulate the sex ratio imbalance. See Parpart, "Sexuality and Power."

133. Burton, *Lake Regions,* 176; Hutley, 27 November 1880; in *Central African Diaries,* ed. Wolf, 231; Thomson, *To the Central African Lakes,* 2:76–77.

134. Speke, 11 November 1861 and 20 April 1862, in *Journal,* 192, 360.

135. Burton, *Lake Regions,* 451.

136. Moloney, *With Captain Stairs,* 54–55.

137. Livingstone, 8 September 1872, in *Last Journals,* 457.

138. Burton, *Lake Regions*, 154,

139. Thomson, *To the Central African Lakes*, 1:263–65, 306; Moloney, *With Captain Stairs*, 160–62.

140. Stanley, *Through the Dark Continent*, 1:68–69; Glassman, *Feasts and Riot*, 90–91.

141. Shabani Kapiga, interview, Kakola, 25 July 2000; Hussen Ally Kalunga, interview, Tabora, 20 July 2000; Mahmood Mohamed Sheikh, interview, Kwihara, 24 July 2000; Chief Abdallah Fundikira, interview, Tabora, 4 July 2000.

142. Kalunde Kongogo, interview, Usule, 29 July 2000. Bibi Kalunde Kongogo's account is rambling and chronologically confused, but full of fascinating detail. Her father was a *mtongi* who traveled to Kigoma (Ujiji?) and Manyema country as well as to the coast. Before colonial times he formed an alliance with an Arab trader, Seif bin Hamis (Sefu bin Hamid, Tippu Tip's son). This was typical of the mutually beneficial relationships between coastal and Nyamwezi traders.

143. Dudu Rajabu Kheli, interview, Tabora, 1 August 2000; Saidi Kitengeremea Fundikira, interview, Tabora, 3 August 2000.

144. Mackay to Wright, Wami River, 18 September 1876, CMS CA6/016; Mackay to Wright, Magubika, 27 May 1877, CMS CA6/016.

145. Grant, *Walk across Africa*, 43.

146. Stairs, "From the Albert Nyanza," 958. See also his comments in the entries for 1 and 10 August 1891, in *Victorian Explorer*, ed. Konczacki, 202, 206–7.

147. The reproduction of labor power in colonial urban centers has been studied by Luise White, "Domestic Labor in a Colonial City: Prostitution in Nairobi, 1900–1952," in *Patriarchy and Class*, ed. Stichter and Parpart, 141–42; White, *Comforts of Home*; Parpart, "Sexuality and Power," among others.

148. *ZEAG*, 11 October 1893. In this case the women were probably slaves. See Renault, "Structures of the Slave Trade," 146–65.

149. Johnson, *My African Reminiscences*, 74; also Livingstone, 22 September 1866, in *Last Journals,*, 100–1.

150. Burton, *Lake Regions*, 184; Cameron, *Across Africa*, 1:47, 108; Moloney, *With Captain Stairs*, 54; Wright, *Strategies of Slaves and Women*, 219n17. The European traders Philippe Broyon and Charles Stokes also traveled with their African wives and children. See Norman R. Bennett, "Philippe Broyon: Pioneer Trader in East Africa," *AA* 62, no. 247 (April 1963): 160; Luck, *Charles Stokes*, 67, 157.

151. This is a euphemism for slaves.

152. Burton, *Lake Regions*, 434.

153. Burton, *Lake Regions*, 184.

154. Coulbois, *Dix années*, 41; Stairs, 10 August 1891, in *Victorian Explorer*, ed. Konczacki, 207.

155. Margaret Strobel, *Muslim Women in Mombasa 1890–1975* (New Haven, CT, 1979), 46–48. For concubinage on the coast, see ibid., 48–50.

156. In more recent times, marriage to a stranger (*mgeni*), usually a migrant laborer, was a good option for Swahili widows and divorcees as it ensured greater independence than did marriage to a local man. See Pamela Landberg, "Widows and Divorced Women in Swahili Society," in *Widows in African Societies: Choices and Constraints*, ed. Betty Potash (Stanford, CA, 1986), 122–24.

157. Bennett, *Stanley's Despatches*, 190–91; Cameron, *Across Africa*, 1:200; Thomson, *To the Central African Lakes*, 2:260–61; Glassman, "Social Rebellion," 93n11. See especially Speke, *Journal*, 167.

158. Hutley, 29 September 1880, in *Central African Diaries,* ed. Wolf, 213; for another case, see Hutley, 28 June 1881, in *Central African Diaries,* ed. Wolf, 272.

159. Raum, "German East Africa," 169.

160. Laura Fair, "Dressing Up: Clothing, Class and Gender in Post-abolition Zanzibar," *JAH* 39 (1998): 64.

161. Laird Jones, "Mapping Consumption: Geographic Patterns in East African Import Sales, 1880–1914" (paper presented at the Canadian Association of African Studies Conference, Université Laval, Quebec, May 2001).

162. Raum, "German East Africa," 169. These comments are part of Raum's larger argument concerning "detribalization." See also Wright, *Strategies of Slaves and Women,* 32.

163. Decle, *Three Years,* 348.

164. Bibi Nelea Nicodemo Msogoti, interview, Isevya, Tabora, 8 August 2000; Bibi Joha Hassan Katalambula, interview, Isevya, Tabora, 8 August 2000.

165. Hodgson and McCurdy, "Wayward Wives."

166. Coquery-Vidrovitch and Lovejoy, "Workers of Trade," 14–15.

167. Quoted in Lamden, "Some Aspects of Porterage," 161.

168. Bennett, *Mirambo,* 146.

169. Coulbois, *Dix années,* 41; Nolan, "Christianity in Unyamwezi," 227.

170. Copy of Cameron's wage book, "Men's Accounts," in Kirk Papers, 21 September 1876. Correspondence block 1871–80, RGS, London, entries for Jacko and Pesa; Wage list, "Royal Geographical Society's East African Expedition of 1879," in Rotberg, *Joseph Thomson,* 314; "Men Engaged for Masai Caravan," nos. 148, 227, in notebook "Stanley's Expedition," ZM. See also William Percival Johnson, "Seven Years Travel in the Region East of Lake Nyassa," *PRGS,* n.s., 6 (1884): 524; Mackay to Wright, Wami River, 18 September 1876, CMS CA6/016; Hore, *To Lake Tanganyika,* 84; Majerus, "Extracts from a History"; Stairs, "From the Albert Nyanza," 957–58.

171. Burton, *Lake Regions,* 384; Decle, *Three Years,* 319, 322; Lloyd, *In Dwarf Land,* 91–92.

172. Madan, *Kiungani,* 78.

173. Madan, *Kiungani,* 111.

174. Livingstone, *Last Journals,* 139.

175. (London, 1889).

176. Clark to Wright, Mpwapwa, 27 September 1876, CMS CA6/07.

177. Roscoe, *Twenty-five Years,* 51.

178. Decle, *Three Years,* 320 See also Jephson, *Diary,* 410, for another account from the Emin Pasha relief expedition. For more on the women among Emin's followers and their work, see Jephson, 6 April 1889, in *Diary,* 343; Parke, 12 July 1889, *My Personal Experiences,* 454.

179. Kalunde Kongogo, interview, Usule, 29 July 2000.

CHAPTER 5: ON SAFARI: THE CULTURE OF LEISURE AND FOOD

1. Seminar für Orientalische Sprachen, "Lieder und Sangesweisen," 56. This song was probably composed much earlier than the 1890s, when it was collected. The German editor notes that it was sung by the merchant caravan leader, although the *kirangozi* usually took the lead in marching songs. The bell refers to those worn by the *kirangozi* or

fastened to ivory tusks and the legs of ivory porters. See Burton, *Lake Regions,* 242, 481. Mwanamumeta was a caravan leader from earlier, perhaps pioneering, times.

2. See Unomah, "Economic Expansion," 217, for attacks on caravans during the war between Unyanyembe and Urambo. The war between the Germans and the coast Arabs threatened missionary caravan traffic. See Pruen, *Arab and the African,* 95–97; Ashe, *Two Kings of Uganda,* 274–83.

3. Mzee Shabani Kapiga, interview, Kakola, 25 July 2000.

4. Mnyampala, *Gogo,* 45; Stairs, 12 August 1891, in *Victorian Explorer,* ed. Konczacki, 208.

5. Burton, *Lake Regions,* 224; Hore, *To Lake Tanganyika,* 116–17.

6. Copplestone to Hutchinson, Uyui, 22 March 1881, CMS G3A6/01.

7. See Burton, *Lake Regions,* 512, on the diplomatic, military, and other powers of chiefs with reference to travelers.

8. Hutley, 27 July 1878, in *Central African Diaries,* ed. Wolf, 44 (Mirambo); Speke, *Journal,* 165–67 (Myonga of Uzinza); James B. Wolf, ed., *Missionary to Tanganyika, 1877–1888* (London, 1971), 43; Sissons, "Economic Prosperity," 91.

9. Hassing and Bennett, "Journey across Tanganyika," 141; Tucker, *Eighteen Years,* 31, 33. For other examples, see Cameron, *Across Africa,* 1:145; Hannington, *Peril and Adventure,* 23; Roscoe, *Twenty-five Years,* 48–50; Moloney, *With Captain Stairs,* 50, 52.

10. Ashe, *Chronicles of Uganda,* 26–27. For earlier incidents in Ugogo involving "Wahumba," "Wataturu," and Maasai, see Southon to Whitehouse, Urambo, 4 May 1880, LMS 3/1/D. An attack by Hehe on a Nyamwezi party in the Marenga Mkali is recorded in Ashe, *Chronicles of Uganda,* 22. For other cases, see Roscoe, *Twenty-five Years,* 48–50; Stokes to Lang, Uyui, 6 October 1884, CMS G3A6/02.

11. White Fathers, *A l'assaut des pays nègres,* 158–59; Hore to Mullens, Kawele, 25 February 1879, LMS 2/1/A; Selemani bin Mwenye Chande in Harries, *Swahili Prose Texts,* 235.

12. Griffith to Thompson, Uguha, 15 January 1882; Southon to Thompson, Urambo, 30 January 1882; Griffith to Thompson, Uguha, 13 March 1882; all LMS 4/4/A; Southon to Thompson, Urambo, 17 April 1882, LMS 4/4/B; Southon to Thompson, Urambo, 12 June 1882, LMS 4/4/B; Griffith to Thompson, Ujiji, 16 October 1882, LMS 4/5/B.

13. Price to Lang, Mpwapwa, 5 August 1884, CMS G3A6/01.

14. Baxter to Hutchinson, Kadali, 7 September 1880, CMS CA6/05.

15. Cameron, *Across Africa,* 1:145; Stanley, *Through the Dark Continent,* 1:383, 385, 397; White Fathers, *A l'assaut des pays nègres,* 158–59; O'Flaherty to Hutchinson, Uyui, 29 November 1880, CMS G3A6/01; Hutley to Thompson, Uguha, 10 May 1881, LMS 4/2/A; Hassing and Bennett, "Journey across Tanganyika," 137; Ashe, *Chronicles of Uganda,* 22.

16. Aylward Shorter, *Nyungu-ya-Mawe: Leadership in Nineteenth Century Tanzania* (Nairobi, 1969), 11–14; Aylward Shorter, "Nyungu ya Mawe and the Empire of the Ruga-Ruga," *JAH* 9 (1968): 235–59; Unomah, "Economic Expansion," 255–64; Kabeya, *King Mirambo.*

17. Burton, *Lake Regions,* 224.

18. Selemani bin Mwenye Chande in Harries, *Swahili Prose Texts,* 235. On the borders of Kenya's Athi Plain, a pride of 27 lions attacked a caravan in 1894. See Decle, *Three Years,* 482–83, and 477–78, 496; French-Sheldon, *Sultan to Sultan,* 182–83, for separate incidents.

19. Southon, "History, Country and People of Unyamwezi," 3:8.

20. Stanley, 24 December 1874, in *Exploration Diaries,* ed. Stanley and Neame, 34; Selemani bin Mwenye Chande in Harries, *Swahili Prose Texts,* 235; Baumann, *Durch Massailand,* 15; Gaetano Casati, *Ten Years in Equatoria and the Return with Emin Pasha,* trans. Mrs. J. R. Clay (1891; repr., New York, 1969), 2:281.

21. New, *Life, Wanderings, and Labours,* 346. I have slightly altered New's rendering of the Swahili. See C. Delmé-Radcliffe, "Extracts from Lt. Col. C. Delmé-Radcliffe's Typescript Diary Report on the Delimitation of the Anglo-German Boundary," *UJ* 11, no. 1 (1947): 28, for an incident involving porters and rhinos.

22. Stanley, *How I Found Livingstone,* 383; McLynn, *Stanley,* 143–44. See Peters, *New Light,* 490; Fortie, *Black and Beautiful,* 127, for incidents in which crocodiles in killed porters.

23. Waller in Livingstone, *Last Journals,* 539. A mamba bit and killed a young girl in Susi and Chuma's party bearing Livingstone's body to the coast.

24. Burton, *Lake Regions,* 140; Isabel Burton, *Life of Captain Sir Richard F. Burton* (London, 1893), 1:288; Thomson, *To the Central African Lakes,* 1:58; Elton, *Travels,* 409–10; Watt, *In the Heart,* 32; Lloyd, *In Dwarf Land,* 46–47.

25. Elton, *Travels,* 394. For termites, tsetse flies, and bees, see Burton, *Lake Regions,* 140, 149–50, 178–49; Murphy to Kirk, Tonda, 25 April 1873, VLC 3/4, RGS; Decle, *Three Years,* 358–60.

26. Clark to Wright, Mpwapwa, 27 September 1876, CMS CA6/07.

27. Thomson, *To the Central African Lakes,* 1:299–302. For similar incidents, see Roger Price, 2 August 1877, in *Private Journal of the Rev. Roger Price* (London, 1878), 50–51; Elton, *Travels,* 362–63. Fires were almost as much a danger in villages, the larger of which were often trading bases. See Livingstone, 24 July and 23 September 1867, in *Last Journals,* 181, 191; Burton, *Lake Regions,* 447.

28. Decle, *Three Years,* 319.

29. For an overview, see Beverly and Walter T. Brown, "East African Trade Towns: A Shared Growth," in *A Century of Change in East Africa,* ed. W. Arens (Geneva, 1976), 183–200.

30. For Mbwamaji, see Rockel, "Safari!" chap. 3; for Saadani, see Glassman, *Feasts and Riot,* 64–68.

31. Burton, "Lake Regions," 78–81; Burton, *Lake Regions,* 450; Speke, 23 October 1860, in *Journal,* 61; Livingstone, 10 October 1870, in *Last Journals,* 335; William Beardall, 11 February 1881, in "Exploration of the Rufiji River under the Orders of the Sultan of Zanzibar," *PRJS,* n.s., 3, no. 11 (1881): 656; In 1878 Johnston believed Zungomero to be "ruinous and abandoned," but he mentions nearby "Kisake." By 1884 Kisaki was the base of Mbunga raiders from Mahenge who threatened the Bagamoyo routes to the north. See Keith Johnston, "Native Routes in East Africa from Dar es Salaam towards Lake Nyassa," *PRGS,* n.s., 1, no. 7 (1879): 419; L. E . Larson, "A History of the Mbunga Confederacy ca. 1860–1907," *TNR* 81/82 (1977): 38. There was probably some confusion between the two settlements.

32. Burton, "Lake Regions," 190; Burton, *Lake Regions,* 269–72.

33. Blackburn to Lang, Uyui, 2 July 1885, CMS G3A6/02; Ashe, *Chronicles of Uganda,* 33; Peters, *New Light,* 500–1; Luck, *Charles Stokes,* 158–59.

34. Huntley, 27 July 1878, 22 July 1881, and 6 September 1881, in *Central African Diaries,* ed. Wolf, 43–4, 277, 280–81; Hore, *To Lake Tanganyika,* 136; AIA, *Rapports sur les marches,* 33–34; Decle, *Three Years,* 348–9; Bennett, *Mirambo,* 101; Unomah, *Mirambo of Tanzania,* 15 (sketch of Iselamagazi), 16, 30; Kabeya, *King Mirambo,* 23–25.

35. Price, *Report,* 37; AIA, *Rapports sur les marches,* 61; Smith, "Earliest Ox-Wagons," 8; Pruen, *Arab and the African,* 13.

36. Brown and Brown, "East African Trade Towns," 183–84.

37. Burton, "Lake Regions," 123; Burton, *Lake Regions,* 174–75.

38. Stuhlmann, *Mit Emin Pascha,* 16; Schmidt, *Geschichte des Araberaufstandes,* 185; T. O. Beidelman, "A History of Ukaguru: 1857–1916," *TNR* 58/59 (1962): 12. See also Wilhelm Langheld, *Zwanzig Jahre in deutschen Kolonien* (Berlin, 1909), 38; Sissons, "Economic Prosperity," 188–89; Bennett, *Arab versus European,* 32.

39. Hore, *To Lake Tanganyika,* 87.

40. Stanley, *Through the Dark Continent,* 1:77; Clark in *CMI* (September 1879): 530–31; O'Flaherty to Hutchinson, Mpwapwa, 20 October 1880, CMS G3A6/01; White Fathers, *A l'assaut des pays nègres,* 121.

41. Pruen, *Arab and the African,* 107. See Stanley, *How I Found Livingstone,* 135, for an earlier description of Mpwapwa and its surroundings.

42. See the discussion of *tembe* size in Sissons, "Economic Prosperity," 207.

43. Last to CMS, Mpwapwa, 24 December 1878, CMS CA6/014; Stanley, *Through the Dark Continent,* 1:77; AIA, *Rapports sur les marches,* 62; Hore, *To Lake Tanganyika,* 85, 88; Stairs, 4 August 1891, in *Victorian Explorer,* ed. Konczacki, 204. Last and Stanley both suggest the stream was perennial. Price and O'Neill differ but state that water could always be obtained by digging in the sandy bed. See Price, *Report,* 36; O'Neill in *CMI* (September 1879): 531.

44. Stanley, *How I Found Livingstone,* 130–32; Cameron, *Across Africa,* 1:85.

45. White Fathers, *A l'assaut des pays nègres,* 121. In December 1874, "provisions were extremely scarce, and at famine prices. Even the natives journeyed far to purchase food for goats and cattle." Stanley, 13 December 1874, in *Exploration Diaries,* ed. Stanley and Neame, 31.

46. On the heterogeneous origins of the people of eastern Ugogo, see Peter Rigby, *Cattle and Kinship among the Gogo* (Ithaca, NY, 1969), 12. On Mpwapwa and more especially neighboring Ukaguru, see Beidelman, "History of Ukaguru."

47. Last to CMS, Mpwapwa, 24 December 1878, CMS CA6/014; Price, *Report,* 36–37.

48. Igor Kopytoff, "The Internal African Frontier: The Making of African Political Culture," in *The African Frontier: The Reproduction of Traditional African Societies,* ed. Igor Kopytoff (Bloomington, 1987), 3–84.

49. The idea presented by Glassman that urban centers along the central routes were fundamentally different from those along the northern (Pangani) routes should be rejected. Glassman writes in *Feasts and Riot,* 69, "Social interaction along the Pangani routes was often intimate, and cultural boundaries relatively loose. Whereas the major way stations of the central routes, such as Tabora and Ujiji, were centers of coastal Muslim culture, dominated by Arabs and garrisoned by Zanzibar, those of the 'Maasai' routes by contrast were multiethnic communities where coastal Muslims and their hosts lived on a more or less equal footing." This sets up a false binary opposition, a methodological flaw found throughout an otherwise valuable book. Tabora and Ujiji were not "garrisoned by Zanzibar," and Arab operations at Tabora depended on alliances with the Unyanyembe elite. The degree of Arab "dominance" at Tabora has been overstated in the literature. The issue was put to rest long ago by Alfred Unomah.

50. Price, *Report,* 37.

51. W. J. Carnell, "Sympathetic Magic among the Gogo of Mpwapwa District," *TNR* 39 (June 1955): 25–38.

52. Price, *Report,* 33, 37; Murphy to Frere, Zanzibar, 7 March 1874, VLC 3/4, RGS.

53. O'Neill in *CMI* (September 1879): 531; T. Griffith-Jones, "Some Notes on Stanley's First and Second Expeditions through Mpwapwa," Dodoma Provincial Book, vol. 1, TNA. Griffith-Jones also provides information on topographical aspects of early Mpwapwa. On Lukole, see also Price to Lang, Mpwapwa, 5 August 1884, CMS G3A6/01. For the early history of the Mpwapwa mission, see Bennett, *Arab versus European,* 95–98.

54. Moloney, *With Captain Stairs,* 43–44; Stairs, 4 August 1891, *Victorian Explorer,* ed. Konczacki, 204; Beidelman, "History of Ukaguru," 19, 24, 27.

55. Pruen, *Arab and the African,* 116–17.

56. Pruen, *Arab and the African,* 125–26.

57. AIA, *Rapports sur les marches,* 61–62. This was probably normal along the main caravan routes.

58. AIA, *Rapports sur les marches,* 61.

59. Baxter to Wright, Mpwapwa, 9 August 1878, CMS CA6/05; White Fathers, *A l'assaut des pays nègres,* 122–23. See Shergold Smith to Kirk, Pembireh Nyambwa, 7 November 1876, CMS CA6/012, for a dispute that led to the death of one mission porter and the wounding of another. The cause is not quite clear, but Shergold Smith had directed some porters to cut grass for thatching, apparently without permission from local authorities. The porters reacted by preparing to desert, when the "Gogo" attacked them. For another dispute over the theft of some goats from an Arab caravan, see Price, *Report,* 38. Many such incidents could be cited for other places along the routes.

60. Brown and Brown, "East African Trade Towns," 192–96.

61. White Fathers, *A l'assaut des pays nègres,* 123.

62. Clark to Wright, Mpwapwa, 27 September 1876, CMS CA6/07. The letter is a copy of Clark's journal, hence the dates progress.

63. Price to Lang, Mpwapwa, 5 August 1884, CMS G3A6/01.

64. Pruen, *Arab and the African,* 135.

65. Brown and Brown, "East African Trade Towns," 196.

66. Singular: *kambi.* The same word was used universally along the central routes. Burton, "Lake Regions," 64n.

67. Burton, "Lake Regions," 159, Burton, *Lake Regions,* 167, 244–45; Hassing and Bennett, "Journey across Tanganyika," 134–35; Sissons, "Economic Prosperity," 117.

68. But see Thomson, *To the Central African Lakes,* 2:217, on visits by women to his porters' camp at night. Abdulrazak Gurnah's novel *Paradise* is quite explicit about sexual activity on caravan journeys.

69. Burton, "Lake Regions," 64n; Thomson, *Through Masai Land,* 57.

70. Burton, "Lake Regions," 111; Burton, *Lake Regions,* 137, 243–44, 245; Moloney, *With Captain Stairs,* 32–33.

71. Burton, *Lake Regions,* 55–56.

72. Burton, "Lake Regions," 159; Price, 18 October 1877, in *Private Journal,* 126; Last to Wright, Zanzibar, 14 June 1878, CMS CA6/014; Hassing and Bennett, "Journey across Tanganyika," 134.

73. Hassing and Bennett, "Journey across Tanganyika," 134; Moloney, *With Captain Stairs,* 54.

74. Burton, "Lake Regions," 139–40, 209; Burton, *Lake Regions,* 244, 245; Thomson, *To the Central African Lakes,* 1:287.

75. Stairs, 1 August 1891, in *Victorian Explorer,* ed. Konczacki, 202.

76. Moloney, *With Captain Stairs,* 33; French-Sheldon, *Sultan to Sultan,* 115; Lloyd, *In Dwarf Land,* 44; E.E. Hassforther, "An Account of a Journey through N.W. German East Africa in 1913–14," *TNR* 61 (September 1963): 210.

77. Burton, *Lake Regions,* 55–56, 245, Price, 18 October 1877, in *Private Journal,* 126–27; Decle, *Three Years,* 321; Charles Stewart Smith, "Explorations in Zanzibar Dominions," in RGS, *Supplementary Papers,* 2 (London: 1889): 107.

78. Hassing and Bennett, "Journey across Tanganyika," 141.

79. Wolf, *Missionary to Tanganyika,* 36, quoted in Sissons, "Economic Prosperity," 116; Stairs, 4 August 1891, in *Victorian Explorer,* ed. Konczacki, 204; also Price, 9 September 1877, in *Private Journal,* 86; French-Sheldon, *Sultan to Sultan,* 180, 190.

80. Pruen, *Arab and the African,* 181 (referring to Stokes); French-Sheldon, *Sultan to Sultan,* 148; Roscoe, *Twenty-five Years,* 14. Stairs also noted how porters sometimes inadvertently polluted water supplies from cisterns. See Stairs, 10 August 1891, in *Victorian Explorer,* ed. Konczacki, 208.

81. Burton, *Lake Regions,* 241, 245, 167; Cameron, *Across Africa,* 1:138.

82. Thomson, *To the Central African Lakes,* 1:95. For similar accounts, see Burton, *Lake Regions,* 244; Cameron, *Across Africa,* 1:38; Pruen, *Arab and the African,* 173–74; Decle, *Three Years,* 321; Lloyd, *In Dwarf Land,* 44; Konczacki, *Victorian Explorer,* 207.

83. Watt, *In the Heart,* 39.

84. Von der Decken, *Reisen in Ost-Afrika,* 1:232.

85. Burton, *Lake Regions,* 246; Grant, *Walk Across Africa,* 43; Livingstone, 7 December 1872, in *Last Journals,* 472; Tucker, *Eighteen Years,* 26; Stairs, "From the Albert Nyanza," 958; Stairs, 1 August 1891, in *Victorian Explorer,* ed. Konczacki, 202.

86. Speke, *Journal,* 52.

87. Atkins writes: "These interpersonal relations united the different parties in the duties of friendship, brotherhood, and matters of social import. Masters [employers] who held this custom in little account, or who attempted to deprive African workers of the deep emotional satisfaction as well as the social support it provided, encountered spirited resistance." Atkins, *The Moon Is Dead!* 122.

88. Rempel, "Exploration, Knowledge, and Empire," 201–2, 246.

89. Iliffe, *Modern History,* 35. For music, see chap.4, above.

90. Fortie, *Black and Beautiful,* 30.

91. Burton, *Lake Regions,* 249; Roscoe, *Twenty-five Years,* 55; Coulbois, *Dix années,* 19–20; Tucker, *Eighteen Years,* 28–29; Thomson, *To the Central African Lakes,* 1:166; Moloney, *With Captain Stairs,* 105.

92. Burton, *Lake Regions,* 462; Parke, 6 December 1888, in *My Personal Experiences,* 327; Price, 18 October 1877, in *Private Journal,* 127. For Tanzanian card games, see M.M. Hartnoll, "Some African Pastimes," *TNR* 5 (April 1938): 32–33.

93. Fortie, *Black and Beautiful,* 30; Johnson, *My African Reminiscences,* 94; Watt, *In the Heart,* 159–60; Last to Whiting, Mamboya, 4 October 1881, CMS G3A6/01.

94. The phrase is Iliffe's, in *Modern History,* 250. Dance has played a major role in Tanzania's history, acting as a unifying force, but expressing social change and regional cultural innovation. For some of this history, see N.V. Rounce, "The Banyamwezi at Home," n.d., RH MSS.Afr.s.424, 300–1; R. de Z. Hall, "The Dance Societies of the Wasukuma, as Seen in the Maswa District," *TNR* 1 (March 1936): 94–96; Ranger, "Movement of Ideas," 167–68; Terence O. Ranger, *Dance and Society in Eastern Africa 1890–1970: The Beni 'Ngoma'* (London, 1975); Iliffe, *Modern History.*

95. Hutley, 4 and 26 July 1878, in *Central African Diaries,* ed. Wolf, 39, 43.

96. See Burton, *Lake Regions,* 269, for the "Circean charms" of the women of Msene. A variation comes from the maritime world, where nineteenth-century American sailors ashore in foreign ports made temporary "marriages" with women, often prostitutes, in order to ensure sexual loyalty: "They called them their 'wives' and they asked for monogamous commitment. Whaleman Ezra Goodnough, who cruised the Indian Ocean in 1847, explained. . . . 'we can hire the girls in Mahe to remember us, that is more than the girls at home will do.'" Margaret S. Creighton, "American Mariners and the Rites of Manhood, 1830–1870," in *Jack Tar in History,* ed. Howell and Twomey, 159.

97. Burton, *Lake Regions,* 248; Johnston to Kirk, Liwela, 25 May 1879, Johnston Corr., RGS. For descriptions, see Thomson, *To the Central African Lakes,* 1:95–96, 178–79, 2:206–7.

98. Speke, *What Led,* 269–70; Burton, *Lake Regions,* 248–49; White Fathers, *A l'assaut des pays nègres,* 195.

99. Stanley, 27 December 1876, in *Exploration Diaries,* ed. Stanley and Neame, 145; Thomson, *To the Central African Lakes,* 1:90, 2:206–7.

100. Moloney, *With Captain Stairs,* 89–90.

101. See Andrew Sherratt, "Introduction: Peculiar Substances," in *Consuming Habits: Drugs in History and Anthropology,* ed. Jordan Goodman, Paul E. Lovejoy, and Andrew Sherratt (London, 1995), 1–2.

102. For datura, see Burton, *Lake Regions,* 81; W.D. Raymond, "Native Materia Medica," *TNR* 5 (April 1938): 74–75.

103. Hore, *To Lake Tanganyika,* 102; Roberts, "Nyamwezi Trade," 57–58.

104. For *pombe,* see Rockel, "Safari!" chap. 4 and especially Justin Willis, *Potent Brews: A Social History of Alcohol in East Africa 1850–1999* (Oxford, 2002). For porters and *pombe,* see Burton, *Lake Regions,* 81; Thomson, *To the Central African Lakes,* 1:256; Wolf, *Central African Diaries,* 247; Mtoro bin Mwinyi Bakari, *Customs of the Swahili,* 114; Willis, *Potent Brews,* 93.

105. Cannabis use was common in the Islamic world in medieval times. Archaeological evidence indicates its use in Ethiopia in the fourteenth century. Presumably it was known along the Swahili coast and in the interior soon afterwards, if not earlier. See Andrew Sherratt, "Alcohol and Its Alternatives: Symbol and Substance in Pre-industrial Cultures," in *Consuming Habits,* ed. Goodman, Lovejoy, and Sherratt.

106. Burton, *Lake Regions,* 81, 323, 343, 456; Burton, "Lake Regions," 224.

107. Smith, "Explorations in Zanzibar Dominions," 111; Mohamed Mangiringiri, interview, Tabora, 20 July 2000.

108. Burton, *Lake Regions,* 483; Reichard, "Wanjamuesi," 328; Casati, *Ten Years,* 2:297–98.

109. For cannabis use amongst the Kololo and Manganja of Nyassaland, see Livingstone and Livingstone, *Narrative,* 214–15; Pringle, *Journey in East Africa,* 153–54. For the Bashilange, see Fabian, *Out of Our Minds,* 151–79.

110. Stanley, 17 May 1876, in *Exploration Diaries,* ed. Stanley and Neame, 120; Stanley, *Through the Dark Continent,* 1:397–98; White Fathers, *A l'assaut des pays nègres,* 193–94; Shorter, *Nyungu-ya-Mawe,* 13; Unomah, "Economic Expansion," 256–57; Unomah, *Mirambo of Tanzania,* 22; Kabeya, *King Mirambo,* 12, 13, 15.

111. White Fathers, *A l'assaut des pays nègres,* 194; Mackay, 11 September 1883, in diary, CMS G3A6/01; Copplestone to Wigram, Uyui, 21 May 1881, CMS G3A6/01. Speke, *Journal,* 99, believed the Nyamwezi to be "desperate smokers and greatly given to drink," although it is not clear if he refers to tobacco or cannabis use. French-Sheldon,

Sultan to Sultan, 119, and Cameron, *Across Africa,* 1:39, refer to porters relaxing by smoking, although they do not specify what.

112. Burton, *Lake Regions,* 243, 246; Stanley and Neame, *Exploration Diaries,* 146; Casati, *Ten Years,* 2:297–98; Tucker, *Eighteen Years,* 29; Stairs, 8 July 1891, in *Victorian Explorer,* ed. Konczacki, 193; See also Livingstone, 3 November 1872, in *Last Journals,* 465; and Palmer to Whitehouse, 12 September 1880, LMS 3/3/A, for an accident involving a porter "intoxicated by bhang."

113. Reichard, "Wanjamuesi," 328. For other descriptions of smoking practices, see Copplestone to Wigram, Uyui, 21 May 1881, CMS G3A6/01; Burton, *Lake Regions,* 81; Casati, *Ten Years,* 2:297–98; Raymond, "Native Materia Medica," 74.

114. Koritschoner, "Some East African Native Songs," 62. I have changed Koritschoner's translation "Indian hemp" back to *bangi.*

115. Fabian, *Out of Our Minds,* 279. Hermann Wissmann and Paul Pogge led an expedition to found a station among the Lunda. Wissmann eventually crossed the continent to the Indian Ocean. Mukenge was the Bashilange chief, and Meta, his sister.

116. Mackay to Wright, Mpwapwa, 14 October 1876, CMS CA6/016; Clark to Wright, Mpwapwa, 4 November 1876, CMS CA6/07; Hore, *Tanganyika,* 173.

117. Burton, *Lake Regions,* 246; Thomson, *To the Central African Lakes,* 1:208–9; Watt, *In the Heart,* 157; Moloney, *With Captain Stairs,* 33; Stanley and Neame, *Expedition Diaries,* 55.

118. Burton, "Lake Regions," 14; Burton, *Lake Regions,* 495, 464; Pruen, *Arab and the African,* 117.

119. Vienne, "De Zanzibar à l'Oukami," 359; Mackay to Wright, Mpwapwa, 14 October 1876, CMS CA6/016; Moloney, *With Captain Stairs,* 33; Southon, "History, Country and People of Unyamwezi," pt. 5, 6; Tippu Tip, *Maisha,* 43 § 55; Mtoro bin Mwinyi Bakari, *Customs of the Swahili,* 161; Mtoro bin Mwinyi Bakari in Harries, *Swahili Prose Texts,* 185; Lloyd, *In Dwarf Land,* 44, 48.

120. Von der Decken, *Reisen in Ost-Afrika,* 1:232; Johnston, *Kilima-Njaro,* 46; Baumann, *Durch Massailand,* 15; Price, 18 October 1877, in *Private Journal,* 127; Thomson, *To the Central African Lakes,* 1:95; Hutley, 5 August 1878, in *Central African Diaries,* ed. Wolf, 47; Southon, "History, Country and People of Unyamwezi," pt. 5, 6; Pilkington to ?, Taro, 20 April 1890, in *Pilkington of Uganda,* by Harford-Battersby, 68; Parke, *My Personal Experiences,* 494.

121. French-Sheldon, *Sultan to Sultan,* 118; Burton, *Lake Regions,* 81.

122. Christopher Ehret, "East African Words and Things: Agricultural Aspects of Economic Transformation in the Nineteenth Century," in *Kenya in the Nineteenth Century (Hadith 8),* ed. Bethwell A. Ogot (Nairobi, 1985), 158. For the introduction of white rice into Unyamwezi, see Rockel, "Safari!" chap. 4.

123. Burton, *Lake Regions,* 81; Thomson, *To the Central African Lakes,* 1:256; Wolf, *Central African Diaries,* 247; Mtoro bin Mwinyi Bakari, *Customs of the Swahili,* 114.

124. See recent research on *konzo* in Hans Rosling, *Cassava Toxicity and Food Security* (Uppsala, 1987); W. P. Howlett, G. Brubaker, N. Mlingi, and H. Rosling, "A Geographical Cluster of Konzo in Tanzania," *Journal of Tropical and Geographical Neurology* 2 (1992): 102–8; N. V. Mlingi, V. D. Assay, A.B.M. Swai, D. G. McLarty, H. Karlen, and H. Rosling, "Determinants of Cyanide Exposure from Cassava in a Konzo-Affected Population in Northern Tanzania," *International Journal of Food Sciences and Nutrition* 44 (1993): 137–44.

125. Decle, *Three Years,* 317.

126. Tippu Tip, *Maisha*, 49–51, § 62–63; Heinrich Brode, *Tippoo Tib: The Story of His Career in Central Africa Narrated from His Own Accounts*, trans. H. Havelock (London, 1907), 64; Casati, *Ten Years*, 2:286; Parke, *My Personal Experiences*, 494; Rempel, "Exploration, Knowledge, and Empire," 186–87; Lloyd, *In Dwarf Land*, 96. Bontinck quotes Didderich and Delcommune on deaths of porters from cassava poisoning during the Belgian expedition to Katanga in 1891–92. See Bontinck, *L'autobiographie de Hamed ben Mohammed*, 221n98.

127. Burton, *Lake Regions*, 495; Copplestone to Lang, Uyui, 4 March 1882, CMS G3A6/01; Mtoro bin Mwinyi Bakari, *Customs of the Swahili*, 140; Speke, 15–20 December 1860, in *Journal*, 88.

128. Burton, *Lake Regions*, 463.

129. Baumann, *Durch Massailand*, 15; Pruen, *Arab and the African*, 173; Luck, *Charles Stokes*, 157.

130. Ashe, *Two Kings of Uganda*, 303; Parke, 14 August 1889, in *My Personal Experiences*, 469.

131. Von der Decken, *Reisen in Ost-Afrika*, 1:228, 2:9; Elton, *Travels*, 395; Pruen, *Arab and the African*, 125; Baumann, *Durch Massailand*, 25–26.

132. Elton, *Travels*, 395. A similar scene is described in Von der Decken, *Reisen in Ost-Afrika*, 2:9.

133. In addition to the sources on elephant hunting in chap. 2, see John M. MacKenzie, *The Empire of Nature: Hunting, Conservation and British Imperialism* (Manchester, 1988).

134. Hassing and Bennett, "Journey across Tanganyika," 145; Watt, *In the Heart*, 151; Cameron, *Across Africa*, 1:214.

135. Moir, *After Livingstone*, 103. The same process for a buffalo took a complete day. Elton, 2 December 1877, in *Travels*, 375. Various techniques for smoking and drying meat are described in Burton, *Lake Regions*, 463.

136. Stanley, *Through the Dark Continent*, 1:104.

137. Burton, "Lake Regions," 178; Burton, *Lake Regions*, 221; Ashe, *Chronicles of Uganda*, 437–48; Pruen, *Arab and the African*, 150–51; Stairs, "De Zanzibar au Katanga," 71.

138. Cameron, *Across Africa*, 1:204; Elton, 2 December 1877, in *Travels*, 375,

139. For examples of "backsliding," see Stanley, 11 January 1875, in *Exploration Diaries*, ed. Stanley and Neame, 44 (wild boar); Moloney, *With Captain Stairs*, 96–97 (hippopotamus).

140. For discussion and examples, see Christie, *Cholera Epidemics*, 311; Hutley, 18 July 1878, in *Central African Diaries*, ed. Wolf, 41; Reichard, "Wanjamuesi," 322.

141. Here is another parallel with merchant mariners, who were often expert fishermen and harvesters of all kinds of animal and marine life. Rediker writes, "Probably no one in the eighteenth century was steeled in the crafty art of self-preservation than the seaman." Rediker, *Between the Devil*, 128–29.

142. Raum, "German East Africa," 196–97. For northeast Tanzania and the northern route, see Kjekshus, *Ecology Control*, 111–16; Koponen, *People and Production*, 103–4, 118–19; Kimambo, "Environmental Control and Hunger"; Meyer, *Across East African Glaciers*, 115–17; Pangani Station to Governor, Pangani, 9 August 1895, TNA G1/35.

143. See Cameron, *Across Africa*, 1:122, on prices in Ugogo in 1873 compared with Burton's time.

144. Sissons, "Economic Prosperity"; Beverly Bolser Brown, "Ujiji: The History of a Lakeside Town, c. 1800–1914" (PhD diss., Boston University, 1973). There is a brief

discussion of the demand for foodstuffs created by the caravan trade and farmer response in Unyamwezi in Unomah and Webster, "East Africa," 296–97.

145. Burton, *Lake Regions,* 147. *Voiandzeia* is maize; *bajri* is millet; *arachis hypogoea* is the pignut.

146. Burton, *Lake Regions,* 182. See also ibid., 81–82, 153, 445, 166–67, 448, 449.

147. Hutley, 17 and 20 June 1878, in *Central African Diaries,* ed. Wolf, 34, 36. For similar accounts from Ugogo, see Sissons, "Economic Prosperity," 93. See also Kjekshus, *Ecology Control,* 47.

148. Decle, *Three Years,* 317, 321. In 1890s central Kenya, peasants responded enthusiastically to the demand for foodstuffs created by increasing caravan traffic. See Charles H. Ambler, *Kenyan Communities in the Age of Imperialism* (New Haven, CT, 1988), 109–10, 115–16.

149. Mackay to Wright, Mpwapwa, 14 October 1876, CMS CA6/016; Moloney, *With Captain Stairs,* 33; Baumann, *Durch Massailand,* 15.

150. Cameron, *Across Africa,* 1:95; Sissons, "Economic Prosperity," 93.

151. As Gleerup noted, porters passing through Uvinza were in great risk of being killed if thefts from fields occurred. See "Journey," 134–35. For an example of Gogo villagers beating porters who had probably stolen food from them, see Stairs, 20 August 1891, in *Victorian Explorer,* ed. Konczacki, 211.

152. Griffith to Whitehouse, Uguha, 24 January 1881, LMS 4/1/A.

153. Tippu Tip, *Maisha,* 43–49 § 55–61.

154. For examples where chiefs or elders negotiated an end to conflicts with caravans, see Hore, *To Lake Tanganyika,* 69–70; Hutley, 7 July 1881, in *Central African Diaries,* ed. Wolf, 275; Stanley, 13 January 1875, in *Exploration Diaries,* ed. Stanley and Neame, 44–45; Stanley, *Through the Dark Continent,* 1:89; Lloyd, *In Dwarf Land,* 95–96; Thomson, *To the Central African Lakes,* 1:273–74.

155. Burton, *Lake Regions,* 416. The "Shashi" of this region were also known to have massacred caravan personnel. See Kollmann, *Victoria Nyanza,* 177.

156. Compare the accounts in Stanley, 23–25 January 1875, in *Exploration Diaries,* ed. Stanley and Neame, 48–51; Stanley, *Through the Dark Continent,* 1:96–101.

157. Harford-Battersby, *Pilkington of Uganda,* 94–95. This was probably the massacre at Makengi, mentioned by Stairs, in which 300 Nyamwezi porters were said to have been killed. See Stairs, 17 August 1891, in *Victorian Explorer,* ed. Konczacki, 210.

158. Moloney, *With Captain Stairs,* 63–65.

159. Baumann, *Durch Massailand,* 18.

160. Lloyd, *In Dwarf Land,* 81–88. The best-known case of the annihilation of an entire caravan occurred in the Kedong Valley in Kenya in November 1895. In response to abuse and thefts, the Maasai killed 646 members including 85 Swahili and 540 Kikuyu porters. For the evidence, see Robert Maxon and David Javersak, "The Kedong Massacre and the Dick Affair: A Problem in the Early Colonial Historiography of East Africa," *HIA* 8 (1981): 261–69.

161. In Harries, *Swahili Prose Texts,* 183. The translation in Bakari, *Customs,* 160, is slightly different.

162. Burton, *Lake Regions,* 180, 181, 167; Hore, *To Lake Tanganyika,* 106; Stairs, 10 August 1891, in *Victorian Explorer,* ed. Konczacki, 208.

163. See Sissons, "Economic Prosperity," chap. 3.

164. In chap. 2.

165. Burton, *Lake Regions,* 181.

166. Pruen, *Arab and the African,* 184.

167. Ashe, *Two Kings of Uganda,* 241–42.

168. Speke, 25–26 January 1861, in *Journal,* 107; Burton, "Lake Regions," 154; Burton, *Lake Regions,* 181.

169. Moloney, *With Captain Stairs,* 53.

170. Tucker, *Eighteen Years,* 33. Another missionary saw the bodies of porters who had died of thirst within reach of the wells, and on one occasion a body inside a well shaft. Roscoe, *Twenty-five Years,* 52.

171. Burton, "Lake Regions," 147; Burton, *Lake Regions,* 177–78.

172. See Stairs, 4, 6, and 7–10 August 1891, in *Victorian Explorer,* ed. Konczacki, 204.

173. See chap. 4.

174. Livingstone, 13 July 1866, in *Last Journals,* 70; Roscoe, *Twenty-five Years,* 52; Swann, *Fighting the Slave Hunters,* 56–57; R.I. Wilfred Westgate, Maureen (Westgate) Carter, and Dorothy (Westgate) Leach, *T.B.R. Westgate: A Canadian Missionary on Three Continents* (Boston, 1987), 52–53.

175. Roscoe, *Twenty-five Years,* 52. Water brought by Gogo villagers cost porters two yards of cloth per gourd in December 1874. See Stanley and Neame, *Exploration Diaries,* 32.

176. Parke, 30 August 1889, in *My Personal Experiences,* 476; Hannington, *Peril and Adventure,* 23–24; Cameron, *Across Africa,* 1:138; Watt, *In the Heart,* 33. For similar accounts, see Thomson, *To the Central African Lakes,* 1:127; Hore, *Tanganyika,* 35–36.

177. Sissons, "Economic Prosperity," chap. 4.

178. Sissons, "Economic Prosperity," 8.

179. Sissons, "Economic Prosperity," 143–44.

180. Price to Lang, Mpwapwa, 5 February 1884, CMS G3A6/01; Price to Lang, Mpwapwa, 5 August 1884, CMS G3A6/01; Stokes to Lang, Uyui, 6 October 1884, CMS G3A6/02; Sissons, "Economic Prosperity," 136, 143–44; Clarke Brooke, "The Heritage of Famine in Central Tanzania," *TNR* 67 (1967): 20; Roscoe to Wigram, Mamboya, 1 November 1884, CMS G3A6/01; Giblin, *Politics of Environmental Control,* 121–24; Cooper, *Plantation Slavery,* 126–28; Hore, *To Lake Tanganyika,* 120, 125, 127.

181. Stokes to Lang, Kulehi camp, 26 July 1884, CMS G3A6/01.

182. Stokes to Lang, Kulehi camp, 26 July 1884, CMS G3A6/01; Baxter to Lang, Zanzibar, 4 August 1884, CMS G3A6/01; ? to Wigram, Mpwapwa, 17 January 1885, CMS G3A6/02; Sissons, "Economic Prosperity," 143.

183. Stokes to Lang, Kulehi camp, 26 July 1884, CMS G3A6/01.

184. Stokes to Lang, Uyui, 6 October 1884, CMS G3A6/02; Stokes to Stock, Uyui, n.d., CMS G3A6/02.

185. Hore, *To Lake Tanganyika,* 76, 77.

186. Hore, *To Lake Tanganyika,* 80–81.

187. Hore, *To Lake Tanganyika,* 97–98, 100–2.

188. Hore, *To Lake Tanganyika,* 102–6.

189. Sissons, "Economic Prosperity," 143.

190. A. Bloyet, "De Zanzibar à la station de Kondoa," *BSG* 7, no. 11 (1890): 361; Roscoe to Lang, Mamboya, 7 September 1885, CMS G3A6/02; ? to Wigram, Mpwapwa, 17 January 1885, CMS G3A6/02.

191. Roscoe to Wigram, Mamboya, 1 June 1885, CMS G3A6/02.

192. Sissons, "Economic Prosperity," 144.

193. Rockel, "Safari!" chap. 6.

CHAPTER 6: CONTESTING POWER ON SAFARI

1. Francis Snyder and Douglas Hay, "Comparisons in the Social History of Law: Labour and Crime," in *Labour, Law, and Crime: An Historical Perspective,* ed. Snyder and Hay (London, 1987), 27–30; Louis A. Knafla and Susan W. S. Binnie, "Beyond the State: Law and Legal Pluralism in the Making of Modern Societies," in *Law, Society, and the State: Essays in Modern Legal History,* ed. Knafla and Binnie (Toronto, 1995), 8–13.

2. Speke, 28 September 1861, in *Journal,* 172.

3. Johannes Fabian, *Language on the Road: Notes on Swahili in Two Nineteenth-Century Travelogues* (Hamburg, 1984). Fabian gives only one side of this story, ignoring porters' construction of caravan culture.

4. See the discussion in chap. 1.

5. David Montgomery, "Workers' Control of Machine Production in the 19th Century," *Labor History* 17, no. 4 (Fall 1976): 485–509.

6. For an 1876 example from Stanley's caravan, see Tippu Tip, *Maisha,* 89 § 117–18; McLynn, *Stanley,* 304; and especially Bontinck, *L'autobiographie de Hamed ben Mohammed,* 250–51n320–21.

7. Cairns, *Prelude to Imperialism,* 92–93; Henrika Kuklick, *The Savage Within: The Social History of British Anthropology, 1885–1945* (Cambridge, 1991), 100–1; George W. Stocking, Jr., *Victorian Anthropology* (New York, 1987), 213, 229.

8. Burton, *Lake Regions,* 491. The White Fathers compared the Waungwana to sailors. *A l'assaut des pays nègres,* 55.

9. Janet J. Ewald, "Crossers of the Sea: Slaves, Freedmen, and Other Migrants in the Northwestern Indian Ocean, c. 1750–1914," *AHR* 105, no. 1 (February 2000): 69–91.

10. See quote p. 121. For similar comparisons in Kenya, see Cooper, *From Slaves to Squatters,* 29, 45.

11. Robin Cohen, "Resistance and Hidden Forms of Consciousness among African Workers," *ROAPE* 19 (1980): 8–22; Bill Freund, *The African Worker* (Cambridge, 1988), 59; Allen F. and Barbara Isaacman, "Resistance and Collaboration in Southern and Central Africa, 1850–1920," *IJAHS,* 10, no. 1 (1977): 31–62; Allen F. Isaacman, "Peasants and Rural Social Protest in Africa," *ASR* 33, no. 2 (1990): 1–121.

12. For similar use of desertion by seamen, see Rediker, *Between the Devil,* 102–6, 115, 291–92.

13. For a typology of state, settler, and mission colonialism, see Comaroff, "Images of Empire."

14. Rempel, "Exploration, Knowledge, and Empire," 53.

15. Comaroff, "Images of Empire."

16. For discussion, see Rempel, "Exploration, Knowledge, and Empire," 151–52, 157–65.

17. See Parke, *My Personal Experiences,* 21. For the contradictions in Stanley's character, see McLynn, *Stanley.*

18. See Stanley, *Through the Dark Continent,* 1:209; Stanley, 6 February 1875, in *Exploration Diaries,* ed. Stanley and Neame, 55. Mounteney Jephson, a member of the Emin Pasha Relief Expedition, noted that *shauri*s always ended "by everyone being brought around to Stanley's way of thinking," quoted in Donald Simpson, *Dark Companions,* 183.

19. See chap. 4.

20. The classic accounts are E. P. Thompson, "Time, Work-Discipline and Industrial Capitalism," reprinted in Thompson, *Customs in Common,* 352–403; Herbert Gutman,

"Work, Culture, and Society in Industrializing America, 1815–1919," in *Work, Culture, and Society in Industrializing America: Essays in American Working-Class and Social History* (New York, 1977); Montgomery, "Workers' Control."

21. See Atkins, *The Moon Is Dead!* especially chap. 4.

22. Chris Lowe on clocks and culture, 1 October 2003, H-Africa listserv.

23. Coquery-Vidrovitch and Lovejoy, "Workers of Trade," 15.

24. For Nyamwezi caravan officials, see chap. 3.

25. Lloyd, *In Dwarf Land,* 43–44.

26. Lloyd, *In Dwarf Land,* 45. We may allow for some twists in the translation and retelling.

27. Moore, *To the Mountains,* 116–17.

28. Wilson and Felkin, *Uganda,* 1:17.

29. Hutley, 29 September 1877 and 15 June 1878, in *Central African Diaries,* ed. Wolf, 10, 34; Dodgshun, 28 September 1877, in *From Zanzibar,* ed. Bennett, 35. See also Livingstone, 23 April 1866, in *Last Journals,* 35–36.

30. Henry to Wright, Mpwapwa, 1 October 1878, CMS CA6/012.

31. Cameron, *Across Africa,* 1:112–13; also 155–56.

32. Hore, *To Lake Tanganyika,* 121.

33. Hassing and Bennett, "Journey across Tanganyika," 133–34.

34. See chap. 3; also Unomah, "Economic Expansion," 286–88; Temu, "Tanzanian Societies," 105; Chief Abdallah Fundikira, interview, Tabora, 4 July 2000.

35. A description from a different context is in C. Gillman, 7 January 1906, in diaries, RH MSS Afr.s.1175(1). For a more problematic example, see Dodgshun, 30 September 1877, in *From Zanzibar,* ed. Bennett.

36. An earlier assessment is in Cairns, *Prelude to Imperialism,* 41–46.

37. Hore, *Tanganyika,* 247–48.

38. For some episodes from the journey, see chap. 5.

39. Hore, *Tanganyika,* 163–64.

40. Dodgshun died at Ujiji soon after arriving in early 1879.

41. Dodgshun, 18–19 August 1877 and 2–8 May 1878, in *From Zanzibar,* ed. Bennett, 26–27, 64.

42. Southon to Whitehouse, Urambo, 18 December 1879, "Hints for Missionaries Proceeding to Central Africa," LMS 2/3/A. Other travelers also found maintaining discipline easier if they shared jokes and banter with their porters. See Hore, *Tanganyika,* 35–36; Smith, "Explorations in Zanzibar Dominions," 107.

43. Southon, "Hints for Missionaries," LMS 2/3/A. Southon uses the labels Waungwana and Swahili interchangeably. Compare Southon's approach with the almost ritual quality of the mutual "boosting" session when Thomson reached Lake Tanganyika with his caravan. He took the roll, gave a speech praising his men, and shook the hand of each of his 150 porters "with many pleasing and encouraging words." Thomson, *To the Central African Lakes,* 1:309–10.

44. Jérome Becker, the Belgian explorer, had similar ideas. See Fabian, *Out of Our Minds,* 141–44.

45. Philip Curtin, *The Image of Africa* (Madison, 1964), 414–31; Andrew Ross, "David Livingstone: The Man behind the Mask," in De Gruchy, *London Missionary Society,* 37–54.

46. Livingstone, 26 March 1866 and 16 February 1867, in *Last Journals,* 26, 160.

47. Hine, *Days Gone By,* 275.

48. Wilson and Felkin, *Uganda,* 1:74, 78–79; Swann, *Fighting the Slave Hunters,* 73; Watt, *In the Heart,* 75–76, 92.

49. Mackay to Wright, Mpwapwa, 14 October 1876; Mackay, Bagamoyo, 19 April 1887, in diary, CMS CA6/016.

50. Dodgshun, 16 and 29 September 1878, in *From Zanzibar,* ed. Bennett, 82–83, Swann, *Fighting the Slave Hunters,* 152–53.

51. French-Sheldon, *Sultan to Sultan;* Dorothy Middleton, *Victoria Lady Travellers* (London, 1965), 96–97.

52. Watt, *In the Heart,* 96–102.

53. Watt, *In the Heart,* 96–99. For a contemporary criticism of Hannington's use of "brute violence," see Cairns, *Prelude to Imperialism,* 41.

54. Quoted in Watt, *In the Heart,* 99.

55. Most other European travelers came to the same conclusion. See Hutley, 14 July 1879, in *Central African Diaries,* ed. Wolf, 117. Exceptions were Burton and CMS missionary Gordon. See Burton, *Lake Regions,* 432; Gordon to Lang, Msalala, 5 November 1883, CMS G3A6/01.

56. Watt, *In the Heart,* 100–1.

57. Watt, *In the Heart,* 102.

58. Bridges, "Nineteenth-Century East African Travel Records," 189.

59. Thomson, *To the Central African Lakes,* 2:104–5. For further slowdowns and protests, see ibid.,106–8.

60. Thomson, *To the Central African Lakes,* 2:114–15.

61. Thomson, *To the Central African Lakes,* 2:115–16. More physical confrontations occurred before Thomson's "conquest" was complete. See ibid., 116–18.

62. See also Thomson, *To the Central African Lakes,* 1:280; Thomson, *Through Masai Land,* 73, 99.

63. For example, Thomson, *To the Central African Lakes,* 2:191.

64. Weule, *Native Life,* 41–42.

65. Hassing and Bennett, "Journey across Tanganyika," 137. See also Johnston, *Kilima-Njaro,* 48–50.

66. Decle, *Three Years,* 321. Decle's clear approval of corporal punishment for Africans is on page 203. A *kiboko* is a hippopotamus-hide whip.

67. Peters, *New Light,* 58.

68. Ewart S. Grogan and Arthur H. Sharp, *From the Cape to Cairo: The First Traverse of Africa From South to North* (London, 1900), 101. This book contains a litany of racist invective and accounts of brutality beyond even the standards of the decades of high imperialism.

69. Grogan and Sharp, *From the Cape,* 122–23. In April 1888, near the Ituri River, Stanley shot at two Waungwana porters "as they were not working as well as they might," grazing the heel of one man. Jephson, *Diary,* 235.

70. Fabian, *Out of Our Minds,* 144–46.

71. Rempel, "Exploration, Knowledge, and Empire," 332.

72. See Mackay to Wright, Mkindo (Mkundi?) River, 22 March 1878; Robb to Mackay, Zanzibar, 11 April 1878; Mackay to Wright, Uyui, 24 May 1878; all CMS CA6/016; Smith to Hutchinson, Zanzibar, 24 June 1878, CMS CA6/03. The incident is not mentioned in the hagiographic *A.M. Mackay.* For comments by a fellow missionary sympathetic to Mackay, see Ashe, *Chronicles of Uganda,* 86. For recent accounts of the incident, see Bennett, *From Zanzibar,* xix–xx; Oliver, *Missionary Factor,* 83; Harman, *Bwana Stokesi,* 24–25.

73. Parke, 20 and 21 September 1887 and 2 May 1889, in *My Personal Experiences,* 111, 418–19; Hoffman, *With Stanley in Africa,* 132–33.

74. Moore, *To the Mountains,* 140, 161–52, 169. Thirty-three of Moore's porters deserted between Ujiji and the south end of Lake Kivu.

75. Peters, *New Light,* 105, 210; Lamden, "Some Aspects of Porterage," 161.

76. Rockel, "Safari!" chap. 6.

77. Grogan and Sharp, *From the Cape,* 95; Fortie, *Black and Beautiful,* 27–28, 52, 101; Weule, *Native Life.*

78. Paternalists mention flogging less than authoritarians. Whether this represents either a reluctance to discuss it or to impose it is difficult to decide. I suspect a little of both. For evidence of Arabs who flogged their porters, see Decle, *Three Years,* 314.

79. Harman, *Bwana Stokesi,* 23; Burton, *Lake Regions,* 183, 432; Speke, *Journal,* 265, also 416; Grant, *Walk across Africa,* 76.

80. Johnson, *My African Reminiscences,* 21; Smith, "Explorations in Zanzibar Dominions," 106; Hutley, 12 August 1878, 27 April 1878, and 14 September 1881, in *Central African Diaries,* ed. Wolf, 49, 24, 279–80; Lloyd, *In Dwarf Land,* 92–93; Meyer, *Across East African Glaciers,* 48, 52; Peters, *New Light,* 62–63; Grogan and Sharp, *From the Cape,* 96, 103; Fortie, *Black and Beautiful,* 58, 100. For further examples, see Livingstone, 7 July 1886, 30 August 1872, 3 November 1872, and 14 February 1873, in *Last Journals,* 69, 456, 465, 488; Cameron, *Across Africa,* 1:241–42, 298; Thomson, *To the Central African Lakes,* 1:114, 155–58; 193; Thomson, *Through Masai Land,* 57; Moloney, *With Captain Stairs,* 40–41.

81. See Bennett, *Stanley's Despatches,* 17; Stanley, *How I Found Livingstone,* 129–32; McLynn, *Stanley,* 114; Rempel, "Exploration, Knowledge, and Empire," 280.

82. Stanley, 4 and 5 July 1875, in *Exploration Diaries,* ed. Stanley and Neame, 86–87 (here Stanley says 100 lashes); Stanley, *Through the Dark Continent,* 1:209 (here Stanley says 50 lashes); Liebowitz, *The Physician and the Slave Trade,* 205, quoting Kirk.

83. Parke, *My Personal Experiences,* 38–39; Jephson, 1 August, 18 October, and 20 October 1887, in *Diary,* 131, 167–68, 170; Stairs, "Shut up in the African Forest," 59. Parke defends Stanley in *My Personal Experiences,* 513. See Rempel, "Exploration, Knowledge, and Empire," 218–19, 266, 279, for John Henry Bishop, and 166–73, 212, for further extreme cases of 100 and 150 lashes.

84. Mary Turner, paper presented at the International Conference on Masters and Servants in History, York University, Toronto, April 1996. In the antebellum plantations in the Deep South of the United States there was no limit, although reforms in the 1840s prohibited flogging to the extent of causing death. Rick Halpern, personal communication.

85. Deut. 25:2–3; 2 Cor. 11:24.

86. Chris Munn, personal communication.

87. David Killingray, "The 'Rod of Empire': The Debate over Corporal Punishment in the British African Colonial Forces, 1888–1946," *JAH* 35, no. 2 (1994): 203.

88. See Killingray, "Rod of Empire," for European justification for the flogging of Africans.

89. Killingray, "Rod of Empire," 203.

90. "Regulations to be Observed by Caravan Leaders and Others in the Engagement and Treatment of Porters," AA12/9, consular records, ZNA; published in *ZEAG,* 17 October 1894, 9–10. For discussion, see Rockel, "Safari!" chap. 5.

91. Koponen, *Development for Exploitation,* 337–38, 359–66, for discussion. See also Iliffe, *Modern History,* 150, for statistics covering the years 1901–13.

92. Michel Foucault, *Discipline and Punish: The Birth of the Prison* (Toronto, 1995), 14, 16.

93. Thomson, *To the Central African Lakes,* 1:221–25. For a case from the Emin Pasha Relief Expedition in which porters preferred flogging to the stopping of rations, see Rempel, "Exploration, Knowledge, and Empire," 281–82.

94. Killingray, "Rod of Empire," 207, notes evidence for a preference for flogging instead of fines and extra duties in colonial armies.

95. Smith, "Explorations in Zanzibar Dominions," 106.

96. Morton to Smith, Unyanyembe, 25 July 1877, CMS CA6/03; Dodgshun, 14 June 1878, in *From Zanzibar,* ed. Bennett, 72; Stairs, 6 July 1891, in *Victorian Explorer,* ed. Konczacki, 192; Rashid bin Hassani, "Story of Rashid bin Hassani," 100; Decle, *Three Years,* 314, 497.

97. Bennett, *Stanley's Despatches,* 61, 62, 63, 64; Stanley, *How I Found Livingstone,* 116; Stanley, 30 December 1874, 24 January 1875, 6 February 1875, 4 July 1875, and 5 July 1875, in *Exploration Diaries,* ed. Stanley and Neame, 37, 50, 55, 86–87; Stanley, *Through the Dark Continent,* 1:209; McLynn, *Stanley,* 137.

98. Bennett, *Stanley's Despatches,* 40.

99. Grogan and Sharp, *From the Cape,* 103–4. A porter at Fort Bodo was sentenced to 30 days' "stone drill" combined with 50 lashes for sleeping while on sentry duty. See Stairs, Diary, 11 July 1888, in Rempel, "Exploration, Knowledge, and Empire," 212.

100. A useful overview from an anthropological perspective is Sherry B. Ortner, "Resistance and the Problem of Ethnographic Refusal," *CSSH* 37 (1995): 173–93.

101. Eric Hobsbawm, *Primitive Rebels* (New York, 1965); Thompson, *Making;* E. P. Thompson, "Eighteenth-Century English Society: Class Struggle Without Class?" *SH* 3, no. 2 (1978): 133–65; Christopher Hill, *The World Turned Upside Down: Radical Ideas during the English Revolution* (London, 1975).

102. Ortner, "Resistance," 174–75; Foucault, *Discipline;* James C. Scott, *Weapons of the Weak: Everyday Forms of Peasant Resistance* (New Haven, CT, 1985).

103. Ortner, "Resistance," 175.

104. Ortner, "Resistance," 176–80. A good example is Allen F. Isaacman, *Cotton Is the Mother of Poverty: Peasants, Work, and Rural Struggle in Colonial Mozambique, 1938–1961* (Portsmouth, NH, 1997).

105. Ortner, "Resistance," 180.

106. Thompson, *Making;* Thompson, *Customs in Common;* Terence O. Ranger, *Revolt in Southern Rhodesia, 1896–97: A Study in African Resistance,* 2nd ed. (London, 1979); Charles van Onselen, *Chibaro: African Mine Labour in Southern Rhodesia* (Nottingham, 1976); Rediker, *Between the Devil;* Dipesh Chakrabarty, *Rethinking Working-Class History: Bengal 1890–1940* (Princeton, NJ, 1989); Jeffrey B. Peires, *The Dead Will Arise: Nongqawuse and the Great Xhosa Cattle-Killing Movement of 1856–7* (Johannesburg, 1989); Isaacman, "Peasants"; Isaacman, *Cotton;* Atkins, *The Moon Is Dead!*

107. Thompson, *Making;* Rediker, *Between the Devil;* Chakrabarty, *Rethinking;* Isaacman, *Cotton.*

108. Van Onselen, *Chibaro.*

109. Freund, *African Worker,* 58–59.

110. In Stanley's Emin Pasha Relief Expedition, working conditions were abysmal, and food entitlements so limited that the odds for survival were poor: only 35 percent of the Rear Column porters lived to see Zanzibar again. See Rempel, "Exploration, Knowledge, and Empire," 282–88.

111.Swann, *Fighting the Slave Hunters,* 174. The evidence for desertion is less clear for Nyamwezi caravans.

112. Rediker, *Between the Devil,* 101. "Desertion was a … trademark of a footloose maritime proletariat" (105).

113. Harries, *Work, Culture, and Identity,* 42.

114. Stichter, *Migrant Laborers,* 3–4.

115. A representative of the Zanzibar-based trading company and caravan outfitter Boustead, Ridley and Company noted of deserters that "whether … slaves or freemen they almost invariably return to Zanzibar." Muxworthy to Wookey, Zanzibar, 28 June 1880, LMS 3/4/C.

116. Stairs, 5 and 10 July 1891, in *Victorian Explorer,* ed. Konczacki, 191, 193– 94.

117. Thomson, *To the Central African Lakes,* 1:vii–viii, 309–10.

118. Burton, *Zanzibar,* 2:294–95. He refers to the free porters as "undisciplinable," while the slaves and ex-slaves were "apt to abscond."

119. Burton, *Zanzibar,* 2:147.

120. Speke, 27 October, 27 November, 5 December, and 10 December 1860, in *Journal,* 64, 75, 80, 86. For a full list of the caravan's losses to Unyanyembe, including the desertions of 25 Zanzibari slaves and 98 Nyamwezi porters, see Speke, 23 January 1861, in ibid., 97. For the Arab's losses, see Speke, 1–3 June and 11–15 September 1861, in ibid., 132–33, 164.

121. Bennett, *Stanley's Despatches,* 19, 50, 61; Simpson, *Dark Companions,* 116; Stanley, 16 January 1875, in *Exploration Diaries,* ed. Stanley and Neame, 46.

122. Cameron to Kirk, Masuwa, 10 April 1873, VLC 3/2, RGS; Cameron, *Across Africa,* 1:47, 72, 75, 122, 138, 139, 179; Foran, *African Odyssey,* 66, 91–94.

123. Giraud, *Lacs,* 51. Giraud writes that the Ganda looked down on porterage, claiming that they should be *askari* instead.

124. Giraud, *Lacs,* 474–78, 509–519.

125. Baumann, *Durch Massailand,* 8.

126. Burton, *Lake Regions,* 100–103.

127. Grant, *Walk across Africa,* 22–23, 42, 121.

128. Tippu Tip, *Maisha,* 43–49 § 55–61. See also chap. 5. For another case of a dispute between porters and a village community leading to desertions, see Herman von Wissman, *My Second Journey through Equatorial Africa,* trans. Minna J.A. Bergman (London, 1891), 267–68.

129. Dodgshun to Mullens, Uyui, 8 January 1879, LMS 2/1/A; Dodgshun, in *From Zanzibar,* ed. Bennett, 114; Bennett, *Mirambo,* 89–90.

130. Harries, *Swahili Prose Texts,* 239. Strikes also occurred when porters demanded that a powerful chief be conciliated before their caravan might proceed. For examples, see Burton, *Zanzibar,* 2:208–9; Thomson, *To the Central African Lakes,* 1:194–5, 197; Johnston, *Kilima-Njaro,* 115–17.

131. Watt, *In the Heart,* 152–56.

132. Cameron, *Across Africa,* 1:156–62, 171–177; Dillon to ?, Unyanyembe, 8 October 1873, VLC 3/6 RGS. For discussion of some consequences of the war, see Rockel, "Nation of Porters."

133. Ashe, *Two Kings of Uganda,* 26; Stokes to Lang, Bembiganda (?), Mgunda Mkali, 9 December 1882, CMS G3A6/01. See also Hannington to Wigram, Kwandi, 26 October 1882; Copplestone to Lang, Urambo, 27 October 1882, CMS G3A6/01.

134. Broyon to McGregor, Zanzibar, 1 October 1879, LMS 2/3/D.

135. Deniaud journal, Maison généralice, 31 August 1878, White Fathers, quoted in Nolan, "Christianity in Unyamwezi," 71; White Fathers, *A l'assaut des pays nègres,* 160.

136. Krapf, *Travels,* 288–89, 292–93.

137. Burton, *Lake Regions,* 153.

138. Hutley, 24 April 1879, in *Central African Diaries,* ed. Wolf, 104. The expedition journal is blank for this period due to an "almost general" attack of "fever." White Fathers, *A l'assaut des pays nègres,* 311.

139. Bennett, *Mirambo,* 86.

140. Dodgshun, 28 January 1878, in *From Zanzibar,* ed. Bennett, 57; Hutley, 27 January 1878, in *Central African Diaries,* ed. Wolf, 14.

141. Dodgshun, 19–25 April, and 11–12, 28, and 29 May 1878, in *From Zanzibar,* ed. Bennett, 63, 66, 69, 114; Dodgshun to Mullens, Uyui, 8 January 1879, LMS 2/1/A; Hutley, 6 April, 11 May, and 31 May 1878, in *Central African Diaries,* ed. Wolf, 19, 27, 30.

142. Grogan and Sharp, *From the Cape,* 65, 99.

143. Shorter, "The Kimbu," 109–110; Shorter, *Nyungu-ya-Mawe,* 13. Nyungu and his allies were well placed to attack caravans, especially in the Mgunda Mkali. The central route was twice temporarily closed, in 1878 and 1880.

144. Burton, *Lake Regions,* 192; Sissons, "Economic Prosperity," 242, 258, 152.

145. Bennett, *From Zanzibar,* 72, 14 June 1878. Dodgshun also refers to chained deserters in an Arab caravan. See 19 June 1878, in *From Zanzibar,* ed. Bennett, 73.

146. Tippu Tip, *Maisha,* 19–21 § 12–15.

147. Morton to Smith, Unyanyembe, 25 July 1877, CMS CA6/03.

148. Pruen, *Arab and the African,* 218.

149. Peters, *New Light,* 94–95.

150. Muxworthy to Southon, Zanzibar, 6 January 1880; Muxworthy to Southon, Zanzibar, 28 June, 1880; Muxworthy to Wookey, Zanzibar, 15 October 1880, LMS 3/4/E.

151. Moore, *To the Mountains,* 162; Grogan and Sharp, *From the Cape,* 103. Captured deserters were also returned to the coast to be dealt with by company authorities there. See French-Sheldon, *Sultan to Sultan,* 106; Decle, *Three Years,* 496–97, for a case in British East Africa.

152. Grogan and Sharp, *From the Cape,* 103.

153. Peters, *New Light,* 84–86, 104–5. By 1896 Peters had gained such a reputation for brutality that he was dismissed from the German colonial service after being tried for various abuses. See W. O. Henderson, "German East Africa 1884–1918," in *History of East Africa,* ed. Harlow and Chilver, 2:146; Koponen, *Development for Exploitation,* 363.

154. Stairs, 25 July 1891, in *Victorian Explorer,* ed. Konczacki, 199–200.

155. Southon to Whitehouse, Urambo, 18 December 1879, "Hints for Missionaries," LMS 2/3/A. Judging by the low number of desertions in Southon's caravan—only 3 out of 168 porters deserted between Saadani and Mpwapwa—his advice was good. See Southon to Whitehouse, Mpwapwa, 16 July 1879, LMS 2/1/D.

156. Baumann, *Durch Massailand,* 7; Murphy to Kirk, Bagamoyo, 19 April 1873, VLC 3/4 RGS; Roscoe, *Twenty-five Years,* 7; Murphy to Kirk, Tonda, 25 April 1873, VLC 3/4 RGS.

157. Bennett, *Stanley's Despatches,* 190.

158. Thomson, *Through Masai Land,* 35.

159. Giraud, *Lacs,* 42.

160. Roscoe, *Twenty-five Years,* 5. Thomson describes a similar scene in *To the Central African Lakes,* 1:66–67, pointing out that most of the crowd were porters' wives, left behind and perhaps never to see their husbands again.

161. Moloney, *With Captain Stairs,* 19–20.

162. Iliffe, *Modern History,* 46.

163. Morton to Smith, Unyanyembe, 25 July 1877, CMS CA6/03; Mackay to Wright, Uyui, 24 May 1878, CMS CA6/016; Thomson, *To the Central African Lakes,* 2:114; Tippu Tip, *Maisha,* 89 § 118; Stairs, "Shut up in the African Forest," 56; Grogan and Sharp, *From the Cape,* 122–23.

164. Porters were not the only laborers to go on strike in nineteenth-century Tanzania. Villagers attached to Holy Ghost Fathers' mission stations protested the lack of "liberty, land, wages." Zanzibaris hired in 1877 to build a road from Dar es Salaam struck over the "hard work" and inadequate rations. Canoemen on Lake Victoria struck work, demanding higher wages. See Brown, "Pre-colonial History," 217–18; Moir, 19 June–14 July 1877, in journal, 1877, MP, box 64, IBEAC file3; Mayes to Mackinnon, SS *Abyssinia,* 26 September 1877, MP, box 65, IBEAC file 7; Hannington, *Peril and Adventure,* 72.

165. For example, in Last to Lang, Mamboya, 7 June 1882; Ashe to Lang, Kagei, 13 March 1883, CMS G3A6/01.

166. Grant, *Walk across Africa,* 24, also 75.

167. White Fathers, *A l'assaut des pays nègres,* 283.

168. Grant, *Walk across Africa,* 32. See also Mrs. Charles E. B. Russell, *General Rigby, Zanzibar and the Slave Trade* (1935; repr., New York, 1970), 239.

169. Cameron, *Across Africa,* 1:68, 196; Foran, *African Odyssey,* 54, 57, 104.

170. Bennett, *Stanley's Despatches,* 69–71, 76–77.

171. Dodgshun, 29 August 1878, in *From Zanzibar,* ed. Bennett, 80.

172. Hannington, *Peril and Adventure,* 52–54. For another case of strikes over rations, see Dodgshun, 7 March 1879, in *From Zanzibar,* ed. Bennett, 105.

173. Gordon to Lang, Msalala, 5 November 1883, CMS G3A6/01. See the discussion of stopping rations as a punishment, above.

174. Cameron, *Across Africa,* 1:152; Foran, *African Odyssey,* 73. Strikes also occurred over unpaid wages. See Speke, *What Led,* 197, 200–1.

175. Speke, 3–6 June 1861, in *Journal,* 133.

176. Giraud, *Lacs,* 99–100. For similar strikes, see Thomson, *To the Central African Lakes,* 1:178–79, 288–89.

177. Speke, *Journal,* 159. This was one of many strikes during the journey; there was a repetition in September (p. 172). Earlier, the expedition's Nyamwezi porters had successfully struck over fear of the Ngoni. See Speke, 17 and 19 June 1861, in *Journal,* 144–46, also 443; Grant, *Walk across Africa,* 112–13, 114–15, 121.

178. Livingstone, 11 February 1871, in *Last Journals,* 357. Livingstone told Stanley at Ujiji, "My men would not budge a step forward. They mutinied and formed a secret resolution that if I still insisted on going on to raise a disturbance in the country, after they had effected it to abandon me . . . the hearts of my people failed, and they set about frustrating me in every possible way." Bennett, *Stanley's Despatches,* 99. Stanley probably exaggerated Livingstone's account.

179. Doghshun, 31 December 1877, 3 January 1878, and 19 January 1878, in *From Zanzibar,* ed. Bennett, 52–53, 55.

180. Speke, *What Led,* 272, 300–1, 327. For another strike over trading rights, see Cameron, *Across Africa,* 1:299–301.

181. AIA, *Rapports sur les marches,* 31.

182. Isaacman, *Cotton,* 205–9. For peasant and rural resistance during the German period, see Sunseri, *Vilimani.*

183. Burton, *Lake Regions,* 384–85.

184. Grant, *Walk across Africa,* 42.

185. Wilson and Felkin, *Uganda,* 1:15–16.

186. Hore, *Tanganyika,* 34–35.

187. Peters, *New Light,* 61–63.

188. Grogan and Sharp, *From the Cape,* 96.

189. Last to MacGregor, Mpwapwa, 9 September 1879; Muxworthy to Whitehouse, Zanzibar, 15 October 1879; Last to MacGregor, Mpwapwa, 27 October 1879; Muxworthy to Whitehouse, Zanzibar, 13 November 1879, LMS 2/3/D. For a similar case, see Muxworthy to Southon, Zanzibar, 28 June 1880, LMS 3/4/E.

190. Muxworthy to Southon, Zanzibar, 6 January 1880, LMS 3/4/D.

191. Boustead, Ridley and Company to Southon, Zanzibar, 6 February 1880, LMS 3/4/D.

192. Moloney, *With Captain Stairs,* 26.

193. Stairs, 5 July 1891, in *Victorian Explorer,* ed. Konczacki, 191. For another case, see Decle, *Three Years,* 314.

194. See chap. 3.

195. Grant, *Walk across Africa,* 32.

196. Rempel, "Exploration, Knowledge, and Empire," 190–91, 243.

197. Cameron, *Across Africa,* 1:236, 241; Thomson, *Through Masai Land,* 56–57.

198. Blackburn to Lang, Mamboya, 5 July 1883, CMS G3A6/01; Watt, *In the Heart,* 393–94; Pilkington to ?, Taro, 20 April 1890, in *Pilkington of Uganda,* by Harford-Battersby, 71.

199. Grogan and Sharp, *From the Cape,* 120–21. The possibility remains that the carriers were speaking the truth. For a similar case, see Decle, *Three Years,* 474. Other cases of theft are mentioned in Hutley, 2 June and 6 July 1880, in *Central African Diaries,* ed. Wolf, 189–90, 193; Griffith to Thompson, Ujiji, 21 October 1882, LMS 4/5/B; Decle, *Three Years,* 483.

200. Fortie, *Black and Beautiful,* 27.

201. See Blohm, *Nyamwezi,* Vol. 1: (plate 10, illustration 142).

202. Rockel, "Safari!" chap. 6.

CHAPTER 7: CUSTOMS IN COMMON

1. Nyamwezi marching songs, in Mtoro bi Mwinyi Bakari, *Customs of the Swahili,* 165–66. Allen, the editor, notes, "Appropriately, the songs are in a Swahili that contains a Kinyamwezi admixture. The Nyamwezi as men in the middle sing songs that insult both the coasters and the inlanders" (297n19).

2. Speke, *Journal,* 194–95.

3. These themes will be more fully explored elsewhere.

4. Anthony Giddens, *The Constitution of Society: Outline of the Theory of Structuration* (Berkeley and Los Angeles, 1984), 164. Intersocietal systems are "social systems which cut across whatever dividing lines exist between societies or societal totalities, including agglomerations of societies" (375).

5. Johnson, *Standard Swahili-English Dictionary,* 453. For fuller discussion of the lexical root, see Stephen A. Lucas, "The Role of Utani in Eastern Tanzanian Clan Histories," in "Utani Relationships in Tanzania," ed. Stephen A. Lucas (Dar es Salaam, 1974–76), 1:16–17.

6. Lucas, "Role of Utani."

7. Circumcised versus uncircumcised peoples; upcountry versus coastal peoples; peoples of the mountains versus peoples of the plains, and so on. See Stephen A Lucas, "On the Non-existence of Tribes in Tanzania: An Utani Conceptualization of Intergroup Relationships," in "Utani Relationships in Tanzania," ed. Lucas, 7:5–6.

8. R. E. Moreau, "Joking Relationships in Tanganyika," *Africa* 14 (1943–44): 386–400.

9. For example, Iliffe, *Modern History,* 46.

10. Dora C. Abdy, "Notes on Utani and Other Bondei Customs," *Man* 14 (October 1924): 152–54.

11. T. V. Scrivenor, "Some Notes on Utani, or the Vituperative Alliances Existing between Clans in the Masasi District, " *TNR* 4 (1937): 72–74; F. J. Pedler, "Joking Relationship in East Africa," *Africa* 13, no. 1 (January 1940): 170–73; E. Spies, "Observations on Utani Customs among the Ngoni of Songea District," *TNR* 16 (1943): 49–53.

12. R. E. Moreau, "The Joking Relationship (*Utani*) in Tanganyika," *TNR* 12 (1941): 1–10; Moreau, "Joking Relationships in Tanganyika," 386–400.

13. Alfred Reginald Radcliffe-Brown, "On Joking Relationships," in *Structure and Function in Primitive Society: Essays and Addresses* (London, 1952), 90–104; Radcliffe-Brown, "A Further Note on Joking Relationships," in *Structure and Function,* 105–16. These articles were originally published in the journal *Africa.*

14. Radcliffe-Brown, "On Joking Relationships," 91.

15. Radcliffe-Brown, "On Joking Relationships," 91–93.

16. Radcliffe-Brown, "On Joking Relationships," 94–95.

17. Radcliffe-Brown, "On Joking Relationships," 101–2.

18. This paragraph relies on Radcliffe-Brown, "A Further Note"; T. O. Beidelman, "*Utani:* Some Kaguru Notions of Death, Sexuality and Affinity," *Southwestern Journal of Anthropology* 22 (1966): 354–56; Rigby, "Joking Relationships," 133.

19. Rigby, "Joking Relationships," 133.

20. Rigby, "Joking Relationships," 133–34, 151–52. The first point is also made by Beidelman in "*Utani:* Some Kaguru Notions," 356.

21. See chap. 2.

22. E. W. Shetto, "Utani Relationships: The Nyamwezi," in "Utani Relationships in Tanzania," ed. Lucas, 4:143.

23. Shetto, "Utani Relationships: The Nyamwezi," 144–52; Mlolwa Nkuli, "Notes on Nyamwezi Utani," in "Utani Relationships in Tanzania," ed. Lucas, 4:166–68; Katunzi, "Utani Relationships: The Sumbwa," in "Utani Relationships in Tanzania," ed. Lucas, 6:19–23.

24. Stephen A. Lucas, "War and Trade: Preliminary Thoughts on Ngoni and Nyamwezi *Utani* Networks," in "Utani Relationships in Tanzania," ed. Lucas, 4:1–19.

25. Lucas, "War and Trade," 10–13.

26. Moreau, "Joking Relationship (*Utani*)," 4. See also Rigby, "Joking Relationships," 135 (Gogo); James Boyd Christensen, "Utani: Joking, Sexual License and Social Obligations among the Luguru," *American Anthropologist* 65, no. 6 (December 1963): 1323 (Luguru); Helena Jerman, *Between Five Lines: The Development of Ethnicity in Tanzania with Special Reference to the Western Bagamoyo District* (Uppsala, Sweden, 1997), 146 (Zaramo); J.A.K. Leslie, *A Survey of Dar es Salaam* (London, 1963), 36 (Zaramo, Ngoni).

27. Lucas, "War and Trade," 16. The "logical necessity" of *utani* (or another institution of consociation) was inferred by Gray and Birmingham: "It has been found that forms

of security other than political authority could be afforded to traders who travelled beyond their homeland." Lucas, "War and Trade," 14, quoting Gray and Birmingham, "Some Economic and Political Consequences of Trade," 13.

28. Stephen A. Lucas, "The *Mtani* in Tanzania: A Socio-historical Analysis of His Role in Crisis Situations," in "Utani Relationships in Tanzania," ed. Lucas, 2:4–6.

29. Lucas, "Role of Utani," 22–23.

30. See J. Clyde Mitchell, "Tribe and Social Change in South Central Africa: A Situational Approach," in *The Passing of Tribal Man in Africa,* ed. Peter C.W. Gutkind (Leiden, 1970) 92, 97; A.J. Mjella, "Political and Economic Aspects of Utani: Makonde Migrant Workers in Korogwe District, Tanga Region," in "Utani Relationships in Tanzania," ed. Lucas, vol. 7; D.M. Haulle, "Utani Relationships: The Kisi," in "Utani Relationships in Tanzania," ed. Lucas, vol. 1; and especially Lucas, "On the Non-existence of Tribes."

31. Mzee Mohamed Mangiringiri, interview, Tabora, 20 July 2000 (fighting and cattle raids); Mzee Hussen Ally Kalunga, interview, Tabora, 20 July 2000 (fighting); Mzee Saidi R. Kaloka, interview, Kwihara, 24 July 2000 (intermarriage and fighting); Bibi Kalunde Kongogo, interview, Usule, 29 July 2000 (fighting); Bibi Dudu Rajabu Kheri, interview, Tabora, 1 August 2000 (fighting); Bibi Nelea Nicodemo Msogoti, interview, Isevya, Tabora, 8 August 2000 (fighting and robbery); Mzee Saidi Kitengerema Fundikira, interview, Tabora, 3 August 2000 (fighting and intermarriage).

32. See chap. 2, p. 46. In Burton's version, the Nyamwezi are identified rather than the Sumbwa.

33. Katunzi, "Utani Relationships: The Sumbwa," 25–26.

34. Burton, *Lake Regions,* 215–16.

35. Mzee Juma S. Nkumbo, interview, Uyui ward, 21 July 2000. Other versions using Gogo cow-skin shoes as the marker of difference were told by Mzee Saidi R. Kaloka, interview, Kwihara, 24 July 2000; Mzee Saidi Kitengerema Fundikira, interview, Tabora, 3 August 2000. See also Katunzi, "Utani Relationships: The Sumbwa," 24; M.S. Kabuaye, "Utani and Related Cultural Institutions of the Sukuma Peoples in Shinyanga," in "Utani Relationships in Tanzania," ed. Lucas, 5:241.

36. Stephen A. Lucas, e-mail, 11 January 2002.

37. Rigby, "Joking Relationships," 135.

38. Shetto, "Utani Relationships: The Nyamwezi," 154–55.

39. Burton, *Lake Regions,* 492.

40. Speke, *What Led,* 271. Another description, without the mock confrontation, of two caravans meeting is in Burton, *Lake Regions,* 204.

41. Speke, *Journal,* 314 (my italics). I have altered some of the punctuation for clarity.

42. Stanley, 6 January 1875, in *Exploration Diaries,* ed. Stanley and Neame, 41.

43. A similar institution existed amongst the Kimbu. See Shorter, *Chiefship in Western Tanzania,* 61.

44. Burton, *Lake Regions,* 297–98; "Lake Regions," 201. A Nyamwezi text in Blohm, *Nyamwezi,* 1:70, emphasizes that the *iwanza* was also the place where the village headman or chief would receive guests and hear disputes.

45. Grant, April–May 1861, in *Walk across Africa,* 65–66, at Mininga in northern Unyamwezi; also Cameron, *Across Africa,* 1:181, for the *iwanza* at the capital of Chief Mrima Ng'ombe, Ugunda, in December 1873. Hutley, having read both Burton and Cameron, did not find *kwiwanza* in Mirambo's capital, although he did in surrounding villages. See 4–8 August 1878, in Hutley, *Central African Diaries,* ed. Wolf, 46–48,

46. Copplestone to Wigram, Uyui, 21 May 1881, CMS G3A6/01.
47. Creighton, "American Mariners," 146–47.
48. Livingstone, 5 August 1866, in *Last Journals,* 84.
49. Hutley, 9 December 1880, in *Central African Diaries,* ed. Wolf, 237.
50. Hutley, 30 June 1881, in *Central African Diaries,* ed. Wolf, 272.
51. Michele Wagner, "Environment, Community and History: 'Nature in the Mind' in Nineteenth and Early Twentieth Century Buha, Western Tanzania," in *Custodians of the Land,* ed. Maddox, Giblin, and Kimambo, 175–99.
52. Wagner, "Environment, Community and History," 188–92.
53. Swann, *Fighting the Slave Hunters,* 69–70.
54. Swann, *Fighting the Slave Hunters,* 69–70.
55. Nolan, "Christianity in Unyamwezi," 54.
56. Grant, *Walk across Africa,* 133–34; Thomson, *To the Central African Lakes,* 1:228, 2:59.
57. For Nyamwezi spiritual beliefs and practices, the reader should consult, among others, Blohm, *Nyamwezi,* vol. 1; F.J. Lake, "Ancestor Worship," "Various Acts of Worship," and "The Organisation of Ancestor Worship," in the Nzega District Book, TNA; R.G. Abrahams, *The Nyamwezi Today: A Tanzanian People in the 1970s* (Cambridge,1981), 19–25.
58. Decle, *Three Years,* 345–64, also 289, 352. See also Puder, Hauptmann, and Stationschef von Tabora, "Beantwortung des Fragebogens," in Gottberg, *Unyamwesi,* 245.
59. Grant, *Walk across Africa,* 77, also 251.
60. [Thomas Carlyle], "Occasional Discourse on the Negro Question," *Fraser's Magazine for Town and Country* (December 1849): 672.
61. For "tropical development," see Andrew Porter, *Critics of Empire* (London, 1968), 48–55; Cairns, *Prelude to Imperialism,* 76–81.
62. Cairns, *Prelude to Imperialism,* 204. For "tropical exuberance," see Curtin, *Image of Africa.*
63. Burton, *Lake Regions,* 235. Nevertheless Burton highlights cultural reasons for porterage. "He sits in hut egg-hatching" sums up the disparaging Nyamwezi view of the stay-at-home.
64. Grant, *Walk across Africa,* 76–77.
65. Grant, *Walk across Africa,* 57, 121; Speke, *Journal,* 131.
66. Livingstone, 22 September 1872, in *Last Journals,* 458; Cameron to Sir B. Frere (?), Shamba Gonera, 18 March 1873, VLC 2/14, RGS.
67. Bennett, *Stanley's Despatches,* 160; Simpson, *Dark Companions,* 115; Sissons, "Economic Prosperity," 104. The dollars referred to are Maria Theresa thaler, discussed below.
68. Thomson to Bates, Zanzibar, 26 February 1883, Thomson Corr., RGS. For some other cases of wage bargaining, and the threat of desertion sometimes used for leverage, see Rev. Dr. Krapf, "Journey to Wadigo, Washinsi, and Usambara, July–Sept. 1848," *CMI* 1–2 (1849–50): 155; Grant, *Walk across Africa,* 112, 121; Bennett, *Stanley's Despatches,* 160; A.M. Mackay, 18 August and 12 September 1883, in diary, Gordon to Lang, Msalala, 5 November 1883, both CMS G3A6/01; Bennett, *Mirambo,* 83. The usual result was a compromise.
69. Bennett, *From Zanzibar,* 51–52. For a similar case, see Giraud, *Lacs,* 58–59.
70. Ashe, *Chronicles of Uganda,* 10–11, 39.

71. Johnston, "Native Routes," 421–22; Stairs, 27 June 1891, in *Victorian Explorer,* ed. Konczacki, 189.

72. Roscoe, *Twenty-five Years,* 48.

73. Dodgshun, 26 November 1877, in *From Zanzibar,* ed. Bennett, 45–46. For another example, see Speke, *Journal,* 127.

74. Freund, *African Worker,* 11–12.

75. Frederick Cooper, "Contracts, Crime, and Agrarian Conflict: From Slave to Wage Labor on the East African Coast," in *Labour, Law, and Crime,* ed. Snyder and Hay (London, 1987); Rockel, "Relocating Labor," 451–52.

76. Published translations of business documents in Arabic include H. Thomas, "Arabic Correspondence Captured in South West Bunyoro in 1895: With a Note on Arab traders in Bunyoro," *UJ* 13 (1949): 31–38; and Abdurrahim Mohamed Jiddawi, "Extracts from an Arab Account Book, 1840–1854," *TNR* 31 (1951): 25–31.

77. Johnson, *My African Reminiscences,* 111; Johnston, *Kilima-Njaro,* 61; Edward A. Alpers, "Towards a History of the Expansion of Islam in East Africa: The Matrilineal Peoples of the Southern Interior," in *The Historical Study of African Religion,* ed. Terence O. Ranger and Isaria N. Kimambo (London, 1972), 187; B.G. Martin, "The Qadiri and Shadhili Brotherhoods in East Africa, 1880–1910," in *Muslim Brotherhoods in Nineteenth-Century Africa* (Cambridge, 1976), 158. For a discussion of nineteenth-century Swahili business literature, see Thomas Geider, "Early Swahili Travelogues," in *Sokomoko. Popular Culture in East Africa (Matatu),* ed. Werner Graebner, 9 (1992): 58–62.

78. An earlier agreement, perhaps verbal, was made between Consul Hamerton and the servants, headmen, and the Baluchi escort of Burton and Speke's expedition. The vagueness of the terms (at least in Burton's mind) and his decision to abrogate responsibility for fulfilling them led to the well-known dispute between Burton, the British authorities in Bombay, and Consul Rigby, Hamerton's successor in Zanzibar. See Burton, *Lake Regions,* 550–55; Burton, *Zanzibar,* 2:388; Russell, *General Rigby,* 244–54, 261; Speke, *What Led,* 194, 197; Simpson, *Dark Companions,* 23–24; Frank McLynn, *Burton: Snow upon the Desert* (London, 1990), 134, 161–62, 165–66.

79. Printed in Speke, *Journal,* 553.

80. Simpson, *Dark Companions,* 57.

81. See the photograph of the original in H. Depage, "Note au sujet de documents inédits relatifs à deux expéditions de H.M. Stanley en Afrique Centrale (1874–1877 et 1887–1888)," *Bulletin de l'Institut royal colonial belge* 25 (1954): 132; also partially quoted in Bontinck, *L'autobiographie de Hamed ben Mohammed,* 250; Tippu Tip, *Maisha,* 89–91 § 117–18.

82. Stanley, *Through the Dark Continent,* 1:51–52.

83. "Royal Geographical Society's East African Expedition 1879: Draft of Agreement with Porters at Zanzibar," Alexander Keith Johnston, Jr., Corr. 1870–80, RGS; copy of contract with a list of 128 names dated 17 May 1879, in AA9/10, consular records, ZNA; Rotberg, *Joseph Thomson,* 307; Thomson, *To the Central African Lakes,* 1:65.

84. Price, 19 and 20 July 1877, in *Private Journal,* 32–33; Price, *Report,* 4–5. Glassman mentions the dispute in "Social Rebellion," 96.

85. Two more contracts are mentioned by Stairs, 15 June 1891, in *Victorian Explorer,* ed. Konczacki, 188, where he writes, referring to C.S. Smith, the British consul in Zanzibar, "the contracts must be submitted to him and signed in front of him. I've obtained [H.H.] Johnston's contract and taken it as a model." Johnston had left for Nyasaland, taking Zanzibari porters.

86. For background, see L.W. Hollingsworth, *Zanzibar under the Foreign Office, 1890–1913* (1953; repr., in Westport, CT, 1975), 88–90. Hollingsworth points as precipitating factors to the drain of porters from Zanzibar during the 1880s and early 1890s to serve in British and German East Africa and the Congo Free State, thus threatening Zanzibar's labor supply, and the harsh conditions suffered by porters, which sometimes led to death. In September 1891, on instructions from the British consul, the sultan had forbidden the recruitment of porters for service in territories beyond his own dominions, particularly the Congo.

87. AA12/9, consular records, ZNA; published in *ZEAG,* 17 October 1894, 9–10.

88. Similar registration procedures were proclaimed by the IBEAC at Mombasa. See *ZEAG,* 12 December 1894, 8.

89. Hollingsworth, *Zanzibar,* 89–90.

90. See the papers of the International Conference on Masters and Servants in History, York University, Toronto, April 1996.

91. Thaddeus Sunseri, *Vilimani: Labor Migration and Rural Change in Early Colonial Tanzania* (Portsmouth, NH, 2002), 32–40.

92. *Zanzibar Gazette,* 14 December 1892, 6, ZNA.

93. "Verordnung des Gouverneurs, betreffend de Anwerbung von Trägern. Vom 20. November 1893," 104. 20.11.93, in *Landes-Gesetzgebung des Deutsch-Ostafrikanischen Schutzgebiets. Systematische Zusammenstellung der in Deutsch-Ostafrika geltenden Gesetze, Verordnungen usw.,* 2nd ed. (Tanga, Dar es Salaam, 1911), 310. Thanks to Harald Sippel for supplying me with a copy of this decree.

94. Koponen, *Development For Exploitation,* 364–65.

95. Burton, *Lake Regions,* 236.

96. For the thaler, see Raymond Gervais, "Pre-colonial Currencies: A Note on the Maria Theresa Thaler," *African Economic History,* 11 (1982): 147–52; Sissons, "Economic Prosperity," 36–37; Sheriff, *Slaves, Spices and Ivory,* 136–37.

97. A *doti* was four yards of cloth, the requirement for female dress. On the mainland the most widely accepted currency was the *doti merikani,* or four yards of American unbleached cotton. Sissons, the authority on currency in late nineteenth-century Tanzania, describes the *doti merikani* as "a complete money in that at various times it fulfilled all the functions of money." For the history of *merikani* and other types of imported cloth, see Burton, *Lake Regions,* 114–15; Price, *Report,* 59–60; Sissons, "Economic Prosperity," 42–52; Sheriff, *Slaves, Spices and Ivory,* 77, 88, 102, 253–6, Appendix B, "Prices of Ivory and *Merekani* Sheeting, 1802/3–1873/74."

98. The rate varied between about 112 and 140. See Sissons, "Economic Prosperity," 37.

99. For details of some of the roughly 400 types of beads used for commercial transactions in the East African interior, see Burton, *Lake Regions,* 113–14; Livingstone, *Last Journals,* 150–51; Sissons, "Economic Prosperity," 52–56.

100. Sheriff, *Slaves, Spices and Ivory,* xix. For *masongo,* see Burton, *Lake Regions,* 115–16, 531; Sissons, "Economic Prosperity," 56–58.

101. Burton, *Lake Regions,* 531–534; Sissons, "Economic Prosperity," 46–52.

102. Unomah and Sheriff make similar arguments but with limited evidence. See Unomah, "Economic Expansion," 98; Sheriff, *Slaves, Spices and Ivory,* 182. In Imerina, there was also a noticeable increase in porters' wages toward the end of the nineteenth century. See Campbell, "Labour and the Transport Problem," 353, 355.

103. Burton, *Lake Regions,* 236.

104. Lamden, "Some Aspects of Porterage," 158–59; Nolan, "Christianity in Unyamwezi," 209; Koponen, *Development for Exploitation,* 377.

105. See oral texts of the Maji Maji Research Project, Dar es Salaam, 1968.

106. Iliffe, *Modern History,* 45.

107. Kirk to Smith, Zanzibar, 10 March 1873, VLC 6/1; Cameron to Sir B. Frere (?), Shamba Gonera, 18 March 1873, VLC 2/14, RGS.

108. Indeed, in Senegal the wages of *laptot* (riverboat men) compared well with wages in contemporary rural France! Manchuelle, *Willing Migrants,* 79–80.

109. Sheriff, *Slaves, Spices and Ivory,* 77, 88, 102, 253–56.

110. Sissons, "Economic Prosperity," 45–46.

111. Sissons, "Economic Prosperity," 46.

112. Leue to Governor, Bagamoyo, 11 February 1899, TNA G1/35.

113. Speke, *Journal,* 174. See also ibid., 108.

114. Cameron, *Across Africa,* 1:95. It was also difficult to hire porters in the interior if the necessary currency, *merikani,* was unavailable. See Burton, *Zanzibar,* 2:198. Compare with Malagasy porters, who were "fastidious in ensuring that they were paid in 'good' money." Campbell, "Labour and the Transport Problem," 353.

115. Cameron's wage book, "Men's Accounts," RGS; "Royal Geographical Society's East African Expedition 1879," Johnston, Corr., RGS; Dodgshun, 25 February 1878, in *From Zanzibar,* ed. Bennett, 60; Hore, "Central African Mission: Labour Account (Ujiji)," LMS 3/3/C; Hore to Whitehouse, Ujiji, 13 October 1880, LMS 3/3/B; Griffith to Thompson, Uguha, 15 January 1882, LMS 4/4/A. See also Unomah, "Economic Expansion," 98, and many other sources.

116. Copy of Cameron's wage book, "Men's Accounts," with two additional names, in Kirk Papers, 21 September 1876, corr. block 1871–80, RGS; wage list, "Royal Geographical Society's East African Expedition of 1879," in Rotberg, *Joseph Thomson,* 314; "Men Hired for Masai Caravan," nos., 148, 227, in notebook "Stanley's Expedition," ZM; Griffith to Thompson, Uguha, 15 January 1882, LMS 4/4/A.

117. Krapf, "Journey," 155. See also Krapf, *Travels,* 230, 248, 258, 266.

118. Krapf, *Travels,* 416.

119. Burton, *Zanzibar,* 2:111–12, 147; Von der Decken, *Reisen in Ost-Afrika,* 1:228, 232, 2:8; Thornton to George ?, Mombasa, 27 June 1861, Richard Thornton, letters, RH MSS.Afr.s.27.

120. Burton, *Lake Regions,* 103; Burton, "Lake Regions," 58.

121. Burton, *Lake Regions,* 453–54; Tippu Tip, *Maisha,* 19 § 12; Brode, *Tippoo Tib,* 26–27. Whitely dates this journey to 1863, whereas Bontinck more accurately argues for 1860 in *L'autobiographie de Hamed ben Mohammed,* 21.

122. Mansfield to Marcy, Zanzibar, 31 January 1856, in Bennett and Brooks, *New England Merchants,* 50; Moses D.E. Nwulia, *Britain and Slavery in East Africa* (Washington, DC,1975), 108, for details.

123. Nwulia, *Britain and Slavery,* 108–9.

124. Speke, *What Led,* 194; Simpson, *Dark Companions,* 14; Mackay to Wright, Ndumi, 2 February 1878, CMS CA6/016.

125. Glassman, "Social Rebellion," 96; Glassman, *Feasts and Riot,* 60.

126. See chap. 4.

127. See chap. 3.

128. See the entry for Johnson in table 7.2.

129. Price, *Report,* 65; Speke, 27 and 28 January 1861 and 4 July 1862, in *Journal,* 108, 411; Livingstone, 20–23 November 1872, in *Last Journals,* 469; Coulbois, *Dix années,*

276; Stairs, 21 July 1891, in "De Zanzibar au Katanga," 38. For other examples, see Stanley, *Through the Dark Continent,* 1:117–18; Thomson, *To the Central African Lakes,* 2:267–70; Stairs, "Shut up in the African Forest," 54.

130. Campbell, "Labour and the Transport Problem," 353.

131. See Cameron, "Men's Accounts," RGS. There was a similar practice in the Merina kingdom. See Campbell, "Labour and the Transport Problem," 353.

CHAPTER 8: CONCLUSION

1. Coupland, *East Africa and Its Invaders;* Marsh and Kingsnorth, *An Introduction to the History of East Africa.*

2. In 2005, a visit to the museum at the Catholic (Holy Ghost Fathers) mission in Bagamoyo confirmed the continuing power of the lineage of slavery to influence popular conceptions of the past.

3. Such as in Kjekshus, *Ecology Control;* Koponen, *People and Production;* Jones, "Mapping Consumption"; Prestholdt, "On the Global Repercussions of East African Consumerism"; Unomah, "Economic Expansion"; Cummings, "A Note on the History of Caravan Porters"; Brown and Brown, "East African Trade Towns".

4. Sheriff, *Slaves, Spices and Ivory,* chap. 3.

5. Unomah, "Economic Expansion."

6. See chap. 1.

7. As we have seen, the Nyamwezi were not the only professional porters, and their neighbors—the Sumbwa, Kimbu, and Sukuma—also played significant roles in the caravan system. I often refer to the Nyamwezi and related peoples rather than the Nyamwezi alone.

8. This is a subject that has yet to receive much scholarly attention.

9. Roberts, "Nyamwezi Trade."

10. The Isaacmans show in their rich study, *Slavery and Beyond,* how the condition of military slavery enhanced Chikunda power as soldiers, elephant hunters, porters, and boatmen.

11. Rockel, "Safari!" chap. 6.

12. See Rockel, "Safari!"

13. Prestholdt, "On the Global Repercussions of East African Consumerism."

GLOSSARY

Note: In normal usage, nouns in Kiswahili are prefixed according to class and whether they are singular or plural, as in other Bantu languages such as Kinyamwezi. For example, a Swahili person is a Mswahili; more than one Mswahili is Waswahili. The country or territory of a people or cultural group is prefixed "U"; thus the country of the Nyamwezi is Unyamwezi. Following scholarly conventions, in this book the prefixes are dropped unless the context demands otherwise.

askari. armed guard, soldier
bangi, bhangi. *cannabis sativa*
bao. East African game similar to checkers (draughts)
barghumi. instrument made from kudu horn
boma. defensive earthwork, stockade, fort
bupogo, bupugu. ritual joking relationships within Nyamwezi society
diwan, madiwan. headman, public official, in Muslim coastal society
doti merikani. 12 feet of unbleached American cotton sheeting; a currency unit
frasila. measure of weight, 35 pounds
fundi, mafundi. artisan; professional elephant hunter
hongo. taxes, tolls, fees
ikulu. capital of a Nyamwezi chief
iwanza, kwiwanza. clubs and public guest house in Nyamwezi villages, divided by sex
jemadar. officer of military garrisons of the sultanate of Zanzibar
jumbe, majumbe. village headman
kambi, makambi. campsite; kitchen club or mess on safari
kaniki. plain cotton sheeting made in India
kaya, makaya. Nyamwezi homestead, small community
kibaba. standard measure of weight for rations, about 1.5 pounds
kiboko. hippopotamus-hide whip
kirangozi, virangozi. caravan leader, guide
konzo. paralytic disease caused by the consumption of unprocessed poisonous varieties of cassava
liwali. local governor in Zanzibari sultanate, usually an Omani

machila. palanquin

madala. porter's load, carried from each end of a pole

mapasa. Nyamwezi ritual of departure

masika. long rainy season

masongo. coils of iron wire

mawele. pennisetum millet

mbuga. wetlands or marshes in Unyamwezi

merikani. unbleached cotton sheeting made in New England

mfumu, mafumu. Nyamwezi diviner

mganga, waganga. traditional doctor

miombo. brachystegia; common woodland tree of western Tanzania

mnyampara, wanyampara. elder or councillor in Nyamwezi chiefdoms; caravan headman

mpagazi, wapagazi. long-distance caravan porter

msafari. caravan specialist; professional porter

mshenzi. barbarian; term of abuse

msigo, misigo. load

mtama, matama. sorghum

mtani, watani. partner in ritualized joking relationship

mtemi, batemi. chief in Unyamwezi and Usukuma

mtepe, mitepe. Swahili sewn boat

mtongi. Nyamwezi trader

murran. Maasai warriors

mwanangwa, banangwa. Nyamwezi, Sukuma subchief

mzigaziga. heavy load lashed to a pole and carried by two men

mzimu, mizimu. ancestral spirit, very important in Nyamwezi cosmology

mzungu, wazungu. white man

nyika. open wilderness

pombe. beer

pori. wilderness; bush country

posho. rations; provisions

rugaruga. standing armies of Nyamwezi chiefs

satini. light cotton cloth made in England

Schutztruppe. German colonial army

shamba, mashamba. farm, garden

shauri. meeting; formal consultation

shuka. six feet of cotton sheeting; half a *doti*

suria, masuria. slave concubine in Muslim society

tembe. quadrilateral, flat roofed structure, a dwelling for families and their livestock. Found in central and western Tanzania

tembo. palm wine made in coastal regions

terekeza, telekeza. double march necessitated by lack of water

Thaler, Maria Theresa. international currency used along the East African coast. Used to reckon porters' wages

Träger, Trägern. caravan porter (German)

ugali. stiff porridge made with flour and water

uungwana.   refined living; coastal civilization
utani.   ritualized joking relationships
vbandevba.   merchant class in Unyamwezi
zomari.   wind instrument sounding something like bagpipes

BIBLIOGRAPHY

PRIMARY SOURCES

Interviews

All interviews were carried out by the author in Tabora district, in Tabora town and
surrounding villages.

Fundikira, Chief Abdallah S. Tabora, 4 August 2000.
Fundikira, Mzee Saidi Kitengerema. Tabora, 3 August 2000.
Kagoda, Mzee Omari Musa. Kakola, 25 July 2000.
Kaloka, Mzee Saidi R. Kwihara, 24 July 2000.
Kalunga, Mzee Hussen Ally. Tabora, 20 July 2000.
Kapiga, Mzee Shabani. Kakola, 25 July 2000.
Katalambula, Bibi Joha Hassan. Isevya, Tabora, 8 August, 2000.
Kheri, Bibi Dudu Rajabu. Tabora, 1 August 2000.
Kongogo, Bibi Kalunde. Usule, 29 July 2000.
Mangiringiri, Mzee Mohamed. Tabora, 20 and 30 July 2000.
Maswa, Mzee Vincent. Tabora, 21 July 2000.
Msogoti, Bibi Nelea Nicodemo. Isevya, Tabora, 8 August, 2000.
Nkumbo, Mzee Juma Samweli. Uyui ward, 21 July 2000.
Ntaba, Mzee Mathias. Mayombo, 26 July 2000.
Sheikh, Mzee Mahmood Mohamed. Kwihara, 24 July 2000.

Archival

Tanzania National Archive, Dar es Salaam

German Caravan File G1/35.
British Secretariat Records:
C. J. Bagenal. 1919 Tour Report. Tabora District, file 2551.
Ethnological Survey of Tribes in Mwanza and Tabora Province, 1927–28, File 11075.
District and Provincial Books.
Dodoma Regional Book.
Mpwapwa District Book.
Tabora Provincial Book.

Mpanda District Book.
Nzega District Book.

Africana Library, University of Dar es Salaam

Hans Cory Collection.

Zanzibar National Archive

British Consulate Records:
Files AA9/10, AA12/9.
Universities Mission to Central Africa:
Mission Diary, UMCA Zanzibar, File CB1/5.

Zanzibar Museum

Notebook. "Stanley's Expedition" (Emin Pasha Relief Expedition).

Robarts Library, University of Toronto

Collected papers of the Maji Maji Research Project. Dar es Salaam, 1968–69.

Anglican Church Archives, Toronto

Westgate Collection.

Rhodes House, Oxford

Richard Thornton, letters. MSS.Afr.s.27.
Clement Gillman, Tanganyika diaries, 1905–6.

Royal Geographical Society, London

Correspondence:
Richard F. Burton .
Sir John Kirk 1871–80: Copy of Cameron's porter wage book.
A.K. Johnston, Jr.: Draft agreement with porters, 1876.
Special Collections:
Verney Lovett Cameron: Account and wage books, 1872; Correspondence, 1872–75;
Diary, October–December 1874; Notebooks, April–June 1873; Miscellaneous
    papers.
Joseph Thomson.

London Missionary Society, School of Oriental and African Studies, London

Missionary correspondence, reports, 1878–1886.
Unpublished Papers:
Walter Hutley. "Mahommadanism in Central Africa." LMS 4/2/D. August 1881.
Ebenezer Southon. "The History, Country and People of Unyamwezi." 5 pts. LMS 3/4/C.
Ebenezer Southon. "Report on a Visit to Kirira." LMS 4/3/A .

Mackinnon Papers, School of Oriental and African Studies, London

Boxes 63, 64, 65, 66, 76, 77, 83, 88, 94 Imperial British East Africa Company:
Files 1A, 3, 4, 5, 6, 7, 9, 10, 11, 12, 55, 57, 59, 60, 61, 62.
Emin Pasha—Miscellaneous Correspondence:
Files 2, 4, 6, 32, 37, 39, 51, 55, 56.

Church Missionary Society (Microfilm)

Nyanza Mission (Tanzania and Uganda). Missionary correspondence, journals, reports, and papers, 1876–1886.

Published

Official

House of Commons Parliamentary Papers.
Report of Sir A. Hardinge for the year 1897–98, C.9125, m.f. 105.547–548.
Dispatches by Dr. Livingstone, H.M. Consul, Inner Africa, to Sec. of State for Foreign Affairs, 1870–1872, C.598, m.f. 78.621.
Reports relating to Uganda by Sir Gerald Portal, C.7303, m.f. 100.506–507.

Newspapers and Periodicals

Anti-Slavery Reporter.
Church Missionary Intelligencer.
Zanzibar and East African Gazette.

Books and Articles

Allbrand, F. "Extrait d'une mémoire sur Zanzibar et sur Quiloa." *Bulletin de la Société de géographie* 2, no. 10 (1838): 65–84.
Anon. "Dr. A. Roscher's Tagebuch über seine Reise nach dem Lufidji, 6 Februar bis 24 Marz 1859." *Petermanns Mitteilungen* 8, no. 2 (1862).
Anon. "Dr. Kirk's Visit to the Dar es Salaam District in East Africa." *Proceedings of the Royal Geographical Society,* n.s., 3 (1881): 308–10.
Anon. "History of Kilwa." *Journal of the Royal Asiatic Society* 54 (1895): 385–430.
Ashe, Robert Pickering. *Chronicles of Uganda.* 1894. Reprinted, London, 1971.
Ashe, Robert Pickering. *Two Kings of Uganda or, Life by the Shores of the Victoria Nyanza.* 1889. Reprinted, London, 1970.
Association internationale africaine. *Rapports sur les marches de la première expédition.* Brussels-Etterbeek, 1879.
Atiman, Adrien. "'Adrien Atiman' by Himself." Translated and arranged by Col. L.B. Cane. *Tanganyika Notes and Records* 21 (June 1946): 46–76.
Baker, Samuel. *The Albert N'yanza, Great Basin of the Nile, and Explorations of the Nile Sources.* 2 vols. London, 1866.
Baumann, Oscar. *Durch Massailand zur Nilquelle: Reisen und Forschungen der Massai-Expedition des deutschen anti-sklaverei Komites in den Jahren 1891–1893.* Berlin, 1894.

Beardall, William. "Exploration of the Rufiji River under the Orders of the Sultan of Zanzibar." *Proceedings of the Royal Geographical* Society, n.s., 3, no. 11 (1881): 641–56.

Bennett, Norman R., ed. *From Zanzibar to Ujiji: The Journal of Arthur W. Dodgshun, 1877–1879.* Boston, 1969.

Bennett, Norman R., ed. *Stanley's Despatches to the New York Herald, 1871–1872, 1874–1877.* Boston, 1970.

Bennett, Norman R., and George E. Brooks, eds. *New England Merchants in Africa.* Boston, 1965.

Beringer, O.L. "Notes on the Country between Lake Nyassa and Victoria Nyanza." *Geographical Journal* 21 (January–June 1903): 25–36.

Bloyet, A. "De Zanzibar à la station de Kondoa." *Bulletin de la Société de géographie* 7, no. 11 (1890): 350–64.

Böhm, Richard. *Von Sansibar zum Tanganjika.* Leipzig, 1888.

Brand, N. "Notice of a Caravan Journey from the East to the West Coasts of Africa." With remarks by W.D. Cooley. *Journal of the Royal Geographical Society* 24 (1854): 266–71.

Brode, Heinrich. *Tippoo Tib: The Story of His Career in Central Africa, Narrated from His Own Accounts.* Translated by H. Havelock. London, 1907.

Broyon-Mirambo, Phillipe. "Description of Unyamwesi, the Territory of King Mirambo, and the Best Route Thither from the East Coast." *Proceedings of the Royal Geographical Society* 22 (1878–79): 28–36.

Burton, Isabel. *Life of Captain Sir Richard F. Burton.* 2 vols. London, 1893.

Burton, Richard F. *Sindh and the Races That Inhabit the Valley of the Indus.* 1851. Reprinted, Karachi, 1973.

Burton, Richard F. "The Lake Regions of Central Equatorial Africa." *Journal of the Royal Geographical Society* 29 (1859): 1–464.

Burton, Richard F. *The Lake Regions of Central Africa.* 1860. Reprinted, St. Clair Shores, MI, 1971.

Burton, Richard F. *Zanzibar, City, Island and Coast.* 2 vols. London, 1872.

Cameron, Verney Lovett. *Across Africa.* Vol. 1. London, 1877.

Capus, A. "Contes, chants et proverbes des Basumbwa dans l'Afrique Orientale." *Zeitschrift für Afrikanische und Oceanische Sprachen* 3 (1897): 1–24.

[Carlyle, Thomas]. "Occasional Discourse on the Negro Question." *Fraser's Magazine for Town and Country* (December 1849): 670–79.

Casati, Gaetano. *Ten Years in Equatoria and the Return with Emin Pasha.* Translated by Mrs. J.R. Clay. 1891. Reprinted, New York, 1969.

Christie, James. *Cholera Epidemics in East Africa.* London, 1876.

Christopher, William. "Extract from a Journal by Lt. W. Christopher, Commanding the H.C. Brig of War Tigris, on the E. Coast of Africa. Dated 8th May 1843." *Journal of the Royal Geographic Society* 14 (1844): 76–103.

Clendennen, G.W., ed. *David Livingstone's Shire Journal, 1861–1864.* Aberdeen, 1992.

Cooley, W.D. "Geography of N'yassi." Pt. 2. *Journal of the Royal Geographical Society* 15 (1845): 185–235.

Coulbois, François. *Dix années au Tanganyka.* Limoges, 1901.

Crawford, T.W.W. "Account of the Life of Mathew Wellington in His Own Words, and the Death of David Livingstone and the Journey to the Coast." *Northern Rhodesia Journal* 6 (1965): 99–102.

Decken, Carl Claus von der. *Reisen in Ost-Afrika in den Jahren 1859 bis 1865.* Edited by Otto Kersten. 4 vols. 1869–79. Reprinted, Graz, Austria, 1978.

Decle, Lionel. *Three Years in Savage Africa.* London, 1898.

Delmé-Radcliffe, C. "Extracts from Lt. Col. C. Delmé-Radcliffe's Typescript Diary Report on the Delimitation of the Anglo-German Boundary, Uganda, 1902–1904." *Uganda Journal* 11, no. 1 (March 1947): 9–29.

Elton, J. Frederick. "On the Coast Country of East Africa, South of Zanzibar." *Journal of the Royal Geographical Society* 44 (1874): 227–51.

Elton, J. Frederick. *Travels and Researches among the Lakes and Mountains of Eastern and Central Africa.* Edited by H. B. Cotterill. 1879. Reprinted, London, 1968.

Erhardt, Rev. J. "Reports Respecting Central Africa, as Collected in Mambara and the East Coast." *Proceedings of the Royal Geographical Society* 1, no. 1 (1855–56): 8–10.

Fortie, Marius. *Black and Beautiful.* London, 1938.

Freeman-Grenville, G.S.P., ed. *The East African Coast: Select Documents from the First to the Earlier Nineteenth Centuries.* Oxford, 1962.

French-Sheldon, May. *Sultan to Sultan.* London, 1892.

Germain, M. Adrien. "Note sur Zanzibar et la côte orientale d'afrique." *Bulletin de la Société de géographie* 5, no. 15 (1868): 530–59.

Giraud, Victor. *Les lacs de l'Afrique Equatoriale.* Paris, 1890.

Gottberg, Achim. *Unyamwesi: Quellensammlung und Geschichte.* Berlin, 1971.

Götzen, Graf von. "Journey across Equatorial Africa." *Geographical Journal* 5 (1895): 354–60.

Grant, James Augustus. "Summary of Observations on the Geography, Climate, and Natural History of the Lake Regions." *Journal of the Royal Geographical Society* 42 (1872): 243–342.

Grant, James Augustus. *A Walk across Africa.* London, 1864.

Grogan, Ewart S., and Arthur H. Sharp. *From the Cape to Cairo: The First Traverse of Africa from South to North.* London, 1900.

Guillain, Charles. *Documents sur l'histoire, la géographie et le commerce de l'Afrique orientale.* Paris, 1856. 3 Vols.

Hannington, James. *Peril and Adventure in Central Africa, being Illustrated Letters to the Youngsters at Home.* London, 1886.

Harford-Battersby, C. F. *Pilkington of Uganda.* London, 1899.

Harries, Lyndon, ed. and trans. *Swahili Prose Texts.* London, 1965.

Hassforther, E. E. "An Account of a Journey though N.W. German East Africa in 1913–14." *Tanganyika Notes and Records* 61 (September 1963): 209–15.

Hassing, Per, and Norman R. Bennett. "A Journey across Tanganyika in 1886." Translated and edited extracts from the journal of Edvard Gleerup. *Tanganyika Notes and Records* 58–59 (1962): 129–47.

Heanley, R. M. *A Memoir of Bishop Steere.* London, 1888.

Hine, J. E. *Days Gone By: Being Some Account of Past Years Chiefly in Central Africa.* London, 1924.

Hobley, C. W. *Kenya: From Chartered Company to Crown Colony.* London, 1929.

Hoffman, William. *With Stanley in Africa.* London, 1938.

Hore, Annie. *To Lake Tanganyika in a Bath Chair.* London, 1886.

Hore, Edward Coode. *Tanganyika: Eleven Years in Central Africa.* London, 1892.

Hutchinson, Edward. "The Best Trade Route to the Lake Regions of Central Africa." *Journal of the Society of Arts* 25 (30 March 1877): 430–40.

Hutchinson, Edward. "The Development of Central Africa." *Journal of the Society of Arts* 24 (2 June 1876): 689–704.

Jackson, Frederick J. *Early Days in East Africa.* 1930. Reprinted, London, 1969.

Jephson, A.J. Mounteney. *The Diary of A.J. Mounteney Jephson: Emin Pasha Relief Expedition 1887–1889.* Edited by Dorothy Middleton. Cambridge, 1969.

Johnson, William Percival. "Seven Years Travel in the Region East of Lake Nyassa." *Proceedings of the Royal Geographical Society,* n.s., 6 (1884): 512–36.

Johnson, William Percival. *My African Reminiscences, 1875–1895.* 1924. Reprinted, Westport, CT, 1970.

Johnston, Harry Hamilton. *British Central Africa.* London, 1897.

Johnston, Harry Hamilton. "Journey North of Lake Nyassa and Visit to Lake Leopold (Rukwa)." *Proceedings of the Royal Geographical Society,* n.s., 12 (1890): 225–27.

Johnston, Harry Hamilton. *The Kilima-Njaro Expedition.* London, 1886.

Johnston, Harry Hamilton. "The People of Eastern Equatorial Africa." *The Journal of the Anthropological Institute* 15 (1886): 3–15.

Johnston, Keith. "Native Routes in East Africa from Dar es Salaam Towards Lake Nyassa." *Proceedings of the Royal Geographical Society,* n.s., 1, no. 7 (1879): 417–22.

Junker, Wilhelm. *Travels in Africa during the Years 1882–1886.* 1892. Translated by A.H. Keane. London, 1971.

Kerr-Cross, David. "Geographical Notes on the Country Between Lakes Nyassa, Rukwa, and Tanganyika." *Scottish Geographical Magazine* 6 (June 1890): 281–93.

Kilekwa, Petro. *Slave Boy to Priest.* Translated by K.H.N. Smith. London, 1937.

Kirk, John. "On a New Harbour Opposite Zanzibar." *Proceedings of the Royal Geographical Society* 11 (1866–67): 35–36.

Kirkman, James S., ed. "The Zanzibar Diary of John Studdy Leigh." Pt. 2. *International Journal of African Historical Studies* 13, no. 3 (1980): 492–507.

Kollmann, Paul. *The Victoria Nyanza.* Translated by H.A. Nesbitt. London, 1899.

Konczacki, Janina M., ed. *Victorian Explorer: The African Diaries of Captain William G. Stairs, 1887–1892.* Halifax, Nova Scotia, 1994.

Krapf, J.L. "Journey to Wadigo, Washinsi, and Usambara, July-Sept. 1848." *Church Missionary Intelligencer* 1–2 (1849–50).

Krapf, J.L. *Travels, Researches and Missionary Labours during an Eighteen Years Residence in Eastern Africa.* 1860. Reprinted, London, 1868.

Langheld, Wilhelm. *Zwanzig Jahre in deutschen Kolonien.* Berlin, 1909.

Last, James T. "A Journey into the Nguru Country from Mamboia, East Central Africa." *Proceedings of the Royal Geographical Society,* n.s., 4 (1882): 148–57.

Last, James T. *Polyglotta Africana Orientalis.* London, n.d.

Last, James T. "A Visit to the Waitumba Iron Workers and the Mangaheri, near Mamboya, in East Central Africa." *Proceedings of the Royal Geographical Society,* n.s., 5 (1883): 581–92.

Livingstone, David. *The Last Journals of David Livingstone.* Edited by H. Waller. New York, 1875.

Livingstone, David. *Livingstone Letters, 1843–1872: David Livingstone Correspondence in the Brenthurst Library, Johannesburg.* Edited by Maurice Boucher. Johannesburg, 1985.

Livingstone, David. *Missionary Travels and Researches in South Africa.* London, 1857.

Livingstone, David, and Charles Livingstone. *Narrative of an Expedition to the Zambesi and Its Tributaries; and the Discovery of the Lakes Shirwa and Nyassa, 1858–1864.* 1865. Reprinted, London, 2001.

Lloyd, A. B. *In Dwarf Land and Cannibal Country.* London, 1900.

Mackay, Alexina Harrison. *A. M. Mackay, Pioneer Missionary of the Church Missionary Society to Uganda, by His Sister.* London, 1890.

MacQueen, James. "Observations on the Geography of Central Africa." *Proceedings of the Royal Geographical Society* 3, no. 4 (1859): 208–14

MacQueen, James. "The Visit of Lief Ben Saeid to the Great African Lake." *Journal of the Royal Geographical Society* 15 (1845): 371–76.

Madan, A. C. trans. and ed. *Kiungani; or, Story and History from Central Africa.* London, 1887.

Meyer, Hans. *Across East African Glaciers. An Account of the First Ascent of Kilimanjaro.* Translated by E.H.S. Calder. London, 1891.

Moir, Frederick L. Maitland. *After Livingstone: An African Trade Romance.* London, 1924.

Moir, Frederick L. Maitland. "Eastern Route to Central Africa." *Scottish Geographical Magazine* 1, no. 4 (April 1885): 95–112.

Moir, Jane F. *A Lady's Letters from Central Africa.* Glasgow, 1891.

Moloney, J. A. *With Captain Stairs to Katanga.* London, 1893.

Moore, J.E.S. *To the Mountains of the Moon.* London, 1901.

Mtoro bin Mwinyi Bakari. *The Customs of the Swahili People.* Translated and edited by J.W.T. Allen. Berkeley and Los Angeles, 1981.

Muhammed, Hamid bin (Tippu Tip). *Maisha ya Hamid bin Muhammed el Murjebi yaani Tippu Tip.* Translated and edited by W. H. Whitely. Nairobi, 1974.

Mullens, Joseph. "A New Route and New Method of Travelling into Central Africa Adopted by the Rev. Robert Price in 1876." *Proceedings of the Royal Geographical Society* 21 (1877): 233–44.

New, Charles. *Life, Wanderings, and Labours in Eastern Africa.* 1873. Reprinted, London, 1971.

Parke, T. H. *My Personal Experiences in Equatorial Africa as Medical Officer of the Emin Pasha Relief Expedition.* London, 1891.

Perham, Marjorie, ed. *Ten Africans: A Collection of Life Stories.* Evanston, IL, 1963.

Peters, Carl. *New Light on Dark Africa.* Translated by H. W. Dulcken. London, 1891.

Pickering, Charles. *The Races of Man and Their Geographical Distribution.* London, 1850.

Price, Roger. *Private Journal of Rev. Roger Price.* London, 1878.

Price, Roger. *Report of the Rev. R. Price of His Visit to Zanzibar and the Coast of Eastern Africa.* London, 1876.

Pringle, M.A. *A Journey in East Africa Towards the Mountains of the Moon.* Edinburgh, 1886.

Pruen, S. T. *The Arab and the African.* 1891. Reprinted, London, 1986.

Rankin, L. K. "The Elephant Experiment in Africa: A Brief Account of the Belgian Elephant Expedition on the March from Dar es Salaam to Mpwapwa." *Prss,* n.s., 4 (1882): 273–88.

Rebmann, J. "Narrative of a Journey to Madjame, in Kirima, during April, May, and June, 1849." *Church Missionary Intelligencer* 1, no. 12 (1850): 272–76; 1, no. 13 (1850): 307–12; 1, no. 14 (1850): 327–30; 1, no. 16 (1850): 376–81.

Reichard, Paul. *Deutsch-Ostafrika: Das Land und seine Bewohner.* Leipzig, 1892.

Reichard, Paul. "Vorschläge zu einer praktischen Reiseausrüstung für Ost- und Central-Afrika." *Zeitschrift der Gesellschaft für Erdkunde zu Berlin* 24 (1889): 1–80.

Reichard, Paul. "Die Wanjamuesi." *Zeitschrift der Gesellschaft für Erdkunde zu Berlin* 24 (1889): 246–60, 304–31.

Roscoe, John. *Twenty-five Years in East Africa.* Cambridge, 1920.

Ross, Robert, ed. "The Dutch on the Swahili Coasts, 1776–1778: Two Slaving Journals." Pts. 1 and 2. *International Journal of African Historical Studies* 19, no. 2 (1986): 305–60; 19, no. 3 (1986): 479–506.

Said bin Habeeb. "Narrative of Said bin Habeeb, an Arab Inhabitant of Zanzibar." *Transactions of the Bombay Geograpical Society* 15 (1860): 146–48.

Salt, Henry. *A Voyage to Abyssinia and Travels into the Interior of That Country.* 1814. Reprinted, London, 1967.

Schmidt, Rochus. *Geschichte des Araberaufstandes in Ost-Afrika.* Frankfurt an der Oder: Trowitzsch & Sohn, 1892.

Schweinitz, Graf von. "Das Trägerpersonal der Karawanen." *Deutsche Kolonialzeitung* 2 (February 1894): 18–20.

Seminar für Orientalische Sprachen. "Lieder und Sangeswesweisen und Geschichten der Wanyamwezi." *Mittheilungen des Seminars für Orientalische Sprachen zu Berlin* 4, no. 3 (1901): 45–62.

Sharpe, Alfred. *The Backbone of Africa.* London, 1921.

Smee, Captain Thomas. "Observations during a Voyage of Research on the East Coast of Africa, from Cape Guardafui South to the Island of Zanzibar, in the H.C.'s Cruisers Ternate (Capt. T. Smee), and Sylph Schooner (Lieutenant Hardy)." In *Zanzibar, City, Island and Coast,* ed. Richard F. Burton. Vol. 2. London, 1872. Previously published in *Transactions of the Bombay Geographical Society* 6 (1844): 23–61.

Smith, Charles Stewart. "Explorations in Zanzibar Dominions," in Royal Geographical Society, *Supplementary Papers* 2 (London, 1889), 101–125.

Southon, Ebenezer. "Notes on a Journey Through Northern Ugogo in East Central Africa." *Proceedings of the Royal Geographical Society* 3 (1881): 547–53.

Speke, John Hanning. "On the Commerce of Central Africa." *Transactions of the Bombay Geographical Society* 15 (1860): 138–45.

Speke, John Hanning. *What Led to the Discovery of the Source of the Nile.* Edinburgh, 1864.

Speke, John Hanning. *Journal of the Discovery of the Source of the Nile.* New York, 1864.

Stairs, William G. "De Zanzibar au Katanga: Journal de Capitaine Stairs (1890–1891)." *Le Congo illustré* 2 (1892): 5–7, 13–15, 21–23, 29–31, etc.

Stairs, William G. "From the Albert Nyanza to the Indian Ocean." *The Nineteenth Century* 29, no. 172 (June 1891): 953–68

Stairs, William G. "Shut up in the African Forest." *The Nineteenth Century* 29, no. 167 (January 1891): 45–62.

Stanley, Henry Morton. *How I Found Livingstone.* London, 1872.

Stanley, Henry Morton. *Through the Dark Continent.* 2 vols. 1899. Reprinted, Toronto, 1988.

Stanley, R., and A. Neame, eds. *The Exploration Diaries of H. M. Stanley.* London, 1961.

Steere, Edward. *Collections for a Handbook of the Nyamwezi Language, as Spoken at Unyanyembe.* London, n.d.

Stevenson, James. *The Arabs in Central Africa and at Lake Nyassa.* Glasgow, 1889.

Stuhlmann, Franz. *Mit Emin Pascha ins Herz von Afrika.* Berlin, 1894.

Swann, A. J. *Fighting the Slave Hunters in Central Africa.* 1910. Reprinted, London, 1969.

Sykes, Colonel. "Notes on the Possessions of the Imaum of Muskat, on the Climate and Productions of Zanzibar, and the Prospects of African Discovery." *Journal of the Royal Geographical Society* 23 (1853): 101–19.

Taylor, William Ernest. *African Aphorisms, or Saws from Swahili-Land.* 1891. Reprinted, London, 1924.

Thomson, Joseph. "Progress of the Society's East African Expedition: Journey along the Western Side of Lake Tanganyika." *Proceedings of the Royal Geographical Society,* n.s., 2 (1880): 306–9.

Thomson, Joseph. *To the Central African Lakes and Back.* 2 vols. 1881. Reprinted, London, 1968.

Thomson, Joseph. "Notes on the Basin of the River Rovuma, East Africa." *Proceedings of the Royal Geographical Society,* n.s., 4 (1882): 65–79.

Thomson, Joseph. *Through Masai Land.* 1885. Reprinted, London, 1968.

Tucker, Alfred. *Eighteen Years in Uganda and East Africa.* London, 1908.

Velten, C., ed. *Safari za Wasuaheli.* Göttingen, 1901.

Velten, C., trans. and ed. *Schilderungen der Suaheli.* Göttingen, 1901.

Vienne, C. de. "De Zanzibar à l'Oukami, route des lacs de L'Afrique Equatoriale." *Bulletin de la Société de géographie* 6, no. 4 (1872): 356–69.

Wainwright, Jacob. "Tagebuch von Jacob Wainright über den Transport von Dr. Livingstone's Leiche 4. Mai 1873–18 Februar 1874." *Petermanns Mitteilungen* 20 (1874): 187–93.

Waller, Horace. "The Two Ends of the Slave-Stick." *Contemporary Review* (April 1889): 532–33.

Ward, Gertrude. *Letters from East Africa, 1895–1897.* London, 1899.

Watt, Rachel Stuart. *In the Heart of Savagedom.* London, n.d., ca. 1912.

Wauwermans, Lieutenant-Colonel. "L'oeuvre africaine dans ses rapports avec les progrès du commerce et de l'industrie," *Bulletin de la Société de géographie d'Anvers* 2 (1878): 346–71.

Weule, Karl. *Native Life in East Africa.* Translated by Alice Werner. 1909. Reprinted, Westport, CT, 1970.

White Fathers. *A l'assaut des pays nègres: Journal des missionaries d'Alger dans l'Afrique Equatoriale.* Paris, 1884.

Wilson, C. T. "From Kagei to Tabora and Back." *Proceedings of the Royal Geographical Society,* n.s., 2 (1880): 616–20.

Wilson, C. T., and R. W. Felkin. *Uganda and the Egyptian Soudan.* Vol. 1. London, 1882.

Wissmann, H. von. *My Second Journey through Equatorial Africa.* Translated by Minna J. A. Bergmann. London, 1891.

Wolf, James B., ed. *Missionary to Tanganyika, 1877–1888.* London, 1971.

Wolf, James B., ed. *The Central African Diaries of Walter Hutley, 1877–1881.* Boston, 1976.

Young, E. D. *The Search after Livingstone.* London, 1868.

SECONDARY SOURCES

Books and Articles

Abdallah, Yohanna B. *The Yaos.* Translated and edited by Meredith Sanderson. 1919. Reprinted, London, 1973.

Abdy, Dora C. "Notes on Utani and Other Bondei Customs." *Man* 14 (October 1924): 152–54.

Abrahams, R.G. *The Peoples of Greater Unyamwezi, Tanzania.* London, 1967.

Abrahams, R.G. *Political Organization of Unyamwezi.* London, 1967.

Abrahams, R.G. *The Nyamwezi Today: A Tanzanian People in the 1970s.* Cambridge, 1981.

Alpers, Edward A. *The East African Slave Trade.* Nairobi, 1967.

Alpers, Edward A. "Trade, State and Society among the Yao in the Nineteenth Century." *Journal of African History* 10, no. 3 (1969): 405–20.

Alpers, Edward A. "The Coast and the Development of the Caravan Trade." In *A History of Tanzania,* ed. Isaria N. Kimambo and A.J. Temu. Nairobi, 1969.

Alpers, Edward A. "Towards a History of the Expansion of Islam in East Africa: The Matrilineal Peoples of the Southern Interior." In *The Historical Study of African Religion,* ed. Terence O. Ranger and Isaria N. Kimambo. London, 1972.

Alpers, Edward A. *Ivory and Slaves in East Central Africa.* Berkeley and Los Angeles, 1975.

Alpers, Edward A. "Gujarat and the Trade of East Africa, c. 1500–1800." *International Journal of African Historical Studies* 9, no. 1 (1976): 22–44.

Alpers, Edward A. "The Story of Swema: Female Vulnerability in Nineteenth-Century East Africa." In *Women and Slavery in Africa,* ed. Claire C. Robertson and Martin A. Klein. Madison, 1983.

Ambler, Charles H. *Kenyan Communities in the Age of Imperialism.* New Haven, CT, 1988.

Amin, Shahid, and Marcel van der Linden. Introduction to *"Peripheral" Labour? Studies in the History of Partial Proletaranization,* ed. Shahid Amin and Marcel van der Linden. Cambridge, 1997.

Amin, Shahid, and Marcel van der Linden, eds. *"Peripheral" Labour? Studies in the History of Partial Proletarianization.* Cambridge, 1997.

Anon. "Some Notes on Kilwa." *Tanganyika Notes and Records* 2 (1936): 92–95.

Atkins, Keletso E. *The Moon Is Dead! Give Us Our Money! The Cultural Origins of an African Work Ethic, Natal, South Africa, 1843–1900.* Portsmouth, NH, 1993.

Austen, Ralph A. *Northwest Tanzania under German and British Rule.* New Haven, CT, 1968.

Austen, Ralph A. "Ntemiship, Trade and State Building: Political Development among the Western Bantu of Tanzania." In *East African History,* ed. Daniel F. McCall, Norman R. Bennett, and Jeffrey Butler. New York, 1969.

Austen, Ralph A. "Patterns of Development in 19th Century East Africa." *African Historical Studies* 4 (1973): 645–57.

Bade, Klaus J. "Imperial Germany and West Africa: Colonial Movement, Business Interests, and Bismarck's 'Colonial Policies.'" In *Bismarck, Europe and Africa: the Berlin Conference 1884–1885 and the Onset of Partition,* ed. Stig Förster, Wolfgang J. Mommsen, and Ronald Robinson. London, 1988.

Barrett-Gaines, Kathryn. "Travel Writing, Experiences, and Silences: What Is Left out of European Travelers' Accounts: The Case of Richard D. Mohun." *HIA* 24 (1997): 53–70.

Beachey, R.W. "The Arms Trade in East Africa in the Late Nineteenth Century." *Journal of African History* 3 (1962): 451–67.

Beachey, R.W. "The East African Ivory Trade in the Nineteenth Century." *Journal of African History* 8 (1967): 269–90.

Beachey, R.W. *The Slave Trade of Eastern Africa.* London, 1976.

Beidelman, T.O. "A History of Ukaguru: 1857–1916." *Tanganyika Notes and Records* 58/59 (1962): 10–39.

Beidelman, T.O. "The Organization and Maintenance of Caravans by the Church Missionary Society in Tanzania in the Nineteenth Century." *International Journal of African Historical Studies* 15, no. 4 (1982): 601–23.

Beidelman, T.O. "*Utani:* Some Kaguru Notions of Death, Sexuality and Affinity." *Southwestern Journal of Anthropology* 22 (1966): 354–80.

Belich, James. *Making Peoples: A History of the New Zealanders, from Polynesian Settlement to the End of the Nineteenth Century.* Auckland, 1996.

Bennett, Norman R. "Captain Storms in Tanganyika: 1882–1885." *TNR* 54 (1960): 51–63.

Bennett, Norman R. "Philippe Broyon: Pioneer Trader in East Africa." *African Affairs* 62, no. 247 (April 1963): 156–64.

Bennett, Norman R. "Mirambo of the Nyamwezi." In *Studies in East African History,* ed. Norman R. Bennett. Boston, 1963.

Bennett, Norman R. "The London Missionary Society of Urambo, 1878–1898." *Tanzania Notes and Records* 65 (March 1966): 43–52.

Bennett, Norman R. "Mwinyi Kheri." In *Leadership in Eastern Africa,* ed. Norman R. Bennett. Boston, 1968.

Bennett, Norman R. *Mirambo of Tanzania 1840? –1884.* New York, 1971.

Bennett, Norman R. "The Arab Impact." In *Zamani: A Survey of East African History,* ed. Bethwell A. Ogot. Nairobi, 1974.

Bennett, Norman R. "Isiki, Ntemi of Unyanyembe." In *African Dimensions,* ed. Mark Karp. Boston, 1975.

Bennett, Norman R. *Arab versus European: Diplomacy and War in Nineteenth-Century East Central Africa.* New York, 1986.

Berger, Iris. *Religion and Resistance: East African Kingdoms in the Precolonial Period.* Tervuren, 1981.

Berntsen, John L. "The Maasai and Their Neighbors: Variables of Interaction." *African Economic History* 2 (1976): 1–11.

Blohm, Wilhelm. *Die Nyamwezi.* 2 vols. Hamburg, 1933.

Bolt, Christine. *Victorian Attitudes to Race.* London, 1971.

Bontinck, François, trans. and ed. *L'autobiographie de Hamed ben Mohammed el-Murjebi Tippo Tip (ca. 1840–1905).* Brussels, 1974.

Bontinck, François. "La double traversée de l'Afrique par trois 'arabes' de Zanzibar (1845–1860)." *Etudes d'histoire africaine* 6 (1974): 5–53.

Bovill, E.W. *The Golden Trade of the Moors.* London, 1970.

Brady, Cyrus Townsend, Jr. *Commerce and Conquest in East Africa with Particular Reference to the Salem Trade with Zanzibar.* Salem, MA, 1950.

Brantlinger, Patrick. "Victorians and Africans: The Genealogy of the Myth of the Dark Continent." *Critical Inquiry* 12 (Autumn 1985): 166–203.

Bridges, Roy C. "Nineteenth-Century East African Travel Records, with an Appendix on 'Armchair Geographers' and Cartography." *Paideuma* 33 (1987): 179–96.

Bridges, Roy C. "Elephants, Ivory and the History of the Ivory Trade in East Africa." In *The Exploitation of Animals in Africa,* ed. Jeffrey C. Stone. Aberdeen, 1988.

Brooke, Clarke. "The Heritage of Famine in Central Tanganyika." *Tanzania Notes and Records* 67 (June 1967): 15–22.

Brown, Beverly. "Muslim Influence on Trade and Politics in the Lake Tanganyika Region." *African Historical Studies* 4, no. 3 (1971): 617–29.

Brown, Beverly, and Walter T. Brown. "East African Trade Towns: A Shared Growth." In *A Century Of Change in Eastern Africa,* ed. W. Arens. Geneva, 1976.

Brown, Walter T. "Bagamoyo: An Historical Introduction." *Tanzania Notes and Records* 71 (1970): 69–83.

Brown, Walter T. "The Politics of Business Relations Between Zanzibar and Bagamoyo in the Late Nineteenth Century." *African Historical Studies* 4, no. 3 (1971): 631–43.

Bujra, Janet M. "Women 'Entrepreneurs' of Early Nairobi." In *Crime, Justice and Underdevelopment,* ed. Colin Sumner. London, 1982.

Bulliet, R. *The Camel and the Wheel.* Cambridge, 1975.

Bülow, Frieda von. *Im Lande der Verheißung: Ein Kolonialroman um Carl Peters.* Dresden, 1899.

Cain, P. J., and A. G. Hopkins. *British Imperialism: Innovation and Expansion 1688–1914.* London, 1993.

Cairns, H.A.C. *Prelude to Imperialism: British Reactions to Central African Society 1840–1890.* London, 1965.

Campbell, Gwyn. "Labour and the Transport Problem in Imperial Madagascar, 1810–1895." *Journal of African History* 21 (1980): 341–56.

Carnell, W. J. "Sympathetic Magic among the Gogo of Mpwapwa District." *Tanganyika Notes and Records* 39 (June 1955): 25–38.

Chakrabarty, Dipesh. *Rethinking Working-Class History: Bengal 1890–1940.* Princeton, NJ, 1989.

Chakrabarty, Dipesh. *Provincializing Europe: Postcolonial Thought and Historical Difference.* Princeton, NJ, 2000.

Channock, Martin. *Law, Custom and Social Order: The Colonial Experience in Malawi and Zambia.* Cambridge, 1985.

Chittick, Neville. "The Early History of Kilwa Kivinje." *Azania* 4 (1969): 153–59.

Chittick, Neville. "The Mosque at Mbuamaji and the Nabahani." *Azania* 4 (1969): 159–60.

Chrétien, Jean-Pierre. *The Great Lakes of Africa: Two Thousand Years of History.* New York, 2003.

Christensen, James Boyd. "Utani: Joking, Sexual License and Social Obligations among the Luguru." *American Anthropologist* 65, no. 6 (December 1963): 1314–27.

Clarence-Smith, Gervase. "Indian Business Communities in the Western Indian Ocean in the Nineteenth Century." *The Indian Ocean Review* 2, no. 4 (1989): 18–21.

Clarence-Smith, William Gervase, ed. *The Economics of the Indian Ocean Slave Trade in the Nineteenth Century.* London, 1989.

Cohen, Robin. "Resistance and Hidden Forms of Consciousness among African Workers." *Review of African Political Economy* 19 (1980): 8–22.

Cohen, Robin. "From Peasants to Workers in Africa." In *Political Economy of Contemporary Africa,* ed. Peter C.W. Gutkind and Immanuel Wallerstein. Beverly Hills, CA, 1985.

Cole-King, P. A. "Transportation and Communication in Malawi to 1891 with a Summary to 1918." In *The Early History of Malawi,* ed. Bridglal Pachai. London, 1972.

Comaroff, John L. "Images of Empire, Contests of Conscience: Models of Colonial Domination in South Africa." In *Tensions of Empire: Colonial Cultures in a Bourgeois World,* ed. Frederick Cooper and Ann Laura Stoler. Berkeley and Los Angeles, 1997.

Connah, Graham. *African Civilizations.* Cambridge, 1987.

Cooper, Frederick. *Plantation Slavery on the East Coast of Africa.* New Haven, CT, 1977.

Cooper, Frederick. *From Slaves to Squatters: Plantation Labour and Agriculture in Zanzibar and Coastal Kenya, 1890–1925.* New Haven, CT, 1980.

Cooper, Frederick. *On the African Waterfront.* New Haven, CT, 1987.

Cooper, Frederick. "Contracts, Crime, and Agrarian Conflict: from Slave to Wage Labor on the East African Coast." In *Labour, Law, and Crime: An Historical Perspective,* ed. Francis Snyder and Douglas Hay. London, 1987.

Cooper, Frederick. "Work, Class and Empire: An African Historian's Retrospective on E. P. Thompson." *Social History* 20, no. 2 (May 1995): 235–41.

Cooper, Frederick. "Conflict and Connection: Rethinking Colonial African History." In *History after the Three Worlds: Post-Eurocentric Historiographies,* ed. Arif Dirlik, Vinay Bahl, and Peter Gran. Lanham, MD, 2000.

Coquery-Vidrovitch, Catherine, and Paul E. Lovejoy, eds. *The Workers of African Trade.* Beverly Hills, CA, 1985.

Coquery-Vidrovitch, Catherine, and Paul E. Lovejoy. "The Workers of Trade in Precolonial Africa." In *The Workers of African Trade,* ed. Catherine Coquery-Vidrovitch and Paul E. Lovejoy. Beverly Hills, CA, 1985:

Cory, Hans. "Religious Beliefs and Practices of the Sukuma/Nyamwezi Tribal Group." *Tanganyika Notes and Records* 54 (March 1960): 14–26.

Coupland, Reginald. *Kirk on the Zambesi: A Chapter of African History.* Oxford, 1928.

Coupland, Reginald. *East Africa and Its Invaders from the Earliest Times to the Death of Seyyid Said in 1856.* Oxford, 1961.

Creighton, Margaret S. "American Mariners and the Rites of Manhood, 1830–1870." In *Jack Tar in History,* ed. Colin Howell and Richard J. Twomey. Fredericton, New Brunswick, 1991.

Cummings, Robert J. "A Note on the History of Caravan Porters in East Africa." *Kenya Historical Review* 1, no. 2 (1973): 109–38.

Cummings, Robert J. "Wage Labor in Kenya in the Nineteenth Century." In *The Workers of African Trade,* ed. Catherine Coquery-Vidrovitch and Paul E. Lovejoy. Beverly Hills, 1985.

Curtin, Philip. *The Image of Africa.* Madison, 1964.

Curtin, Philip, Steven Feierman, Leonard Thompson, and Jan Vansina. *African History.* London, 1978.

De Gruchy, John. ed. *The London Missionary Society in Southern Africa, 1799–1999: Historical Essays in Celebration of the Bicentenary of the LMS in Southern Africa.* Athens, 2000.

Depage, H. "Note au sujet de documents inédits relatifs à deux expéditions de H.M. Stanley en Afrique centrale (1874–1877)." *Bulletin de l'Institut royal colonial belge* 25 (1954): 129–52.

Deutsch, Jan-Georg. "The 'Freeing' of Slaves in German East Africa: The Statistical Record, 1890–1914." *Slavery and Abolition* 19, no. 2 (August 1998): 109–32.

Duffill, M. B., and Paul E. Lovejoy. "Merchants, Porters, and Teamsters in the Nineteenth-Century Central Sudan." In *The Workers of African Trade,* ed. Catherine Coquery-Vidrovitch and Paul E. Lovejoy. Beverly Hills, CA, 1985.

Ebner, Elzear. *The History of the Wangoni.* Peramiho, Tanzania, 1987.

Ehret, Christopher. "East African Words and Things: Agricultural Aspects of Economic Transformation in the Nineteenth Century." In *Kenya in the Nineteenth Century (Hadith 8),* ed. Bethwell A. Ogot. Nairobi, 1985.

Ehret, Christopher. *An African Classical Age: Eastern and Southern Africa in World History, 1000 B.C. to A.D. 400.* Charlottesville, 1998.

Eigler, Friederike. "Engendering German Nationalism: Gender and Race in Frieda von Bülow's Colonial Writings." In *The Imperialist Imagination: German Colonialism and Its Legacy,* ed. Sara Friedrichsmeyer, Sara Lennox, and Susanne Zantop. Ann Arbor, (1998): 69–85.

Essner, Cornelia. "Some Aspects of German Travellers' Accounts from the Second Half of the 19th Century." *Paideuma* 33 (1987): 197–205.

Ewald, Janet J. "Crossers of the Sea: Slaves, Freedmen, and Other Migrants in the Northwestern Indian Ocean, c. 1750–1914." *American Historical Review* 105, no. 1 (February 2000): 69–91.

Eze, Emmanuel Chukwudi, ed. *Race and the Enlightenment: A Reader.* Cambridge, MA, 1997.

Fabian, Johannes. *Language on the Road: Notes on Swahili in Two Nineteenth-Century Travelogues.* Hamburg, 1984.

Fabian, Johannes. *Out of Our Minds: Reason and Madness in the Exploration of Central Africa.* Berkeley and Los Angeles, 2000.

Fair, Laura. "Dressing Up: Clothing, Class and Gender in Post-abolition Zanzibar." *Journal of African History* 39 (1998): 63–94.

Fair, Laura. *Pastimes and Politics: Culture, Community, and Identity in Post-abolition Urban Zanzibar, 1890–1945.* Athens, 2001.

Falola, Toyin. "The Yoruba Caravan System of the Nineteenth Century." *International Journal of African Historical Studies* 24, no. 1 (1991): 111–32.

Falola, Toyin, and Paul E. Lovejoy, eds. *Pawnship in Africa: Debt Bondage in Historical Persepective.* Boulder, CO, 1994.

Farar, Caras, and Mathew Welland. "David Livingstone: Two Accounts of His Death and the Transportation of His Body to the Coast." *Northern Rhodesia Journal* 6 (1965): 95–102.

Feierman, Steven. *The Shambaa Kingdom: A History.* Madison, 1974.

Feierman, Steven. "African Histories and the Dissolution of World Histories." In *Africa and the Disciplines: The Contributions of Research in Africa to the Social Sciences and Humanities,* ed. Robert Bates, V. Y. Mudimbe, and Jean O'Barr. Chicago, 1993.

Foran, W. Robert. *African Odyssey; The Life of Verney Lovett Cameron.* London, 1937.

Fosbrooke, H. A. "Richard Thornton in East Africa." *Tanganyika Notes and Records* 58/59 (March–September 1962): 43–63.

Foucault, Michel. *Discipline and Punish: The Birth of the Prison.* Toronto, 1995.

Freeman-Grenville, G.S.P. "The German Sphere, 1884–98." In *History of East Africa,* ed. Roland A. Oliver and Gervase Mathew. Vol. 1. Oxford, 1963.

Freeman-Grenville, G.S.P. "The Coast, 1498–1840." In *History of East Africa,* ed. Roland A. Oliver and Gervase Mathew. Vol. 1. Oxford, 1963.

Freeman-Grenville, G.S.P. *The French at Kilwa Island.* Oxford, 1965.

Freund, Bill. *The Making of Contemporary Africa.* Bloomington, 1984.

Freund, Bill. *The African Worker.* Cambridge, 1988.

Galbraith, J. S. *Mackinnon and East Africa, 1878–1892: A Study in the "New Imperialism."* Cambridge, 1972.

Geertz, Clifford. "Thick Description: Toward an Interpretive Theory of Culture." Chap. 1 in *The Interpretation of Cultures.* New York, 1973.

Geider, Thomas. "Early Swahili Travalogues." Ed. Werner Graebner. *Sokomoko: Popular Culture in East Africa (Matatu)* 9 (1992): 27–65.

Genovese, Eugene. *Roll, Jordan, Roll: The World the Slaves Made.* New York, 1976.

Gervais, Raymond. "Pre-colonial Currencies: A Note on the Maria Theresa Thaler." *African Economic History* 11 (1982): 147–52.

Giblin, James L. "Famine and Social Change during the Transition to Colonial Rule in Northeastern Tanzania, 1880–1896." *African Economic History* 15 (1986): 85–105.

Giblin, James L. "Trypanosomiasis Control in African History: An Evaded Issue?" *Journal of African History* 3 (1990): 59–80.

Giblin, James L. *The Politics of Environmental Control in Northeastern Tanzania, 1840–1940.* Philadelphia, 1992.

Giblin, James L. "Pawning, Politics and Matriliny in Northeastern Tanzania." In *Pawnship in Africa: Debt Bondage in Historical Perspective,* ed. Toyin Falola and Paul E. Lovejoy. Boulder, CO, 1994.

Giddens, Anthony. *The Constitution of Society: Outline of the Theory of Structuration.* Berkeley and Los Angeles, 1984.

Gilbert, E. "The *Mtepe:* Regional Trade and the Late Survival of Sewn Ships in East African Waters." *International Journal of Nautical Archaeology* 27, no. 1 (1998): 43–50.

Glassman, Jonathon. "The Bondsman's New Clothes: The Contradictory Consciousness of Slave Resistance on the Swahili Coast." *Journal of African History* 32, no. 2 (1991): 277–312.

Glassman, Jonathon. *Feasts and Riot: Revelry, Rebellion, and Popular Consciousness on the Swahili Coast, 1856–1888.* Portsmouth, NH, 1995.

Gottberg, Achim. "On the Historical Importance of the Crisis of the Fundikira Empire." In *Afrika-Studien,* ed. W. Markov. Leipzig, 1967.

Gray, John M. "Ahmed bin Ibrahim: The First Arab to Reach Buganda." *Uganda Journal* 11, no. 1 (1947): 80–97.

Gray, John M. "Acholi History, 1860–1901." Pt. 3. *Uganda Journal* 16, no. 2 (1952): 132–44.

Gray, John M. "Trading Expeditions From the Coast to Lakes Tanganyika and Victoria Before 1857." *Tanganyika Notes and Records* 49 (1957): 226–46.

Gray, John M. "The British Vice-Consulate at Kilwa Kivinji, 1884–1885." *Tanganyika Notes and Records* 51 (December 1958): 174–93.

Gray, John M. "Arabs on Lake Victoria, Some Revisions." *Uganda Journal* 22 (1958): 76–81.

Gray, John M. *History of Zanzibar from the Middle Ages to 1856.* London, 1962.

Gray, Richard, and David Birmingham, eds. *Pre-colonial African Trade.* London, 1970.

Gray, Richard, and David Birmingham. "Some Economic and Political Consequences of Trade in Central and Eastern Africa in the Pre-colonial Period." In *Pre-colonial African Trade,* ed. Richard Gray and David Birmingham. London, 1970.

Gregory, Robert G. *South Asians in East Africa: An Economic and Social History.* Boulder, CO, 1993.

Gunderson, Frank. "From 'Dancing with Porcupines' to 'Twirling a Hoe:' Musical Labour Transformed in Sukumaland, Tanzania." *Africa Today* 48, no. 4 (2001): 3–26.

Gurnah, Abdulrazak. *Paradise.* London, 1994.

Gutkind, Peter C. W. "The Boatmen of Ghana: The Possibilities of a Pre-colonial African Labor History." In *Confrontation, Class Consciousness, and the Labour Process: Studies in Proletarian Class Formation,* ed. Michael Hanagan and Charles Stephenson. New York, 1986.

Gutkind, Peter C. W. "Trade and Labor in Early Precolonial African History: The Canoemen of Southern Ghana." In *The Workers of African Trade,* ed. Catherine Coquery-Vidrovitch and Paul E. Lovejoy. Beverly Hills, CA, 1995.

Gutman, Herbert, *Work, Culture, and Society in Industrializing America: Essays in American Working-Class and Social History.* New York, 1977.

Guyer, Jane I. "Household and Community in African Studies." *African Studies Review* 24, no. 2/3 (1981): 87–137.

Gwassa, G.C.K., and J. F. Mbwiliza. "Social Production, Symbolism and Ritual in Buha: 1750–1900." *Tanzania Notes and Records* 79/80 (1976): 12–21.

Hadjivayanis, George, and Ed Ferguson. "The Development of a Colonial Working Class." In *Zanzibar under Colonial Rule,* ed. Abdul Sheriff and Ed Ferguson. London, 1991.

Hall, R. de Z. "The Dance Societies of the Wasukuma, as Seen in the Maswa District." *Tanganyika Notes and Records* 1 (March 1936): 94–96.

Harlow, Vincent, and Elizabeth Chilver, eds. *History of East Africa.* Vol. 2. Oxford, 1965.

Harman, Nicholas. *Bwana Stokesi and His African Conquests.* London, 1986.

Harms, Robert W. *River of Wealth, River of Sorrow: The Central Zaire Basin in the Era of the Slave and Ivory Trade, 1500–1891.* New Haven, CT, 1981.

Harries, Patrick. *Work, Culture, and Identity: Migrant Laborers in Mozambique and South Africa, c. 1860–1910.* Portsmouth, NH, 1994.

Hartnoll, M. M. "Some African Pastimes." *Tanganyika Notes and Records* 5 (April 1938): 31–36.

Hartwig, Gerald W. "The Victoria Nyanza as a Trade Route in the Nineteenth Century." *Journal of African History* 11 (1970): 535–52.

Hartwig, Gerald W. *The Art of Survival in East Africa: The Kerebe and Long-Distance Trade 1800–1895.* New York, 1976.

Hassani, Rashid bin. "The Story of Rashid bin Hassani of the Bisa Tribe Northern Rhodesia." Recorded by W. F. Baldock. In *Ten Africans,* ed. Margery Perham. Evanston, IL, 1963.

Hegel, Georg Wilhelm Friedrich. *The Philosophy of History.* Toronto, 1956.

Helly, Dorothy O. *Livingstone's Legacy: Horace Waller and Victorian Mythmaking.* Athens, 1987.

Henderson, W. O. "German East Africa 1884–1918." In *History of East Africa,* ed. Vincent Harlow and E. M. Chilver. Vol. 2. Oxford, 1965.

Hill, Christopher. *The World Turned Upside Down: Radical Ideas during the English Revolution.* London, 1975.

Hill, Mervyn F. *Permanent Way.* 2 vols. Nairobi, 1950.

Hobsbawm, Eric. *Primitive Rebels.* New York, 1965.

Hochschild, Adam. *King Leopold's Ghost: A Story of Greed, Terror, and Heroism in Colonial Africa.* New York, 1999.

Hodges, Geoffrey W. T. *The Carrier Corps.* New York, 1986.

Hodgson, A.G.O. "Some Notes on the Hunting Customs of the Wandamba of the Ulanga Valley, Tanganyika Territory." *Journal of the Royal Anthropological Institute of Great Britain and Ireland* 56 (1926): 59–70.

Hodgson, Dorothy, and Sheryl McCurdy. "Wayward Wives, Misfit Mothers, and Disobedient Daughters: 'Wicked' Women and the Reconfiguration of Gender in Africa." *Canadian Journal of African Studies* 30, no. 1 (1996): 1–9.

Hogendorn, Jan, and Marion Johnson. *The Shell Money of the Slave Trade.* Cambridge, 1986.

Hollingsworth, L.W. *Zanzibar under the Foreign Office, 1890–1913.* 1953. Reprinted, Westport, CT, 1975.

Holmes, C.F. "Zanzibari Influence at the Southern End of Lake Victoria: The Lake Route." *African Historical Studies* 4, no. 3 (1971): 477–503.

Holmes C.F., and R.A. Austen. "The Pre-colonial Sukuma." *Journal of World History* 14, no. 2 (1972): 377–405.

Howell, Colin, and Richard J. Twomey, eds. *Jack Tar in History: Essays in the History of Maritime Life and Labour.* Fredericton, New Brunswick, 1991.

Howlett, W.P., G. Brubaker, N. Mlingi, and H. Rosling. "A Geographical Cluster of Konzo in Tanzania." *Journal of Tropical and Geographical Neurology* 2 (1992): 102–8.

Hoyle, B.S. *Gillman of Tanganyika 1882—1946: The Life and Work of a Pioneer Geographer.* Aldershot, 1987.

Iliffe, John. "The Age of Improvement and Differentiation (1907–45)." In *A History of Tanzania,* ed. Isaria N. Kimambo and A.J. Temu. Nairobi, 1969.

Iliffe, John. *Tanganyika under German Rule, 1905–1912.* Cambridge, 1969.

Iliffe, John. *A Modern History of Tanganyika.* Cambridge, 1979.

Iliffe, John. "Wage Labour and Urbanisation." In *Tanzania Under Colonial Rule,* ed. M.H.Y. Kaniki. London, 1980.

Iliffe, John. *Africans: The History of a Continent.* Cambridge, 1995.

Isaacman, Allen F. "Peasants and Rural Social Protest in Africa." *African Studies Review* 33, no. 2 (1990): 1–12.

Isaacman, Allen F. *Cotton Is the Mother of Poverty: Peasants, Work, and Rural Struggle in Colonial Mozambique, 1938–1961.* Portsmouth, NH, 1997.

Isaacman, Allen F., and Barbara Isaacman, "Resistance and Collaboration in Southern and Central Africa, 1850–1920." *International Journal of African Historical Studies* 10, no. 1 (1977): 31–62.

Isaacman, Allen F., and Barbara Isaacman, *Slavery and Beyond: The Making of Men and Chikunda Ethnic Identities in the Unstable World of South-Central Africa, 1750–1920.* Portsmouth, NH, 2004.

Isaacman, Allen F., and Elias Mandala. "From Porters to Labor Extractors: The Chikunda and Kololo in the Lake Malawi and Tchiri River Area." In *The Workers of African Trade,* ed. Catherine Coquery-Vidrovitch and Paul E. Lovejoy. Beverly Hills, 1985.

Jeal, Tim. *Livingstone.* London, 1973.

Jeeves, Alan H. *Migrant Labour in South Africa's Mining Economy: The Struggle for the Gold Mine's Labour Supply, 1890–1920.* Kingston, Ontario, 1985.

Jerman, Helena. *Between Five Lines: The Development of Ethnicity in Tanzania with Special Reference to the Western Bagamoyo District.* Uppsala, 1997.

Jiddawi, Abdurrahim Mohamed. "Extracts from an Arab Account Book, 1840–1854." *Tanganyika Notes and Records* 31 (1951): 25–31.

Johnson, Frederick. *A Standard Swahili-English Dictionary.* Nairobi, 1939.

Johnson, Marion. "The Cowrie Currencies of West Africa." *Journal of African History* 3 (1970): 17–49, 331–51.

Johnson, Marion. "Cloth as Money." *Textile History* 11 (1980): 193–202.

Jones, Stephanie. *Two Centuries of Overseas Trading: The Origins and Growth of the Inchcape Group.* Basingstoke, UK, 1986.

Kabeya, J. B. *King Mirambo.* Kampala, 1976.

Kalinga, Owen J. "The Balowoka and the Establishment of States West of Lake Malawi." In *State Formation in Eastern Africa,* ed. Ahmed Idha Salim. Nairobi, 1984.

Kaniki, M.H.Y., ed. *Tanzania under Colonial Rule.* London, 1980.

Katoke, Israel K. *The Karagwe Kingdom: A History of the Abanyambo of North-West Tanzania.* Nairobi, 1975.

Killingray, David. "'A Swift Agent of Government': Air Power in British Colonial Africa, 1916–1939." *JAH* 25 (1984): 429–44.

Killingray, David. "Labour Exploitation for Military Campaigns in British Colonial Africa 1870–1945." *Journal of Contemporary History* 24, no. 3 (July 1989): 483–501.

Killingray, David. "The 'Rod of Empire': The Debate over Corporal Punishment in the British African Colonial Forces, 1888–1946." *Journal of African History* 35, no. 2 (1994): 201–16.

Kimambo, Isaria N. *A Political History of the Pare of Tanzania c. 1500–1900.* Nairobi, 1969.

Kimambo, Isaria N. "The East African Coast and Hinterland, 1845–80." In *UNESCO General History of Africa.* Vol. 6, *Africa in the Nineteenth Century until the 1880s,* ed. J. F. Ade Ajayi. Paris, 1984.

Kimambo, Isaria N. "Environmental Control and Hunger in the Mountains and Plains of Northeastern Tanzania." In *Custodians of the Land: Ecology and Culture in the History of Tanzania,* ed. Gregory Maddox, James Giblin, and Isaria N. Kimambo. London, 1996.

Kimambo, Isaria N., and A. J. Temu, eds. *A History of Tanzania.* Nairobi, 1969.

King, J. W. "An Historical Note on Nile Transport." *Uganda Journal* 30, no. 2 (1966): 219–23.

Kirknaes, Jesper, and John Wembah-Rashid. *Bagamoyo: A Pictorial Essay.* Denmark, n.d.

Kjekshus, Helge. *Ecology Control and Economic Development in East African History.* London, 1977.

Kjekshus, Helge. *Ecology Control and Economic Development in East African History.* 2nd ed. London, 1996.

Knafla, Louis A., and Susan W. S. Binnie. "Beyond the State: Law and Legal Pluralism in the Making of Modern Societies." In *Law, Society, and the State: Essays in Modern Legal History,* ed. Louis A. Knafla and Susan W. S. Binnie. Toronto, 1995.

Koponen, Juhani. *People and Production in Late Precolonial Tanzania: History and Structures.* Jyväskylä, Finland, 1988.

Koponen, Juhani. *Development for Exploitation: German Colonial Policies in Mainland Tanzania, 1884–1914.* Helsinki, 1994.

Koponen, Juhani. "Population: A Dependent Variable." In *Custodians of the Land: Ecology and Culture in the History of Tanzania,* ed. Gregory Maddox, James L. Giblin, and Isaria N. Kimambo. London, 1996.

Kopytoff, Igor, ed. *The African Frontier: The Reproduction of Traditional African Societies.* Bloomington, 1987.

Koritschoner, Hans. "Some East African Native Songs." *Tanganyika Notes and Records* 4 (October 1937): 51–64.

Kuklick, Henrika. *The Savage Within: The Social History of British Anthropology, 1885–1945.* Cambridge, 1991.

La Fontaine, J. "The Zinza." From notes by J. W. Tyler. In *East African Chiefs,* ed. Audrey I. Richards. London, 1959.

Lamden, S. C. "Some Aspects of Porterage in East Africa." *Tanganyika Notes and Records* 61 (September 1963): 155–64.

Lamphear, John. "The Kamba and the Northern Mrima Coast." In *Pre-colonial African Trade,* ed. Richard Gray and David Birmingham. London, 1970.

Landberg, Pamela. "Widows and Divorced Women in Swahili Society." In *Widows in African Societies: Choices and Constraints,* ed. Betty Potash. Stanford, CA, 1986.

Langworthy, Harry W. "Swahili Influence in the Area Between Lake Malawi and the Luangwa River." *African Historical Studies* 4, no. 3 (1971): 575–602.

Larson, L. E. "A History of the Mbunga Confederacy ca. 1860–1907." *Tanzania Notes and Records* 81/82 (1977): 35–42.

Law, Robin C. C. *The Horse in West African History.* Oxford, 1980.

Law, Robin C. C. "Wheeled Transport in Pre-colonial West Africa." *Africa* 50, no. 3 (1980): 249–62.

Leslie, J.A.K. *A Survey of Dar es Salaam,* London, 1963.

Liebowitz, Daniel. *The Physician and the Slave Trade: John Kirk, the Livingstone Expeditions, and the Crusade against Slavery in East Africa.* New York, 1999.

Linebaugh, Peter, and Marcus Rediker, "The Many-Headed Hydra: Sailors, Slaves and the Atlantic Working Class in the Eighteenth Century." In *Jack Tar in History: Essays in the History of Maritime Life and Labour,* ed. Colin Howell and Richard J. Twomey. Fredericton, New Brunswick, 1991.

Linebaugh, Peter, and Marcus Rediker, *The Many-Headed Hydra: Sailors, Slaves, Commoners, and the Hidden History of the Revolutionary Atlantic.* Boston, 2000.

Loomba, Ania. *Colonialism/Postcolonialism.* London, 1998.

Lovejoy, Paul E. *Caravans of Kola: The Hausa Kola Trade, 1700–1900.* Zaria, 1980.

Lovejoy, Paul E. *Salt of the Desert Sun: A History of Salt Production and Trade in the Central Sudan.* Cambridge, 1986.

Low, D. A. "The Northern Interior, 1840–84." In *History of East Africa,* ed. Roland A. Oliver and Gervase Mathew. Vol. 1. Oxford, 1963.

Luck, Anne. *Charles Stokes in Africa.* Nairobi, 1972.

Lynn, Martin. "From Sail to Steam: The Impact of the Steamship Services on the British Palm Oil Trade with West Africa, 1850–1890." *JAH* 30 (1989): 227–45.

Lynn, Martin. "Technology, Trade and 'A Race of Native Capitalists': The Krio Diaspora of West Africa and the Steamship, 1852–95." *JAH* 33, no. 3 (1992): 421–40.

MacDonald, Kenneth Iain. "Push and Shove: Spatial History and the Construction of a Portering Economy in Northern Pakistan." *Comparative Studies in Society and History* 40 (1998): 287–317.

Mackay, Duncan. "The Orderly Frontier: The World of the Kauri Bushmen, 1860–1925." In *The Shaping of History: Essays from the New Zealand Journal of History,* ed. Judith Binney. Wellington, 2001.

MacKenzie, John M. *The Empire of Nature: Hunting, Conservation, and British Imperialism.* Manchester, 1988.

Maddox, Gregory. "Environment and Population Growth in Ugogo, Central Tanzania." In *Custodians of the Land: Ecology and Culture in the History of Tanzania,* ed. Gregory Maddox, James L. Giblin, and Isaria N. Kimambo. London, 1996.

Maddox, Gregory, James L. Giblin, and Isaria N. Kimambo, eds. *Custodians of the Land: Ecology and Culture in the History of Tanzania.* London, 1996.

Maganga, Clement, and Derek Nurse. "Nyamwezi." In "Description of Sample Bantu Languages of Tanzania." Ed. D. Nurse. *Langues africaines/African Languages* 5, no. 1 (1979): 57–66.

Maganga, Clement, and Thilo C. Schadeberg *Kinyamwezi, Grammar, Texts, Vocabulary.* Cologne, 1992.

Manchuelle, François. *Willing Migrants: Soninke Labor Diasporas, 1848–1960.* Athens, 1997.

Mandala, Elias C. *Work and Control in a Peasant Economy: A History of the Lower Tchiri Valley in Malawi 1859–1960.* Madison, 1990.

Mangat, J.S. "Aspects of Nineteenth Century Indian Commerce in Zanzibar." *Journal of African and Asian Studies* 2, no. 1 (Autumn 1968): 17–27.

Marsh, Z.A., and G.W. Kingsnorth. *An Introduction to the History of East Africa.* 3rd ed. Cambridge, 1965.

Martin, B.G. "The Qadiri and Shadhili Brotherhoods in East Africa, 1880–1910." In *Muslim Brotherhoods in Nineteenth-Century Africa.* Cambridge, 1976.

Matson, A.T. "Sewa Haji: A Note." *Tanzania Notes and Records* 65 (March 1966): 91–94.

Maxon, Robert, and David Javersak. "The Kedong Massacre and the Dick Affair: A Problem in the Early Colonial Historiography of East Africa." *History in Africa* 8 (1981): 261–69.

Mbilinyi, Marjorie. "Women's Resistance in 'Customary' Marriage: Tanzania's Runaway Wives." In *Forced Labour and Migration: Patterns of Movement within Africa,* ed. Abebe Zegeye and Shubi Ishemo. London, 1989.

McIntosh, Susan Keech, ed. *Beyond Chiefdoms: Paths to Complexity in Africa.* Cambridge, 1999.

McLynn, Frank. *Burton: Snow upon the Desert.* London, 1990.

McLynn, Frank. *Stanley: The Making of an African Explorer.* Chelsea, MI, 1990.

Middleton, John. *The World of the Swahili: An African Mercantile Civilization.* New Haven, CT, 1992.

Mitchell, J. Clyde. "The Causes of Labour Migration." In *Forced Labour and Migration: Patterns of Movement within Africa,* ed. Abebe Zegeye and Shubi Ishemo. London, 1989.

Mitchell, J. Clyde. "Tribe and Social Change in South Central Africa: A Situational Approach." In *The Passing of Tribal Man in Africa,* ed. Peter C.W. Gutkind. Leiden, 1970.

Mlingi, N.V., V.D. Assay, A.B.M. Swai, D.G. McLarty, H. Karlen, and H. Rosling. "Determinants of Cyanide Exposure from Cassava in a Konzo-Affected Population in Northern Tanzania." *International Journal of Food Sciences and Nutrition* 44 (1993): 137–44.

Mnyampala, Mathias E. *The Gogo: History, Customs and Traditions.* Translated by Gregory Maddox. New York, 1995.

Monson, Jamie. "Canoe-Building under Colonialism: Forestry and Food Policies in the Inner Kilombero Valley, 1920–1940." In *Custodians of the Land: Ecology and Culture in the History of Tanzania,* ed. Gregory Maddox, James L. Giblin, and Isaria N. Kimambo. London, 1996.

Montgomery, David. "Workers' Contol of Machine Production in the 19th Century." *Labor History* 17, no. 4 (Fall 1976): 485–509.

Moore, E.D. *Ivory Scourge of Africa.* New York, 1931.

Moore, Henrietta L., and Megan Vaughan. *Cutting down Trees: Gender, Nutrition, and Agricultural Change in the Northern Province of Zambia, 1890–1990.* London, 1994.

Moreau, R.E. "The Joking Relationship (*Utani*) in Tanganyika." *Tanganyika Notes and Records* 12 (1941): 1–10.

Moreau, R.E. "Joking Relationships in Tanganyika." *Africa* 14 (1943–44): 386–400.

Munro, J. Forbes "Shipping Subsidies and Railway Guarantees: William Mackinnon, Eastern Africa and the Indian Ocean, 1860–93." *JAH* 28 (1987): 209–30.

Napier Bax, S. "The Early Church Missionary Society Missions at Buzulima and Usambiro in the Mwanza District." *Tanganyika Notes and Records* 7 (June 1939): 39–55.

Newbury, David. *Kings and Clans: Ijwi Island and the Lake Kivu Rift, 1780–1840.* Madison, 1991.

Northrup, David. *Beyond the Bend in the River: African Labor in Eastern Zaire, 1865—1940.* Athens, 1988.

Nwulia, Moses D.E. *Britain and Slavery in East Africa.* Washington, DC, 1975.

Ogot, Bethwell A., ed. *Zamani: A Survey of East African History.* Nairobi, 1974.

Ogot, Bethwell A., ed. *Kenya in the Nineteenth Century (Hadith 8).* Nairobi, 1985.

Ogunremi, Gabriel Ogundeji. "Human Porterage in Nigeria in the Nineteenth Century: A Pillar in the Indigenous Economy." *Journal of the Historical Society of Nigeria* 8, no. 1 (December 1975): 37–59.

Ogunremi, Gabriel Ogundeji. *Counting the Camels: The Economics of Transportation in Pre-industrial Nigeria.* New York, 1982.

Oliver, Roland A. "Discernible Developments in the Interior c. 1500–1840." In *History of East Africa,* ed. Roland A. Oliver and Gervase Mathew. Vol. 1. Oxford, 1963.

Oliver, Roland A. *The Missionary Factor in East Africa.* 2nd. ed. London, 1965.

Oliver, Roland A. *The African Experience.* London, 1991.

Oliver, Roland A., and Anthony Atmore. *Africa Since 1800.* 3rd ed. Cambridge, 1981.

Oliver, Roland A., and Gervase Mathew, eds. *History of East Africa.* Vol. 1. Oxford, 1963.

Ollendorff, Robert. "Bagamoyo, 1883–1945." *Tanganyika Notes and Records* 19 (June 1945): 62–63.

Olukoju, Ayodeji. "Elder Dempster and the Shipping Trade of Nigeria during the First World War." *JAH* 33, no. 2 (1992): 255–72.

Ortner, Sherry B. "Resistance and the Problem of Ethnographic Refusal." *Comparative Studies in Society and History* 37 (1995): 173–93.

Ortner, Sherry B. *Life and Death on Mt. Everest: Sherpas and Himalayan Mountaineering.* Princeton, NJ, 1999.

Page, Melvin E. "The Manyema Hordes of Tippu Tip: A Case Study in Social Stratification and the Slave Trade in Eastern Africa." *International Journal of African Historical Studies* 7, no. 1 (1974): 69–84.

Page, Melvin E. "Tippu Tip and the Arab 'Defense' of the East African Slave Trade." *Etudes d'histoire africaine* 6 (1974): 105–17.

Parpart, Jane L. "Sexuality and Power on the Zambian Copperbelt: 1926–1964." In *Patriarchy and Class: African Women in the Home and the Workforce,* ed. Sharon B. Stichter and Jane L. Parpart. Boulder, CO, 1988.

Pearson, Michael N. *Port Cities and Intruders: The Swahili Coast, India, and Portugal in the Early Modern Era.* Baltimore, 1998.

Pedler, F.J. "Joking Relationship in East Africa." *Africa* 13, no. 1 (January 1940): 170–73.

Peires, Jeffrey B. *The Dead Will Arise: Nongqawuse and the Great Xhosa Cattle-Killing Movement of 1856–7.* Johannesburg, 1989.

Phiri, Kings M. "Political Change among the Chewa and Yao of the Lake Malawi Region, c. 1750–1900." In *State Formation in Eastern Africa,* ed. Ahmed Idha Salim. Nairobi, 1984.

Porter, Andrew. *Critics of Empire: British Radical Attitudes to Colonialism in Africa 1895–1914.* London, 1968.

Porter, Andrew. "Trusteeship, Anti-slavery and Humanitarianism." In *The Oxford History of the British Empire: The Nineteenth Century,* ed. Andrew Porter. Oxford, 1999.

Posnansky, Merrick. "Connections between the Lacustrine Peoples and the Coast." In *East Africa and the Orient: Cultural Synthesis in Pre-colonial Times,* ed. H. Neville Chittick and Robert I. Rotberg. New York, 1975.

Prakash, Gyan. *Bonded Histories: Genealogies of Labor Servitude in Colonial India.* Cambridge, 1990.

Prakash, Gyan. "Introduction: After Colonialism." In *After Colonialism: Imperial Histories and Postcolonial Displacements,* ed. Gyan Prakash. Princeton, NJ, 1995.

Prakash, Gyan. "Colonialism, Capitalism and the Discourse of Freedom." In *"Peripheral" Labour? Studies in the History of Partial Proletarianization,* ed. Shahid Amin and Marcel van der Linden. Cambridge, 1997.

Pratt, Mary Louise. "Fieldwork in Common Places." In *Writing Culture: The Poetics and Politics of Ethnography,* ed. James Clifford and George E. Marcus. Berkeley and Los Angeles, 1986.

Pratt, Mary Louise. *Imperial Eyes: Travel Writing and Transculturation.* London, 1992.

Prestholdt, Jeremy. "On the Global Repercussions of East African Consumerism." *American Historical Review* 109, no. 3 (June 2004): 755–81.

Radcliffe-Brown, Alfred Reginald. "On Joking Relationships." Chap. 4 in *Structure and Function in Primitive Society: Essays and Addresses.* London, 1952.

Radcliffe-Brown, Alfred Reginald. "A Further Note on Joking Relationships." Chap. 5 in *Structure and Function in Primitive Society: Essays and Addresses.* London, 1952.

Radforth, Ian. "The Shantymen." In *Labouring Lives: Work and Workers in Nineteenth-Century Ontario,* ed. Paul Craven. Toronto, 1995.

Ranger, Terence O. "The Movement of Ideas, 1850–1939." In *A History of Tanzania,* ed. Isaria N. Kimambo and A.J. Temu. Nairobi, 1969.

Ranger, Terence O. "African Reactions to the Imposition of Colonial Rule in East and Central Africa." In *Colonialism in Africa 1870–1960.* Vol. 1, *The History and Politics of Colonialism 1870–1914,* ed. L.H. Gann and Peter Duignan. Cambridge, 1969.

Ranger, Terence O. *Dance and Society in Eastern Africa 1890—1970: The Beni 'Ngoma.'* London, 1975.

Ranger, Terence O. *Revolt in Southern Rhodesia, 1896–97: A Study in African Resistance.* 2nd ed. London, 1979.

Raum, O.F. "German East Africa: Changes in African Tribal Life Under German Administration, 1892–1914." In *History of East Africa,* ed. Vincent Harlow and E.M. Chilver. Vol. 2. Oxford, 1965.

Raymond, W.D. "Native Materia Medica." Pt. 3 *Tanganyika Notes and Records* 5 (April 1938): 72–75.

Rediker, Marcus. *Between the Devil and the Deep Blue Sea: Merchant Seamen, Pirates, and the Anglo-American Maritime World, 1700–1750.* Cambridge, 1987.

Redmayne, Alison. "The Hehe." In *Tanzania Before 1900,* ed. Andrew Roberts. Nairobi, 1968.

Redmayne, Alison. "Mkwawa and the Hehe Wars." *Journal of African History* 9, no. 3 (1968): 409–36.

Renault, François. "The Structures of the Slave Trade in Central Africa in the 19th Century." In *The Economics of the Indian Ocean Slave Trade in the Nineteenth Century,* ed. William Gervase Clarence-Smith. London, 1989.

Richards, Audrey I., ed. *East African Chiefs.* London, 1959.

Rigby, Peter. "Joking Relationships, Kin Categories, and Clanship among the Gogo." *Africa* 38, no. 2 (1968): 133–55.

Rigby, Peter. *Cattle and Kinship among the Gogo: A Semi-pastoral Society of Central Tanzania.* Ithaca, NY, 1969.

Roberts, Andrew, ed. *Tanzania Before 1900.* Nairobi, 1968.

Roberts, Andrew. "The Nyamwezi." In *Tanzania Before 1900,* ed. Andrew Roberts. Nairobi, 1968.

Roberts, Andrew. "Political Change in the Nineteenth Century." In *A History of Tanzania,* ed. Isaria N. Kimambo and A. J. Temu. Nairobi, 1969.

Roberts, Andrew. "Nyamwezi Trade." In *Pre-colonial African Trade,* ed. Richard Gray and David Birmingham. London, 1970.

Roberts, Andrew. *A History of the Bemba.* London, 1973.

Roberts, Andrew. *A History of Zambia.* London, 1976.

Robertson, Claire C. "Gender and Trade Relations in Central Kenya in the Late Nineteenth Century." *International Journal of African Historical Studies* 30, no. 1 (1997): 23–47.

Robinson, Ronald, and John Gallagher. *Africa and the Victorians: The Climax of Imperialism.* With Alice Denny. New York, 1968.

Rockel, Stephen J. "Relocating Labor: Sources from the Nineteenth Century." *History in Africa* 22 (1995): 447–54.

Rockel, Stephen J. "Wage Labor and the Culture of Porterage in Nineteenth Century Tanzania: The Central Caravan Routes." *Comparative Studies of South Asia, Africa and the Middle East* 15, no. 2 (1995): 14–24.

Rockel, Stephen J. "'A Nation of Porters': The Nyamwezi and the Labour Market in Nineteenth-Century Tanzania." *Journal of African History* 41, no. 2 (2000): 173–95.

Rockel, Stephen J. "Enterprising Partners: Caravan Women in Nineteenth Century Tanzania." *Canadian Journal of African Studies* 34, no. 3 (2000): 748–78.

Rodney, Walter. "The Political Economy of Colonial Tanganyika 1890–1930." In *Tanzania under Colonial Rule,* ed. M.H.Y. Kaniki. London, 1979.

Rosling, Hans. *Cassava Toxicity and Food Security.* Uppsala, 1987.

Ross, Andrew. "David Livingstone: The Man behind the Mask." In *The London Missionary Society in Southern Africa, 1799–1999: Historical Essays in Celebration of the Bicentenary of the LMS in Southern Africa,* ed. John de Gruchy. Athens, 2000.

Ross, Doran H., ed. *Elephant: The Animal and Its Ivory in African Culture.* Los Angeles, 1992.

Rotberg, Robert I. *Joseph Thomson and the Exploration of Africa.* London, 1971.

Rounce, N. V. "Ingereza Ng'wana Sweya: His Own Story and His Agricultural Practices."
    East African Agricultural Journal 5 (1939): 211–15.
Russell, Mrs. Charles E. B. *General Rigby, Zanzibar, and the Slave Trade.* 1935. Reprinted,
    New York, 1970.
Said, Edward. *Orientalism.* London, 1978.
Salim, Ahmed Idha, ed. *State Formation in Eastern Africa.* Nairobi, 1984.
Samarin, William J. "The State's Bakongo Burden Bearers." In *The Workers of African
    Trade,* ed. Catherine Coquery-Vidrovitch and Paul E. Lovejoy. Beverly Hills, CA,
    1985.
Samarin, William J. *The Black Man's Burden: African Colonial Labor on the Congo and
    Ubangi Rivers, 1880–1900.* Boulder, CO, 1989.
Sandbrook, Richard, and Robin Cohen, eds. *The Development of African Working Class:
    Studies in Class Formation and Action.* Toronto, 1975.
Scott, James C. *Weapons of the Weak: Everyday Forms of Peasant Resistance.* New Haven,
    CT, 1985.
Scrivenor, T. V. "Some Notes on Utani, or the Vituperative Alliances Existing between
    Clans in the Masasi District." *TNR* 4 (1937): 72–74.
Seidenberg, D. A. *Merchant Adventurers: The World of East African Asians 1750–1985.*
    New Delhi, 1996.
Senior, H. S. "Sukuma Salt Caravans to Lake Eyasi." *Tanganyika Notes and Records* 6
    (1938): 87–90.
Sheriff, Abdul M. H. "Tanzanian Societies at the Time of the Partition." In *Tanzania under
    Colonial Rule,* ed. M.H.Y. Kaniki. London, 1980.
Sheriff, Abdul M. H. "Ivory and Commercial Expansion in East Africa in the Nineteenth
    Century." In *Figuring African Trade,* ed. S. Liesegang, H. Pasch, and A. Jones.
    Berlin, 1986.
Sheriff, Abdul M. H. *Slaves, Spices and Ivory in Zanzibar: Integration of an East African
    Commercial Empire into the World Economy 1770–1873.* London, 1987.
Sheriff, Abdul M. H. "Localisation and Social Composition of the East African Slave
    Trade, 1858–1873." In *The Economics of the Indian Ocean Slave Trade in the
    Nineteenth Century,* ed. William Gervase Clarence-Smith. London, 1989.
Sheriff, Abdul M. H., and E. Ferguson, eds. *Zanzibar under Colonial Rule.* London,
    1991.
Sheriff, Abdul M. H. ed. *The History and Conservation of Zanzibar Stone Town.* London,
    1995.
Sherratt, Andrew. "Introduction: Peculiar Substances." In *Consuming Habits: Drugs in
    History and Anthropology,* ed. Jordan Goodman, Paul E. Lovejoy, and Andrew
    Sherratt. London, 1995.
Sherratt, Andrew. "Alcohol and Its Alternatives: Symbol and Substance in Pre- industrial
    Cultures." In *Consuming Habits: Drugs in History and Anthropology,* ed. Jordan
    Goodman, Paul E. Lovejoy, and Andrew Sherratt. London, 1995.
Shorter, Aylward. "The Kimbu." In *Tanzania Before 1900,* ed. Andrew Roberts. Nairobi,
    1968.
Shorter, Aylward. "Nyungu ya Mawe and the Empire of the Ruga-Ruga." *Journal of
    African History* 9 (1968): 235–59.
Shorter, Aylward. *Nyungu-ya-Mawe: Leadership in Nineteenth Century Tanzania.* Nairobi,
    1969.

Shorter, Aylward. *Chiefship in Western Tanzania: A Political History of the Kimbu.* Oxford, 1972.

Shorter, Aylward. "The Rise and Decline of Bungu Power, a Forgotten Episode in the History of Nineteenth Century Tanzania." *Tanzania Notes and Records* 73 (1974): 1–18.

Shorter, Aylward. "An Incident on the White Fathers Journey in 1878." *Tanzania Notes and Records* 88/89 (1982): 57–61.

Simpson, Donald Herbert. *Dark Companions: The African Contribution to the European Exploration of East Africa.* London, 1975.

Sippel, Harald. "'Wie erzieht man am besten den Neger zur Plantagen-Arbeit?' Die Ideologie der Arbeitserziehung und ihre rechtliche Umsetzung in der Kolonie Deutsch-Ostafrika." In *Arbeit in Afrika,* ed. Kurt Beck and Gerd Spittler. Hamburg, 1996.

Smith, Alison. "The Southern Section of the Interior, 1840–84." In *History of East Africa,* ed. Roland A. Oliver and Gervase Mathew. Vol. 1. Oxford, 1963.

Smith, Edwin W. "The Earliest Ox-Wagons in Tanganyika: An Experiment Which Failed." Pts. 1 and 2. *Tanganyika Notes and Records* 40 (September 1955): 1–14; 41 (December 1955): 1–15.

Smith, MacKenzie and Company. *The History of Smith, MacKenzie and Company, Ltd.* London, 1937.

Snyder, Francis, and Douglas Hay. "Comparisons in the Social History of Law: Labour and Crime." In *Labour, Law, and Crime: An Historical Perspective,* ed. Francis Snyder and Douglas Hay. London, 1987.

Spear, Thomas, and Richard Waller, eds. *Being Maasai: Ethnicity and Identity in East Africa.* London, 1993.

Spies, E. "Observations on Utani Customs among the Ngoni of Songea District." *TNR* 16 (1943): 49–53.

St. John, Christopher. "Kazembe and the Tanganyika-Nyasa Corridor, 1800–1890." In *Precolonial African Trade,* ed. Richard Gray and David Birmingham, London, 1970.

Stedman Jones, Gareth. *Languages of Class: Studies in English Working Class History, 1832–1982.* Cambridge, 1983.

Steinhart, Edward I. "Elephant Hunting in 19th-Century Kenya: Kamba Society and Ecology in Transformation." *International Journal of African Historical Studies* 33, no. 2 (2001): 335–49.

Stichter, Sharon B. *Migrant Laborers.* Cambridge, 1985.

Stichter, Sharon B., and Jane L. Parpart, eds. *Patriarchy and Class: African Women in the Home and the Workforce.* Boulder, CO, 1988.

Stichter, Sharon B. "The Migration of Women in Colonial Central Africa: Some Notes towards an Approach." In *Demography from Scanty Evidence: Central Africa in the Colonial Era,* ed. Bruce Fetter. Boulder, CO, 1990.

Stocking, George W., Jr. *Victorian Anthropology.* New York, 1987.

Stoecker, Helmuth, ed. *German Imperialism in Africa.* Translated by Bernd Zöllner. Atlantic Highlands, NJ, 1986.

Strobel, Margaret. *Muslim Women in Mombasa 1890–1975.* New Haven, CT, 1979.

Sunseri, Thaddeus. "Slave Ransoming in German East Africa, 1885–1922." *International Journal of African Historical Studies* 26, no. 3 (1993): 481–511.

Sunseri, Thaddeus. "Labour Migration in Colonial Tanzania and the Hegemony of South African Historiography." *African Affairs* 95 (1996): 581–98.

Sunseri, Thaddeus. "'Dispersing the Fields': Railway Labor and Rural Change in Early Colonial Tanzania." *Canadian Journal of African Studies* 32, 3 (1998): 558–83.

Sunseri, Thaddeus. *Vilimani: Labor Migration and Rural Change in Early Colonial Tanzania.* Portsmouth, NH, 2002.

Sutton, J.E.G. "Dar es Salaam: A Sketch of a Hundred Years." *Tanzania Notes and Records* 71 (1970): 1–19.

Sutton, J.E.G. *Early Trade in Eastern Africa.* Nairobi, 1973.

Sutton, J.E.G., and Andrew D. Roberts. "Uvinza and Its Salt Industry." *Azania* 3 (1968): 45–86.

Temu, A.J. "Tanzanian Societies and the Colonial Invasion 1875–1907." In *Tanzania under Colonial Rule,* ed. M.H.Y. Kaniki. London, 1980.

Thomas, H.B. "Arabic Correspondence Captured in South West Bunyoro in 1895: With a Note on Arab Traders in Bunyoro." *Uganda Journal* 13, no. 1 (March 1949): 31–38.

Thomas, H.B. "Church Missionary Society Boats in East Africa." *Uganda Journal* 25, no. 1 (1961): 43–53

Thompson, E.P. *The Making of the English Working Class.* Harmondsworth, UK, 1968.

Thompson, E.P. "Patrician Society, Plebeian Culture." *Journal of Social History* 7, no. 4 (1974): 382–405.

Thompson, E.P. "Eighteenth-Century English Society: Class Struggle Without Class?" *Social History* 3, no. 2 (1978): 133–65.

Thompson, E.P. *Customs in Common.* London, 1991.

Tosh, John. "The Northern Interlacustrine Region." In *Pre-colonial African Trade,* ed. Richard Gray and David Birmingham. London, 1970.

Unomah, Alfred C., and J.B. Webster. "East Africa: The Expansion of Commerce." In *The Cambridge History of Africa,* ed. John E. Flint. Vol. 5. London, 1976.

Unomah, Alfred C. *Mirambo of Tanzania.* London, 1977.

Vail, Leroy, and Landeg White. "'Paiva': The History of a Song." In *Power and the Praise Poem: Southern African Voices in History,* ed. Leroy Vail and Landeg White. Charlottesville, 1991.

Van Onselen, Charles. *Chibaro: African Mine Labour in Southern Rhodesia.* Nottingham, 1976.

Vaughan, Megan. "Colonial Discourse Theory and African History, or Has Postmodernism Passed Us By?" *Social Dynamics* 20, no. 2 (1994): 1–23.

Versteijnen, F. *The Catholic Mission of Bagamoyo.* Bagamoyo, 1968.

Wagner, Michele. "Environment, Community and History: 'Nature in the Mind' in Nineteenth and Early Twentieth Century Buha, Western Tanzania." In *Custodians of the Land: Ecology and Culture in the History of Tanzania,* ed. Gregory Maddox, James L. Giblin, and Isaria N. Kimambo. London, 1996.

Waller, Richard. "Economic and Social Relations in the Central Rift Valley: The Maa Speakers and Their Neighbours in the Nineteenth Century." In *Kenya in the Nineteenth Century,* ed. Bethwell A. Ogot. Nairobi, 1985.

Waller, Richard. "Emutai: Crisis and Response in Maasailand 1883–1902." In *The Ecology of Survival: Case Studies from Northeast African History,* ed. Douglas H. Johnson and David M. Anderson. London, 1988.

Washbrook, D.A. "Orients and Occidents: Colonial Discourse Theory and the Historiography of the British Empire." In *The Oxford History of the British Empire.* Vol. 5, *Historiography,* ed. Robin Winks. Oxford, 1999.

White, Landeg. *Magomero: Portrait of an African Village.* Cambridge, 1987.

White, Luise. "Domestic Labor in a Colonial City: Prostitution in Nairobi, 1900–1952." In *Patriarchy and Class: African Women in the Home and Work Force,* ed. Sharon B. Stichter and Jane L. Parpart. Boulder, CO, 1988.

White, Luise. *The Comforts of Home: Prostitution in Colonial Nairobi.* Chicago, 1990.

Whiteley, W. H. *Swahili: The Rise of a National Language.* London, 1969.

Willis, Justin. *Potent Brews: A Social History of Alcohol in East Africa 1850–1999.* Oxford, 2002.

Wolf, James B. "Commerce, Christianity, and the Creation of the Stevenson Road." *African Historical Studies* 4, no. 2 (1971): 363–71.

Woods, Tony. "Capitaos and Chiefs: Oral Tradition and Colonial Society." *International Journal of African Historical Studies* 23, no. 2 (1990): 259–68.

Worger, William H. *South Africa's City of Diamonds: Mine Workers and Monopoly Capitalism in Kimberley, 1867–1895.* New Haven, CT, 1987.

Wright, Marcia. "East Africa, 1870–1905." In *History of East Africa,* ed. Roland A. Oliver and Gervase Mathew. Vol. 6. Oxford, 1963.

Wright, Marcia, and Peter Lary. "Swahili Settlements in Northern Zambia and Malawi." *African Historical Studies* 4, no. 3 (1971): 547–73.

Wright, Marcia. "Women in Peril." *African Social Research* 20 (1975): 800–19.

Wright, Marcia. "Bwanikwa: Consciousness and Protest among Slave Women in Central Africa, 1886–1911." In *Women and Slavery in Africa,* ed. Claire Robertson and Martin A. Klein. Madison, 1983.

Wright, Marcia. *Strategies of Slaves and Women: Life Stories from East/Central Africa.* New York, 1993.

Yeo, P. H. "Caput-Nili: The Travels of Richard Kandt in German East Africa." *Tanganyika Notes and Records* 63 (September 1964): 207–12.

Zegeye, Abebe, and Shubi Ishemo, eds. *Forced Labour and Migration: Patterns of Movement within Africa.* London, 1989.

Zeleza, Tiyambe. *A Modern Economic History of Africa.* Vol. 1, *The Nineteenth Century.* Dakar, 1993.

UNPUBLISHED PAPERS AND THESES

Anthony, David. "Culture and Society in a Town in Transition: A People's History of Dar es Salaam, 1865–1939." PhD diss., University of Wisconsin–Madison, 1980.

Brown, Beverly Bolser. "Ujiji: The History of a Lakeside Town, c.1800–1914." PhD diss., Boston University, 1973.

Brown, Walter Thaddeus. "A Pre-colonial History of Bagamoyo: Aspects of the Growth of an East African Coastal Town." PhD diss., Boston University, 1971.

Cummings, Robert J. "Aspects of Human Porterage with Special Reference to the Akamba of Kenya: Towards an Economic History, 1820–1920." PhD thesis, University of California, Los Angeles, 1975.

Deutsch, Jan-Georg. "What Happened to All the Slaves? Colonial Policy, Emancipation, and the Transformation of Slave Societies in German and British East Africa (Tanganyika), c. 1890–1930." Paper presented at the annual meeting of the African Studies Association, Orlando, FL, November 1995.

Glassman, Jonathon. "Social Rebellion and Swahili Culture: The Response to German Conquest of the Northern Mrima." PhD thesis, University of Wisconsin–Madison, 1988.

Haulle, D.M. "Utani Relationships: The Kisi." In "Utani Relationships in Tanzania," ed. Stephen A. Lucas. Vol. 1. Dar es Salaam, Tanzania, 1974–76.

Holmes, C.F. "A History of the Bakwimba of Usukuma, Tanzania, from Earliest Times to 1945." PhD diss., Boston University, 1969.

Home, David Lawrence. "Mode of Production in the Social and Economic History of Kilwa to 1884." PhD thesis, University of California, Los Angeles, 1984.

Honey, Martha Spencer. "A History of Indian Merchant Caital and Class Formation in Tanganyika c. 1840–1940." PhD thesis, University of Dar es Salaam, 1982.

Itandala, A. Buluda. "A History of the Babinza of Usukuma, Tanzania, to 1890." PhD thesis, Dalhousie University, 1983.

Jones, Laird. "Mapping Consumption: Geographic Patterns in East African Import Sales, 1880–1914." Paper presented at the Canadian Association of African Studies Conference, Université Laval, Quebec, May 2001.

Kabuaye, M.S. "Utani and Related Cultural Institutions of the Sukuma Peoples in Shinyanga." In "Utani Relationships in Tanzania," ed. Stephen A. Lucas. Vol. 5. Dar es Salaam, Tanzania,l 1974–76.

Katunzi. "Utani Relationships: The Sumbwa." In "Utani Relationships in Tanzania," ed. Stephen A. Lucas. Vol. 6. Dar es Salaam, Tanzania, 1974–76.

Kieran, John A.P. "The Holy Ghost Fathers in East Africa 1863–1914." PhD thesis, University of London, 1966.

Kolmin, F.W., and C. Whybrow. "Not Only Nazis." Unpublished Manuscript. File 10829. Vol. 6. British Secretariat Records. Tanzania National Archives.

Loomba, Ania. "Can the Subaltern Speak? Postcolonialism, Postmodernism and Writing Subaltern History." Paper presented at the History and African Studies Seminar, University of Natal, Durban, South Africa, 6 May 1998.

Lucas, Stephen A., ed. "Utani Relationships in Tanzania." 7 vols. Dar es Salaam, Tanzania, 1974–76.

Lucas, Stephen A. "The Role of Utani in Eastern Tanzanian Clan Histories." In "Utani Relationships in Tanzania," ed. Stephen A. Lucas. Vol. 1. Dar es Salaam, Tanzania, 1974 –76.

Lucas, Stephen A. "The *Mtani* in Tanzania: A Socio-historical Analysis of His Role in Crisis Situations." In "Utani Relationships in Tanzania," ed. Stephen A. Lucas. Vol. 4. Dar es Salaam, Tanzania, 1974–76.

Lucas, Stephen A. "War and Trade: Preliminary Thoughts on Ngoni and Nyamwezi *Utani* Networks." In "Utani Relationships in Tanzania," ed. Stephen A. Lucas. Vol. 4. Dar es Salaam, Tanzania, 1974 –76.

Lucas, Stephen A. "On the Non-existence of Tribes in Tanzania: An Utani Conceptualization of Intergroup Relationships." In "Utani Relationships in Tanzania," ed. Stephen A. Lucas. Vol. 7. Dar es Salaam, Tanzania, 1974–76.

Mjella, A.J. "Political and Economic Aspects of Utani: Makonde Migrant Workers in Korogwe District, Tanga Region." In "Utani Relationships in Tanzania," ed. Stephen A. Lucas. Vol. 7. Dar es Salaam, Tanzania, 1974 –76.

Myers, Garth Andrew. "The Early History of the Other Side of Zanzibar Town." Paper presented at the International Conference on the History and Culture of Zanzibar, 14–16 December 1992.

Nkuli, Mlolwa. "Notes on Nyamwezi Utani." In "Utani Relationships in Tanzania," ed. Stephen A. Lucas. Dar es Salaam, Tanzania, 1974 –76.

Nolan, Francis Patrick. "Christianity in Unyamwezi 1878–1928." PhD diss., University of Cambridge, 1977.

Podruchny, Carolyn. "Sons of the Wilderness: Work, Culture and Identity among Voyageurs in the Montréal Fur Trade, 1780–1821." PhD thesis, University of Toronto, 1999.

Rempel, Ruth. "Exploration, Knowledge, and Empire in Africa: The Emin Pasha Relief Expedition, 1886–1892." PhD thesis, University of Toronto, 2000.

Rockel, Stephen J. "Caravan Porters of the *Nyika:* Labour, Culture and Society in Nineteenth Century Tanzania." PhD thesis, University of Toronto, 1997.

Rockel, Stephen J. "Safari! The East African Caravan System in the Nineteenth Century." Unpublished manuscript.

Rounce, N. V. "The Banyamwezi at Home." MSS.Afr.s.424.ff 297–303, Rhodes House, n.d.

Salaita, John. "Colonialism and Underdevelopment in Unyanyembe ca. 1900–1960." MA thesis, University of Dar es Salaam, 1975.

Shetto, E. W. "Utani Relationships: The Nyamwezi." In "Utani Relationships in Tanzania," ed. Stephen A. Lucas. Vol. 4. Dar es Salaam, Tanzania, 1974–76.

Sissons, Carol Jane. "Economic Prosperity in Ugogo, East Africa, 1860–1890." PhD thesis, University of Toronto, 1984.

Stigger, Philip. "The Late 19th. Century Caravan Trade and Some of Its Modern Implications: The Shinyanga Example." Unpublished Paper. Simon Fraser University, n.d.

Turner, Mary. Paper presented at the International Conference on Masters and Servants in History, York University, Toronto, April 1996.

Unomah, Alfred C. "Economic Expansion and Political Change in Unyanyembe, c. 1840–1900." PhD thesis, University of Ibadan, 1972.

Walji, Shirin Remtulla. "A History of the Ismaili Community in Tanzania." PhD thesis, University of Wisconsin–Madison, 1974.

MAPS

Bagamoyo, Surveys and Mapping Division, Ministry of Lands, Housing, and Urban Development, Tanzania, 1987.

Burton and Speke's Route. *Tanganyika Notes and Records* 49 (1957): opp. 300.

Gulliver, P. H. "A Tribal Map of Tanganyika." *Tanganyika Notes and Records* 52 (March 1959): 61–74.

Hildebrands Urlaubskarte, Ostafrika, 1989.

Republic of Tanzania, Ordnance Survey, 1987.

Shell Map of Tanzania, 1973.

Tabora and Urambo Districts, Surveys and Mapping Division, Ministry of Lands, Housing, and Urban Development, Tanzania, 1976.

INDEX